JUSTIFIED IN JESUS CHRIST

Evangelicals and Catholics in Dialogue

Edited by Dr. Steven Hoskins
and Dr. David Fleischacker

University of Mary Press
Bismarck, North Dakota

© 2017 by University of Mary
First published in 2017

All rights reserved. No part of this book may be reproduced in any form without written permission of the copyright owners.

Published in the United States of America by
University of Mary Press
7500 University Drive
Bismarck, ND 58504
www.umary.edu

ISBN-10: 0-9988728-2-2
ISBN-13: 978-0-9988728-2-7

Design: Jerry Anderson

Printed in Canada

In Memoriam

Dr. Ralph Del Colle

1954-2012

We remember Ralph Del Colle, who was with us
from the beginning and departed this world in 2012.
Ralph dedicated himself to the service of healing the rifts
that have torn so many of us apart in the Christian world.
He worked with great faith and diligence to clarify the
issues, find the agreements, and resolve the differences.
He was a good friend and colleague to all of us.
He is sorely missed.

To his memory this volume is dedicated.

Contents

Foreword 1
A Short History of the Dialogue 5

Section 1: Original Sin and the Fallen State of the Human Race

Common Statement: Original Sin 11

Background Papers

Original Sin and Prevenient Grace: An Effective
Evangelical Synergistic Perspective on Salvation 17
Dr. Steven Hoskins

Original Sin and Its Effects
Within the Economy of Salvation 33
Dr. Dennis W. Jowers

The Patristic Background to Original Sin 51
Dr. Daniel Keating

Original Sin: A Catholic Introduction 65
Dr. David P. Fleischacker

Section 2: Initial Justification

Common Statement: Initial Justification. 77

Background Papers

Crucified Monergism: A Theological
Interpretation of Justification in Galatians 83
Dr. Malcolm Yarnel

Initial Justification: A "Synergist" Explanation.................. 101
Dr. Glen W. Menzies

Ex inimico amicus: Catholic Teaching on Initial Justification 123
Dr. Christian D. Washburn

Section 3: Sanctification and Justification

Common Statement: Justification and Sanctification 149

Background Papers

An Evangelical Reformed Perspective on the
Relation between Justification and Sanctification 155
Dr. Dennis W. Jowers

Life in the New Creation: Justification
and Sanctification Revisited 173
Dr. Jackie David Johns & Dr. Cheryl Bridges Johns

Justification and Sanctification in
Scripture and the Church Fathers 183
Dr. Daniel Keating

Justification and Sanctification in the
Catechism of the Catholic Church 197
Dr. David P. Fleischacker

Engrafted into Christ: Sanctification
and the Transformative Power of Grace
in the Catholic Tradition................................. 211
Dr. Christian D. Washburn

Section 4: Justification and the Final Judgment

Common Statement: Justification and the Final Judgment...... 235

Background Papers

The Relationship between Justification and
Final Judgment: A Wesleyan View of Judgment,
the Goal of Salvation, and Heaven 241
Rev. Bruce N.G. Cromwell, Ph.D.

Theological Contours of Monergism in the
Final Judgment: A Reformed Understanding 261
Rev. Chris Castaldo, Ph.D.

"Saved, But Only As Through Fire:" Notes on
the Scriptural and Theological Foundations
for the Doctrine of Purgatory 279
Dr. William B. Stevenson

Nothing Unclean Will Enter Heaven:
Justification and Eschatology 293
Dr. Christian D. Washburn

Contributing Authors: Background Papers.................... 313

Annual Dialogue Participants and Consultants............... 315

Index of Names... 317

Subject Index.. 325

Foreword

IN THE EARLY 1980S, several Christian groups were promoting moral and ethical issues in the Minneapolis, MN area. Interestingly, almost all the participants in these groups were either Evangelicals or Catholics. Both groups found themselves fighting side by side in the trenches for these causes. This was not coincidental. These common efforts resulted not only from similar interests in social issues but also from a common approach to Scripture. Both Catholics and Evangelicals take Scripture seriously!

A question arose: why had Evangelicals and Catholics not established formal, bilateral ecumenical discussions, as dozens of other denominations had done. Inquiries were made, and a local discussion began between Bonn Clayton and Father Arthur Kennedy, who was the Chair of the Ecumenical Commission for the Archdiocese and also Chair of the Theology Department at the University of St. Thomas. In those early years, most of these discussions focused on the correspondences between Evangelical and Catholic theology.

In 1993, more participants were invited into the discussion. A group of about 10 Evangelical and Catholic theologians from seminaries and colleges in the greater Minneapolis-St. Paul area began meeting quarterly at St. John Vianney, the Minor Seminary at St. Thomas, to discuss theology and to establish fellowship. A decade into those discussions, Fr. Kennedy became the Ecumenical Director of the United States Conference of Catholic Bishops, and this ecumenical group considered establishing a national Evangelical-Catholic dialogue. Twenty-three of the presidents of the largest Evangelical denominations in the United States were contacted, and most of them were very interested in the idea of an ecumenical dialogue with the Catholic Church. They appointed permanent representatives to the dialogue, and the USCCB also appointed several scholars. The first meeting of the national dialogue met in 2003.

Initially the participants seriously considered focusing on justification, partly because the Vatican and the Lutheran World Federation had recently concluded their "Joint Declaration on the Doctrine of Justification" (1999). After much consideration, however, the dialogue decided to consider several other topics first to become better acquainted with each other and with the dynamic between the Evangelical and Catholic traditions. The dialogue spent a decade discussing Scripture, tradition, church, and atonement, along with a variety of other topics. At last, in 2013, the participants decided to create a four-year round of dialogues to find common ground on the topic of justification. This book is the product of those discussions and has borne much good fruit between Evangelicals and Catholics.

During this period from 2014 to 2017, many convergences on this subject were discovered, many of them quite unexpected. It is hoped that this work will make that goal more easily attainable in the future, whether by the present participants or their successors. The warm ecumenical relations between Pope Francis and evangelicals have been a source of encouragement and inspiration to us.

It is important that the readers understand that the dialogue group and its individual members do not speak officially for the churches they represent. Nevertheless, the views of these theologians and pastors merit serious attention and carry considerable weight. It is hoped that their endeavors will contribute to an increased unity between our various denominations and help to spur on others in the quest for unity.

Finally, it would be remiss not to give heartfelt thanks both to our Lord and to those who have helped put this text together. First, a great thank you goes out to Monsignor Shea, the Sisters of Annunciation Monastery, and the University of Mary for hosting the latest round of the dialogues starting in 2015. Their hospitality has surpassed all expectations, and the location has provided the dialogue with a beautiful and fruitful environment. Thank you to Bishop David Kagan for welcoming us into the

Diocese of Bismarck, North Dakota. Thanks to our editors, Kateri Krebs, Andrea Gleiter, Gretchen K. Washburn, and Barbara Spindel for their diligent care, and to Patrick McCloskey and Jerry Anderson for helping to construct a beautiful book that manifests so well the friendships and the discussions that have developed over the years in this dialogue.

Co-Chairmen:

John Gaydos
Bishop of Jefferson City
United States Conference of Catholic Bishops

Bonn Clayton
Former Judicatory Executive
Conservative Congregational Christian Conference

A Short History of the Dialogue

A Dialogue in Testament of Friendship

Christian dialogue, especially ecumenical dialogue, is a testament to friendship. Dialogue, an ongoing work of the Spirit in the churches, is not relationship. It is neither short nor spontaneous, as relationship indicates. Friendship of this kind is indicative of friendship first with God, who then makes friendship with one another possible over time. Over the last two millennia this kind of friendship has produced the Christian Scriptures and resulted in councils and dialogues ranging from Nicaea to Trent and beyond. Ecumenical dialogue between Catholics and Evangelicals is the result of key developments that began in the 20th century and continue to take place in the 21st. Key in this is the secularization of culture that has largely become ignorant, apathetic, or hostile to Christianity. This age deems it necessary that we stand together in response to the persistent confusion of those who are not Christian due to the splintering of our communions. Others need to hear and see that we recognize that the world's only hope is in the Christ who has shown us the face of God. Through him, we are granted access into the divine life of the Trinity.

This particular kind of Christian friendship, known as ecumenical dialogue, is not necessarily indicative that we are fond of each other on the personal level, though in this dialogue charity and kindness in the enterprise have brought about real affection for one another. Ecumenical dialogue is indicative of the testament of friends who employ the gift of language and logic in order to test and attest to one another's judgment so that we might be joined together by common judgments and by God for the good of God's church and our witness to the world. Unlike some dialogues and like others, the common task of this dialogue is understanding. In order to achieve that understanding, the members of this Evangelical-Catholic dialogue present papers to one another, bringing together wisdom that we trust for our salvation and the work of friends who have written in the Scriptures and across the Christian era. It is not unusual for our dialogue to be marked by the wisdom of Jesus and the prophets recorded in the Scriptures. Our conversations express the hearts and minds of theologians ranging from Saint Paul to Saint Augustine to Luther to Karl Barth. Their inclusion in our conversations points to the truth that friendship is the way God works among us and has continually for centuries. The lives of living saints are the hermeneutical key to understanding one another for those of us who bear the title and burden of Christianity in this world. For this task, we take up common theological concerns from the testimonies of the Scripture and the Creeds (like justification, the church, and atonement) and background papers to one another on our respective traditions, opening up dialogue among us that leads to understanding.

As a way of testifying to one another, this method of dialogue risks many things: understanding, misunderstanding, agreement, and disagreement among them. In this we are vulnerable to God and to one another, and we seek a way beyond the separation of our traditions in both theology and time and the structures we academics and pastors have set up to keep ourselves at a distance from one another. In this we risk, for the good of God's church, the truth and telling it to one another in the structured format of ecumenical dialogue. This dialogue is then a way into friendship and a way beyond the superficiality of relationships, for such friendship takes both expertise and time.

This dialogue was held in its formative years as a regional dialogue and then as an official dialogue sponsored by the United States Council of Catholic Bishops on the campus of the University of St. Thomas in St. Paul, Minnesota. Two years ago, we moved to the campus of the University of Mary in Bismarck, North Dakota. We are a host of theologians that has now spanned beyond two decades as a gathering of friends that encompasses the Roman Catholic Church and several Evangelical communities and denominations.

Evangelical-Catholic Dialogue
Structure and Meetings, 2003-2011

The Evangelical-Catholic Dialogue of the United States of America began as a regional dialogue in 1993 in the Minneapolis-Saint Paul area. It met to discuss theology and ecumenical concerns under the co-direction of Father Arthur Kennedy, then Professor of Theology at the University of St. Thomas and now bishop in Boston, Massachusetts, and Bonn Clayton, staff member of the National Association of Congregational Christian Churches representing the Conservative Congregational Christian Churches. After a decade of regional meetings, the meeting became a national dialogue sponsored by the United States Council of Catholic Bishops (USCCB), gaining that recognition during Bishop Kennedy's tenure as Executive Director of the Secretariat for Ecumenical and Interreligious Affairs, of the USCCB (2002-2005). From 2004 to 2007, the Most Reverend Frederick Campbell, Bishop of the Diocese of Columbus, Ohio, served as sponsoring bishop for the Catholic contingent. From 2008 until 2015, the same group continued to meet to finalize and expand discussions. The Most Reverend John Gaydos, Bishop of the Diocese of Jefferson City, Missouri oversaw the Catholic members, and he was instrumental in initiating a second round of full and formal discussions sponsored by the USCCB in 2015. Catholic participants include Dr. David P. Fleischaker, Dr. Christian D. Washburn, Dr. Daniel A. Keating, and Dr. William B. Stevenson. Bonn Clayton has continued to serve as the organizing force of the Evangelical contingent of our dialogue, which includes representatives from the Assemblies of God (Dr. Glen Menzies), independent Baptist churches (Dr. Malcolm Yarnell), the Korean Baptist Church (Dr. Dennis Jowers), the New Covenant Church (Dr. Christopher Castaldo), the Free Methodist Church (Dr. Bruce Cromwell), the Four Square Church (Dr. Dennis Moore), the Salvation Army (Rev. Paul Fleeman, Rev. Jeff Strickler), the Church of the Nazarene (Dr. Steven Hoskins), Converge Worldwide (Dr. Chris Armstrong), the Wesleyan Church (Rev. Duane Fisher), the Church of God (Dr. Cheryl Bridges Johns, Dr. Jackie Johns), Cleveland, and others. The dialogue currently meets in October of every calendar year.

Until 2014, the dialogue met yearly at the University of St. Thomas, establishing an important ecumenical voice between Catholics and Evangelicals. Since 2015, the dialogue has met at the University of Mary at the generous invitation of the campus and its president, Monsignor James P. Shea.

With its inauguration as an official dialogue of the USCCB in 2003, the dialogue conscientiously spent two years exploring several topics, seeking to find its voice. Initial explorations around the topics of Scripture, authority, the Joint Declaration of 1999, and the Eucharist were held in order to discover potential common ground between the groups and, in so doing, lead the dialogue to a fruitful avenue of discussion and establish an agenda coordinated to promote mutual understanding. In 2004, a report from the Catholics and the World Evangelical Alliance was read to help with guidance.

These were important years for the dialogue as it considered topics that proved to be both polemical and agreeable to both sides. A considerable time was spent getting to know one another. The corporate nature of Catholicism provided much of the discussion, a topic on which the Evangelical traditions held varying positions. Most importantly, a sense of shared faith arose within the ranks of the group. A common belief that conversion was necessary to the Christian faith became apparent in the discussions, that everyone from both sides was a "born again" child of God, and, by consent, that if you put faithful Catholics and Evangelicals in a room together they would come to recognize one another as faithful Christians. With this measure of goodwill becoming pervasive in the meetings, two things emerged from the first two years of the dialogue: 1) a decision to make a methodical survey of topics that would be mutually beneficial for discussion, and 2) the need to create a "Common Statement" each year based on areas of agreement and disagreement between the two sides based on that year's dialogue. These statements, at times more informal and at other times more formal, reflect the measure of common ground and clarity of differing ideals that have come to characterize our interactions. As "Common Statements," they have continued to be important to the dialogue, giving it a dedicated and repeatable format and a galvanizing center that continues to serve the dialogue well.

After the first two years of meeting, a systematic exploration of topics began in 2005 covering Authority (2005), Scripture (2006), Tradition (2007), Atonement—Objective (2008), Atonement—Subjective (2009), The Church—Essence (2010), and The Church—Structures (2011). In each year, papers were read from both sides and opened up for consideration and dialogue. The papers provided a starting point for conversation and for clarifications of positions.

From 2005 to 2009, one paper was read from each side. As the dialogue continued, it seemed appropriate that more than one paper would be read from each side. Since 2010, the Catholics have read two or three position papers discussing the year's theme, and Evangelicals have offered two papers discussing the theme, one from the classical Reformed or Monergist perspective and one from the Synergist perspective of Evangelical theology.[1] This structure has led to a fruitful representation of theological positions from both sides and to the articulation of common statements and of key differences between the groups.[2] These papers served the same purpose in the current round of dialogues leading to this book. In 2013, the members of the dialogue decided on a four-year round that would cover the topic of justification and bring us to the commemoration of the 500th anniversary of the Protestant Reformation in 2017.

2014—Original sin and its effects within the economy of salvation

2015—Initial justification

2016—The relationship between justification and sanctification

2017—The relationship between justification and final judgment

The following sections of this book will include the common statements generated by each of these dialogues along with the accompanying background papers that were delivered.

Dr. Steven Hoskins, Ph.D
Trevecca Nazarene University
Nashville, Tennessee

Notes

[1] In the traditions represented by Evangelicals in this dialogue, monergist theology proceeds from the idea that human beings possess no will or inclination toward holiness or God until regeneration is complete in salvation. Synergists, on the other hand, believe that God's grace is operative and active in the life of humans before regeneration. These two positions represent distinct and differing positions in regards to the doctrine of the Holy Spirit and theological anthropology.

[2] In some years, the statements also included passages where the two sides could not come to agreement.

Section 1

Original Sin and the Fallen State of the Human Race

This first of four dialogues on justification took place at the University of Saint Thomas, St. Paul, October 9-12, 2014. The conversations of the dialogue were rich in debate and interest about the state and life of the Garden of Eden and the nature and character of the first man and woman before and after their fall.

Common Statement

Original Sin

PART OF THE GOSPEL, the Good News, is a discussion of the sin and evil to which it is an answer. The sin of Adam and Eve, their fall from their primitive state, and the effects of this upon their progeny is generally labeled "original sin."

1. **Evangelicals and Catholics agree that before Adam and Eve fell or lapsed, they were in a type of right relationship with God, with each other, and with the whole of creation. However...**
    i. Calvinists hold that God could not originally have created human beings without original righteousness.
    ii. Catholics hold that Adam and Eve were given at their creation an intimacy with God that was both natural and supernatural. Naturally, God gave Adam and Eve souls that were lacking perfection but that had an unimpeded finality toward perfection. As well, God gave perfections to their souls that were not acquired by Adam and Eve; these are called the preternatural gifts and include the right ordering of the powers of the soul (integrity) and immortality. Catholics hold that God did not need to give these

preternatural gifts to Adam and Eve because God did not owe these to a nature that has an unimpeded finality toward its own perfection. In other words, the preternatural gifts are not necessary to a right ordering of human nature. Supernaturally, God out of abundant goodness gave Adam and Eve original grace and original righteousness. God did not need to do so. Overall, the intimacy of Adam and Eve to God included a right ordering of the entire soul of Adam and Eve to God, a soul endowed with natural powers, provided with some preternatural perfections of those natural powers, and given supernatural perfections centered in original grace and original righteousness.

2. **Catholics and Evangelicals agree that the solidarity of the human race originates in its first parents, Adam and Eve.**

3. **Evangelicals and Catholics agree that the origin of the Fall of Adam and Eve was not self-initiated but initiated by the prince of lies, Satan.**

4. **Catholics and Evangelicals agree that the sin of Adam and Eve is the primary cause of the loss of original righteousness; this loss is transmitted to all of the children of Adam and Eve unless God causes otherwise. Jesus did not inherit original sin. The sin of Adam and Eve is the primary cause of this loss because God had given original righteousness (not understood the same way for Catholics, Wesleyans/Arminians, and Calvinists) to all of their children on the condition that they remained in original righteousness. Hence, Adam and Eve lost a right relationship to God, to each other, and to the whole of creation. Sinning, Adam and Eve became culpable for their actions and estranged from their Creator. All would agree that this leads to death. However...**

    i. From the Wesleyan/Arminian perspective, every human son and daughter inherits death and a propensity to sin, but not Adam's guilt. Once they become responsible moral agents, they invariably commit actual sins for which they are culpable.

    ii. Catholics would add that this is first a "death of the soul" (the loss of original grace that was a supernatural gift) and then a death that involves a separation of the body and soul. As well, the Catholics hold that Adam's sin is the reason why all of the children of Adam and Eve are privated of original grace, original righteousness, and the preternatural gifts and placed into a state that is inclined to sin and that will be transmitted by means of generation to their children. Catholics would add that through the merits of the redemptive acts of Christ, Mary was preserved from original sin at the moment of her conception in order to be able to receive the Son of God in her womb as an unstained tabernacle.

5. **Evangelicals and Catholics agree that original sin has a damaging impact upon the human body, mind, and will. In this fallen state, the body is subject to death, the mind is darkened to the ways of God's salvation, and the will by its own natural powers has no capability of living in a loving relationship to God. Both would agree that it is the cause of death. Both would agree that the children of Adam and Eve can be redeemed by Christ even though concupiscence remains. However...**

   i. Wesleyan/Arminians affirm that Adam is the only one guilty of original sin. The children inherit a propensity to sin but not the guilt of punishment that is due to Adam as a result of the sin he committed. Infants who die before the age of accountability would not be damned. Similarly, they consider those who have not yet become responsible moral agents to be neither righteous nor unrighteous and, while deserving neither punishment nor reward, still hope for God's gracious blessings.

   ii. The Wesleyans who practice infant baptism hold that while the human race inherits many defects from its primal fallen parents, it does not inherit guilt for the original sin. Consequently, infants are not born guilty, but neither are they born righteous or as part of God's kingdom. The baptism of infants marks the intention of their parents, godparents, or the believing community to claim for them the promises of God's kingdom.

   iii. Wesleyan/Arminians argue that God's love is so abundant that he universally bestows prevenient grace that allows even unregenerate humans to understand God's salvific way so that God can bring them to an act of faith that is salvific.

iv. Both the Calvinists and the Catholics, on the other hand, emphasize that the human race inherits the guilt of Adam and Eve and the punishment due that guilt though they would differ on the nature of that guilt.

v. Calvinists hold that concupiscence is an integral aspect of original sin—that the propensity to sin is actually sin—and separates us from God. Thus, as long as it remains, the person is in a state of sin that would be damnable. The children of Adam inherit the guilt of Adam and therefore inherit the punishment of Adam's sin, which is eternal damnation. And so, though the concupiscence is damnable, if Christ is their savior, they can be saved even with the reality of concupiscence remaining in this life.

vi. Catholics affirm that the privation of original grace and original righteousness is also transmitted with the disorders of the soul that include an inclination to sin (concupiscence), and that without God's healing and salvation, the children of Adam and Eve would be left in eternal separation from God and hence in hell. The children of Adam contract the sin of Adam, though they do not have the personal guilt of having committed the sin. This contraction is not merely an imputation of Adam's sin and guilt; rather, Adam's sin causes an actual privation of the grace in the son or daughter, a grace necessary to make him or her holy, and thus a privation of that which makes it possible to be in union with God.

vii. Furthermore, the inclination to sin for Catholics and Wesleyan/Arminians is not sin, although it is disordered. Thus a person can be in a state of sanctity (holy) even if this inclination remains. However, in order to be in the full presence of God in eternal life, even this inclination to sin must be purged.

6. **Catholics and Evangelicals agree that even after being regenerated, the children of Adam and Eve retain a propensity to sin.**

Background Paper

Original Sin and Prevenient Grace: An Effective Evangelical Synergistic Perspective on Salvation

Dr. Steven Hoskins

EVANGELICALS OF THE Arminian/Wesleyan persuasion, also known as Evangelical Synergists, affirm with Catholics and Evangelical Monergists that all humans are born in original sin, thus declaring that all humans are conceived in sin and shaped in wickedness. Hence, there is in every human a carnal mind, which is enmity against God and which is not, indeed cannot, be subject to the law of God. This infects the whole soul so much that there dwells in all humans, in the flesh, no good thing, even so that every imagination of the thoughts of said humans is evil, only evil, and that continually.[1] Ergo, by nature we who are human do neither know, love, nor fear God and can be said to be atheists in the world. Unassisted by the grace of God, humans cannot but be anything else.

Fortunately, such grace is also the dual condition of everyone born human. Arminians/Wesleyans refer to this as prevenient grace (or preventing grace or the grace that goes before), that state in which God, from birth until death, by his empowering grace seeks to enlighten, convict, and save all humans and then sufficiently lead them into all righteousness/sanctification. This is only accomplished by God as an act of grace and not through any ability inherent in humans. Thus said, such grace is co-operant and inbeing, requiring responsibility from both God and humans, affirming a role for meaningful human participation in salvation. Further, it should be noted that the Arminian/Wesleyan position contends that accepting a gift graciously offered does not imply that the gift is earned or deserved; the gift is all of grace. Without a willingness to accept the gift, the gift-giving is not completed. To force someone to accept a gift against his or her own will is a kind of coercion that has nothing to do with grace.[2]

WESLEY AS A GUIDE

In his *John Wesley's Theology Today,* Colin Williams begins his explanation of Wesley's theology by noting the essential doctrines that Wesley held to that shaped and formed his theology. They are in Williams' order as follows: original sin, the deity of Christ, atonement, justification by faith alone, the work of the Holy Spirit, and the Holy Trinity.[3] Williams' book was one of the most important works in setting the tone for the revolution in Wesley studies in the 20th century that has now spanned the last six decades. This revolution has sought to cement the legacy of John Wesley as the theological fountainhead of churches that stand as his ongoing legacy, particularly solidifying the theology of the Methodist churches, British and American, with the holiness churches that began to populate the American landscape in the late 19th and early 20th centuries. It has also sought to prove the orthodoxy of Wesleyan theology and show that Wesley's orthodoxy was actually a *via media* theology, an orthodox way between the classical doctrinal positions of Roman Catholicism and Reformed theology. This via media approach opens the doors for discussion in this dialogue.

This revolution in Wesley studies has produced quite a body of literature on both Wesley and his understanding of the underpinnings of his theology.[4] Admittedly, Wesley has proved quite a theological knot to unravel. His writing was not systematic but pastoral and episodic by rule.[5] He did not write according to systematic principles, but drew his theology from the disparate sources, both Western and Eastern (so Maddox below), and usually wrote his theology in the light of the Book of Common Prayer and the liturgies, prayer books, and tomes of the ancient church fathers (the Ante-Nicene Fathers) that he studied while a student at Christ Church, Oxford.

The debate about his "place" in the Christian tradition, something noted by his critics and friends during his lifetime, has continued during this revival of Wesley scholarship:

> Given his Western Christian location, this debate has generally focused on whether Wesley is more "Protestant" or more "Catholic." Early studies generally assumed that he was Protestant, but differed over which branch of Protestantism he more nearly resembled or depended upon. Some argued strongly that he was best construed in terms of the Lutheran tradition. Others advocated a more Reformed Wesley. Most assumed that such general designations must be further refined. Thus, there were readings of Wesley in terms of Lutheran Pietism or Moravianism, English (Reformed) Puritanism, and the Arminian revision of the Reformed tradition.[6]

Dominantly Protestant readings of Wesley proved to be inadequate. There are clearly typical "Catholic" themes in his thought and practice as well. This clearly appeals to Wesley scholars who see his work as a *"via media"* between the two Western theological traditions and provides a direct line of theological dialogue to Wesley. His famous dictum, "If thy heart is as my heart, then give me thine hand," holds much promise for both mutual understanding and dialogue on the subject at hand between Evangelicals and Catholics.[7]

However, as Maddox notes, "the unique nature of Anglicanism has suggested a related reading of Wesley that deserves more consideration. Early Anglican theologians did not mediate directly between contemporary Protestantism and Catholicism. Rather, they called for a recovery of the faith and practice of the first four centuries of the Christian church."[8] This order of theological thinking, revived in Wesley's days at Oxford, acknowledges a more Eastern theological bent depending as much, if not mostly, upon the Eastern Fathers of the pre-Nicene church. "Wesley gives lists of those he admires or recommends for study. Frequently cited were Basil, Chrysostom, Clement of Alexandria, Clement of Rome, Ephraem Syrus, Ignatius, Irenaeus, Justin Martyr, Origen, Polycarp and (Pseudo-) Macarius. By contrast, references to Augustine, Cyprian and Tertullian were relatively rare."[9] If this is true, and this paper would argue that it is, then yet another reading of Wesley presents itself, one dependent upon a synthesis of both East and West, one that enters into the parameters of this dialogue for both Evangelicals and Catholics.

An Understanding of the Difficulties of Original Sin

The purpose of this paper is to explain the Wesleyan-Arminian understanding of original sin and its companion doctrine, for Wesley and Arminius, prevenient grace. For the purposes of this ecumenical dialogue, this is an Evangelical synergist approach to the idea. To be fair and clear, in his discussions of original sin Wesley does often opt for an "Eastern perspective." In his discussions of prevenient grace, Wesley follows the theology of James Arminius, thus writing from a more "Western perspective." However, Wesley's understanding of original sin and prevenient grace is enmeshed in an approach that brings the two sides together. What emerges from the combining of these two understandings of the doctrines is consistent with his *via media* approach to theology, in this instance a synthesis of Eastern/Western theology. Further, and perhaps more importantly, it should be noted that for Wesley (and Arminius to a degree) this discussion was set in a pastoral context, to set the work of God's grace in an *ordo-salutis* (salvific order) in which God's grace was constantly evangelistic, accomplished salvation and sanctification in the same work of the initial conversion of the believer, and demanded responsibility from humans in response to the grace given from the beginning until the end of life.

A Wesleyan Understanding of Original Sin

To state it simply and straightforwardly, the Wesleyan position on the doctrine of original sin is argued as follows:

- Sin came into the world through the disobedience of our first parents.
- The Fall led to death by sin.
- There are two kinds of sin: original sin/depravity and actual/personal sin.
- The Fall led to the corruption of nature.

- The Fall led to the loss of original righteousness.
- All humans are born averse to God.
- Humans are born without spiritual life.
- Humans are inclined to evil.
- Original sin continues to exist in the life of the regenerate.
- Original sin can be cleansed by the Holy Spirit.
- Original sin differs from actual sin in that it is an inherited propensity to actual sin.
- Humans are not accountable for sin until its divinely provided remedy is neglected or rejected.
- Actual sin is the voluntary violation of a known law of God by a morally responsible person.
- Sin is not involuntary, inescapable shortcomings, infirmities, faults, mistakes, failures, or other deviations from perfect conduct. This does not include attitudes contrary to the Spirit of Christ (sins of the spirit).
- Personal sin is primarily a violation of the law of love, and it can be called unbelief.[10]

Wesley began to deal with this problem in the middle of the Methodist revival, sometime around the year 1750. As usual, Wesley's coming to the idea arose from the pastoral questions that were raised to him by his Methodist followers. If one is born in original sin, then how does one have the capacity to respond to God? Does the guilt of original sin so overwhelm us that we are incapacitated from being able to respond to God's overtures to us to accept the salvation offered in Christ? How do humans born sinful distinguish and acknowledge God in their sinful state? Is there any way to comprehend the work of God given original sin? Further, are we responsible for the guilt incurred by being born evil? How does one decide to become a Christian in the first place?

Wesley wrestled with these questions by adopting a *via media* position affirming the condition of original sin and the conviction that humans cannot in any honorable way be held eternally culpable of guilt of a sin they did not commit. Holding to a classic synergistic approach, Wesley dealt with the theological crisis of 1750 by acknowledging that God's first activity in fallen human lives is one of grace. This grace is universally available, but resistible. Prevenient grace is both pardon and power, because Wesley was increasingly uneasy with the idea of inherited universal guilt. The Wesleyan position can be stated, according to Randy Maddox, as: "Any present human culpability for our fallen condition results from our rejection of God's restoring work in our lives, not any continuing responsibility for the Original Sin."[11]

The key that unlocks the door of understanding these questions for Wesley, and now Wesleyan/Arminians, is that the doctrine of original sin establishes the need of the grace of God for a human being to wake up to sin or even to do any good. In his sermon "Awakest thou that Sleepest," John Wesley notes, "…as to the sleepers here spoken to. By sleep is signified the natural state of man; that deep sleep of the soul, into which the sin of Adam hath cast all who spring from his loins."[12] The plain fact for Wesley and his followers is that we human beings, because of original sin, do not have the capacity of good without God's grace. Hence, he writes,

> And yet I do not know that ever it was controverted in the primitive Church. Indeed there was no room for disputing concerning it, as all Christians agreed. And so far as I have ever observed, the whole body of ancient Christians, who have left us anything in writing, declare with one voice, that even believers in Christ, till they are "strong in the Lord and in the power of his might," have need to "wrestle with flesh and blood," with an evil nature, as well as "with principalities and powers."[13]

Wesley, following an orthodox understanding of both original sin and justification, establishes the need of the grace of God in the lives of human beings in order to awaken them to the knowledge of sin so that they can do any kind of good. The idea of prevenient grace affirms that even when we are lost, the Holy Spirit is at work attempting to awaken all sinners to accept Jesus as savior as a work of God's doing, a grace that awakens us to our need for salvation. Hence, Wesley affirmed that one does not just decide to become a Christian. We are invited and awakened by the Spirit of God's grace, bestowing that knowledge before we even know we are sinners.

The Effective Role of Prevenient Grace

For Wesley, especially and given the list above, this means that original sin is a call not only to understand the immensity of sin, but the universality of sin in all humans and the universality of an effective grace available to all humans. Such universality of grace is for Wesley, following Arminius and the Catholic tradition as shown below, a more basic and preceding condition than original sin. Ergo, grace is also the dual condition, along with original sin, of everyone born human. This grace for Arminian/Wesleyans is referred to as prevenient grace (also known as preventing grace or the grace that goes before, i.e., grace preceding the condition of universal sin), that state in which God, from birth until death, by his empowering grace seeks to enlighten, convict, and save all humans and then sufficiently lead them into all righteousness/sanctification. In summarizing Wesley's position on prevenient grace, Randy Maddox notes,

> Wesley understood Prevenient Grace to be God's initial move toward restored relationship with fallen humanity. As a first dimension, this involved God's merciful removal of any inherited guilt, by virtue of Christ. A second dimension of God's initial move to restored Presence is a partial healing of our debilitated human faculties, sufficient for us to sense and respond to God. The final dimension of God's specific overtures to individuals, inviting closer relationship. If these overtures are welcomed, a grace-empowered relationship of co-operative and progressive transformation sets forth. Since God's grace is universal, so is the possibility of such a relationship. Since God's grace is resistible, no individual's participation is inevitable.[14]

The history of the doctrine of prevenient grace is instructive here. The theological pedigree of the doctrine in the Western Christian tradition is confirmed and codified at the Second Council of Orange (529 AD), which stated that though faith is a free act, it results even in its beginnings from the grace of God.[15] The inclusion of prevenient grace as a "predisposing grace of God through Jesus Christ" by the Council of Trent cemented its place in Catholic theology as a cautioning against the idea of total and complete depravity as affirmed by Luther, Calvin, and the classical Reformed theologians.[16]

For Wesley, the doctrine of prevenient grace was rooted in the works of the Dutch theologian James Arminius (1560-1609) and his followers, known as Remonstrants, affirming that divine grace precedes human decision. This, of course, flies in the face of the idea that grace is only given by God to the elect, contra the historic Reformed or monergist position on justifying grace, and affirms that grace exists prior to and without reference to anything humans have done or initiated, contra Pelagianism. As humans are corrupted by the effects of sin, prevenient grace allows persons to engage their God-given free will to choose the salvation offered by God in Jesus Christ or to reject that salvific offer. Whereas Augustine held that prevenient grace cannot be resisted, Wesleyan/Arminians believe that such grace enables, but does not ensure, personal acceptance of the gift of salvation. Arminius thus taught: "Concerning grace and free will, this is what I teach according to the Scriptures and orthodox consent: Free will is unable to begin or to perfect any true and spiritual good, without grace.... This grace goes before, accompanies, and follows; it excites, assists, operates that we will, and co-operates (by and through grace) lest we will in vain."[17] In appropriating the thought of Arminius, John Wesley states that prevenient grace elicits "the first wish to please God, the first dawn of light concerning His will, and the first slight transient conviction of having sinned against Him."[18]

For Wesley, the doctrine of prevenient grace serves as a *via media* solution between the two great problems that divided Christianity: the belief of original sin and the Protestant doctrine of salvation by grace alone. It is also particularly effective in doing so: i.e., in some great way, prevenient grace grants power to humans from God. Developing the idea based upon the witness of Scripture, Wesley believed that prevenient grace enabled the doctrines of original sin and salvation by grace to co-exist while still maintaining God's sovereignty and holy character as well as human freedom. Wesley's doctrine of prevenient grace can be plainly stated thus:

- God is at work in the world, seeking to regenerate the lost.
- Moral acts are possible in the unregenerate through prevenient grace.
- Prevenient grace is the work of God drawing all people to a salvation.

- Prevenient grace does not save a person.
- Prevenient grace is resistible by all persons.[19]

Prevenient grace has thus proven a distinctive doctrine of the followers of Arminius and Wesley. For both thinkers and their followers, it represents a bridge between the issue of revelation (and thus several other doctrines—salvation, original sin, inherited depravity among them) that divided the theology of Roman Catholicism on the one hand and the monergists of the Continental Reformation on the other. Augustine and Aquinas both argued that the ideal of grace is active before even revelation to the human person; the former saw it as a vestige of the Trinitarian life in creation and the latter cited reason as a way of pointing to revelation. Luther and Calvin, on the other hand, felt that humans are so bereft of God apart from the direct intervention of the Cross of Christ that any prevenient grace was unthinkable. The Roman Catholic position, or at least that of Augustinians and Thomists, holds that enough of the image remains, so that some recognition of God is possible, hence the idea of prevenient grace.[20] This represents a real impasse and an important point for ecumenical dialogue.

Wesleyan/Arminian theology attempts to bridge this impasse with a strategic move on the theological chessboard. The genius of Wesley is that he acknowledges the doctrine of original sin as taught just as the Lutheran tradition and the Protestant tradition has affirmed it. However, the doctrine of prevenient grace asserts that the Holy Spirit begins the regeneration of the image of God in the human person before salvation occurs. H. Ray Dunning, a noted Wesleyan theologian, argues that

> Wesley only avoided the morass of Calvinism (or the classic Reformed theological positions of total depravity and irresistible grace) by a "hair's breadth" to use his own words. But that "hair" was enough to stand as a continental divide so that the two theologies (perspectives) lie miles apart in their fully developed expressions. The truth that holds them but a hair's breadth apart at the point of the watershed is the doctrine of *prevenient grace*. It could even be argued that this teaching was the most far-reaching and pervasive aspect of Wesley's thought.[21]

Further, Wesleyan synergism argues that the work of prevenient grace is the work of the Holy Spirit and thus Christological by method and nature:

"As the work of the Holy Spirit and preventing grace are virtually synonymous concepts, the work of the Spirit is seen by Wesley as Christological in nature."[22] This means that prevenient grace is a glimpse into the life of the Trinity as the Holy Spirit testifies to the work of Christ and Christ testifies to the work of the Father. In affirming this, Wesleyan theology opens Christian (read ecumenical) dialogue not only in studying justifying grace, but also to the issues of the Trinitarian ontology of god (i.e., God's being and nature) and epistemology (i.e., the question of how humans are known by and know God) by arguing that prevenient grace is the way that God first knows human beings and, consonantly, the way that human beings first know God.

Accordingly, the prevailing theological paradigm of Western theology as invoked by Wesley, which is indicative of the synergist tradition in Evangelical theology, humankind originally included the ability to choose between right and wrong and thus responsibility. Hence, following the *ordo salutis* for Wesley as noted above in Colin Williams, because of the Fall all human beings have become depraved and are created sinful. Thus, human beings cannot turn to God. Prevenient grace, the grace that comes before justifying grace, is given to all humans in creation. The grace of God through Jesus Christ is freely bestowed upon all people, enabling all who will to turn from sin to righteousness, or justifying grace, and believe in Jesus Christ for pardon and cleansing from sin. This grace can be resisted and lost—both at the point of prevenient grace and justifying grace. This grace can also be accepted. For those who accept God's grace, sanctification follows and allows for good works that are pleasing and acceptable to God. To state the matter clearly: "The plain fact is that we human beings do not have the capacity of good without God's grace."[23]

Following this, what prevenient grace means—or, perhaps more correctly stated, does—is give humans the power to do good. Prevenient grace is God's effective way of awakening us now and continually all our lives long to the fact that we are creatures, created in a divine image and for the purpose of relationship with our divine Creator. Prevenient grace is the power of God that restores by God's grace the ability to respond to God's offer of salvation. In its rudimentary form, this grace awakens our need to respond to God's offer of salvation and grants us the power so to do. Given our ongoing need for salvation and the sanctification that is established in us at the moment of our justification, prevenient grace goes before and beyond any basic knowledge of right and wrong and demands an ongoing effective exercise of theological power. In its beginnings, prevenient grace partially restores our liberty and will, i.e., our theological sensibilities and powers. As we grow in sanctifying grace over time, it includes "all the drawings of the Father... [and] all the convictions which his Spirit from time to time works in every person."[24] Prevenient grace, at least according to Wesley, continues over time. As Randy Maddox articulates it: "Put in other terms, we might silence the overtures of Prevenient Grace, but would not drive its very Presence from our lives. Therein lies our only hope of a latter 'awakening' to God's further overtures."[25] Thus, prevenient grace goes before our justification and awakening to God at the first acknowledgement of God's work in our lives and continues to do so all our lives long as we continue in relationship with God.

The Means of Prevenient Grace in Theological/Ecumenical Dialogue

As noted above, the Wesleyan/Arminian understanding of original sin was never simply juridical. It is articulated in a pastoral context, setting the work of God's grace in an *ordo salutis* (salvific order) in which God's grace is constantly evangelistic, accomplishes salvation and sanctification in the same work of the initial conversion of the believer, and demands theological responsibility from humans in response to the grace given from the beginning until the end of life. For Wesleyan/Arminians the cogent issue is the relationship between God—gracious, relentless, and universally available—and humans—fallen, created in God's image, and created with free will to accept or reject God's grace. The synthesis of Wesley, based on his reading of Arminius and the Western and the Eastern Fathers, is to center on the need for responsible human participation in the divine life, through the means that God has graciously provided.

So what does this mean for ecumenical dialogue? I argue here that the doctrine of prevenient grace means several things that are useful for our dialogue. First, prevenient grace can help us account for our being in this dialogue. The question often comes, "Why ecumenical dialogue?" Prevenient grace helps us to account for this and other dialogues as the ongoing evangelistic work of God in the creation, bringing us together in relationships aimed at mutual understanding of God and each other. As an effective power that grants us sanctified insight into our own relationships, the doctrine is one way of establishing the need for such dialogues.

Second, prevenient grace provides us the power to do theology together with a "continual awakening" of God's overtures to us in understanding the God who has come in Jesus in better and ever-deepening ways. Prevenient grace is a "theological key" to understanding all sorts of theological discussions. It provides us common ground in affirming God's first activity in fallen human lives, something all our traditions share. The continuing effectiveness of this grace gives us the power and opportunity to discuss the nature of grace and how our faculties, sin-corrupted as they may be, are continually awakened and enlightened to the need for theological dialogue and understanding. This includes the ideas as to whether and how grace is universally available to us as humans and whether and how it may be resistible, a point of some disagreement among us. Prevenient grace, as a common idea among theologians like us in the Western tradition, demands an accounting of how original sin is effective. This is certainly a point at which synergists have affinity with the Catholic position on original sin and disagree with Evangelical monergists. This point should be carefully wrestled with as we seek convergence and understanding together.

Additionally, and to the point of ecumenical dialogue like ours, prevenient grace is one way of discussing our understandings of ontology and epistemology as theological ways into understanding one another. As an ontological tool, prevenient grace is a way of seeing God, or at least one way of understanding the Trinitarian works of God as a unified yet independent trinity of co-equal persons. It proclaims a unity of Father-Son-Spirit bearing witness to Godself before and then with human participation and understanding. This way of seeing also accounts for prevenient grace as an epistemological tool, an effective way of witnessing to the grace of God at work in the world. Epistemology is certainly one of the crucial points of this or any ecumenical dialogue. How do we understand grace to operate and to effect salvation? While we will not always agree, making clear our understanding of the operation of grace is a grace in itself and one worthy of ongoing discussion.

To end this paper, the discussion of original sin and prevenient grace reflects an affirmation of theology as a way into salvation, a second-order grace following the worship of Christ's holy church with its continual affirmation of God as gracious. The power to ponder grace and offer answers to its great mysteries of both revelation and power are both gifts of God to us. For Wesleyan synergists, this is the point, and it is a pastoral one. The ongoing pastoral role of theologians is a testimony to the idea that prevenient grace is an enduring and effective power. The pastoral results of ecumenical dialogue—understanding our differences, whether historical, ontological, or epistemological, and finding ways to articulate and affirm what we can—illustrate that prevenient grace remains with us throughout our lives. Thus, prevenient grace represents for the Wesleyan/Arminian a power that reflects, even in dialogue with those with whom we both agree and disagree, at least a partial restoring of our sin-corrupted human faculties by an act of God's gracious power at work in us. Ecumenical dialogue and the understandings that come with it, both what we affirm and what we deny, mean that from time to time we affirm that God works in every person and through our theological faculties. In this we affirm that grace will not be silenced and that God never, despite even our occasional anathemas to the contrary, abandons any of us. In this, we are given a way forward as a kind of common testimony to both the universal condition of our sin and misunderstandings and, even more so, to the universal pre-condition of God's grace in our work. So it was that Pope Benedict XVI lauded ecumenical dialogue in his address at the ecumenical prayer gathering during his New York City visitation of 2008, noting,

> Too often those who are not Christians, as they observe the splintering of Christian communities, are understandably confused about the Gospel message itself. Fundamental Christian beliefs and practices are sometimes changed within communities by so-called "prophetic actions" that are based on a hermeneutic not always consonant with the datum of Scripture and Tradition.[26]

Ecumenical dialogue is a work of God's grace and an answer to our own pastoral situation. As a way beyond confusion and toward understanding, it is a testimony to such work. Confessing the universality of our sinfulness and believing that the greater, preceding, and ongoing work of God's grace is with us are the basis of our labor.

Notes

1. Rom. 8:7-8.
2. The gift of the thinking done in this paper has come to me through my teacher H. Ray Dunning and my colleague Henry Spaulding, both of whom are quoted in this work. I am indebted to them as friends who have instructed most of my thinking on the subjects of original sin and prevenient grace.
3. Colin Williams, *John Wesley's Theology Today* (Nashville: Abingdon Press, 1960), 16-17.
4. For an account of the ongoing research into Wesley and his theology, see Ted Runyon, *The New Creation: John Wesley's Theology Today* (Nashville: Abingdon Press, 1998).
5. Randy Maddox, *Responsible Grace: John Wesley's Practical Theology* (Nashville: Abingdon Press, 1994).
6. Ibid., 28.
7. See, for example, John Wesley, "Letter to a Roman Catholic" (Nashville: Abingdon, 1968). The letter was written by Wesley to a friend in Dublin, Ireland, in 1749.
8. Maddox, *Responsible Grace*, 29.
9. Ibid., 30.
10. Henry Spaulding, *We Believe: Engaging the Doctrinal Heritage of the Church of the Nazarene* (Mount Vernon, OH: Mount Vernon Nazarene University Human Resources, 2011), 24.
11. Maddox, *Responsible Grace*, 87.
12. John Wesley, "The Sermons of John Wesley – Sermon 3: Awakest Thou That Sleepest," Wesley Center Online, http://wesley.nnu.edu/john-wesley/the-sermons-of-john-wesley-1872-edition/sermon-3-awake-thou-that-sleepest/ (accessed February 1, 2017).
13. John Wesley, "The Sermons of John Wesley – Sermon 13: On Sin In Believers," Wesley Center Online, http://wesley.nnu.edu/john-wesley/the-sermons-of-john-wesley-1872-edition/sermon-13-on-sin-in-believers/ (accessed February 1, 2017).
14. Maddox, *Responsible Grace*, 90.
15. Heinrich Joseph Dominicus Denzinger, "Second Council of Orange," in *Enchiridion Symbolorum et Definitionum: A Compendium of Creeds, Definitions, and Declarations of the Catholic Church, 43rd ed.* (San Francisco: Ignatius Press, 2012), 375-77.
16. Council of Trent, Session 6, Chapter 5, Hanover Historical Texts Projects, https://history.hanover.edu/texts/trent/ct06.html (accessed February 1, 2017).
17. James Arminius, *The Works of James Arminius, D.D., Formerly Professor of Divinity in the University of Leyden* (Auburn, NY: Derby and Miller, 1853), 4:472
18. John Wesley, "The Sermons of John Wesley – Sermon 85: On Working Out Our Own Salvation," Wesley Center Online, http://wesley.nnu.edu/john-wesley/the-sermons-of-john-wesley-1872-edition/sermon-85-on-working-out-our-own-salvation/ (accessed February 1, 2017).
19. Spaulding, *We Believe*, 34.
20. Ibid., 35.
21. H. Ray Dunning, *Grace, Faith and Holiness: A Wesleyan Systematic Theology* (Kansas City: Beacon Hill Press, 1988), 48-49.

22 Ibid., 50.
23 Spaulding, *We Believe*, 26.
24 John Wesley, "The Sermons of John Wesley – Sermon 43: The Scripture Way of Salvation," Wesley Center Online, http://wesley.nnu.edu/john-wesley/the-sermons-of-john-wesley-1872-edition/sermon-43-the-scripture-way-of-salvation/ (accessed February 1, 2017).
25 Maddox, *Responsible Grace*, 88.
26 Pope Benedict XVI, "Remarks at the Church of St. Joseph in Yorkville, Manhattan," *The New York Times*, April 19, 2008, http://www.nytimes.com/2008/04/19/nyregion/19ecumtext.html (accessed February 1, 2017).

Background Paper

Original Sin and Its Effects Within the Economy of Salvation

Dr. Dennis W. Jowers

Scripture, as understood by monergist Evangelicals, teaches that original sin, which plagues all human beings save Christ alone, consists in three distinct elements: viz. the guilt of Adam's first sin, the want of original righteousness, and the corruption of fallen human beings' entire nature.[1] This paper constitutes an attempt to clarify what monergist Evangelicals understand original sin to be and why, in their view, Adam's descendants, Christ alone excepted, suffer from it.

The Guilt of Adam's First Sin

The first of original sin's three fundamental constituents, as we have already observed, is the guilt of Adam's first sin. Scripture teaches that God imputes Adam's first sin to all persons descended from him by way of seminal generation most clearly in Romans 5:12-21:

> Therefore, just as sin entered the world through one man and death through sin, and so death passed to all men, inasmuch as all sinned—for before the law sin was in the world. Yet sin is not imputed where there is no law. But death reigned from Adam

until Moses even over those who did not sin in the likeness of the transgression of Adam, who is the pattern of him who is to come. But not as the trespass, so also is the gift. For if through the transgression of one many died, much more has the grace of God and the gift through the grace of the one man Jesus Christ abounded to many. And not as through the one who sinned is the gift; for the judgment of one transgression was unto condemnation, but the gift is of many transgressions unto justification. For if on account of one transgression, death reigned through one, much more will those who receive the abundance of grace of the gift of righteousness reign through the one Jesus Christ. Therefore, as through one transgression condemnation came to all men, so also through one righteousness justification of life came to all men. For just as through the disobedience of one man, many were constituted sinners, so also through the obedience of one will many be constituted righteous. The law entered that sin might abound, but where sin abounded, grace superabounded so that as sin reigned through death, so grace might also reign through righteousness unto eternal life through Jesus Christ our Lord."[2]

Monergist Evangelicals admit that Paul attributes the universality of death to the universality of sin: "death passed to all men inasmuch as all sinned."[3] All who die, however, are not guilty of actual sin, i.e., sin committed by one's own act in one's own person. For "death reigned from Adam until Moses even over those who did not sin in the likeness of the trespass of Adam,"[4] i.e., even over infants who, being ignorant of good and evil,[5] could do neither in their own person.[6] Yet Paul asserts that all die, because all sin.[7] God, who slays not the righteous with the wicked,[8] furthermore, would hardly recompense infants with the wages of sin[9] if they were free of all fault. Of what sin, one might reasonably ask, are infants guilty? For what crime does God condemn them?

Paul answers this question almost immediately by asserting that human beings suffer death "on account of the transgression of one."[10] "The judgment of one transgression was unto condemnation."[11] "Through the transgression of one death reigned through one transgression."[12] "Through one transgression condemnation was unto all men."[13] Four times Paul asserts that the sin God punishes in all persons, including infants, is Adam's.[14] Because God imputes Adam's first sin to all persons descended from him by way of seminal generation, God's justice not only allows but requires him to exact the penalty of death from them.

Those who insist *a priori* on the salvation of all infants, admittedly, might conjecture that death, in the case of infants, constitutes not a punishment, but a blessing, because God whisks dead infants away, without exception, to heavenly bliss. One who reasons thus might conclude that one need attribute no crime to infants because God inflicts on them no punishment. This argument fails because death would never have afflicted any human being if neither Adam nor Eve had sinned; penalizing the human race for original and actual sin is death's *raison d'être*. Though God often inflicts death mercifully, Scripture characterizes death in language that strongly suggests that it is intrinsically evil. Death, according to Scripture, is the one who feeds on the corpses of the wicked,[15] whom those who hate wisdom love,[16] whose firstborn is calamity,[17] who rides the pale horse while Hades follows,[18] and whom God will cast into the lake of fire:[19] "the last enemy to be destroyed."[20] One would be hard-pressed, furthermore, to characterize the slaughter of infants as benevolence human or divine. Death constitutes punishment, therefore, which presupposes sin to be punished. "In Adam all die,"[21] because in Adam all sinned.[22]

The universality of death proves that God imputes Adam's first sin to all those descended from him by way of seminal generation. The same conclusion follows from the universal prevalence of original sin's second and third components, the want of original righteousness and the corruption of human nature in its entirety. Each of these is a punishment, and each afflicts persons guilty of no actual sin. Each of these presupposes the imputation of Adam's guilt to all of his descendants, excepting Christ.

Notwithstanding all of this, one might object, the doctrine that God imputes Adam's first sin to all of his descendants by way of seminal generation seems inconsistent with the teaching of Ezekiel 18:20: "The soul who sins shall die. The son shall not suffer for the iniquity of the father, nor shall the father suffer for the iniquity of the son. The righteousness of the righteous shall be upon him, and the wickedness of the wicked shall be upon him." A glance at the context of this passage shows that the son whom God exempts from the punishment due his father is an adult son who leads a consistently righteous life. After describing the vices of a wicked son, who, notwithstanding the righteousness of his father, will suffer eternal condemnation (Ezekiel 18:10-13), Ezekiel remarks:

> Now, behold, if he [the wicked son of a righteous father mentioned in the previous verses] begets a son, and he sees all the sins that his father has done, and he sees and does not do the like: on the mountains he does not eat and does not lift up his eyes to the idols of the house of Israel. He does not defile his friend's wife, does not oppress a man, does not take a pledge, and does not commit robbery. He gives his bread to a hungry man and covers a naked man with a garment. He withholds his hand from iniquity,[23] does not take usury or profit, performs my judgments, [and] walks in my statutes. He shall not die for the iniquity of his father. He shall surely live. His father, because he practiced extortion, robbed his brother, and did what is not good in the midst of his people, behold, he shall die for his iniquity. Yet you say, "Why does not the son suffer for the iniquity of the father?" If the son does judgment and righteousness, if he keeps all my statutes and does them, he shall surely live.[24]

Only after uttering these words does Ezekiel declare, "The soul who sins shall die. The son shall not suffer for the iniquity of the father, nor the father suffer for the iniquity of the son."[25] Ezekiel does not proclaim a universal principle to the effect that no one shall suffer for his father's iniquity.[26] He asserts that a quite exceptionally righteous person, who "has done what is just and right, and has been careful to observe all my statutes, he shall surely live."[27] No unregenerate person can truthfully lay claim to such exceptional righteousness. No unregenerate person can reasonably claim that Ezekiel 18:20 exempts him from punishments merited by other persons' sins.[28]

Scripture attests that God punishes some quite harshly for the sins of others to whom they bear some special relation. God punished Canaan and his descendants for the sin of Canaan's father, Ham.[29] God slew the firstborn sons of all Egypt as punishment for Pharaoh's refusal to allow the Israelites to depart.[30] God permanently excluded Ammonites and Moabites from the congregation of Israel to punish sins committed by Balak and his generation.³¹ God excluded distant generations of Eli's descendants from the priesthood as punishment for crimes committed by Eli and his two sons.³² He condemned the child born of David and Bathsheba's adultery to death to punish their sin.³³ He inflicted three years of famine on Israel as punishment for Saul's attempt to annihilate the Gibeonites.³⁴ He slew 70,000 persons as punishment for the census that David ordered.³⁵ God slew all of Jeroboam's house to punish Jeroboam's sins,³⁶ all of Baasha's house to punish his sins,³⁷ and all of Ahab's house to punish his sins.³⁸ God condemned the prophet Amaziah's wife to prostitution and his children to death by the sword to punish his sins.³⁹ One could continue this list indefinitely.

While Scripture never impugns God's justice in the slightest, it consistently reports that God punishes human beings for the sins of certain persons who constitute their heads or representatives. Passages like Romans 5:12–21 and 1 Corinthians 15:22 seem to teach that Adam constitutes a head or representative of the entire human race in the same way in which Christ is head or representative of those whom he saves. The parallel between Adam and Christ drawn in Romans 5:18–19 seems especially telling: "As (ὡς) through one transgression came condemnation to all men, so also (οὕτως καὶ) through one righteousness justification of life came to all men. For just as (ὥσπερ γὰρ) through the disobedience of one man, many were constituted (κατεστάθησαν) sinners, so also (οὕτως καὶ) through the obedience of one will many be constituted (κατασταθήσονται) righteous." As God imputes Christ's righteousness to believers,⁴⁰ these passages strongly suggest, God in the same way imputes Adam's first sin to his posterity, *sans* Christ.

Scripture appears to teach that God imputes Christ's righteousness to those whom he represents as substitute and high priest before his Father; it also teaches that God likewise imputes Adam's first sin to the great mass of humanity, of whom Adam is the source and head. By thus imputing the status of covenantal, or federal, heads to those whom they represent, God does not contravene the principle enunciated in Ezekiel 18:20, which applies only to quite exceptional persons. Rather, God acts in accordance with patterns of divine behavior that appear frequently throughout Scripture.

A persistent objector might complain that a benevolent God, "a God merciful and gracious, abounding in steadfast love,"⁴¹ would hardly impose a trial on Adam in which failure meant eternal death for himself and his posterity without promising Adam some comparably far-reaching reward for success. This would constitute a compelling objection to the views advanced above only if such a promise were demonstrably lacking, which is not the case. Scripture contains no sentence that explicitly states, "If the prelapsarian Adam had obeyed for a specified period, he and his posterity would have received eternal life as a reward." Yet precisely this conclusion follows from various passages of Scripture, which, taken together, imply the same.

In Romans 7:10, Paul evidently refers to the 10th commandment, which he quotes in verse, writing of ἡ ἐντολὴ ἡ εἰς ζωήν, "the commandment unto life." He does not shrink from describing the service of Moses in bringing Israel the two tables of the law as "the ministry of death in letters carved on stone tablets."[42] Paul even claims that "the letter kills"; the commandments written in letters on tablets of stone, that is to say, kill. "By the works of the law no flesh will be justified before him [i.e., God], for through the law is the knowledge of sin."[43] In what sense could the 10th commandment, an integral aspect of the natural and the Mosaic law, be unto life? This seems conceivable only in the case of Adam. If Adam had obeyed God as he ought, he would have received life as a reward, and as his descendants suffered the guilt and the penalty of his initial crime, so, it seems, they would have received Adam's righteousness and its reward if he had remained righteous.[44]

Perfect obedience to the moral law by an individual human being now would secure him eternal life, if such obedience were conceivable;[45] Christ's perfect obedience of the law actually does secure eternal life now for all to whom God imputes this obedience.[46] If perfect righteousness achieved by human beings would secure them eternal life, and such righteousness, when imputed to them, actually secures them eternal life, parity of reasoning strongly suggests that the righteousness of Adam that God would have imputed to his descendants, if Adam had persevered in righteousness, would secure for them eternal life as well. The absence of an explicit promise in Scripture that God would have rewarded Adam and his posterity with eternal life if Adam had obeyed the mandates imposed on him in no way discredits the thesis that God imputes Adam's first sin to all persons descended from him by way of seminal generation.

The Want of Original Righteousness

The contention of monergist Evangelicals that God imputes Adam's first sin to his descendants by way of seminal generation seems amply warranted. That Adam's first sin deprived him and his descendants, *sans* Christ, of original righteousness seems equally evident. As employed by Protestant theologians, the term "original righteousness" typically denotes those elements of the image of God, which human beings forfeited by the Fall, and which they regain through the grace of Christ: viz.: knowledge at least *de facto* inaccessible to the unregenerate,[47] righteousness, and true holiness.[48] Those who deny that Adam possessed these traits, alleging that he began his existence as an intellectual and moral infant, flagrantly contradict Scripture, which identifies knowledge, righteousness, and holiness as constituents of the divine image[49] in which God created the first human beings.[50] Such persons, moreover, severely impugn God's wisdom by implying that he entrusted lordship over the entire subhuman creation[51] to an unprincipled imbecile.[52] That the human race, excepting Christ, lost original righteousness in Adam seems scarcely to require proof. If the human race had retained original righteousness, why would God need to restore it in the regenerate? We consider it established, therefore, that by his fall, Adam forfeited original righteousness for himself and his descendants.

The Corruption of Fallen Human Beings' Entire Nature

The corruption of human beings' entire nature as a consequence of Adam's Fall seems evident from Scripture, if one accurately conceives of this corruption. When monergist Evangelicals ascribe comprehensive corruption to fallen human beings, they do not mean to suggest that fallen human beings lack any essential constituent of human nature. Adam's children by way of natural descent, although fallen, remain human beings. Neither do monergist Evangelicals mean to suggest that every fallen person is as corrupt as he conceivably could be. The corruption they ascribe to ordinary human beings is comprehensive in its extent, not in its intensity.

This corruption suffices to render unregenerate human beings incapable of performing any spiritual good. "The mind of the flesh," asserts Paul, "is enmity against God, for it is not subject to the law of God, nor can it be."[53] Sin, according to Scripture, is lawlessness (ἀνομία).[54] If unregenerate human beings cannot be subject to the law of God, their deeds must necessarily be lawless and sinful without exception. Paul writes, "To the unclean and unbelieving is nothing clean, but their mind and conscience are defiled. They profess to know God, but by their works deny him, being abominable, disobedient, and unfit for any good work."[55] It is only reasonable, therefore, that Jesus says to his disciples: "Without me you can do nothing,"[56] for apart from Christ, in their unregenerate state, human beings are utterly incapable of doing spiritual good.

While unregenerate, human beings cannot accept the saving truths of the gospel. "The natural man does not receive the things of the Spirit of God, for to him they are foolishness, and he cannot know them, because they are spiritually discerned."[57] Regeneration must come first, in being if not in time; only then can faith follow. As 1 Corinthians 2:14 attests, he who is capable of receiving the truths of the gospel is no longer a natural man.

Scripture describes the spiritual bondage to which fallen human beings are subject on account of original sin in highly expressive language. The unregenerate are "dead in trespasses and sins,"[58] "by nature children of wrath,"[59] children of the devil,[60] slaves of sin.[61] This thoroughgoing corruption of human nature in all of its aspects issues in a deluge of actual sin. Paul assesses the moral accomplishments of unregenerate humanity:

Both Jews and Gentiles are all under sin. As it is written:

> No one is righteous: not even one.
>   There is no one who understands,
>   no one who seeks God.
> They have all turned aside. They have together become worthless.
>   There is none who does good.
>   There is not even one.
> Their throat is an empty sepulcher.
>   With their tongues they have deceived.
> The venom of asps is under their lips.
>   Their mouth is full of cursing and bitterness.
>   Their feet are swift to shed blood.
>   Destruction and misery are in their ways,
>   and the way of peace they have not known.
>   There is no fear of God before their eyes.[62]

The behavior Paul depicts, though deplorable, is only to be expected of a creature every intention of the thoughts of whose heart is only evil continually.[63] That the Fall rendered human nature in its entirety thoroughly corrupt, then, seems evident from Scripture and bitter experience.

How Evangelical Monergist and Catholic Views of Original Sin Differ

This understanding of original sin's constituents agrees remarkably well with the Catholic conception of original sin articulated by Aquinas, who grants:

1) that all of Adam's descendants, Christ alone excepted,[64] share in the guilt of Adam's first sin;[65]

2) that God punishes Adam's descendants by way of seminal generation for this primal sin by depriving them of original justice;[66] and

3) that the want of original justice in human beings introduces various disorders into their constitution and especially concupiscence.[67]

Where lies the differences that divide monergist Evangelicals' opinions from the views of Catholics on this subject? Two differences lie at the heart of divisions between Catholics and monergist Evangelicals about original sin. First, Evangelicals typically regard the disorders introduced by the want of original righteousness in fallen humanity as more severe than most Catholics grant. Few Evangelicals would assert that a just God originally could have created man, prior to any sin, in the miserable estate in which he finds himself now. Yet Pius V condemned the proposition of Michel du Bay: "God could not from the beginning have created man, such as he is now born."[68]

Second, and even more consequentially, monergist Evangelicals consider original righteousness exacted, *naturae debita*.[69] They believe that God could not have justly created Adam without original righteousness and that no human being can fulfill his most basic duties to God and his neighbor without the original righteousness that Adam forfeited in the Fall. The Catholic Church teaches that original righteousness is unexacted, *naturae indebita*: good, but not so indispensable to the performance of human beings' basic duties that a good God could not have created Adam without it.

The Catholic Church considers original righteousness unexacted for at least three reasons. First, she rightly deems original righteousness an accident, not a constitutive element, of human nature. That one can be a human being without possessing original righteousness follows inexorably from two considerations: Christ possessed original righteousness in its fullness, and he assumed the nature that all human beings share, like them in all but sin.[70]

Monergist Evangelicals also condemn the error that the Fall rendered Adam and his descendants subhuman animals. A property of human beings can constitute an accident, without being unnecessary for human flourishing. Someone born blind, lame, deaf, and dumb would be a human being in spite of his disabilities, for the abilities to see, walk, hear, and speak are accidents, not constitutive principles, of human nature. This does not imply that a just God could have created Adam, prior to any sin on his part, blind, lame, deaf, and dumb, for the abilities to see, walk, hear, and speak, although they do not constitute human beings as human, seem indispensable to ordinary human flourishing. *Pace* Aquinas,[71] it is not the case that one who regards original righteousness as an accident of human nature must, in order to safeguard original righteousness' accidental character, deem it a *donum superadditum*.[72]

The Catholic Church's second principal reason for considering original righteousness unexacted appears considerably weightier than the first. This second reason concerns whether and to what extent concupiscence constitutes an offense against the moral law. The Catholic Church grants that concupiscence, i.e., unlawful desire, if it arises spontaneously, constitutes a mortal sin only if the human being subject to unlawful desire lends it the consent of his will. She can hardly do otherwise if she wishes to remain faithful to the Council of Trent's Decree *on Justification*. In this decree, the Council Fathers anathematize anyone who affirms that "through the grace of our Lord Jesus Christ, which is conferred in baptism…the whole of that which has the true and proper nature of sin is not taken away";[73] yet they affirm that "in the baptized remains concupiscence or kindling [*fomitem*]."[74] One can hold these two positions consistently only if one denies that concupiscence constitutes a mortal sin. Today's Roman magisterium affirms with the aforementioned decree, that "this concupiscence, which the Apostle sometimes calls sin, the holy synod declares, the Catholic Church has never understood to be called sin, because it truly and properly is sin in the renewed, but because it is from sin and inclines to sin."[75]

If Adam's merely natural endowments included immunity from concupiscence, this spontaneous, disordered desire would constitute even in renewed persons something unnatural, something incompatible with the rectitude of which human beings are naturally capable and which God requires of them. If immunity from concupiscence were natural to human beings, concupiscence would be sin in the full and proper sense of the term. To avoid this conclusion, as one must in order consistently to uphold the Council of Trent's teaching on baptism and justification, one must deem Adam's immunity from concupiscence an unexacted *donum superadditum*: something his nature did not, in the strictest sense of the term, need.

Evangelical monergists typically find this teaching exceedingly difficult to reconcile with Scripture. Paul writes in Romans 7:7: "What shall we say, then? Is the law sin? Let it not be. Yet I would not have known sin unless through the law; for I would not have known lust [ἐπιθυμίαν] unless the law had said, 'You shall not lust' [οὐκ ἐπιθυμήσεις]." Paul asserts that he learned what sin was from the law's prohibition of ἐπιθυμία. Ἐπιθυμία, in Pauline thought, is the paradigm case of sin. Yet ἐπιθυμία, which the Vulgate renders as *concupiscentia*,[76] is nothing but concupiscence. It seems difficult reasonably to dispute that in Paul's judgment, concupiscence constitutes sin.

Second, Scripture defines sin as lawlessness: "sin is lawlessness" (1 John 3:4b). An essential component of the moral law that binds Old and New Testament saints alike is the command, "You shall love the Lord your God with all your heart and with all your soul and with all your strength" (Deuteronomy 6:5; Mark 12:30; Matthew 22:37; Luke 10:27). One subject to concupiscence, i.e., subject to even one unlawful desire, cannot love God with all of his heart, soul, and strength. He who experiences unlawful desire behaves lawlessly. He violates the moral law; he sins.

Third, Scripture identifies death as the penalty of sin: the penalty, not of some particular kind of sin, but of sin as such, sin *simpliciter*. "The wages of sin," writes Paul, "is death."[77] To construe the term "sin" here in the sense of mortal sin alone would be to reduce Paul's statement to a tautology, for the term "mortal sin" means "sin that merits death." If by "sin" in Romans 6:23a, Paul meant not sin in general, but "sin that merits death" alone, that is to say, he would communicate in this passage only the tautology: "The wages of sin that merits death is death." It hardly seems plausible to suppose that Paul intends to express no more than this.[78]

Paul confirms that he regards death as the divinely appointed penalty for all violations of God's law in Galatians 3:10b, in which he quotes Deuteronomy 27:26: "Cursed is everyone who continues not in all things written in the book of the law to do them." The book of the law referred to here is manifestly the Pentateuch, which includes the commands to love God with all one's heart, soul, and strength,[79] to love one's neighbor as oneself,[80] and to love the stranger as oneself.[81] That the curse in question here is death appears from Galatians 3:13: "Christ redeemed us from the curse of the law by becoming a curse on our behalf, as it is written, 'Cursed is everyone who is hanged on a tree.'" Christ redeemed the saints from the curse of death by dying in their stead. In Galatians 3:10b, Paul implies that even one violation of any of the Pentateuch's moral precepts merits death. Every sin is a mortal sin.[82]

This biblical doctrine, viz. that every sin whatsoever merits eternal death, renders certain of the Catholic Church's teachings on the subjects of justification and baptism's effects untenable. If all failures to love God with all the heart, soul, and strength constitute sins in the proper sense of the term, and if the motions of concupiscence, which not only issue in but constitute such failures, remain after the new birth, then justification cannot consist in the utter removal from the regenerate of all that renders them worthy of damnation. The Council of Trent notwithstanding, it cannot be the case that "in the renewed, God hates nothing."[83] God hates the law in one's members that wars against the law of one's mind.[84] God hates the defilement of which even the regenerate must cleanse themselves.[85] God hates the flesh that lusts against the Spirit.[86] God hates the law of sin to which even the apostle Paul's flesh is enslaved,[87] and Christ does not shrink from calling even his own disciples evil.[88] It is true that "there is no condemnation to those who are in Christ Jesus,"[89] but this is because God has imputed Christ's righteousness to them and their sin to

Christ,[90] not because they no longer deserve eternal death. Evangelical monergists consider concupiscence a mortal sin and believe that all sins, even the slightest, merit the punishment of eternal death. This explains why they find the Catholic Church's second principal reason for deeming original righteousness unexacted and unpersuasive.

The third principal reason for the Catholic Church's insistence that original righteousness constitutes a *donum superadditum* to Adam's nature rather than a natural accident seems to consist in the fear that if the Church granted that original righteousness were natural to Adam and therefore exacted, she would compromise its gratuity.

This would be problematic, Evangelical monergists respond, only if God, by endowing Adam with original righteousness as a natural rather than a supernatural accident, thereby rendered himself less thankworthy. He does not. Arguably, God renders himself more thankworthy by laying himself under a certain theoretical necessity to supply the being he envisioned creating with original righteousness than he would have been if he had bestowed original righteousness on Adam as an unexacted appendage. As Anselm of Canterbury explains:

> There is a necessity, which diminishes or eliminates gratitude to a benefactor; and there is a necessity in terms of which a greater gratitude is owed for a benefit. For example, when because of the necessity to which someone is subject he confers a benefit against his will, little or no gratitude is owed to him. But when he willingly submits himself to the necessity of doing a good work, and does not merely endure this necessity against his will, surely he deserves greater gratitude for his good work. For this "necessity" ought not really to be called a necessity, but a grace, since he voluntarily incurred it or holds to it, without anyone's constraining him.[91]

God's willingness to endow Adam with original righteousness as an accident of nature rather than grace hardly renders him less worthy of thanks and praise. The Catholic Church's third principal reason for regarding original righteousness as a *donum superadditum* seems inadequate to debunk the Evangelical monergist position.

The chasm that separates Catholics from Evangelical monergists on the subject of original sin seems to derive principally from their disagreement about whether original righteousness is exacted: whether a just and benevolent God could have created the first human being without endowing him with original righteousness. Disagreements between Catholics and Evangelical monergists over this subject reflect deeply rooted disagreements about which sins do or do not render those who commit them worthy of eternal death. Evangelical monergists and Catholics agree in 1) deeming all merely human beings culpable from the first moment of their existence on account of Adam's first sin; 2) regarding concupiscence and mortality as consequences of and punishments for Adam's first sin; 3) believing that Christ will free his sheep entirely from the curse of concupiscence at their death; and 4) trusting that Christ, who has already triumphed over death himself, will liberate his flock from the curse of mortality on the Last Day.

Notes

[1] The answer to the *Westminster Shorter Catechism*'s question 18, accordingly, reads: "The sinfulness of that estate whereinto man fell, consists in the guilt of Adam's first sin, the want of original righteousness, and the corruption of his whole nature, which is commonly called Original Sin; together with all actual transgressions which proceed from it." *Westminster Shorter Catechism Project*, http://www.shortercatechism.com/resources/wsc/wsc_018.html (accessed April 6, 2017).

[2] Unless otherwise noted, all translations are my own.

[3] Rom. 5:12b.

[4] Rom. 5:14.

[5] Deut. 1:39.

[6] Rom. 9:11. Augustine (*Epistula* 157.19 and *Contra Julianum opus imperfectum* 6.4.9), Anselm (*De conceptu virginali et de originali peccato* 22), and Aquinas (*Super epistolam ad Romanos lectura*, cap. 5, lect. 4), likewise, identify infants as those to whom Paul refers in Rom. 5:14, who "did not sin in the likeness of the trespass of Adam."

[7] Rom. 5:12b.

[8] Gen. 18:25.

[9] Rom. 6:23.

[10] Rom. 5:15.

[11] Rom. 5:16.

[12] Rom. 5:17.

[13] Rom. 5:18.

[14] As John Murray rightly observes in his *The Imputation of Adam's Sin* (Grand Rapids: W.B. Eerdmans, 1959), 66-68, these verses imply that God imputed Adam's sin immediately to each person descended from him by way of seminal generation. Those who assert that everyone inherits depravity and becomes worthy of eternal death only by virtue of this depravity, that is to say, err by interposing a medium, viz. inherited depravity, between Adam and his condemned descendants. These texts do

not assert, however, that God condemns all human beings except Christ, because Adam's sin caused them to inherit a depraved nature, which renders them sinful in and of themselves. In Rom. 5:15-18, Paul characterizes the entire human race *sans* Christ as condemned for the sin of Adam. Inherited depravity constitutes a punishment for this sin, not its source. On this last point, see Francis Turretin, *Institutes of Elenctic Theology*, trans. George Musgrave Giger, ed. James. T. Dennison, Jr., 3 vols. (Phillipsburgh, NJ: P&R, 1992-97 [orig. 1679-85]) vol. 1, loc. 9, q. 9, c. 21, 622.

15 Ps. 49:14.
16 Prov. 8:36.
17 Job 18:12-13.
18 Rev. 6:8.
19 Rev. 20:14.
20 1 Cor. 15:26.
21 1 Cor. 15:22.
22 Thomas Aquinas mounts substantially the same argument in his *Summa contra Gentiles* 4.50.3.
23 The Masoretic text here reads "מֵעָנִי," i.e., "from a poor man" or "from the poor." Like most contemporary translators, for reasons of coherence and because of the parallel with verse 8, I follow the suggestion in the critical apparatus of BHS to emend the text at the beginning of verse 17 to "מֵעָוֶל" so that it agrees with the *LXX* rendering, "καὶ ἀπὸ ἀδικίας."
24 Ezek. 18:14-19.
25 Ezek. 18:20.
26 "For Ezekiel, too," writes Walter Eichrodt, "the connection between the destiny of the individual and the guilt of his ancestors was and remained an undeniable fact. We must not be so hasty as to accuse him of thoughtless inconsistency when in other passages he...presupposes almost as a matter of course a common national destiny, within which good and evil are inextricably intertwined and where the collective guilt meets with its punishment." Eichrodt, *Ezekiel: A Commentary* (Philadelphia: Westminster Press, 1970), 237.
27 Ezek. 18:19.
28 We owe our interpretation of Ezek. 18:20 principally to Turretin, *Institutes*, vol. 1, loc. 9, q. 9, c. 27, 624-25.
29 Gen. 9:25.
30 Exod. 11:5.
31 Deut. 23:3-4.
32 1 Sam. 3:30-36; 1 Kings 2:26-7.
33 2 Sam. 12:14.
34 2 Sam. 21:1.
35 2 Sam. 24:15; 1 Chron. 21:14.
36 1 Kings 14:10, 15:29-30.
37 1 Kings 16:3, 11-12.
38 1 Kings 21:21-22; 2 Kings 9:8-9, 10:6-11.
39 Amos 7:17.
40 2 Cor. 5:21; Rom. 4:5-8.

41 Exod. 34:6; Cf. Neh. 9:17; Ps. 86:15, 103:8, 145:8; Joel 2:13; Jon. 4:2.
42 2 Cor. 3:7.
43 Rom. 3:20.
44 Our argument from Rom. 7:10 derives from ibid., vol. 1, loc. 8, q. 6, c. 4, 583.
45 Matt.19:17b; Luke 10:25-28; Leviticus 18:5; Cf. Rom. 10:5, Gal. 3:12.
46 Rom. 4:5-8, 5:18-19; 2 Cor. 5:21
47 Col. 3:10, Eph. 4:24.
48 "These three elements," writes Louis Berkhof, "constitute the original righteousness, which was lost by sin, but is regained in Christ." Berkhof, *Systematic Theology* (Grand Rapids: W.B. Eerdmans, 1938), 204.
49 Col. 3:10; Eph. 4:24
50 Gen. 1:26-27.
51 Gen. 1:26, 28; Ps. 8:5-8.
52 We owe this point to Samuel Niles, *The True Scripture Doctrine of Original Sin* (Boston: S. Kneeland, 1757), 54-55.
53 Rom. 8:9.
54 1 John 3:4.
55 Titus 1:15-16.
56 John 15:5.
57 1 Cor. 2:14.
58 Eph. 2:1; cf. Eph. 2:5.
59 Eph. 2:3.
60 John 8:47.
61 John 8:34.
62 Rom. 3:9-18.
63 Gen. 6:5.
64 Thomas Aquinas, *Summa Theologiae* I-II, 81, 3 corp.
65 Ibid. I-II, 81, 1 corp.
66 Ibid. I-II, 85, 5 corp.
67 Ibid. I-II, 82, 3 corp.
68 DH *Enchiridion symbolorum, definitionum, et declarationum de rebus fidei et morum*, ed. Peter Hünermann, 44th ed. (Freiburg: Herder, 2014), 1955. Among the other propositions condemned by Pius V in his bull against Michel du Bay, *Ex omnibus afflictionibus*, are the following:
    (a) That which is without charity is not true obedience to the law (ibid. 1916);
    (b) There is no sin that is by its nature venial, but every sin merits eternal punishment (ibid. 1920);
    (c) Free will, without the assistance of God's grace, is not capable of abstaining from sin (*nonnisi ad peccandum valet;* ibid. 1927);
    (d) Everything that a sinner or slave of sin does is a sin (ibid. 1935).
69 See, for example, Charles Hodge, *Systematic Theology*, 3 vols. (1872-73) 2:104-5. One who contends that original righteousness is *humanae naturae debita* does not imply that any creature possesses a right to any bounty from God. For, as Turretin explains, in supplying original righteousness, God pays a debt that he owes to his own fidelity, not to Adam, who can give God nothing and therefore merit nothing *de condigno* (*Institutes,*

vol. 1, loc. 8, q. 3., cc. 16, 17, 578). Aquinas likewise asserts that Adam is due certain natural gifts only inasmuch as God owes it to his own justice and goodness to bestow them, *ST* I, 21, 1 ad. 3 and *ST* I-II, III, 1 ad 2.

70 Heb.2:17, Heb. 4:15.

71 See Aquinas, *Summa contra Gentiles*, Book 4.52.14 and *ST* I, 95, 1 corp.

72 Cf. Herman Bavinck's argument *per reductionem ad absurdum* against this notion: "Adam also had natural, original righteousness. This natural righteousness, though it is natural and flows from the basic principles and powers of the natural man without supernatural assistance…can nevertheless still be lost and is in fact lost by many persons. Yet, even the most degenerate sinner, one devoid of all natural justice, is still a human being. The possibility of losing and the actual loss of original righteousness, therefore, can absolutely not serve as an argument against its natural character. If that were the case, the natural justice that Rome also teaches would have to be called supernatural." Bavinck, *Reformed Dogmatics*, trans. John Vriend, ed. John Bolt, 4 vols. (Grand Rapids: W.B. Eerdmans, 2003-8), 2:546.

73 DH 1515.

74 Ibid.

75 Ibid.

76 In the Vulgate, Rom. 7:7 reads: "Quid ergo dicemus? Lex peccatum est? Absit. Sed peccatum non cognovi nisi per legem. Nam concupiscentiam nesciebam nisi lex diceret, 'Non concupisces.'"

77 Rom. 6:23a.

78 We owe this argument to William Jenkin, who states it in "No Sin Venial," his contribution to *The Morning Exercises at Cripplegate*, ed. James Nichol, 6 vol. (London: Thomas Tegg, 1845) 6:150-82 at 168-69.

79 Deut. 6:5.

80 Levi. 19:18b.

81 Levi. 19:34b.

82 Cf. James 2:10. Some may consider the punishment of eternal death disproportionate to the offense committed in the slightest of sins. William Ames addresses such persons' concerns thus: "The evil of sin, even of the slightest, is greater than the evil of any punishment…. Any fault, therefore, may justly be punished by God with any penalty, even eternal death." Ames, *Bellarminus enervatus*, 4 vols. (Amsterdam: Apud Ioannem Iansonnium, 1628), vol. 4, book 2, c. 1, §17, 22.

83 DH 1515.

84 Rom. 7:23.

85 2 Cor. 7:1.

86 Gal. 5:17.

87 Rom. 7:25.

88 Matt. 7:11; Luke 11:13.

89 Rom. 8:1.

90 2 Cor. 5:21.

91 *Cur Deus Homo Complete Philosophical and Theological Treatises of Anselm of Canterbury*, trans. Jasper Hopkins and Herbert Richardson (Minneapolis: Banning Press, 2000), 352.

Background Paper

The Patristic Background to Original Sin

Dr. Daniel A. Keating

Orientation

The teaching of the Church Fathers on "the sin of Adam" or "original sin" does not strictly determine what the various churches have taught or how we ought to think about the consequences of Adam's sin today. Yet, this background is crucial for understanding: 1) how the first generations of Christians thought about Adam's sin; 2) the differences among them in emphasis and in doctrine; and 3) where our various views on original sin (may) derive from.

Scholarly surveys of original sin in the Fathers can serve as resources for us.[1] I find all of them helpful but none of them fully satisfactory. They tend to be driven by the Augustinian account and by later disputes, with the authors hunting for evidence for one view or another, and at points are tone-deaf to the significant *similarities* across the Fathers when charting where the crucial differences lie.

I hope to show underlying similarities in the various approaches and to indicate lines of differences between one view and another. *The difference cannot be neatly summed up as differences between the East and the*

West. My aim is to help us see, amidst the detail and complexity, the salient questions that shape the history of this issue.

Survey of the Fathers

Justin Martyr (Died c.165 AD)

By all accounts, the first appearance of the sin of Adam in the Fathers is found in Justin Martyr. He speaks of the human race falling under the serpent's power of death, but he does not develop this idea.[2] He is the first to take up and develop the typology of Eve and Mary, and so he extends the Adam-Christ typology with a further contrast. But there is little theological development of this notion in Justin.

Theophilus of Antioch (Died c. 183 AD)

Theophilus is the first Christian writer to present Adam and Eve as *children* who were called to obey their Father:

> But Adam, being yet an infant in age, was on this account as yet unable to receive knowledge worthily. For now, also, when a child is born it is not at once able to eat bread, but is nourished first with milk, and then, with the increment of years, it advances to solid food. Thus, too, would it have been with Adam.... But He wished also to make proof of him, whether he was submissive to his commandment. And at the same time he wished man, infant as he was, to remain for some time longer simple and sincere. For this is holy, not only with God, but also with men, that in simplicity and guilelessness subjection be yielded to parents.... So also for the first man, disobedience procured his expulsion from Paradise. Not, therefore, as if there were any evil in the tree of knowledge; but from his disobedience did man draw, as from a fountain, labor, pain, grief, and at last fall a prey to death.[3]

For Theophilus, death is the primary consequence of Adam's sin, human beings remain free in regard to their wills, and the devil is assigned the primary blame in the Fall.[4]

Irenaeus of Lyons (c. 125-200 AD)

Irenaeus takes up and develops the idea of Adam and Eve as grown children, not yet fully mature, who were deceived by the devil.[5] It is important to note that in *Adversus Haereses*, Irenaeus sets himself the task of rejecting the error of Tatian, who taught that Adam is not in the end saved by God but lost forever. Thus, Irenaeus describes Adam's sin as a real transgression but one in which he was deceived by the devil, and he places the greatest blame upon the devil himself:

> For [God] knew that [the serpent] had been the prime mover in the guilty deed; but he pronounced the curse upon him in the first instance, that it might fall upon man with a mitigated rebuke. For God detested him who had led man astray, but by degrees, and little by little, he showed compassion to him who had been beguiled.[6]

For Irenaeus, Adam actually repents after the Fall, and though he is required to leave paradise, this "exile" is an expression of the mercy of God, who did not want the human race to live eternally under the power of sin. Following his sin, Adam admits, "I have by disobedience lost that robe of sanctity which I had from the Spirit," and waits for his redemption in Christ.[7] For Irenaeus, all this is the prelude to the new Adam who would come to redeem those who had fallen under sin and the power of death: "Now Adam had been conquered, all life having been taken away from him: wherefore, when the foe was conquered in his turn [by Christ], Adam received new life; and the last enemy, death, is destroyed, which at the first had taken possession of man."[8]

Tertullian (Died c. 220 AD)

This early African writer considers Adam's fall to have had very serious effects, but at the same time he rejects the practice of infant baptism.[9] Rejecting the Platonic belief in the pre-existence of souls, he also proposed an avenue for the passing on of Adam's sin known as "traducianism." On this view the soul as well as the body is generated by the human parents, and through this generation the fault of Adam is passed to all his descendants.[10] This theory was on offer during the Patristic Period, and Augustine of Hippo was initially drawn to it, though he also recognized the problems with it and increasingly distanced himself from the materialistic implications of this theory of the soul's origin.[11]

Clement of Alexandria (c. 150-215 AD)

Clement appears to follow in the path set by Theophilus and Irenaeus, viewing Adam as a child who was led astray and became an "adult" as a result of his disobedience:

> The first man, when in Paradise, sported free, because he was the child of God; but when he succumbed to pleasure... was as a child seduced by lusts, and grew old in disobedience; and by disobeying his Father, dishonored God. Such was the influence of pleasure. Man, that had been free by reason of simplicity, was found fettered to sins.[12]

The dominant concern in Clement's writings is to oppose Gnosticism and specifically the gnostic rejection of marriage and sexuality. Though recognizing Adam's sin and the effects on the human race, Clement emphasizes the role of human freedom. "Clement's notion of baptism corresponds with his conception of sin as sickness and conversion as healing. Baptism is a rebirth and regeneration."[13]

Origen (185-254 AD)

Origen is credited by some as being the first to use the phrase "original sin,"[14] though when examined closely this is not precisely the expression he employs. Origen speaks of every soul contracting "a stain of sin and iniquity,"[15] and he understands the rite of infant baptism to reveal the need for this stain of sin to be removed. In his commentary on Romans 5, he writes, "For those entrusted with the divine mysteries knew that there are inborn stains of sin present in all that must be washed off by water and the Spirit."[16] Origen appeals to what would become the standard biblical texts (Psalm 51, texts from Job) to ground this conviction. It is striking that in Origen—a Greek writer—we find such a strong sense of the need to cleanse the defilement of sin in newborn infants, and on some occasions he ties this stain of sin to Adam.[17] At the same time, he vigorously defends human freedom and judges that each one is condemned or acquitted for what he has freely done. His overall conception of the problem of sin is unique, in detail unlike any who followed him.

Cyprian of Carthage (Died 258 AD)

Cyprian is commonly identified as the figure who combined the key elements that later came to full development in Augustine and the Western tradition: "The achievement of a correlation between the practice of infant baptism and the doctrine of original sin was first made visible in Cyprian."[18] In this matter he seems *not* to have followed his mentor Tertullian. Cyprian holds to the sin of Adam still present in us and ties this closely to the practice of infant baptism: "How much rather ought we to shrink from hindering an infant, who, being lately born, has not sinned, except in that, being born after the flesh according to Adam, he has contracted the contagion of the ancient death at its earliest birth."[19] The practice of infant baptism for Cyprian demonstrates the remedy that is needed for all those born of Adam's stock. Augustine will later cite Cyprian as an authority on this very point.

The Cappadocian Fathers: Basil (330–379 AD), Gregory of Nazianzus (c. 332–395 AD), Gregory of Nyssa (329–389 AD)

In their reading of the opening chapters of Genesis, the Cappadocian Fathers follow the lines set down by Philo (and by Origen, but less closely). On this account, Adam was created with great and high attributes, "endowed with the freedom of will, filled with love for his creator and blest with the most intimate intercourse with him."[20] Thus, there is among the Cappadocians a high or exalted view of what Adam originally possessed, in contrast to the Irenaean view. Nonetheless, "their tendency is to view original sin as a wound inflicted on our nature."[21] It is primarily the *effects* of Adam's sin that need remedy. Still, Basil speaks in terms of the transmission of *sin* from Adam,[22] while Gregory of Nyssa describes the transmission of sin in plain terms:

> Just as in the natural propagation of the species each animal engenders its like, so man is born from man, a being subject to passions from a being subject to passions, a sinner from a sinner. Thus sin takes its rise in us as we are born; it grows with us and keeps us company till life's term.[23]

Despite this sense of transmitted sin, the Cappadocians hold the conviction that human beings are responsible only for their own sins; they do not speak about the human race as being *guilty* in Adam.

John Chrysostom (347-407 AD)

In their dispute over original sin, Augustine and Julian of Eclanum each claimed John as supporting their rival views. John takes the view that as a result of Adam's sin we are inclined to sin and are made mortal:

> Now this is why Adam is a type of Christ. How a type? it will be said. Why in that, as the former became to those who were sprung from him, although they had not eaten of the tree, the cause of that death which by his eating was introduced; thus also did Christ become to those sprung from Him.[24]

But while John understands Adam's sin to make us liable to punishment and death, he demurs from acknowledging that we are properly "sinners" because of Adam's sin:

> For the fact that when he had sinned and become mortal, those who were of him should be so also, is nothing unlikely. But how would it follow that from his disobedience another would become a sinner? For at this rate a man of this sort will not even deserve punishment, if, that is, it was not from his own self that he became a sinner. What then does the word "sinners" mean here? To me it seems to mean liable to punishment and condemned to death.[25]

Notably, John appears to deny that sin properly speaking exists in infants.[26]

Athanasius (c. 296-373 AD), Didymus (c. 313-398 AD), Cyril (c. 378-444 AD)

Athanasius presents Adam in the Garden as in a state of supernatural blessedness. J.N.D. Kelly concludes that in Athanasius, "we see the idea of original righteousness and perfection in embryo."[27] For Athanasius, the sin of Adam had repercussions for the whole human race, as Adam's initial fault unloosed, with evils both physical and moral, the multitude of sins from which Christ redeemed us. The primary focus is the inheritance of death: "For all other men, being merely born of Adam, died, and death reigned over them."[28] But Athanasius also speaks of the passage of sin from Adam to his descendants, though he does not expand upon it: "When Adam had transgressed, his sin reached unto all men."[29] In the following selection from his work against the Arians, Athanasius presents a fuller picture of how Christ redeemed what was lost in Adam:

For no longer according to our former origin in Adam do we die; but henceforward our origin and all infirmity of flesh being transferred to the Word, we rise from the earth, the curse from sin being removed, because of Him who is in us, and who has become a curse for us. And with reason; for as we are all from earth and die in Adam, so being regenerated from above of water and Spirit, in the Christ we are all quickened.[30]

Didymus appears to follow Origen more closely (and there is no surprise in this). He holds that infants are born with a sin transmitted through their parents and so need cleansing from this sin through baptism. Didymus also accents the new life we receive through the Holy Spirit in baptism, including the renewal of the image and likeness of God.[31] From Didymus' writings we can glean many of the elements of the Augustinian view of original sin, but with less expansion and explanation.

Cyril of Alexandria, interestingly, also holds a "strong" view of Adam's sin; that is, he considers the Fall as a serious disobedience that brought all kinds of baleful effects in its wake. He uses the image of a root being corrupted and working its way through the whole plant to describe how Adam's sin has infected the entire race: "Paul shows that corruption extends to the entire human nature because of the transgression in Adam."[32] We are all directly affected by one man's sin, and this leads to the corruption of our nature, estrangement from God, and eventual physical and spiritual death. In his commentary on Romans 5:18, he specifically asks how it is that we are infected with Adam's sin when Scripture says that a man will die only for his own sins. His answer: through Adam's sin, desires and impurities ran into the nature of the flesh, and "our nature has become sick with sin through the disobedience of one, namely, Adam." Our nature fell under "the law of sin," and thus our nature became feeble in Adam.[33] From this Christ set us free. At the same time, Cyril holds that we are only personally guilty for our own sins, and earlier in the Romans commentary describes how we become imitators of Adam's sin in our own life.

Ephrem (c. 306-373 AD) and the Macarian Homilies (c. 300-391 AD)

Two important witnesses from the late fourth century speak about Adam's sin in terms of leaven introduced into the "dough" or "lump" of humanity. In a commentary on Romans 5:12, Ephrem the Syrian presents our plight and rescue through the metaphor of leaven in dough: "Just as the first Adam sowed impure sin in pure flesh, and so the leaven of wickedness was buried in our entire dough, so our Lord sowed justice in the sinful flesh, and changed our dough with his leaven."[34] In the Macarian Homilies, an important source for Byzantine spirituality, the author is even more overt than Ephrem about how the leaven of Adam's sin worked its way thoroughly into the dough of our humanity:

> Just as Adam by his transgression received into himself the leaven of the evil of the passions, and by participation his descendants and the entire human race partook of that leaven, and afterwards, by natural progress the passions of sin have so grown in men that they committed every sort of crime and wrongdoing so that all of humanity was leavened with evil... so the Lord in his time on earth was pleased to die on behalf of all and redeem them with his blood and to put the heavenly leaven of goodness into the faithful souls suffering under the weight of sin.[35]

The picture gained from this image is of sin as a power that spreads like a contagion through the entire human race. These Eastern sources make use of the biblical language of "dough" or "lump" (in Greek, *phurama*; in Latin, *massa*) to describe our humanity infected by Adam's sin.[36] Notably, the language of *massa* becomes Augustine's characteristic way of describing humanity under the influence of Adam's sin.

Ambrose (337-397 AD)

In the estimation of Piero Beatrice, in Ambrose "one finds almost all of the essential elements of the doctrine of original sin" as are later found in Augustine.[37] Ambrose rejects the view that Adam and Eve were simply children, and he follows Philo and the Cappadocians in holding to an exalted view of what Adam possessed. For Ambrose, pride was the root cause of Adam's sin. Rondet sums up the teaching of Ambrose: "Adam's sin was a sin of pride; this sin was our sin, for Adam is in each one of us."[38] Ambrose himself writes:

> Adam existed, and in him we all existed; Adam perished, and in him all perished.... In Adam I fell, in Adam I was cast out of Para-

dise, in Adam I died. How should God restore me, unless he find in me Adam, justified in Christ, exactly as in that first Adam I was subject to guilt and destined to death?[39]

Augustine heard this teaching on the sin of Adam with his own ears from the preaching of Ambrose and appears to have made it his own.

Augustine of Hippo (354-430 AD)

Augustine's views on original sin have been exhaustively treated. He held that nothing is more difficult to understand than the nature of "the ancient sin."[40] He begins his account by carrying "to its highest pitch the growing tendency to attribute original righteousness and perfection to the first man."[41] For Augustine, the only persuasive cause of the Fall of Adam was pride—the Fall was due to Adam alone—and he underscores the immensity of the evil consequences of this fall. For Augustine, the practice of infant baptism and the accompanying exorcisms together display the reality of original sin. The sacramental practice of the church reveals what the church believes.

Augustine was divided in his own mind regarding the propagation of original sin; he wavered between the traducianist theory (the soul is passed to the child from the parents), from which he increasingly drew back, and a creationist theory in which the soul is understood to be created directly by God. However the transmission of sin occurs, for Augustine Adam's sin and the guilt of his sin were transmitted to all descendants of Adam, whereas in Christ both original sin and our personal sins are all remitted:

> And from this we gather that we have derived from Adam, in whom we all have sinned, not all our actual sins, but only original sin; whereas from Christ, in whom we are all justified, we obtain the remission not merely of that original sin, but of the rest of our sins also, which we have added. Hence it runs: "Not as by the one that sinned, so also is the free gift." For the judgment, certainly, from one sin, if it is not remitted—and that the original sin—is capable of drawing us into condemnation; whilst grace conducts us to justification from the remission of many sins,—that is to say, not simply from the original sin, but from all others also whatsoever.[42]

As Henri Rondet sums up, "St. Augustine did not invent original sin, but he rendered explicitly a tradition which, through various formulas, was slowly coming to the surface."[43] Piero Beatrice makes an even stronger claim: "Augustine did not invent the doctrine of hereditary guilt. He did make considerable efforts to elaborate it and provide it with a systematic underpinning.... It already existed before him and was widespread in the Christianity of his time, particularly in the West."[44] Augustine offered the fullest account to date of original sin, but he drew from it a set of consequences, such as the eternal condemnation of infants who die without baptism, that many Fathers before him (including Ambrose) did not affirm.

Analysis of Positions

I offer the following summary conclusions from this brief survey of the Fathers on Adam's sin and its effects.

1) For the Fathers, Adam's sin had a decisive and corporate effect on the entire human race that could only be remedied by the redemption brought by Christ the new Adam. In this they were simply following what Paul states so plainly in Romans 5. Adam did not merely establish a poor example that we all have imitated (as some of the Pelagians were assumed to claim); Adam's sin conferred evil effects upon the human race as a whole.

2) Regarding differences between the Fathers, one notable distinction concerns how Adam's original state is conceived and what level of blame or excuse he is charged with. The line taken by Theophilus, Irenaeus, and Clement of Alexandria considers Adam and Eve to be something like adult children, not yet in full possession of their intellectual faculties, who were deceived by the devil. They are still at fault, but the primary blame is attached to the devil, who is the real culprit in this story. For this reason the Son of God appeared: "to destroy the works of the devil."[45]

The line taken in much of the Eastern tradition, following a path set by Philo, sees Adam in possession of great powers and abilities, such that the Fall was from a more highly developed position. Yet in general these Easterners do not attach fault or blame to Adam's *followers* as strongly as they see this fault in Adam, and the primary result of Adam's sin is an inherited *condition*: proneness to sin and liability to death.

The line taken by Ambrose and Augustine sees Adam in full possession of his faculties and enticed fundamentally by his own pride (even if the devil was the occasion for rousing this pride). Thus, the Fall was devastating to Adam's condition and to us who are born from him. We inherit not only the penalty of that fall but also in some real sense the culpability for it that requires remission.

3) Another line of distinction concerns what is actually passed down from Adam to us. All the Fathers agree that we inherit debilitating consequences from Adam's sin. But what are those consequences? For most of the Fathers of the Eastern tradition, the emphasis falls on the inherited *conditions* of Adam's sin, not the sin itself. Thus, the primary consequences are: a) estrangement from God (shown by exile from the Garden); b) the punishment of physical death as we now experience it; c) a strong propensity toward sin—concupiscence; and d) a broken world and a broken relationship between the human race and the world. It is worth underlining that for Origen and Didymus, infants are born with a stain of sin that genuinely requires cleansing through baptism, but Origen also upholds that we are guilty and so punished only for our own personal sins.

Cyprian, Ambrose, and Augustine are in general agreement with the Eastern Fathers regarding the consequences that accrue to us because of Adam's sin. But they add this conclusion, that we are born actually *infected* with the sin of Adam, and though this is not a *personal* sin, it retains the nature of a sin and requires "remission" through baptism.

One way to state this difference is to use the analogy of disease and its effects. Have we in Adam contracted the actual contagion of disease (that is, are we actively *infected*, like an actual virus), or have we contracted the *effects* of his contagion, like someone who inherited a body broken by disease, but not the disease itself? While the analogy is imperfect, it captures something of the difference between the Eastern and Augustinian views.

4) Of the writers surveyed here, only Tertullian speaks against the baptism of infants (the earlier writers, e.g., Justin, do not address the issue). The Fathers who postdated Tertullian were committed to the baptism of infants and saw this as a port of entry into the kingdom of God. Some of these (from both East and West) view baptism as essential to wiping away the stain of sin with which we are born; others do not view it in this way, but rather see baptism as a requirement for our new birth into the life and grace of God that enables us to overcome the inherited *effects* of original sin.

What can we draw from the results of this survey? First, there is a broad consensus on the basic condition that we inherited from Adam that is healed only through baptism into Christ and the new life in the Holy Spirit. Second, the differences among the Fathers are more subtle than is often stated. There are not just two camps or positions, but several different factors that are weighed differently. Recognizing the variety of views can aid us in evaluating the similarities and differences found among our own positions today.

Notes

[1] Henri Rondet, *Original Sin: The Patristic and Theological Background*, trans. Cajeta Finegan (New York: Alba House, 1972); Tatha Wiley, *Original Sin: Origins, Developments, Contemporary Meanings* (New York: Paulist Press, 2002); Pier Franco Beatrice, *The Transmission of Sin: Augustine and the Pre-Augustinian Sources,* trans. Adam Kamesar (Oxford: Oxford University Press, 2013). See also the treatments of original sin in Jaroslav Pelikan, *The Christian Tradition: A History of the Development of Doctrine* (Chicago: University of Chicago Press, 1971), and J.N.D. Kelly, *Early Christian Doctrines*, rev. ed. (New York: Harper Collins, 1978).

[2] See Justin Martyr, *Dialogue with Trypho*, 87.4.

[3] Theophilus, *Ad Autolycum*, 2.25, in *Fathers of the Second Century: Hermas, Tatian, Athenagoras, Theophilus, and Clement of Alexandria*, vol. 2 of *Ante-Nicene Fathers (ANF)*, eds. A. Roberts, J. Donaldson, and A.C. Coxe, trans. M. Dods (Grand Rapids: W.B. Eerdmans, 1979), 104.

[4] Rondet, *Original Sin*, 35.

[5] See Irenaeus, *Demonstration of the Apostolic Teaching*, 14.

[6] Irenaeus, *Adv. Haer.*, lll.23.5, in *The Apostolic Fathers with Justin Martyr and Irenaeus*, vol. 1 of *ANF*, ed. and trans. A. Roberts, J. Donaldson, and A.C. Coxe (Grand Rapids: W.B. Eerdmans, 1978), 457.

[7] Irenaeus, *Adv. Haer.*, lll.23.5

[8] Irenaeus, *Adv. Haer.*, lll.23.7.

[9] Beatrice, *Transmission of Sin*, 233, argues that Tertullian's rejection of infant baptism shows that his account of Adam's sin is markedly different from the position Augustine came to hold.

[10] Rondet, *Original Sin: Patristic*, 55-58.

[11] For Augustine's distancing himself from the traducianist theory, see Beatrice, *Transmission of Sin*, 74.

12 Clement of Alexandria, *Protrep*. 11, in vol. 2 of *ANF*, 202-03.

[13] Wiley, *Original Sin: Origins*, 40.

[14] Ibid., 46.

[15] Origen, *Comm. in Lev.* 8.2-3, trans. by Rondet in *Original Sin: Patristic*, 75.

[16] Origen, *Hom. in Rom.* 5.9, trans. by the author from *PG*, vol. 14, 1017B.

[17] Beatrice, *Transmission of Sin*, 178-79.

18 Jaroslav Pelikan, *The Emergence of the Catholic Tradition (100-600)*, vol. 1 of *The Christian Tradition: A History of the Development of Doctrine* (Chicago: University of Chicago Press, 1971), 291.

19 Cyprian of Carthage, *Ep.* 58.5 (to Fidus), in *Fathers of the Third Century: Hippolytus, Cyprian, Novatian, Appendix*, vol. 5 of *ANF*, eds. A. Roberts, J. Donaldson, and A.C. Coxe, trans. R.E. Wallis (Grand Rapids: W.B. Eerdmans, 1979), 354.

20 Kelly, *Early Christian Doctrines*, 348.

21 Ibid., 350.

22 See Basil, *Hom.* 8.7.

23 Gregory of Nyssa, *On the Beatitudes*, oration 6, trans. by Kelly in *Early Christian Doctrines*, 351.

24 John Chrysostom, *Comm. Ep. Rom., Hom.* 10, in *Saint Chrysostom: Homilies on the Acts of the Apostles and the Epistle to the Romans*, vol. 11 of *NPNF*, ed. P. Schaff, trans. J.B. Morris, W.H. Simcox, and G.B. Stevens, 1st ser. (Grand Rapids: W.B. Eerdmans, 1978), 402.

25 Ibid., 403.

26 See *In Matt. Hom.* 28.3.

27 Kelly, *Early Christian Doctrines*, 346.

28 Athanasius, *Contra Arian*, I.11.44, in *St. Athanasius: Select Works and Letters*, vol. 4 of *NPNF*, eds. P. Schaff and H. Wace, trans. J.H. Newman and A.T. Robertson, 2nd ser. (Grand Rapids: W.B. Eerdmans, 1979), 332.

29 Athanasius, *Contra Arian*, I.12.51, 336.

30 Ibid., III.26.33, 412.

31 See Didymus, *De Trinitate*, 2.12.

32 Cyril, *Comm. Jn. 1:9*, in *Cyril of Alexandria: Commentary on John*, vol. 2 of *Ancient Christian Texts*, trans. David R. Maxwell (Downer's Grove, IL: IVP Academic, 2015), 55.

33 Cyril, *Comm. Rom. 5:18*, trans. by the author from *Sancti patris nostri Cyrilli Archiepiscopi Alexandrini in d. Joannis Evangelium*, vol. 3, ed. P.E. Pusey (Oxford: The Clarendon Press, 1872), 186.

34 Trans. by Beatrice, *Transmission of Sin*, 54-55.

35 *Macarian Homilies*, 24.2-3, trans. by Beatrice, *Transmission of Sin*, 55.

36 For Paul's use of "dough" or "lump" (*phurama*) to designate the people of God or the body of believers, see Rom. 9:21, 11:16; 1 Cor. 5:6-7; Gal. 5:9. Paul does not apply this term to Adam's sin, but he does employ it to show the harmful effects of sin and evil working through the body of believers.

37 Beatrice, *Transmission of Sin*, 144.

38 Rondet, *Original Sin: Patristic*, 112.

39 Ambrose, *Expos. Luc.* 7; *De excess. Satur.* 2.6; trans. by Kelly, *Early Christian Doctrines*, 354.

40 Augustine of Hippo, *De mor. eccl. cath.* 1.40, trans. by Kelly, *Early Christian Doctrines*, 363.

41 Ibid., 362.

42 Augustine, *De Pec. Mer. et Rem.*, 16, in *Saint Augustin: Anti-Pelagian Writings*, vol. 5 of *NPNF*, ed. P. Schaff, trans. P. Holmes, 1st ser. (Grand Rapids: W.B. Eerdmans, 1978), 447.

43 Rondet, *Original Sin: Patristic*, 122.

44 Beatrice, *Transmission of Sin*, 257.

45 1 John 3:8. RSVCE.

Background Paper

Original Sin: A Catholic Introduction

Dr. David P. Fleischacker

THE HISTORY OF THE CATHOLIC teachings on original sin is long and rich. There are many facets of it that have contributed to clarifications about original sin, especially the teachings on baptism, reconciliation, Mary, and the nature of sanctification.[1] For Catholics, golden nuggets of this history are summarized in the *Catechism of the Catholic Church*, which we know to be an authoritative guide. As we Catholics have discussed in the past, the teachings of the Church are the teachings of Christ. The gifts that He gave are the gifts given by the Church of Christ, the Church that subsists in the Catholic Church.[2] All of this is a reminder of the backdrop that has come to the fore over the last decade in our conversations with each other as Evangelicals and Catholics.

Original sin is the great tragedy of the human race and of all history.[3] If it is true that most tragedies spring from the flaws in human character, the case of Adam and Eve is rather different. No flaws existed in them before they sinned. They were created as man and woman by God's love, goodness, and power. Nothing in them could have predicted what was to take place. Reinforcing this point is that Adam and Eve did not turn from God the moment they were created. On their own, they did not attempt to eat of the forbidden fruit. Rather, they stayed with God. One really has to turn to a different source to find the flaw that unravels history.

As the *CCC* enlightens us: "Behind the disobedient choice of our first parents lurks a seductive voice, opposed to God, which makes them fall into death out of envy."[4] The original sin of Adam and Eve springs from an earlier sin, that of the great fallen angel Lucifer. And here is where we stop at a great mystery. Evil has no real explanation.[5] Lucifer was created by God just as were Adam and Eve. He was a great light made for heaven. No flaws in that creation. But from the moment of his creation, he turned away from the source of his light and his life. His disobedience is one of self-glorification. Envy is the motive attributed to him that originates his fall.[6] But there is no explanation for his envy. He had everything in God, who loved him deeply and abidingly.[7] He was made to receive that love, to shine with it, to illumine the created world with God's love and glory. No flaw here. His envy was absurd. Evil is not rational because it simply does not make sense. It has no intelligible being, as Augustine discovered after a long struggle over the nature of evil.[8] The flaw that was to spring to all of humanity through the original man and the original woman started in a flaw of creatures who had been made as angels but who became serpents.

Eve is tempted with the identical sin that was committed by the serpent, one of pride, namely to be her own god, springing from envy because the fruit is beautiful to behold.[9] God is beautiful to behold. The tree of good and evil manifested this reality. Their happiness was to behold their Creator. The tree manifests that they are creatures and only God is the creator and the one who is the source of goodness. God gave them a concrete reality to manifest their decision to trust him or to turn from him.[10] The fruit of this tree was that reality. But they embraced the temptation of Lucifer. They wanted to be God by a spiritual violence. In this envy, this pride, the attempt to become God is realized. It is impossible, of course. Entirely foolish. Absurd. But they tried. And when they did, what remained? They existed, but without the light of God's being shining in their souls. They were privated of God's sanctifying grace. They became unholy, blemished, fallen. Their minds became dark. Their wills became weak. And at the end, their souls would be separated from their bodies.[11] They were to die. They could no longer eat of the tree of life.

The first thing to be lost in Genesis was their relationship with God. They had to hide, but why? Because they were naked. They hid in the shame of their disobedience. But with that disobedience to God came the disobedience of their own bodily desires to their minds. Immediately with their fall was the emergence of lust. The relationship between the man and the woman who were made for each other became deformed and perverted. The beauty and harmony of the Garden, where all was in right order and relation, was lost. They could no longer stay.

Theologically, as St. Thomas would say, before the Fall Adam and Eve possessed original justice, original grace, and gifts that would strengthen all the powers of the soul.[12] This grace was sanctifying grace, the grace that made them pure and holy, which was the light and life of God present in their souls. Sanctifying grace is not something as such that human beings naturally deserve. More profoundly, human beings cannot naturally merit this grace. It was a grace given to Adam and Eve, because they were made not only in the image of God but in a graced image. Sanctifying grace in its fundamental form, as St. Thomas would formulate, is placed in the very essence of the human soul itself.[13] The *Catechism of the Catholic Church* repeats this point.[14] Even without that grace, the human being is a being made to know and to love God, who created human beings with this natural orientation. But God, being gracious, has always given us even more. He made Adam and Eve to be holy like He is holy, so that He could converse with them and they could receive that conversation.[15] Thus, it is understood in Tradition that Adam and Eve had been elevated supernaturally, to a relationship with God and each other that not only fulfilled their natural capacities but elevated those very capacities to be like God's love and knowledge.[16] A great gift. Pride and envy destroyed it. Original sin resulted in the death of sanctified souls.[17]

The loss of holiness permeates the entire soul. In other words, the privation of sanctity caused by a fundamental stain at the very heart of the soul then deforms the unfolding of every capability that human beings possess in their bodies, senses, minds, and wills. Death, sickness, lust of the eyes, gluttony, darkness of mind, weakness of will are just a few of the effects.[18]

There is an important clarification to make. Though original sin begets a rudimentary disordering of the entire soul, right down into its essence, this disorder does not make the nature of the human person evil. What is created and continues to be sustained in our souls and minds is not evil. Our soul was made to love God. Our minds were made to know the Truth. Our wills were made to embrace the Good. It is the privation of this in the death of the body, the disordered desires, the darkness of the mind, and the weakness of the will that is evil. But even with those privations, the body that seeks life, the mind that seeks truth, the will that seeks the good are all good. Our created nature is not evil and sin does not destroy that nature as such. As the Catechism reads,

> ... but human nature has not been totally corrupted: it is wounded in the natural powers proper to it, subject to ignorance, suffering and the dominion of death, and inclined to sin—an inclination to evil that is called concupiscence.[19]

The point is that nature as created remains the same, and thus good, because it is what God created us to be. However, the realization of that nature, its general state, and its orientation to become what it was meant to be has been deformed or stained. That is where the evil of original sin lies, and its heart is the privation of sanctifying grace.

As mentioned, this deformation is passed on. It is communicated to all human beings born as sons and daughters of Adam and Eve. This presents a difficulty, however. God creates the soul, yet certainly does not transmit any evil or sin into it, including original sin.[20] So, one must look to another source that causes the transmission of original sin. That source is centered in the generative unity of the man and woman. The Fall tells us something about this transmission. Eve was the first to be seduced, and through her, her husband fell. And then with both fallen, they no longer could remain in the Garden, and neither could any of the children that would be born to them. Their choice to remain in God would have meant that their children would have been born in that Garden, in God's loving presence, in a state of love with God, in a state of holiness. But their expulsion meant that they lost this mediating role of a gift that only God can give. All of their children would be born outside of the Garden, without the harmony of the Garden, and most important, without God's grace.[21]

St. Augustine, the first to clearly formulate original sin, speculated that concupiscence is the cause. It was this concupiscence that one finds immediately after Adam falls with Eve. They are ashamed of their bodies and the disordered desires that twist a pure, loving relationship between them. This concupiscence is tied to the heart of the Fall itself, standing next to the envy that springs forth pride to take in violence what only belongs to God, namely to be God. It is the state of impurity that results from the Fall. And it is this state that is to exist between every man and every woman for the rest of history, and it is the one thing that they then mediate to their children. St. Thomas builds on this, noting how the mother and the father generate the body, and they impart with that body a disposition that is disordered, and it is this disorder that then "instrumentally causes" the soul to be privated of the holiness and the love of God.[22] The Catechism does not settle on specifics, but it does note that though the state of original grace and righteousness was an undeserved gift to Adam and Eve, it was given to them and to the whole human race that would be born to them. In this way, they were meant to transmit original grace to their children.[23] And, as they lost the mediating role of grace, so they lost the mediating role in transmitting harmony to the souls and civilizations of their children. With Adam and Eve, the great tragedy of the human race had begun.

At the root of this transmission is the unity of the human race, a unity to which many throughout history have been blind because of the very evil that original sin begets.[24] Because it is a unity of persons, it follows the kind of unity that is found in kingdoms, cities, or families, but it is a unity of persons centered around the Holy Trinity as three persons who are the one God (note the family terms, Father and Son). Two points are noteworthy with regard to this unity. First, the perfection of each human being is interiorly related to all that exists, including all other human beings. It is a perfection both of knowledge and will. The human mind as an unrestricted potentiality for receiving all that exists is perfected not by understanding and knowing this or that particular finite being, but only by the concrete totality, which is why it is made for wisdom and for the unrestricted God. Likewise, the human will has an unrestricted potency for the good. As a result of both the potentiality of the mind and the will, what brings about true human beatitude is to be present to all else in knowledge and love including the unrestricted Good who is God. We experience glimpses of this in everyday life. Stop for a moment and think about what happens to you when something good comes to a friend or a child. You rejoice when they rejoice. You experience sorrow when they experience sorrow.

Second, the perfection of each human person necessarily takes place in relationship to other human beings. Only through the mediation of others down through the whole of history do we move toward the beatitude that we seek. This is the intrinsic developmental element to human existence that takes place by the mediational activities that occur between people. Through the life of the parents comes the life of a child. Through the language of a community comes the language of an individual. Through the common good of a civilization comes the common good of each man, woman, and child. Human beings mediate the goods of life to each other every day, as one sees in every home or civic economy and polity. God created us this way.

The second point links to the first. Even with the mediation of others, no individual human being becomes perfected in this life. In other words, in this life, we do not come to be present in knowledge and love to all that exists, especially the totality of the unrestricted love, truth, and goodness of God. What is needed? This is the kind of unity to which Catholics point in the beatific vision. In short, unity is necessary for human beatitude and it is centered around the Triune God.

Hence, it should be no surprise that God saves us through this same kind of unity, using mediation to bestow his grace. It forms a kind of kingdom, city, or family that unfolds developmentally. In other words, it forms the economy of salvation. Revelation unfolds developmentally from the beginning of the Old Covenant to its perfection in Christ. Then the reception of this Revelation continues to grow in dogmatic development.[25] Mediation is the key to how all of this takes place. Christ is the one mediator of all salvation. He becomes the one who descends to reunite us with his Father. His mediating role is made real by becoming one of us, through the incarnation. One can see God's desire to make us into cooperators of his grace at the very beginning of the human race. God gave to Adam and Eve both the image and the likeness, a likeness that they were to mediate to their children. But this was lost with their first sin and not regained until Christ, the one mediator of salvation, when God reintroduces the mediation of grace into the human race through his Son, and his mediation continues through the sacraments, prayers of the saints, intercessions, Mary his mother, and the whole Church.[26]

Though original sin included the loss of the ability of man and woman to mediate original grace and righteousness to their children, mediation did not stop. It is a necessity of how we are created. So, instead of grace, the fallen state is begotten of man and born of woman. This will continue to the end of history, even though mediating grace will return to the human race when God becomes man in Jesus Christ.[27] After Jesus, baptism becomes possible. But even with baptism, much of original sin will remain. The Garden is not restored. Man and woman continue to beget and bear children in and with sin. Many of the effects of original sin remain, playing out as a lifelong battle of faith.[28] As I mentioned at the beginning, this history of the teachings on original sin is long and rich, so this introduction to the topic is simply a little window unto a much larger world. Original sin begins with Adam and Eve and remains with us until the second coming of Christ.

One last question is sometimes asked: Why would God allow this? The answer is not merely because human beings have freedom. God is all-powerful and could have created a human being who did not fall yet remained entirely free while staying in that state. After all, Adam and Eve started that way. Instead, God permits evil to bring about greater goods.[29] Self-sacrificing love would not exist without evil. Neither would courage. The Crucifixion would not have taken place. The sacraments would never be. Evil makes possible a love that is greater because it is responding to evil. Not freedom, but goodness is the explanation for why God permits original sin and all evil acts. Only this explains one of the great statements that Catholics make in the Exsultet said at Easter.

"O happy fault that earned for us so great, so glorious a Redeemer."

Notes

[1] *Catechism of the Catholic Church* (*CCC*) 387: "Only the light of divine Revelation clarifies the reality of sin and particularly of the sin committed at mankind's origins. Without the knowledge Revelation gives of God we cannot recognize sin clearly and are tempted to explain it as merely a developmental flaw, a psychological weakness, a mistake, or the necessary consequence of an inadequate social structure, etc. Only in the knowledge of God's plan for man can we grasp that sin is an abuse of the freedom that God gives to created persons so that they are capable of loving him and loving one another." And *CCC* 388: "With the progress of Revelation, the reality of sin is also

illuminated. Although to some extent the People of God in the Old Testament had tried to understand the pathos of the human condition in the light of the history of the fall narrated in Genesis, they could not grasp this story's ultimate meaning, which is revealed only in the light of the death and Resurrection of Jesus Christ [cf. Rom. 5:12-21]. We must know Christ as the source of grace in order to know Adam as the source of sin. The Spirit-Paraclete, sent by the risen Christ, came to 'convict the world concerning sin' [cf. John 16:8], by revealing him who is its Redeemer."

2   CCC 830: "The word 'catholic' means 'universal,' in the sense of 'according to the totality' or 'in keeping with the whole.' The Church is catholic in a double sense: First, the Church is catholic because Christ is present in her. 'Where there is Christ Jesus, there is the Catholic Church' [St. Ignatius of Antioch, *Ad Smyrn.* 8, 2; *Apostolic Fathers*, II/2, 311]. In her subsists the fullness of Christ's body united with its head; this implies that she receives from him 'the fullness of the means of salvation' [UR 3; AG 6; Eph. 1:22-23] which he has willed: correct and complete confession of faith, full sacramental life, and ordained ministry in apostolic succession. The Church was, in this fundamental sense, catholic on the day of Pentecost [cf. AG 4] and will always be so until the day of the Parousia." Vatican Web site, http://www.vatican.va/archive/ENG0015/__P29.HTM.

3   CCC 390: "The account of the fall in Genesis 3 uses figurative language, but affirms a primeval event, a deed that took place at the beginning of the history of man [cf. GS 13 # 1]. Revelation gives us the certainty of faith that the whole of human history is marked by the original fault freely committed by our first parents" [cf. Council of Trent: DS 1513; Pius XII: DS 3897; Paul VI: AAS 58 (1966), 654].

4   CCC 391.

5   This is where the patristics borrowed from the formulation of evil given to us by Plato and Aristotle, namely that evil is a privation of being or a privation of the good. See Augustine, *Confessions*, 7.10-13, or his *City of God*, 11.9, for two of many examples. A key in this is to realize that mere words about something do not mean that there is an existent reality with an intelligibility. Some sensate examples may help, such as "darkness" or "silence." Neither of these name being but rather an absence of being. However, the absence of being alone is not evil, rather there is needed a privation of being. A privation includes the affirmation that something should be which is not, and there is no intelligible reason as to why there is the absence.

6   CCC 392: "Scripture speaks of a sin of these angels. This 'fall' consists in the free choice of these created spirits, who radically and irrevocably rejected God and his reign. We find a reflection of that rebellion in the tempter's words to our first parents: 'You will be like God.' The devil 'has sinned from the beginning'; he is 'a liar and the father of lies.'"

7   Lucifer will forever possess a nature that is good and created by God. At the same time, his fall is permanent and irrevocable. He will be in an eternal state in which his nature will be deprived of God (CCC 393).

8   Augustine, *The Confessions*, 7.10.

9   CCC 392: "Scripture speaks of a sin of these angels [cf. 2 Pt 2:4]. This 'fall' consists in the free choice of these created spirits, who radically and irrevocably rejected God and his reign. We find a reflection of that rebellion in the tempter's words to our first parents: 'You will be like God' [Gen. 3:5]. The devil 'has sinned from the beginning'; he is 'a liar and the father of lies' [1 John 3:8; → 1 John 8:44]."

¹⁰ *CCC* 396: "God created man in his image and established him in his friendship. A spiritual creature, man can live this friendship only in free submission to God. The prohibition against eating 'of the tree of the knowledge of good and evil' spells this out: 'for in the day that you eat of it, you shall die' [Gen. 2:17]. The 'tree of the knowledge of good and evil' [Gen. 2:17] symbolically evokes the insurmountable limits that man, being a creature, must freely recognize and respect with trust. Man is dependent on his Creator, and subject to the laws of creation and to the moral norms that govern the use of freedom."

¹¹ *CCC* 1006-1008. Augustine, *City of God*, 13.1-3, 6.

¹² St. Thomas Aquinas, *Summa Theologiae* I, Q. 90-95.

¹³ Aquinas, *ST* I-II, Q. 110, a. 4.

¹⁴ The *CCC* refers to these states of original justice and original grace in several different sections:

> 398: "In that sin man preferred himself to God and by that very act scorned him. He chose himself over and against God, against the requirements of his creaturely status and therefore against his own good. Created in a state of holiness, man was destined to be fully 'divinized' by God in glory. Seduced by the devil, he wanted to 'be like God,' but 'without God, before God, and not in accordance with God'" [St. Maximus the Confessor, Ambigua: PG 91, 1156C; cf. → Gen. 3:5].

> 399: "Scripture portrays the tragic consequences of this first disobedience. Adam and Eve immediately lose the grace of original holiness [cf. Rom. 3:23]. They become afraid of the God of whom they have conceived a distorted image--that of a God jealous of his prerogatives [cf. Gen. 3:5-10]."

> 400: "The harmony in which they had found themselves, thanks to original justice, is now destroyed: the control of the soul's spiritual faculties over the body is shattered; the union of man and woman becomes subject to tensions, their relations henceforth marked by lust and domination [cf. Gen. 3:7-16]. Harmony with creation is broken: visible creation has become alien and hostile to man [cf. Gen. 3:17, 19]. Because of man, creation is now subject 'to its bondage to decay' [Rom. 8:21]. Finally, the consequence explicitly foretold for this disobedience will come true: man will 'return to the ground' [Gen. 3:19; cf. 2:17], for out of it he was taken. Death makes its entrance into human history [cf. Rom 5:12]."

¹⁵ *CCC* 398.

¹⁶ I capitalize Tradition because it is affirmed not only by theologians, such as St. Thomas Aquinas, but by the Magisterium. *CCC* 78: "This living transmission, accomplished in the Holy Spirit, is called Tradition, since it is distinct from Sacred Scripture, though closely connected to it. Through Tradition, 'the Church, in her doctrine, life and worship, perpetuates and transmits to every generation all that she herself is, all that she believes' [DV 8 # 1]. 'The sayings of the holy Fathers are a witness to the life-giving presence of this Tradition, showing how its riches are poured out in the practice and life of the Church, in her belief and her prayer' [DV 8 # 3]."

¹⁷ *CCC* 399. Augustine, *City of God*, 13.9-12, 16.

¹⁸ *CCC* 407: "The doctrine of original sin, closely connected with that of redemption by Christ, provides lucid discernment of man's situation and activity in the world. By our first parents' sin, the devil has acquired a certain domination over man, even though man remains free. Original sin entails 'captivity under the power of him who thenceforth had the power of death, that is, the devil' [Council of Trent (1546): DS 1511; cf. → Heb 2:14]. Ignorance of the fact that man has a wounded nature inclined to evil

gives rise to serious errors in the areas of education, politics, social action [cf. John Paul II, CA 25] and morals."

19 CCC 405.

20 Catholic Tradition holds that man and woman transmit the "material" of the human person, but God and God alone creates, via infusion, the human soul.

21 CCC 402: "All men are implicated in Adam's sin, as St. Paul affirms... "By one man's disobedience many [that is, all men] were made sinners" [Rom. 5:12, 19]. The Apostle contrasts the universality of sin and death with the universality of salvation in Christ. 'Then as one man's trespass led to condemnation for all men, so one man's act of righteousness leads to acquittal and life for all men' [Rom. 5:18]."

22 For St. Thomas, the formal cause is Adam's sin. See Aquinas, ST l-ll, Q. 81, t. 1, r.o. 2.

23 CCC 404.

24 Ibid.: "How did the sin of Adam become the sin of all his descendants? The whole human race is in Adam 'as one body of one man' [St. Thomas Aquinas, De malo 4, 1]. By this 'unity of the human race' all men are implicated in Adam's sin, as all are implicated in Christ's justice. Still, the transmission of original sin is a mystery that we cannot fully understand. But we do know by Revelation that Adam had received original holiness and justice not for himself alone, but for all human nature. By yielding to the tempter, Adam and Eve committed a personal sin, but this sin affected the human nature that they would then transmit in a fallen state [Cf. Council of Trent: DS 1511-1512]. It is a sin which will be transmitted by propagation to all mankind, that is, by the transmission of a human nature deprived of original holiness and justice. And that is why original sin is called 'sin' only in an analogical sense: it is a sin 'contracted' and not 'committed'--a state and not an act."

25 Revelation is completed in Christ and his apostles (CCC 54-67), and then dogmatic development begins with the reception of that Revelation by the Church (CCC 88-90). Even prayer is developmentally revealed (CCC 2566-619).

26 CCC 65, 480, 618, 771, 846, 956 and many other locations (Jesus as one mediator); 168-69 and 197 (Church); 970 and 2673-75 (Mary); 1369 (Eucharist); 1456 (confession); 1544 and 1546 (priesthood); 2574ff (in Old Testament).

27 This does not mean that God does not use human beings for mediation. The "Law and the Prophets" in the Old Testament communicate abundant types of gifts through the mediation of many people, especially the people of Israel. Think of Moses, for example, or David. The point here is that the kind of mediation that is effective in sanctifying is what is missing in the Old Covenant. It, as such, does not save.

28 CCC 405: "Baptism, by imparting the life of Christ's grace, erases original sin and turns a man back towards God, but the consequences for nature, weakened and inclined to evil, persist in man and summon him to spiritual battle."

CCC 407: "The doctrine of original sin, closely connected with that of redemption by Christ, provides lucid discernment of man's situation and activity in the world. By our first parents' sin, the devil has acquired a certain domination over man, even though man remains free. Original sin entails 'captivity under the power of him who thenceforth had the power of death, that is, the devil' [Council of Trent (1546): DS 1511; cf. → Heb 2:14]. Ignorance of the fact that man has a wounded nature inclined to evil gives rise to serious errors in the areas of education, politics, social action [cf. John Paul II, CA 25] and morals. Faith tried is a greater good than faith that is not."

CCC 408: "The consequences of original sin and of all men's personal sins put the world as a whole in the sinful condition aptly described in St. John's expression, 'the sin of the world' [Jn 1:29]. This expression can also refer to the negative influence exerted on people by communal situations and social structures that are the fruit of men's sins [cf. John Paul II, RP 16]."

CCC 409: "This dramatic situation of 'the whole world [which] is in the power of the evil one' [1 John 5:19; cf. 1 Pt 5:8] makes man's life a battle:

> The whole of man's history has been the story of dour combat with the powers of evil, stretching, so our Lord tells us, from the very dawn of history until the last day. Finding himself in the midst of the battlefield man has to struggle to do what is right, and it is at great cost to himself, and aided by God's grace, that he succeeds in achieving his own inner integrity [GS 37 3 2]."

[29] CCC 412.

Section 2

INITIAL JUSTIFICATION

This second of four dialogues centered on initial justification took place at the University of Mary, Bismarck, North Dakota, October 8-10, 2015. Catholics and Evangelicals discussed the conditions and the effects of initial justification, as well as the nature of the event itself.

Common Statement

Initial Justification

1. **Catholics and Evangelicals agree that every aspect of initial justification is initiated by God rather than man. Human merit in no way precedes or causes initial justification. Nevertheless, the human being is not inert as God works upon him. All agree that human beings must accept Christ's gift of justification. However...**
   i. Evangelical monergists consider saving grace to be irresistible and unfailingly efficacious.
   ii. Both Catholics and Evangelical synergists regard the human will as capable of rejecting God's gracious offer.
   iii. Catholics and Evangelical synergists would also teach a graced cooperation in human reception of justification. God's operation includes within it man's cooperation.
2. **Evangelicals and Catholics have similar pastoral practices in leading sinners toward Christ prior to Justification.** Evangelicals and Catholics help to lead sinners to Christ in various ways: We proclaim the Gospel, provide examples of holy living, read the Sacred Scriptures, provide examples of personal piety, teach and model

that we are our brother's keeper, feed the hungry, clothe the naked, bury the dead, visit those in prison, and welcome the refugee. Sinners are encouraged to do these things prior to justification and often do them. However...

> Catholics often speak of some of these as a preparation of the adult sinner that is necessary prior to justification taking place. This is often confusing to Evangelicals because it sounds as if some work on the part of the sinner is necessary to merit justification. This, however, is a mistaken understanding of Catholic teaching. Catholics understand these acts to begin with God's prevenient grace and be sustained by and brought to completion by God's grace. Nevertheless, these works cannot be said to merit "initial justification." Evangelicals agree that the sinner's preparation of justification can in no way be construed as merit earning justification.

3. **Catholics and Evangelicals hold that faith is necessary in God's work of salvation of each human soul. Faith means a trusting belief in the atoning work of Jesus Christ. However...**

   i. Catholics hold that faith is a trusting assent to all that God has revealed to us and that is proposed through the Church.

   ii. Evangelicals hold that faith in Christ comes through the work of the Holy Spirit principally as the believer is engaged by the Scriptures and the proclamation of the Gospel. For Evangelicals, faith means more than intellectual assent but includes the movement of the will.

4. **Evangelicals and Catholics hold that God justifies through faith. However...**

   i. Evangelicals hold that justification comes through "faith alone" (*sola fide*). Faith is the reception of, but not the cause of, that reconciliation. "Although the sinner is justified by faith alone, the faith that justifies is never alone" (Westminster Shorter Catechism).

   ii. Catholics hold that justification does not come through "faith alone," but through faith working through love, the action of the intellect and will toward God and what he has revealed. In the adult, man cannot be justified without this faith. For Catholics, in this initial justification, God's offer of "righteousness" is received through "faith in Jesus Christ" (CCC 1991). This reception of initial justification then pours into our hearts "faith, hope, and charity."

5. **Catholics and Evangelicals hold a central place for Justification. However...**

   i. Catholics define justification as "not only a remission of sins but also the sanctification and renewal of the inward man through the voluntary reception of the grace and gifts whereby an unjust man becomes just and from being an enemy becomes a friend, that he may be an heir according to hope of life everlasting" (*Decree on Justification*, 1547, Council of Trent).

   ii. Evangelicals believe that justification consists in the imputation of Christ's righteousness to the sinner and the non-imputation of past sins to the sinner.

6. **Evangelicals and Catholics agree that this justification includes positive elements. However...**

   i. Catholics hold that there is another element in initial justification, which is "the sanctification and renewal of the inner man." In this sanctification of the inner man, man is made holy by sanctifying grace.

   ii. Evangelicals believe in the imputation of Christ's righteousness to the sinner. They do not usually speak of this sanctification of the inner man as part of justification, but rather use the language of regeneration and sanctification.

7. **Catholics and Evangelicals agree that justification includes the forgiveness of sins. However...**

   i. Catholics hold that this forgiveness of sin makes man "innocent, immaculate, pure, guiltless, and beloved sons of God" (Trent, session 5, *Decree on Original Sin*, 5).

   ii. Evangelicals believe that initial justification consists in part in a non-imputation of past sins to the sinner. Many, but not all, Evangelicals agree with Luther's declaration that at the moment of justification the individual is *simil iustus et peccator* ("at the same time just and a sinner").

Background Paper

Crucified Monergism: A Theological Interpretation of Justification in Galatians

Dr. Malcolm Yarnell

ON THE ONE HAND, Paul's epistle to the Galatians is clear regarding the ineffectiveness of works vis-à-vis the justification of the human being: "A man is not justified by the works of the law but through faith in Jesus Christ."[1] On the other hand, the book of Galatians is also clear that works have profound meaning: "For in Christ Jesus neither circumcision nor uncircumcision means anything, but faith working through love."[2] It is the logical placement of these two great New Testament truths—the ineffectiveness of works yet the importance of works—within diverse ecclesiastical dogmatics that complicates Christian discourse. In regard to the question of justification, this is true within Christianity broadly and within dialogues between Roman Catholics and Evangelicals, as well as between various groups of Evangelicals.

Theological conversation may be aided by the clarification of theological terms, so a review of the context and meanings of the various issues at stake may be helpful. Our primary concern in this particular part of the dialogue is the initial aspect of salvation, particularly "justification." To be clear, most understand justification to be, in major part at the least, a forensic or legal term that is related in the New Testament to personal salvation and applied historically to the initial grant of salvation. As a result, I will focus primarily on the context of justification in our discussion of faith and works. I have treated the doctrine of justification at length elsewhere and will assume that scholarship herein.[3]

Second, two important extrabiblical terms that have been offered for us to use within this discussion are "monergism" and "synergism." Monergism is defined summarily by Millard Erickson as "[t]he view that conversion is accomplished totally by the working of God."[4] Synergism, in contrast, is "[t]he idea that man works together with God in certain aspects of salvation, for example, faith or regeneration."[5] Both terms are used to describe how works either relate or do not relate to Christian salvation.

These latter terms are not used without controversy among Evangelical Protestants. A well-known Lutheran theologian, John Theodore Mueller, is adamant that "[s]cripture positively ascribes conversion, or the engendering of faith in man's heart, exclusively to God." Citing various scriptural passages, he concludes they "exclude from [conversion] man's operation or cooperation."[6] Mueller then, at length, provides answers to objections to monergism. He also argues that synergism, which in his definition suggests that "the will of man from its own natural powers can add something," is itself "pernicious."[7] However, a highly revered Reformed theologian, Herman Bavinck, for instance, accuses Evangelical Lutherans of adopting "a synergistic position."[8]

John Calvin fostered the method by which the Reformed, on their part, sought to avoid synergism. Calvin cited Peter Lombard and Bernard of Clairvaux, some of the "sounder Schoolmen," as offering a distinction between "operating" and "co-operating" grace. God's operating grace first ensures that we can will to do good, while co-operating grace then helps the will to do good. Calvin says the problem with this solution is that it "hints that man by his very own nature somehow seeks after the good."[9] To get around the problem of synergism, Calvin allows for the scholastic problem of the exercise of the free will as a good work, but then solves the problem by ascribing its movement entirely to God. It is "indisputable that free will is not sufficient to enable man to do good works, unless he be helped by grace, indeed by special grace, which only the elect receive through regeneration."[10]

So, in Reformed theology, the human free will is key to personal salvation, but only as a means of applying the predestined will of God. This solution has caused no end of anxiety for Reformed dissenters, such as Jacobus Arminius, who wanted to mitigate the automatic and impersonal description of salvation that this system suggested to him. In the mid-twentieth century, Emil Brunner also registered discomfort with the predestinarianism of the Reformers. He believed that the industrial, scientific, and various social revolutions had altered recent culture and that historical determinism and material determinism were now turning human beings into witless actors. "To-day our slogan must be: No determinism on any account!"[11]

More recently, Donald Bloesch, in his *Essentials of Evangelical Theology*, agrees that synergism is "a real danger," but "we must also recognize the complementary danger of monergism in which God is portrayed as the sole actor in our salvation."[12] Bloesch, who represents a broad and irenic strain of contemporary evangelicalism, sees a danger in synergism because it "makes salvation wholly conditional on man's free response," while monergism provides "the peril of a divine determinism or fatalism which makes a mockery of human freedom; this is more Stoic than Christian."[13] Monergism is firmly opposed to the danger of synergism, but monergism is itself a theological peril. Most recently, recognizing the problems with rank monergism, the Evangelical philosopher-theologian Kevin Vanhoozer sought to construct his theology on the presupposition that Reformed theology is fundamentally unchallengeable[14] even while he modified his system of effectual calling and irresistible grace in an (ultimately unsuccessful) attempt to remove its "impersonal" "coercion" and "violence."[15]

Operating from my own tradition's theological presupposition that a return to the biblical text with a prayer for the Spirit's guidance is the best approach to any difficult theological matter, I suggest we review some of the scriptural underpinnings of this question. Then, after a cursory survey of the history of interpretation, I will offer some preliminary systematic proposals for solving a problem that intractably divides Roman Catholics from Evangelicals and even divides the Evangelical community itself. In our biblical discussion, I shall focus upon the epistle to the Galatians even as it is treated in a canonical context.

Galatians 2:15-16

This is a complex yet important text in the interpretation of Galatians, and in the subsequent historical discussion of faith and works. In these two verses, Paul "set forth the central thesis he wanted to impress upon the Galatians."[16] However, to do so, he used "a single, overloaded sentence in the Greek,"[17] which contains "some of the most compressed language found anywhere in his epistles."[18] Complicating the situation further is that while he is primarily addressing a Gentile congregation in this letter, Paul now focuses on his Jewish (and Judaizing) interlocutors, particularly the apostle Peter. Momentarily, the Galatian Christians have become "awed onlookers at a battle of giants."[19] What has incensed Paul so much that he is willing to challenge the "Rock," the leading apostle, and the peace of the church? Paul believes the gospel itself is at stake, not in its formal definition of the death and resurrection of Jesus Christ, but in its material reception by those who claim to be the people of God.[20] Must the Gentiles be circumcised in obedience to the law, or is righteousness before God based exclusively upon faith in the gospel?

It is in answer to this critical issue in the life of the Galatian church that Paul responds thrice in quick succession that justification occurs not through doing the works demanded by the law but in faith in the gospel of Christ Jesus. Taken in somewhat wooden translation, these three statements are: "knowing that a man is justified not by works of law but through faith of Jesus Christ"; "we believed in Christ Jesus that we might be justified by faith of Christ and not by works of law"; and "no flesh shall be justified by works of law." The first statement regards the Jewish response to the gospel in potentiality; the second regards the Jewish Christians' response to the gospel in actuality; and the third regards both Jewish and Gentile responses to the gospel in potentiality. It is fairly clear that justification, the right standing of a human being before the divine court of law, is due to faith alone. It is also clear that here the antithesis of faith is works of law. The subjects in all three cases are human beings, who seek right standing before God either by responding to the law with works unsuccessfully or by responding to the gospel with faith successfully.

This last claim must be qualified, however, for some scholars have recently argued that the faith "of Jesus Christ" in the first statement should be taken as an objective genitive, such that πίστεως Ἰησοῦ χριστοῦ ought to be translated as "the faith or faithfulness of Jesus Christ." According to this reading, the justification of believers is based not upon the faith of believers but upon the faithfulness of Jesus Christ.[21] Many if not most commentators have, however, retained the traditional idea that this is a subjective genitive, especially in light of the evidence of the use of εἰς, "in," following the verbal for human faith that finds its direction toward Jesus Christ in the second statement.[22] According to this reading, the justification of believers requires the faith of a human being in Jesus Christ as at the least causative, though preferably as a responsive and thus instrumental cause. Richard Longenecker concludes that the Pauline treatment of faith requires both a basis in the faithfulness of Jesus Christ and "mankind's necessary subjective response." He cites Romans 3:22, Galatians 3:22, and Philippians 3:9 as similar examples of where Paul "balances out" the objective work of Christ on behalf of humanity and the subjective response from humanity.[23]

The antithesis of "faith" and "works of law" within the human response to the law and the gospel should be fairly well established. However, there are other definitional issues that need to be addressed. What exactly does Paul mean by "faith"? What exactly is entailed in the human response of faith? Where does faith originate, and what does faith cause? Moreover, what exactly are "works of law"? From the monergistic perspective, might not faith itself be considered a good work because of the free decision of the human will? Of course, this also raises the question of how the will and the act of willing are treated in Galatians.

Faith

James Leo Garrett, after reviewing the biblical scholarship on the various meanings of "faith," concluded that Paul meant by the term "the sinner's absolute reliance on God and God's grace." Justifying faith is "contrasted with reliance upon works."[24] According to this definition, faith is not the human reliance upon human ability whatsoever but human reliance upon divine grace. It is interesting, therefore, that Reformed commentators often feel compelled to warn against faith itself becoming a work of law. Timothy George writes, "Evangelical Christians must ever guard against the temptation to turn faith itself into one of the 'works of the law.'"[25] On the one hand, it is evident that Calvinists are continually concerned that faith itself may be a good work. On the other hand, Paul's letter to the Galatians does not even consider the possibility. To this, I shall return below.

If faith is absolute reliance upon God, whence does faith originate and whither does faith proceed? "Faith," according to Garrett's summation, "is 'in' Christ Jesus and 'of' Christ Jesus."[26] Galatians says that the Spirit comes through the hearing of faith.[27] In Romans, a letter that closely tracks Paul's logic in Galatians, faith is said to come through the hearing of the preaching of the Word.[28] It would seem that the second and third persons of the Trinity are coordinately and actively responsible for the origin of faith in the human being. First, the external proclamation of the Word of God enters through the ear to bring faith to the realm of the human heart and enable an answering word from the human tongue.[29] Second, the ability to confess the saving confession, that "Jesus is Lord," is itself possible only through the working of the Holy Spirit.[30] I have discussed this phenomenon at length elsewhere and subtly demonstrated that it correlates with both Evangelical and Catholic theology.[31]

However, faith not only originates with the Word of God and the Spirit of God, faith also brings access to the Holy Spirit and life in Christ. Galatians 3:14 states that Christ came so that "we might receive the promise of the Spirit through faith." This passage's use of διά, which indicates a channel, requires the Christian theologian to recognize that the active presence of the Holy Spirit in a Christian's life is also the result of faith. The same thing, as noted above, can be said about the relationship of faith and Christ. Christ is not only the subject or origin of faith; Christ is also the object or end of faith. To round out this Trinitarian movement, it is noteworthy that Paul teaches that the Father sends the Word and the Spirit to bring about union with the Word and the Spirit and thus union with himself. Galatians 4:7 considers the movement from the divine *terminus a quo*: "But because you are sons, God sent forth the Spirit of his Son into your hearts, crying, 'Abba, Father.'" Ephesians 2:18 considers the movement to the divine *terminus ad quem*: "For through him [Christ] we both [Jews and Gentiles] have our access in one Spirit to the Father."[32]

Regarding the definition of "faith," we may conclude that faith is the gift of God through his Son and his Spirit; that faith is the believer's entire reliance upon God and his grace; that justification by faith is antithetical to justification by works of the law; and that faith brings life with God through his Son and his Spirit. This theological interpretation should not be controversial to an orthodox theologian, whether he or she is Roman Catholic, Lutheran Evangelical, Reformed Evangelical, Arminian Evangelical, or some other type of Evangelical. However, it is with the next subject that divisions soon appear and have historically remained insurmountable for the various church traditions.

Free Will?

Systematic theologians often begin their anthropology with biblical descriptions of the human being. Hans Schwarz, for instance, considers the Hebrew terms *nephesh, batsar, ruach,* and *leb* and the Greek terms *soma, psyche, nous, sarx,* and *pneuma.* It is interesting that Schwarz does not offer a parallel term for "the free will" among these Hebrew or Greek terms that he says describe the "essentials of a human being."[33] Within his list of "the constituents of the human," James Leo Garrett considers the Old Testament terms *nephesh, pneuma, batsar, leb, kelayot,* and *me'im* and the New Testament terms *psyche, pneuma, sarx, soma, kardia, splanchna, nephros, nous, dianoia,* and *noema*.[34] While Garrett's approach to biblical anthropology is more exhaustive than that of Schwarz, he also does not offer any biblical term for the free will. Both agree that these terms are not to be taken in a compartmental manner and that the biblical terms have meanings and uses that often diverge from their modern language translations.

Augustine of Hippo

The biblical absence of free will as an aspect, organ, or faculty of human nature has not kept theologians, however, from offering it as an important term to describe the human being. In a highly speculative account, Augustine wrote a treatise on free will that was very popular in his day. Augustine's doctrine of free will must be understood as an aspect of his personal development. He first addressed the doctrine in *On Free Choice of the Will,* reacting against the Manichean dualism of an equivalent principle of evil alongside the good. In other words, in order to explain the existence of evil, Augustine took recourse to the philosophical concept of a human (and angelic) faculty of *liberum arbitrium,* free will. Evil exists not as a result of divine fiat but as a result of the choices of God's free creatures: "[A]ll sins come about when someone turns away from divine things that truly persist and toward changeable and uncertain things."[35] Augustine construes free will as a powerful and key internal faculty that may choose either the eternal or the mutable. If it chooses the eternal, it is a "good will"; if not, it is evil. "It is up to our will whether we enjoy or lack such a great and true good."[36] This internally omnicompetent ability to choose good or evil is inherent within the created being, and it is absolutely fundamental to the future of the creature: "It is by the will that human beings deserve, and therefore receive, either a happy or an unhappy life."[37]

Phillip Cary has written perceptively about Augustine's invention of an inner self. For the bishop of Hippo Regius, God is attained through going inward and then going upward.[38] It is in that momentary bend between the inward and the upward that the intense psychology of Western philosophy and theology is rooted. Within that private space, Augustine placed the will as the powerful unitary arbiter of the creature's future. The free will is "something immutable in the soul" and remains powerful, even after the Fall. Augustine at first even ascribes something divine to it but rejects that view as soon as he finds himself a leader responsible for the church.[39] However, while modifying the deified aspect of nature of the free will, Augustine retains both the powerful and arbitrary aspects of the human will.

After the Pelagians began to appeal to Augustine's own writings on free will in support of their affirmations that creatures could remain sinless through the correct use of the will, he placed the will within a revised version of the Genesis narrative.[40] Augustine never disavowed his doctrine of the free will, but placed it in motion. He continued to build a case for a created and continuing free will, for instance, by noting that the commands of God implied its existence.[41] After the Fall, Adam's will was perverted so that it continued to choose freely but only to sin. Building on an early Latin mistranslation of Romans 5:12, Augustine argued that Adam's descendants inherited Adam's evil will through natural generation. In this way, the doctrine of original sin was coupled with a doctrine of original guilt. Through Adam, the human will freely operated in all humanity to bring about its own condemnation.

However, Augustine taught, the will could now be cured by grace. This grace occurs for infants through the regenerative grace of baptism. Moreover, men may now choose to do good works that will justify. Justification occurs through "the good works which faith achieves through the love that is shed abroad by the Holy Ghost which is given to us."[42] Augustine proceeds to couple grace and the will in such a way that the exercise of the free will in faith is both a good work and now itself the source of justification. Grace is maintained through a predestinarian system, for this faith is only given to those whom God has ordained salvation. Yes, faith is in our power, but faith is first a divine gift. God gives to us the ability to believe.[43] The Spirit of God comes to transform the human life by changing the free will from choosing evil to choosing good. This gracious transformation continues such that the human being may now continually merit eternal life.

Martin Luther

Augustine's identification of justification with the grace of willing good works went unchallenged until Martin Luther's protest against medieval abuses in the Roman church. Luther, as is well known, rejected the idea that the human being's justification occurred through merits earned as the result of grace. Rather, grace is directly given to the human soul through the application of Christ's merit with faith. Luther agreed with Augustine that the free will is bonded to sin, as he famously argued against Erasmus. However, God can and does grant faith to the elect through the preaching of the Word. In his reading of Galatians and Romans, Luther saw Paul as teaching that the law's spiritual (as opposed to civil) work is to bring about despair of one's own ability. The law "does nothing else but reveal sin, accuse and terrify men so that it brings them to the very brink of desperation." At this point, when the law can no longer help, the gospel steps in. "Contrariwise, the gospel is a light which lightens, quickens, comforts, and raises up fearful consciences."[44] The internal psychology of Luther's own conversion shapes his presentation of grace and faith. Faith, to Luther, is the cessation of good works and the beginning of justification. There is no good work in faith, only the passive reception of Christ's alien righteousness.

Does this mean that Luther lacks a viable doctrine of good works in the Christian life? Far from it! He continues in his commentary on Galatians, "Now what about those verses in Scripture that speak of the value of good works? When we are out of the matter of justification we cannot sufficiently praise and magnify those works that are commended by God."[45]

In other words, for Luther, good works are necessary as an expression of the faith that justifies, but good works themselves never justify. Faith is not a good work, but faith should result in good works.

A careful reading of the *Joint Declaration on the Doctrine of Justification* reveals where the Roman Catholic and Lutheran doctrines of justification, faith, and good works coalesce and depart. While both communions affirm that justification is by grace alone, the Roman Catholics "say that persons 'cooperate' in preparing for and accepting justification by consenting to God's justifying action." In other words, the Catholic position remains firmly Augustinian in seeing the free will as active and as a good work that cooperates in salvation. On the other hand, the Lutherans affirmed that "human beings are incapable of cooperating in their salvation." However, although faith itself is nevertheless a grace that comes to human beings, this saving faith is a grace that can then be rejected.[46] In this way, we can see that Roman Catholics are synergists, though it is a synergism under grace, while Lutherans are monergists. However, Calvinists tend to view Lutheran monergism with suspicion if not condemnation.

John Calvin

John Calvin retained much of the Augustinian anthropology adopted by Luther, as well as much of his doctrines of election and faith. However, there is a notable sharpening of the emphasis on the human will in Calvin. Luther is more interested in the Word than he is in anthropology, and his doctrine of the free will is dominated by his emphasis on human inability and the need for God's Word and Spirit to turn man. Man has "lost every capacity to do good in matters concerned with his relationship to God," but a "passive capacity" to receive God's grace remains.[47]

In a partial return to medieval scholasticism, Calvin says that "understanding" and "will" are the two fundamental "faculties" of the human soul.[48] Calvin accepts the idea of "will" as fundamental to Christian anthropology and then centers his understanding of what happens to human nature as a result of the Fall around the will.[49] However, Calvin is also less positive about the term "free will," preferring instead to speak of the "unfree will" of sinners.[50] Only the elect are given the ability to exercise free will through a special grace. It is only because of the regeneration worked by the Holy Spirit that the will can work rightly again.[51] Calvinists deny any cooperating grace in human salvation. They protect monergism, however, in a way that elevates the role of the human will. Because faith is seen as an exercise of the will, it always remains under the suspicion of becoming a good work. The good work can be avoided by requiring the will to be activated toward salvation only by an external grace applied internally by the Holy Spirit. The Spirit, of course, comes only upon those who have been eternally elected. Because a soul is elected, it will be irresistibly drawn to salvation through the Spirit.

The Reformed protest against Catholicism and Lutheranism is dominated by the concern for the originating point of salvation. Bavinck admits that Luther's and Calvin's variant doctrines of salvation arose from their diverse experiences.[52] However, he blames the problem of synergism not on Luther, but on Melanchthon and later Lutheranism. The Reformed critique of Lutheran salvation as synergistic rests upon the concern that the crux of the salvation decision is with man rather than God. Bavinck summarizes what he sees in the Lutheran *ordo salutis*: "Human beings hold the power of decision: by their resistance they can nullify the whole work of the Father, the Son, and the Spirit. And they have that power till the moment of their death. More precisely, the center of gravity in the order of salvation is located in faith and justification. Calling, contrition, and regeneration only have a preparatory function."[53] While both Lutherans and Calvinists recognize that the Spirit both precedes and follows faith, the Calvinists place the decisive point before the gift of faith, while the Lutherans place it contemporaneously. Calvin's vigorous doctrine of free will kept him from allowing the regenerating work of the Spirit to be placed anywhere but prior to faith. He argues that any reference to faith as being the conduit of the Spirit, such as in Galatians 3:2, is really just a reference to another less significant spiritual gift.[54]

Herman Bavinck thus requires that faith be placed further down the chain in the *ordo salutis*. Moreover, an eternal divine covenant,[55] particular election, effectual calling, and regeneration must necessarily be located prior to faith; irresistible grace must be maintained so as not to lose the crisis point of salvation to a subsequent human decision.[56] Reformed theologians like Bavinck seem to be motivated in their rigid ordering through their vigorous anthropology, an anthropology whose very optimism regarding the power of the will requires a countervailing pessimism regarding faith.

The dilemma that Calvinism senses with any hint of synergism, even with faith, is prompted by a desire to protect the origination of a chain of causation. In the ancient, medieval, and modern philosophical debates over libertarianism and determinism, the conversation often fell upon origination. According to *The Oxford Companion to Philosophy*, origination considers "the creation of new causal chains by free human choices." On the one side, the "traditional doctrine of free will or libertarianism asserts that there are such genuine creations." On the other side, "Determinists argue that origination does not exist."[57] Likewise, Calvinists, concerned to prevent the cause of salvation from being ascribed to man, deny that origination should be placed in the free will of man (as with Pelagius), or even in the bonded free will of man (as with Augustine and Luther).

A Preliminary Proposal

My own question is whether the Augustinian doctrine of free will, which so bedazzled Augustine, Pelagius, Luther, Calvin, and their followers, is Pauline. Paul gives us Scripture's most complete doctrine of justification; and Pauline justification, as exemplified in his epistle to the Galatians, emphasizes the gospel, the Spirit, Christ, and faith over against the law, the flesh, and works. For Paul, the antitheses are clear, and free will is not a key factor within this soteriological system. Both freedom and willing are evident in Galatians (and Romans), but not in the same way that Augustine proposes with his invention of the free will, the good will, and the evil will. In a similar vein, my students are often puzzled when they first encounter the Pauline doctrine of freedom, for it does not correspond with libertarian free will. Pauline freedom indicates opposition to sin and obedience to God. Calvin recognized the philosophical origin of "free will" and preferred, he said, not to use it.[58] However, he retained the "will" as a fundamental faculty, in spite of its less than biblical basis, and invested it with critical importance.

My own proposal, as neither a Roman Catholic, nor a Lutheran, nor a Calvinist, but as a free church biblicist, is that we reconsider the weight, the competence, and the critical placement that Western Christianity has given to the human faculty of the free will. This proposal has a threefold shape.

First, I propose that one might arrive at an implicit doctrine of the human will from the biblical text but should be very reluctant to grant it much substance, especially when Scripture does not explicitly identify it as a faculty of the human soul, much less a fundamental faculty. I have already noted that Augustine and Calvin derived the doctrine of the human will from the philosophers. In his discussion of free will, Anthony C. Thiselton, a typically adept commentator upon Scripture, hermeneutics, philosophy, and theology, locates the concept's origin in the context of popular philosophical debate regarding determinism. Thiselton describes it as "a purely anthropocentric notion of freedom as the ability to choose to do any action."[59] Gottlob Schrenk declares that the use of θέλημα in later conciliar debates to describe "an organ of volition" is not derived from Scripture: "The psychological presuppositions are that the νοῦς is active in the θέλημα and that what is willed is then expressed in words and acts (ἐνεργεῖται). The New Testament itself has no interest in this type of psychology, which is Greek in source."[60] The Zürich theologian was not using "Greek in source" to indicate fidelity to the faith of the early Christian community.

Second, I propose that the human will thus arrived at is rather impotent and controverted. While Scripture does not explicitly present the human will as a fundamental faculty of the human being, Scripture does indicate the activity of both divine and human willing. As early as Genesis 4, subsequent to the fall, the Lord tells Cain that sin has a desire for Cain, but Cain must rule over sin. The imagery is of an almost visible enemy hiding in order to vanquish Cain, who must, however, conquer it. Sin's internal desire or urge (*teshuqa*) and Cain's rule or conquest (*timshol*) oppose one another. Cain "has a free choice. When facing the alternatives, he is capable of making the right choice. Otherwise, God's words to him about 'doing well' would be meaningless and comic." At the very least, Cain has a "personal responsibility."[61]

If there is a choice given to fallen humanity by God, it could be concluded that it is something within humanity. However, this thing within humanity is neither given form nor is it unitary, even for Christians. The Greek verbs θέλω and βούλομαι are used often in the New Testament, but they have a range of meanings from inclination and desire to decision and command. The willing of God is sovereign and effective. The willing of Jesus is omnipotent in his deity and obedient in his humanity. The willing of the fallen human being is characterized by impotence and disconnection between willing and doing.[62]

The divine and human characteristics of willing are seen in Galatians, too. On the divine side, God is praised for centering the redemption of humanity and history in Christ's cross according to his will.[63] On the human side, Paul presents the conflict between the Judaizers and himself, and the resulting conflict within the Galatians themselves, as a clash of zealous willings with no clear victor as yet.[64] Paul also warns the Galatians that life is a conflict zone between the desiring of the flesh (σάρξ), the human nature that is weak and inclined toward sinfulness, and the desiring of the Spirit (πνεῦμα), the power of God at work in the believer.[65] While there is apparently a willing at work in the Christian, it is composed of things in opposition to one another (ἀντίκειται ἀλλήλοις), so much so that human willing and the doing are contradictory.[66] Calvin's doctrine that the will is moved by the reason, which in turn moves the human soul, is hereby seriously thrown in doubt.[67]

It is only in the Christ that one sees a human will that is without compromise. Christ submitted his human willing to the willing of his Father. He achieved the integrity between willing and working that the flesh, the human nature apart from Christ, is incapable of achieving.[68] The Christian is capable of experiencing integrity between life in the flesh and life in the faith only because the crucified Christ lives in the Christian being crucified.[69] For Christ's life to become my life, his death must first become my death, and this means I have nothing good to offer God, only God himself, the God on the cross, who graces me with the calling to take up my cross.[70]

Third and finally, on the basis of these findings, I propose that theologically we remove the critical origination of faith from the invented anthropological locus of the free will and return it to the revealed theological locus of the Trinity. In a paradoxical move, it appears that the only possible means by which a human being can reach a unitary integrity is if it ceases its own efforts at self-justification and surrenders in faith to the will of God through the crucified Son in the power of the Spirit. This, of course, may only happen because the Son's crucifixion has been appointed as my crucifixion, his surrender to the Father has become my surrender, all of which is a work of his Spirit. In this way, justification remains monergistic, not because it has removed the human actor, but because the human actor has ceased acting on his own behalf in any way and has collapsed into the undeserved grace of God at the call of God. Faith is not a work; the will is not at work; faith is the end of all working and willing; faith is the human person crucified with Christ.⁷¹

I regard this proposal as preliminary primarily because in even allowing for a human aspect, organ, or faculty called "the will," as weak as it is and as ultimately defeated as it must become in faith, we recognize that we are taking one step beyond the biblical text. Whenever you go beyond the divine text, especially if one constructs a loadbearing wall for a humanly-devised theological structure, any humanly-devised theological structure, be it Roman, Reformed, Lutheran, or Free Church, one is preparing that house for a turbulent existence.

Notes

1. Gal. 2:16b.
2. Gal. 5:6.
3. Malcolm Yarnell, "Christian Justification: A Reformation Baptist View," *Criswell Theological Review* 2, no. 2 (2005): 71-90.
4. Millard J. Erickson, *Concise Dictionary of Christian Theology* (Grand Rapids: Baker, 1987), 107. On page 37 of this text, Erickson defines "conversion" thusly: "The action of a person in turning to Christ. It includes repentance (renunciation of sin) and faith (acceptance of Christ)."
5. Ibid., 163.
6. John Theodore Mueller, *Christian Dogmatics: A Handbook of Doctrinal Theology for Pastors, Teachers, and Laymen* (St. Louis: Concordia, 1934), 343.
7. Ibid., 321, 355-62.
8. Herman Bavinck, *Sin and Salvation in Christ*, vol. 3 of *Reformed Dogmatics*, ed. John Bolt, trans. John Vriend (Grand Rapids: Baker, 2006), 521. Bavinck considers even the ideas of resistible grace and amissable grace as placing "the center of gravity" with the human person rather than with God.
9. John Calvin, *Institutes of the Christian Religion*, ed. John T. McNeill, trans. Ford Lewis Battles, Library of Christian Classics (Philadelphia: Westminster Press, 1960), 2.2.6.
10. Ibid.
11. "Even when the extreme formula, *L'homme machine*, is avoided it is still assumed that man is as fixed by his nature as the function of the machine is determined by its construction and its mass, and the energy supplied to it." Emil Brunner, *Man in Revolt: A Christian Anthropology*, trans. Olive Wyon (London: Lutterworth Press, 1939), 257.
12. Donald G. Bloesch, *Essentials of Evangelical Theology*, vol. 1, *God, Authority, and Salvation* (Peabody, MA: Prince Press, 1978), 200.
13. Ibid.
14. Kevin J. Vanhoozer, *Is There a Meaning in This Text? The Bible, the Reader and the Morality of Literary Knowledge* (Leicester, England: Apollos, 1998), 10.
15. Kevin J. Vanhoozer, *First Theology: God, Scripture & Hermeneutics* (Downers Grove, IL: InterVarsity Press, 2002), 100-03.

16 Timothy George, *Galatians*, New American Commentary (Nashville: Broadman & Holman Publishers, 1994), 187.

17 Ronald Y.K. Fung, *The Epistle to the Galatians*, New International Commentary on the New Testament (Grand Rapids: W.B. Eerdmans, 1988), 112.

18 George, *Galatians*, 187.

19 R. Alan Cole, *Galatians*, rev. ed., Tyndale New Testament Commentaries (Grand Rapids: W.B. Eerdmans, 1989), 119.

20 Gal. 1:6-10.

21 The literature is gathered in Richard N. Longenecker, *Galatians*, Word Biblical Commentary (Dallas: Word Books, 1990), 87. See also the summary in George, *Galatians*, 195-96n.

22 Fung, *The Epistle to the Galatians*, 114-15; Cole, *Galatians*, 20; George, *Galatians*, 195.

23 Longenecker, *Galatians*, 87-88.

24 James Leo Garrett, Jr., *Systematic Theology: Biblical, Historical, and Evangelical*, vol. 2 (Grand Rapids: W.B. Eerdmans, 1995), 237.

25 George, *Galatians*, 196.

26 Garrett, *Systematic Theology*, 2:237.

27 Gal. 3:2, 5.

28 Rom. 10:14-18.

29 Rom. 10:8-10.

30 1 Cor. 12:3.

31 Malcolm B. Yarnell III, *The Formation of Christian Doctrine* (Nashville: B&H Academic, 2007), 25-27, 36-38, 82-90, 144-47; idem, *God the Trinity: Biblical Portraits* (Nashville: B&H Academic, 2016), 81.

32 NASB.

33 Hans Schwarz, *The Human Being: A Theological Anthropology* (Grand Rapids: W.B. Eerdmans, 2013), 5-20. The closest Schwarz comes to a discussion of the free will at this point is with the Hebrew *leb*, which he says means primarily "the center of the consciously living person," but which may also indicate "the seat of our intellectual and rational human motions." Ibid., 12-13.

34 James Leo Garrett, Jr., *Systematic Theology: Biblical, Historical, and Evangelical*, vol. 1 (Grand Rapids: W.B. Eerdmans, 1990), 430-39.

35 Augustine of Hippo, *On Free Choice of the Will*, trans. Thomas Williams (Indianapolis: Hackett Publishing, 1993), 1.16.

36 Ibid., 1.12.

37 Ibid., 1.14.

38 This is a persistent pattern that is clearly perceptible, for instance, in Augustine's *De Trinitate* as well as his famous *Confessions*.

39 Phillip Cary, *Augustine's Invention of the Inner Self: The Legacy of a Christian Platonist* (New York: Oxford University Press, 2000), 109-12.

40 Augustine later explained that his first treatise primarily was an argument against the Manicheans but had anti-Pelagian intimations, too.

41 Augustine of Hippo, *A Treatise on Grace and Free Will*, 2-5, in *Nicene and Post-Nicene Fathers*, First Series, vol. 5, ed. Philip Schaff (reprint, Peabody, MA: Hendrickson, 1994), 444-46.
42 Augustine, *A Treatise on the Spirit and the Letter*, 57, in ibid., 109.
43 Augustine, *A Treatise on the Spirit and the Letter*, 54, 60, in ibid., 107, 110.
44 Martin Luther, *Commentary on Galatians* (Grand Rapids: Baker, 1988), 205.
45 Ibid., 218.
46 The Lutheran World Federation and the Roman Catholic Church, *Joint Declaration on the Doctrine of Justification* (Grand Rapids: W.B. Eerdmans, 2000), 15-17.
47 Paul Althaus, *The Theology of Martin Luther*, trans. Robert C. Shultz (Philadelphia: Fortress Press, 1966), 157.
48 Calvin, *Institutes*, 1.15.7.
49 Ibid., 1.15.8.
50 Ibid., 2.2.8.
51 Ibid., 2.2.6, 26-27.
52 Bavinck, *Sin and Salvation*, 3:518.
53 Ibid., 3:522.
54 Calvin, *Institutes*, 3.2.33.
55 Karl Barth deconstructs and disparages this key Reformed axiom as a "mythology." Thanks are expressed to David Allen for reminding me of this critique. Karl Barth, *Church Dogmatics*, IV/1: *The Doctrine of Reconciliation*, eds. G.W. Bromiley and T.F. Torrance (Edinburgh: T&T Clark, 1956), 54-66.
56 Bavinck, *Sin and Salvation*, 3:522-28.
57 *The Oxford Companion to Philosophy*, ed. Ted Honderich (New York: Oxford University Press, 1995), 636-37.
58 Calvin, *Institutes*, 2.2.8.
59 Anthony C. Thiselton, *The Thiselton Companion to Christian Theology* (Grand Rapids: W.B. Eerdmans, 2015), 333.
60 Gottlob Schrenk, "θέλημα," in *Theological Dictionary of the New Testament*, ed. Gerhard Kittel, trans. Geoffrey W. Bromiley (Grand Rapids: W.B. Eerdmans, 1965), 3:62.
61 Victor P. Hamilton, *The Book of Genesis, Chapters 1-17*, New International Commentary on the Old Testament (Grand Rapids: W.B. Eerdmans, 1990), 227-28.
62 Schrenk, "θέλω," in *Theological Dictionary of the New Testament*, 3:44-52.
63 Gal. 1:4.
64 Gal. 4:17-21, 6:12-14.
65 Gal. 5:16-26; cf. Rom. 7:14-25.
66 Gal. 5:17.
67 Calvin, *Institutes*, 1.15.7; 2.2.12, 26.
68 Mark 14:36.
69 Gal. 2:19-20.
70 Christ's very calling to follow him is itself the grace that enables the obedience of faith. Dietrich Bonhoeffer, *Discipleship*, eds. Geffrey B. Kelly and John D. Godsey, trans. Barbara Green and Reinhard Krauss (Minneapolis: Fortress Press, 1996), 66.

Cf. Michael D. Wilkinson, "Suffering the Cross: The Life, Theology, and Significance of Leonhard Schiemer," in *The Anabaptist and Contemporary Baptists: Restoring New Testament Christianity: Essays in Honor of Paige Patterson*, ed. Malcolm Yarnell (Nashville: Broadman & Holman Publishing, 2013), 49-64.

[71] "Faith is not in itself a meritorious work that we offer to God. It justifies only because it alone is the appropriate form of accepting the promise." Wolfhart Pannenberg, *Systematic Theology*, trans. Geoffrey W. Bromiley (Grand Rapids: W.B. Eerdmans, 1998), 3:141-42.

Background Paper

Initial Justification: A "Synergist" Explanation

Dr. Glen W. Menzies

> Eph. 2:8-10:
> For by grace you have been saved through faith; and this is not your own doing, it is the gift of God — not because of works, lest anyone should boast. For we are his workmanship, created in Christ Jesus for good works, which God prepared beforehand, that we should walk in them.

Introduction

At the close of Iustitia Dei, his magisterial history of the doctrine of justification, Alister McGrath, concluding his discussion of the tumultuous debates over justification that roiled the 16th century, notes in contrast the diminished place justification came to hold in the modern era:

> No longer was justification a matter for dispute between Christian groups; it was a matter of debate between Christianity and a secular culture which was increasingly of the view that humanity did not require reconciliation to anything or anyone, for any reason.[1]

This grim summary should serve as a reminder to all of us involved in this Evangelical-Catholic dialogue of how much we hold in common, despite our differences, and how hostile to the gospel are the hearts of those who have not experienced saving grace.

While this essay will focus on many points of disagreement both with Catholic dialogue partners and with other Evangelicals, I should make clear at the outset that we are talking about problems "within the family" and that our agreements far surpass our disagreements. We are brothers and sisters in Christ, and we have all experienced divine grace, even if we may understand and explain this grace differently.

Among the issues in the past debates about justification is a matter of definition. What sort of a term is "justification," and what is the semantic field it implies? Is it a "forensic" term, as the Reformers generally maintained? Or is it a "moral" term? Is "regeneration" a constituent part of justification, or is it a parallel term? Is it logically prior to justification or logically posterior? And how does "adoption" fit in? While these are all legitimate questions, this essay cannot be a comprehensive treatment of soteriology, so issues of the location of justification in the ordo salutis will be discussed only briefly.

As to the agenda of this essay: this essay is about "initial justification," which I believe reflects a distinction evident in the Tridentine Decree on Justification, in which the first nine chapters discuss initial justification, the next four chapters discuss a second justification that in Protestant circles is more commonly labeled "sanctification," and the final three chapters discuss the justification of the lapsed and the sacrament of penance.[2] Therefore, this essay is neither about sanctification, about the relationship of sanctification to justification, nor about the entire suite of blessings associated with initiation into Christ and the Church.

I confess that I am somewhat uncomfortable with the title of this essay, as perhaps is evident by my use of scare quotes around the word "synergist." The word "synergist" is, of course, a compound of the Greek words for "with" and "work," implying that the believer "works with" God to obtain his or her salvation. Since I flatly deny that anyone performs works antecedent to his or her justification that in any way merit this justification, this label seems less than apt. It does not really help to speak of "cooperation" with God in justification since that merely replaces Greek roots with Latin equivalents. "Cooperation" also means to "work with."

The only way I might affirm a "work" prior to justification is in the benign and colorless sense in which the word "work" is used twice in the New Testament when it speaks of "the work of faith."[3] As I believe faith is logically prior to justification, I will affirm that "the work of faith" is antecedent to justification, but without any meritorious implications.

I am also aware that "synergism" is a term of opprobrium coined by its opponents. Nevertheless, it has become part of the standard theological lexicon, so I will use it. The central idea we synergists uphold is that a gift, any gift, must be accepted for the intended transaction to take place. In modern American jurisprudence there are three constituent parts to a gift: a) an offer; b) acceptance of the offer; and c) delivery of the gift. Without all three parts, no gift is given.

As far as I know, this legal principle has no statutory basis. It flows out of common law, not merely from British common law but from the anterior Roman common law. This principle was operative before the birth of Christ, and it is no wonder, for it is based on what might be described as a "self-evident principle" or perhaps even "the laws of nature."

I am sure no one here will dispute the gracious character of justification. Whether or not one believes an individual's merit may contribute to his or her justification by God, all in this dialogue will affirm that justification cannot occur without the application of divine grace. Another way to say this is that justification is experienced as a gift.

Synergists merely affirm that a gift must be accepted and that the acceptance of the gift is not a "work." Moreover, the acceptance of this gift does not in any way impugn the gratuitous character of the gift-giving act.

The Objective Basis of Initial Justification

At a previous meeting, this dialogue considered the matter of Christ's atoning death on the cross as the objective foundation of the righteousness of Christ, which, when applied to the individual, leads to salvation. That year's conference was marked by a surprising degree of agreement between the two delegations. Therefore, it seems unnecessary in this essay to say much about Christ's atonement as the objective basis for all of God's redemptive work, including the grace of justification. The primary locus of our agreement was in Anselm's "Satisfaction Theory of the Atonement."

However, the matter of the "objective basis" of initial justification may also be considered from a different perspective. Is initial justification "forensic," bringing to mind a courtroom and legal theory? Or is it "moral," a category from the domain of behavior and ethics? Put rather baldly, when the New Testament speaks of the conversion of an adult and he is labeled as being *dikaios*, should we hear the echoes of a courtroom decree—"Not guilty!"—or should we picture in our minds' eyes a positive moral appraisal such as we might have for those who feed the poor and care for the sick? While this is an important issue, we will not address it fully right now; rather, readers should keep this topic in the back of their minds, as this essay invokes it throughout its course. Toward the close of this essay, we will return to this topic and discuss it more formally.

Augustine and Pelagius

It is hard to overstate the impact Augustine has had on the theology of the West. Perhaps his most important and enduring contribution came through his controversy with the British monk Pelagius (and his followers), who accused Augustine of promoting lax morality in the Church. To simplify a rather complex story, Pelagius taught that God was the great judge who was able without error to separate those who by their deeds showed themselves to be righteous from those who by their deeds showed themselves to be wicked. God would reward the righteous with life eternal. In contrast, God would send the unrighteous to punishment everlasting. Thus, every human's fate was in his or her own hands (although equally it was in God's hands as well). The legacy of Adam's sin meant no more than that it set a bad example for his descendants.

Pelagius' account of things agreed with neither Augustine's personal experience nor his reading of Scripture, particularly Genesis. Augustine posited that Adam's free will had been taken captive, and the effects were transmitted to all his posterity, with the exception only of Jesus, who was not born of natural generation, and his mother, Mary. Against this notion, the Pelagian bishop Julian of Eclanum argued that in Adam's heirs the human will remained morally neutral, as Adam's will had been when he was created. These morally neutral wills dispassionately weighed arguments for and against any possible course of action. Augustine objected, claiming that in Adam's descendants their free will had been "taken prisoner" and every deliberation was tainted with a moral bias, so the scales always tipped in the direction of evil. Therefore, that person who possessed an inoperative "free will" was not really free. As McGrath explains:

> The free will is not lost, nor is it non-existent; it is merely incapacitated, and may be healed by grace. In justification, the *liberum arbitrium captivatum* ["free will taken captive"] becomes the *liberum arbitrium liberatum* ["liberated free will"] by the action of this healing grace.[4]

Further, this healing grace must come from God. Since the *liberum aritrium captivatum* is incapable of healing itself or of doing any good thing, the initiative lay with God alone. Nevertheless, there is a clear synergistic quality to Augustine's theology. McGrath summarizes:

> According to Augustine, the act of faith is itself a divine gift, in which God acts upon the rational soul in such a way that it comes to believe. Whether this action on the will leads to its subsequent assent to justification is a matter for humanity, rather than for God. "The one who created you without you will not justify you without you" ("*Qui fecit te sine te, non te iustificat sine te*").[5] Although God is the origin of the gift which humans are able to receive and possess, the acts of receiving and possessing themselves can be said to be the humans'.[6]

As it developed, Protestant theology came to insist with Augustine that the initiative leading to the reconciliation of humans to God must come from God. The question that remains is whether there is any role for human beings to play in response to that divine initiative.

The Heritage of the Reformation: Positives and Negatives

The Reformation was about many things, and it would be wrong to characterize it simply as a debate over justification with a few unimportant trifles attached. While justification was not the all-important epicenter of Reformation theology, it was an important topic, and the image of Luther waging war against works-righteousness still looms large in the minds of many who consider the topic of justification in the present day.

Careful analysis suggests that the Reformers and their immediate successors held a variety of viewpoints on justification. In fact, I do not agree completely with Luther or his successor Melanchthon or with Calvin or his successor Beza or with either of the scholastic orthodoxies that emerged within the Lutheran and Reformed camps.

The seminal insight that launched the Reformation was Luther's discovery that "the righteousness of God" (mentioned in Rom. 1:16-17), which is at the center of the gospel, was not the lofty standard of righteousness intrinsic to God himself that seemed to condemn all of humanity by its demands, but rather was a righteousness that comes from God and is applied to the account of the struggling sinner.[7] To Luther it was important that God justified the ungodly even as that person was still unbelieving and still understood himself or herself to be alienated from God. That person's sins were not imputed to him or her, while the alien righteousness of Christ was imputed instead. Thus, *coram Deo* ("before God") the person was counted as righteous, while *coram hominibus* ("before humanity")— most notably in the person's own eyes—he is counted as unrighteous. This is what stands behind Luther's famous phrase *simil iustus et peccator* ("at the same time justified and a sinner").

God initiated this gratuitous salvific act without the cooperation of the individual.

This was necessary because the *liberium arbitrium* ("free will") with which Adam had been endowed had become a *servum arbitrium* ("enslaved will") in all the heirs of fallen Adam. Although at one time Luther had held the view that in the fall free will was not lost, a key moment in the development of his distinctive theology came when he broke with the prevailing theory of his day by concluding that the will of fallen humanity was helpless apart from grace.

Luther's viewpoint was not maintained unmodified by his followers. In 17th-century Lutheran dogmatics, faith itself came to be seen as a cause of justification, and therefore faith must logically come prior to justification. As humans were unable to believe without divine grace first freeing their *servum arbitrium* ("bound will"), it became necessary to postulate that regeneration preceded faith. So later Lutheranism modified Luther's *ordo salutis*, making regeneration precede faith and faith precede justification. No longer did God justify the unbeliever, but rather the believer.[8]

Calvin's theory of justification was very similar to Luther's. In fact, Calvin and the Reformed tradition as a whole remained closer to Luther's position on justification than did the Lutheran orthodoxy that emerged in the 17th century.[9] Calvin's main innovation was to ground justification in predestination, finding some precedent for this idea in Augustine.[10] On the basis of God's eternal decrees of election, the unrighteous and unbelieving elect are justified through the non-imputation of their sins and the imputation of Christ's alien righteousness to them. The elect are also regenerated, adopted, and are indwelt by the Holy Spirit. At this point the protracted process of sanctification also begins.

Calvin insists, like Luther, that the righteousness imputed to the ungodly in justification is alien and extrinsic. However, he differs from Luther by not envisioning a continuing situation in which the justified person views himself or herself as unrighteous at the same time as God views this person as being righteous.

For Calvin, the grace involved in justification (and in regeneration, adoption, etc.) is irresistible, and the individual has no role in effecting any part of it. The chief innovation of Theodore Beza, Calvin's successor at Geneva, was explicitly to affirm the doctrine of limited atonement, the notion that in justification Christ did not die for all people but, rather, only for the elect. Even though a number of passages imply the universal character of Christ's work (e.g., John 1:29, "Behold the Lamb of God who takes away the sin of the world"), Calvin certainly would never have maintained that all humans were therefore counted among the elect. He was no Universalist! But Calvin was also unwilling to follow the logic of the doctrine of irresistible grace to its logical conclusion: limited atonement. Beza, in contrast, did not hesitate in this regard.

While I cannot speak for all Evangelical synergists, I find the position of 17th-century Lutheran orthodoxy the most congenial of the positions sketched above, but still ultimately untenable. This is the only one of the major Reformation positions that suggests the individual must accept or reject the divine offer of justification, which comes in the form of a gift. The problem with this position is that it presumes that a major part of the larger gift of salvation, that being regeneration, has already been accomplished prior to the moment when the individual accepts or rejects God's offer of justification. Is it possible to imagine a person who, after having been regenerated, rejects God's gracious offer and so is not justified? I think not. This would result in a half-saved theological monstrosity, regenerated but not justified.

Resistible Prevenient Grace[11]

More compelling than the theory of Lutheran orthodoxy are approaches that locate the divine initiative not in regeneration but rather in a "prevenient grace" associated with the divine calling (*vocatio*) either as part of it or as a grace that follows immediately on its heels. Prevenient grace, which is initiated entirely by God and apart from any human merit, restores to the unbelieving sinner whose will has been continually enslaved the freedom to accept or to reject God's gracious offer of justification along with regeneration and the other gifts of salvation. While much about this grace remains a mystery known only to God, it does not seem to be a grace perpetually offered and instead seems episodic and in some way linked to the proclamation of the gospel and the wooing of the Holy Spirit.

"Prevenient grace" or "preventing grace," meaning "the grace that comes beforehand," is not mentioned as such in the Bible. While it is usually associated with Jacobus Arminius and John Wesley, it is a much older term and long predates the Protestant Reformation. While used rather differently than by Arminius or Wesley, it finds a place in Augustine's theological system and even is used constructively in Chapter 5 of Trent's Decree *on Justification*:

> *Declarat praeterea, ipsius justificationis exordium in adultis a Dei per Chrisum Iesum praeveniente gratia sumendum esse.* ... ("It [the Synod] furthermore declares that in adults the beginning of that justification must be derived from the prevenient grace of God through Jesus Christ. ...").

The doctrine of prevenient grace is closely tied to the doctrines of original sin and human fallenness. If fallen humans were simply able to choose to turn to God for reconciliation and salvation at their own initiative, then there would be no need for prevenient grace and the concept would be robbed of its meaning.

While Protestants, including Evangelicals, often speak of "total depravity," this is language Catholic theologians usually resist. Some of this reluctance may turn on a misunderstanding of what Protestants mean by the term. It does not mean unsaved, fallen people are as depraved as they could possibly be, cloned Hitlers or worse, roaming everywhere. Instead, it means that every aspect of an unsaved fallen person, including his or her psychology, spiritual nature, will, physicality, social capacity, cognitive or intellectual ability, and moral capacity has been marred or damaged or in some way has been made less than fully operative. It is not enough for prevenient grace simply to remedy an intellectual deficit such as ignorance of the gospel message; it must also remedy the enslavement or captivity of the will to make it free and able to accept God's free offer of salvation.

Catholic doctrine certainly teaches a kind of depravity "transmitted with human nature" from Adam to his descendants.[12] This deficit inherited from Adam precludes fallen people from saving themselves. Chapter 5 of the Council of Trent's Decree *on Justification* makes clear that divine grace can be resisted when it says, *abicere potest* ("he is able to reject it"). But it clearly affirms that no one can be justified without the grace of God by relying on his or her own free will: *...neque tamen sine gratia Dei movere se ad iustitiam coram illo libera sua voluntate possit* ("...however, neither without the grace of God can one move himself to righteousness before Him [i.e., God] by his own free will").[13]

The *Canons on Justification* are perhaps even clearer than the Decree. Canon 3 stresses that justification comes only through the divine initiative:

> If anyone shall say that without the anticipatory inspiration of the Holy Spirit (*sine præveniente Spiritus Sancti inspiratione*) and without His assistance man can believe, hope, and love or be repentant, as he ought, so that the grace of justification may be conferred upon him: let him be anathema.

Canon 4 is equally clear in its commitment to a synergist position:

> If anyone shall say that man's free will moved and aroused by God does not cooperate by assenting to God who rouses and calls, whereby it disposes and prepares itself to obtain the grace of justification, and that it cannot dissent, if it wishes, but that like something inanimate it does nothing at all and is merely in a passive state (*passive se habere*): let him be anathema.

So what sort of "prevenient grace" does the *Decree on Justification* suggest? It seems to be largely the proclamation of the gospel, the offer of God's salvation in a clear and persuasive manner. As Chapter 6 of the *Decree* says:

> Now they are disposed to that righteousness when aroused and assisted by divine grace, receiving faith "by hearing" [Rom. 10:17], they are freely moved toward God, believing that to be true which has been divinely revealed and promised. ...

No doubt part of what constitutes God's prevenient grace is the proclamation of the gospel. But if the Protestant doctrine of "total depravity" is correct, this sort of prevenient grace is inadequate. There has to be the application of prevenient grace that enables the *servum arbitrium* ("enslaved will") to be restored to its natural status as *liberium arbitrium* ("free will"), or for the *liberum arbitrium captivatum* once again to become the *liberum arbitrium liberatum*. The simple addition of intellectual knowledge, even if it is knowledge of the gospel message, is not enough.

Divine Sovereignty and Human Freedom

Much of the difficulty encountered over the centuries when justification has been discussed turns on disagreements over how to understand both divine sovereignty and human freedom. Some "high Calvinists" (e.g., Vincent Cheung, John Frame, and John Piper) argue that not a single atom in the universe moves without God's direction and that therefore God directs even evil actions. While not morally culpable, God directly mandated that the ovens of Auschwitz be built and used. And yet despite their affirmations that God is in meticulous control of everything, such Calvinists still claim that human freedom remains completely operative throughout it all.[14]

The motivation behind such thinking is understandable, even laudable: If the entire universe and all of history exist to herald the glory of God, then if theologians are to err, they should err on the side of the sovereignty of God. To diminish God's sovereignty is to diminish God and his glory, and this is something to be avoided at all costs.

The problem with this is that in the end the doctrine of God's meticulous providence, i.e., his meticulous direction of everything, ends up diminishing God's glory and renders him impersonal, unlike the Sovereign Lord depicted in Scripture. This is because, as high Calvinists see things, all things are predetermined. God's eternal decrees must necessarily reflect the one best situation possible, and once they have been decreed, they cannot be changed. Isaac Watts describes this well:

> Let us then consider what will be the Consequences of supposing that the Divine Will in all its Determinations and Decrees whatsoever, is universally, certainly and unalterably influenced by the superior Fitness of Things....Then there is nothing amongst all the Works of God's Creation, or his Providence, or his Government of Creatures thro' Time or Eternity, left free to him with a *Liberty of Choice or Indifference*, since this Opinion supposes there is but one single Train of fittest Things, or one Set of Things supremely fit among all the Millions of Possibles that come within the Divine Survey. Then every Atom in the Creation, together with the Shape of it, and the Size and Situation of it through the whole Universe, every Motion in the World of corporeal Nature appointed by God, together with the Times and Periods, Minutes and Moments of every Event, the least as well as the greatest, ... are all eternally necessary, because they are the fittest that could be. ...
>
> What strange Doctrine is this, contrary to all our ideas of the Dominion of God? Does it not destroy the Glory of his Liberty of Choice, and take away from the Creator and Governor and Benefactor of the World, that most free and sovereign Agent, all the Glory of this sort of Freedom? Does it not seem to make him a kind of intelligent Instrument of eternal Necessity, an almost mechanical medium of Fate, and introduce Mr. *Hobbes*'s Doctrine of *Fatality* and *Necessity* into all things that God hath to do with? Doth it not seem to represent the blessed God as a Being of vast Understanding and Consciousness, as well as of Power and Efficiency, but still to leave him *without a Will* to chuse [sic] among all the Objects within his view? In short, it seems to make the Blessed God a sort of Almighty Minister of Fate under its universal and supreme Influence.[15]

One of the sorrows of modern life in America is recognition of how little God is acknowledged in popular culture today. It used to be common to hear people say things like, "God seems to be telling me something" or "I guess God wants me to...." Today those sentiments are still widely expressed, but with "the Universe" taking the place of God.

Googling "the Universe wants..." results in over 79 million hits. Googling "the Universe seems to be telling..." results in over 54 million hits. It does not seem people substitute "the Universe" for "God" as an expression of philosophical materialism. The anthropomorphic way in which they think of that great throng of atoms we call the Universe "wanting" or "saying" something suggests this is not the case. Instead they think of "the Universe" as being a metaphysical force—a karmic force, really—rather than a personal being. And if we reduce God to a being so constrained by the logic of his own decrees that he has no real choice, we have boxed him in and reduced him to something like the karma of American pop culture.

But how can humans be free if God is sovereign? Theories abound, including those "compatibilist" theories that suggest humans can be free even when every decision they make has been fixed and made certain by another (i.e., God). But there is a simpler and more obvious solution to this problem. To use the language of Baylor theologian Roger E. Olson, "God is sovereign over his sovereignty."[16] In other words, it is no insult to God's sovereignty to claim he chooses to limit himself. In fact, Scripture teaches that God created man in his image and also that he delegated to Adam the authority to name the animals. Adam's is not an absolute sovereignty, unlimited and without restraint, but it is a kind of sovereignty. It is for this reason, as Elaine Pagels has perceptively pointed out, that when the church fathers before Augustine read the first three chapters of Genesis, they beheld a story of human freedom and moral accountability.[17] It is only with Augustine that this narrative becomes primarily (and oxymoronically) a story of "captive free will" (*liberum arbitrium captivatum*).

What is at stake here is nothing less than the internal coherence of soteriology. The pithy comment of Bernard of Clairvaux makes the point well: "Take away free will and there is nothing that needs to be saved." While every theologian will affirm some theory of free will, some are too fainthearted to concede a free will that involves "libertarian freedom" and true choice between alternatives. In the end, this diminishes the gospel.

This is one point where Evangelical synergists appear to track more closely with Catholics than with Evangelical monergists. While personally I would be unwilling to anathematize anyone over this point, I agree with the analysis of the issue that lies behind Trent's Canon 6 *on Justification*:

> If anyone shall say that it is not in the power of man to make his ways evil, but that God produces the evil as well as the good works, not only by permission, but also properly and of Himself, so that the betrayal of Judas is no less His own proper work than the vocation of Paul: let him be anathema.

Similarly, Canon 23 appears to be aimed squarely at Calvinism. In this matter too Evangelical synergists would agree with the Catholic critique, if not the application of an anathema, on these grounds. The canon reads:

> If anyone shall say that the grace of justification is attained by those who are predestined unto life, but that all others, who are called, are called indeed, but do not receive grace, as if they are by divine power predestined to evil: let him be anathema.

Canon 23 appears to be aimed in large part, although perhaps not exclusively, at the Calvinistic doctrine of "perseverance of the saints." Since Evangelical synergists typically hold, in contradistinction to Evangelical monergists, that it is possible for a person who has been truly justified and regenerated later to fall away from the faith and to renounce the gift of salvation that once had been accepted and received, there would appear to be some alignment of the Catholic and Evangelical synergist positions. Canon 23 reads:

> If anyone shall say a man once justified can sin no more, nor lose grace, and that therefore he who fails and sins was never truly justified; or, on the contrary, that throughout his whole life he can avoid all sins even venial sins, except by a special privilege of God, as the Church holds in regard to the Blessed Virgin: let him be anathema.

However, it would be a mistake to conclude that Evangelical synergists are in total (or even substantial) agreement with this canon. Woven throughout the fabric of the canon's argument is the assumption that to be saved by God a human must possess a righteousness that is properly his or her own and not simply imputed to him or her on the basis of Christ's alien righteousness. Thus, when a person sins after justification, this results in his or her justification, understood as a state of righteousness, being lost. In contrast, Evangelical synergists hold that after a person has been (initially) justified, Christ's righteousness continues to serve as the primary basis, although not usually the sole basis, for that person's continuing righteousness. Thus, the person continues to be righteous *coram Deo* unless that person willfully renounces his or her faith, choosing to despise God's gift of salvation, thereby apostatizing or "falling way" from a state of grace. In such a case, God accedes to the free choice of the person and no longer imputes Christ's righteousness to him or her. In addition, God begins imputing anew whatever sins the person may newly commit, including the sin of unbelief, damning him or her to eternal punishment.

Works and Sola Fide

Within Reformation theology justification is famously regarded as the *articulus stantis et cadentis ecclesiae*, "the article on which the Church stands or falls." While Luther never used these exact words, he came close: *quia isto articulo stante stat Ecclesia, ruente ruit Ecclesia* ("Because if this article [of justification] stands, the church stands; if this article collapses, the church collapses").[18] Moreover, for Luther the article of justification means justification *sola fide*, "by faith alone." Without *sola fide*, the gospel simply was not the gospel and without the gospel the church could not remain standing.

The question, of course, is whether or not Luther was right about this. An obvious problem is that the one time "faith alone" is mentioned in Scripture, in James 2:24, the text seems specifically to deny Luther's contention: "You see that a person is justified by works and not by faith alone" (ὁρᾶτε ὅτι ἐξ ἔργων δικαιοῦται ἄνθρωπος καὶ οὐκ ἐκ πίστεως μόνον).[19] Protestants have often wrestled with this issue, and I will offer a few observations.

First, it seems that Paul and James are working with very different definitions of faith. In 2:19 James says, "Even the demons believe—and shudder!" While clearly the intention of this passage is to diminish the role of faith in comparison to works, the passage makes clear that faith is understood by James to mean intellectual understanding, not a commitment of the will to love God and follow Christ. Demons may believe God exists, but they can hardly be envisioned as committed to God in these ways. Therefore, the deeper commitment of the will that Paul contemplates when he speaks of faith serves as the sole basis of justification in a way that mere intellectual assent could not.

This explanation is helpful, but it does not fully solve the problem. James does not merely limit the role of such intellectual knowledge: he also asserts that "works" justify.

The key question, however, is this: Does James envision works that are antecedent to faith, or does he envision works subsequent to faith? If these works are subsequent to faith, justification, and regeneration, then such works are simply the normal expression of a transformed life. Even Calvin suggests something along these lines: "We are not saved by works, but neither are we saved without them."[20] By depicting a contest in which two people demonstrate evidence of having been justified by God, James makes clear that he is not discussing the basis on which justification was predicated, but rather the subsequent outward evidence for a contested justification dating from a prior time.

James has in his sights those who claim to have faith in Christ and yet, by their lack of the Christian fruit that normally accrues in Christian life, call into question their claim to have been justified. Key to this argument is the fact that works are visible to others in a way that subjective faith is not.

Chapter 10 of the Tridentine Decree *on Justification* encourages that the justified be "further justified" by whatever means available. A number of passages of Scripture are cited in support of this assertion. Among them is James 2:22, which states of Abraham that "faith cooperated with his works" (ἡ πίιστις συνήργει τοῖς ἔργοις αὐτοῦ).

In the illustration James gives of this cooperation between "faith" and "works," Abraham's offering of his son Isaac in sacrifice shows the particular way the cooperation occurs. In Genesis 15:6 Abraham trusts in God and his faith is "reckoned to him as righteousness." At that time Isaac had not even been born. It is only later, in Genesis 22, that Abraham shows himself to be willing to sacrifice his son, even though this deed would make believing God's promises to him even more unfathomable than it already was. This act of obedience was the fruit that resulted from a life of faith, faith that was prior to the "works" James cites, faith that had already resulted in Abraham's justification.

I would maintain that a person might by good works provide further evidence of an initial faith that led to justification. A person might by good works demonstrate fruit validating an earlier personal transformation, of which justification was a part. However, Evangelicals do not understand how one could be "further justified," as Trent suggests. If one has been accorded a standing of righteousness before the divine judge, what more is there to justify? It would be as if a judge rendered two verdicts upon two defendants and found one "not guilty" and the second one "really not guilty." What would be the actual distinction in meaning or impact between these two verdicts?

Also problematic is the unfortunate way in which the Greek word *metanoēsate* ("repent") of Acts 2:38 is translated, first in the Vulgate and then with only the slightest variation in Chapter 6 of the *Decree on Justification*. In the Vulgate, the expression *poenitentium agite* ("do penance") is used. In Chapter 6 of the *Decree, pænitentiam agite* ("do penance") appears. In both cases, rather than calling for a change of mind, the mistranslated text demands an action, a "work," so to speak.

Infusion or Imputation of Grace

At the heart of the differences between Catholicism and Evangelicalism over initial justification is whether Christ's righteousness is infused into the believer and perhaps joined to an actual righteousness proper to the person himself or herself, or is imputed ("reckoned") to the person as something "alien," coming from the outside and not being properly his or her own, but rather being counted that way legally. Another way to frame the issue, as was suggested at the beginning of this essay, is to inquire whether the term *dikaios* should be understood, on the one hand, as a forensic term, pictured using courtroom imagery, or, on the other hand, as a moral term, evoking considerations of character and behavior.

While Evangelicals do sometimes think of the terms *dikaios* ("righteous") and *dikaiosynē* ("righteousness") in moral terms, particularly when speaking of sanctification (what Catholics sometimes call "second justification"), they normally think of initial justification in forensic terms. In contrast, Catholics almost always think of justification, including initial justification, in moral terms. The result is that sometimes Catholics and Evangelicals talk past each other or use the same language to mean quite different things.

Trent's Canons 10 and 11 *on Justification* are clear in their rejection of the idea that Christ's alien righteousness is imputed onto the individual. Canon 10 reads:

> If anyone shall say that men are justified without the righteousness (*iustitia*) of Christ by which He merited for us, or that by that righteousness itself (*per eam ipsam*) he is formally just (*iustos*): let him be anathema.

As Canon 11 makes clear, when the bishops of Trent speak of the grace of Christ being received by the individual, they speak not only of Christ's graciousness toward humanity, which is received entirely as a gift, but rather of a gracious character that is implanted within the soul of the individual. Thus, to receive "grace" at justification is understood quite differently by Evangelicals and Catholics. For the Evangelical it entails no change in the person's character; for the Catholic a change of character is precisely what is meant. Canon 11 reads:

> If anyone shall say that men are justified either by the sole imputation of the righteousness of Christ (*iustitiæ Christi*), or by the sole remission of sins, to the exclusion of grace and charity, which is poured forth into their hearts by the Holy Spirit and remains in them, or even that the grace by which we are justified is only the favor of God: let him be anathema.

Evangelicals are certainly not opposed to the development of, and even infusion from God of, virtues such as grace and charity in the individual Christian. What we find contrary to the gospel message, as we understand it, is that the presence of these virtues in the individual could serve as a basis of her initial justification. As Ephesians 2:8 says, "For by grace you have been saved through faith; and this is not your own doing, it is the gift of God." The infusion of righteousness into the individual to make that individual worthy of salvation—both in her own eyes and in the eyes of other humans—suggests that it is a matter of merit and not of grace. Similarly, the notion of infused virtues making a person worthy of divine acceptance and reward runs entirely counter to the normal Evangelical conception of initial justification.

Preparation for Justification

Evangelical synergists believe that individuals may reject God's free offer of reconciliation, of which initial justification is a part. However, we affirm the doctrine of total depravity and its necessary implication that fallen humans are utterly lost and unable to save themselves. If people are to be reconciled to God, God himself must take the initiative through the application of divine grace. While this must include more than supplying the intellectual content of the gospel message, the exact working of this grace remains something of a mystery and likely differs in its specific form depending on the specific situation of each individual.

God may use anointed preaching, a situation of great personal pain, the winsome influence of a godly friend, or some similar situation to refocus the person's mind and heart on spiritual things. These are not merely mechanical, external events, but rather situations and actions that the Holy Spirit uses in his exercise of prevenient grace. In fact, Evangelicals understand the Holy Spirit to be at work even before one is called to become a Christian; the Holy Spirit convicts the ungodly of their sin. Synergism is especially common in traditions that have grown out of revivalism and "the sawdust trail," and these traditions frequently pay great attention to preparing people for encounter with the gospel, mediated and enlivened by the Holy Spirit.

To express this differently, the idea of "preparation" for conversion is very much a part of the Evangelical heritage, although generally this preparation differs considerably from the notion of preparation in the Catholic tradition. Within the Catholic tradition, preparation is something a person does himself or herself in anticipation of the infusion of divine grace. To the extent that, according to Catholic theology, human action preceding initial justification is understood to be necessary (although by itself not sufficient) for initial justification to occur, this is problematic for Evangelicals.

Trent's Canon 9 on *Justification* illustrates the Catholic perspective:

> If anyone shall say that by faith alone the sinner is justified, so as to understand that nothing else is required to cooperate in the attainment of the grace of justification, and that *it is in no way necessary that he be prepared and disposed by the action of his own will*: let him be anathema (emphasis added).

Conclusion

While the agreements between Evangelical synergists and Catholics with respect to the doctrine of initial justification are greater than our differences, our differences are real and significant. Because of their rejection of the Protestant doctrine of total depravity, Catholics conclude that humans are able to, and in fact must, contribute to their own salvation through acts of preparation, even though, due to the greater and absolutely necessary contribution of Christ's merit in one's justification, they clearly assert that humans are unable to save themselves. They also assert that Christ's righteousness and the virtues of grace and charity are infused into the individual at justification, making that person worthy to be saved both *coram Deo* ("before God") and *coram hominibus* ("before humans").

Evangelical synergists maintain that for a gift to be a gift three things must take place: a) an offer; b) acceptance of the offer; and c) delivery of the gift. Evangelical synergists differ from Evangelical monergists because we maintain that, aided by prevenient grace, people are able to accept or to reject God's gracious gift of salvation, including initial justification. We differ from Catholicism in our denial of any ability (or necessity) to contribute to our own initial justification. We also assert that in initial justification Christ's alien righteousness is imputed to us even while we are not properly righteous in and of ourselves. Thus, we accept the slogan *simil iustus et peccator* as an apt description of things at the moment of justification, although we also contend that after regeneration and sanctification the disciple of Christ should begin the process of developing an intrinsic character more and more like that of his or her master and exemplar, Jesus Christ.

Evangelical synergists affirm that, as Eph. 2:10 tells us, God's people were "created in Christ Jesus for good works." Following justification good works should characterize the lives of the justified. However, initial justification is not and cannot be anchored in good works that precede that justification. Thus, the solution to the challenge posed by James 2:24, "...a person is justified by works and not by faith alone," is that initial justification is *sola fide*, while this initial justification is later manifested to others by subsequent good works that flow out of it.

NOTES

[1] Alister E. McGrath, *Iustitia Dei: A History of the Christian Doctrine of Justification*, 3rd ed. (Cambridge: Cambridge University Press, 2005), 357.

[2] McGrath, *Iustitia*, 339.

[3] 1 Thess. 1:3; 2 Thess. 1:11.

[4] Ibid., 42.

[5] Augustine, *Sermon 169*, 13.

[6] McGrath, *Iustitia*, 42.

[7] Chapter 7 of the Council of Trent's *Decree on Justification* concurs with Luther's interpretation of this phrase, as it states: "...the unique formal cause [of justification]" is "the righteousness [*iustitia*] of God, not that by which He Himself is righteous [*iustus*], but by which he makes us righteous [*iustos*]." See Denzinger, Henricus, *Enchiridion Symbolorum*, 26th ed. (Rome: Herder, 1976), 371. See also Denzinger, Henry, *The Sources of Catholic Dogma*, trans. by Roy J. Defarrari from the 30th ed. of the *Enchiridion Symbolorum* (Fitzwilliam, NH: Loreto, 2002), 251. In the several quotations of Trent's *Decree on Justification* and its *Canons on Justification* found in this essay, I have started with Defarrari's translation, but in a number of cases I have felt the need to modify it. I have tried to include the relevant Latin in such cases.

[8] McGrath, *Iustitia*, 275-76.

[9] Ibid., 277.

[10] See Augustine, *Ad Simplicianum*, 1.2.6 and McGrath's mention of this, *Iustitia*, 40.

[11] While most adherents of the doctrine of "prevenient grace" understand this to be "universal" in the sense that this grace is given to all, some adhere to a doctrine of "individualistic" prevenient grace, wherein only those who hear an intelligent presentation of the Gospel experience it. Theopedia.com, s.v. "Resistible prevenient grace." Accessed Sept. 28, 2015.

[12] Pope John Paul II, *Catechism of the Catholic Church* (Vatican City: Libreria Editrice Vaticana, 1992), §419.

[13] Chapter 5 continues: "Hence, when it is said in the Sacred Writings: 'Turn to me and I will turn to you' [Zach. 1:3], we are reminded of our liberty; when we reply: 'Convert us to you, O Lord, and we shall be converted' [Lam. 5:21], we confess that the grace of God comes to us first" [Author's translation].

[14] Two descriptions of "meticulous providence" help explain the perspective. Both are borrowed from Roger E. Olson, *Against Calvinism* (Grand Rapids: Zondervan, 2011), 78, 80. R. C. Sproul (in *What Is Reformed Theology?* [Grand Rapids: Baker, 1997], 72) writes: "The movement of every molecule, the actions of every plant, the falling of every start, the choices of every volitional creature, all of these are subject to his sovereign will. No maverick molecules run loose in the universe, beyond the control of the Creator. If one such molecule existed, it could be the critical fly in the eternal ointment." Similarly, Loraine Boettner (in *The Reformed Doctrine of Predestination* [Grand Rapids: W.B. Eerdmans, 1948], 30) writes: "Even the sinful actions of men [including Adam's first sin] can occur only by his [God's] permission. And since he permits not unwillingly but willingly, all that comes to pass--including the actions and ultimate destiny of man— must be, in some sense, in accordance with what he desired and purposed."

15 Isaac Watts, *An Essay on the Freedom of the Will in God and in Creatures* (London: Roberts, 1732), 82-86.
16 Olson, *Against Calvinism*, 66.
17 Elaine Pagels, "Adam and Eve and the Serpent in Genesis 1-3," 412-23 in Karen L. King, *Images of the Feminine in Gnosticism* (Philadelphia: Fortress, 1988).
18 WA 40/3.352.3.
19 Here the Vulgate does not use *sola fide*, but rather *fide tantum*.
20 John Calvin, *Institutes*, 3.16.1.

Background Paper

Ex inimico amicus:
Catholic Teaching on Initial Justification

Dr. Christian D. Washburn

Underlying the difference between Protestant thought and Catholic thought are divergent understandings of whether the gifts given to man are natural or supernatural. Protestant theology has generally deemed this distinction deeply problematic. In its view, it suggests that God created man to be damned, since man's nature on its own was incapable of obtaining his end, heaven.[1] Catholic theology, on the other hand, has seen heaven as natural only to God. Man's supernatural end, which is participation in God's own inner life, transcends the capacity and claims of the natural order. Hence, no creature, not even the highest angel, could, without grace, merit the Beatific Vision. According to Catholic doctrine, no creature is naturally proportioned to any supernatural end. This distinction between natural and supernatural gifts leads to very divergent views concerning not only the nature of original justice but also all subsequent discussion of the Fall and the restoration of man through justification and sanctification. This essay will explain the Catholic teaching on initial justification, in which the supernatural power of grace acts to expel sin and transform one from an enemy of God into a friend of God (*ex inimico amicus*).[2] To this end, this article will first examine the Catholic Church's teaching on the grace of the first man, original sin, the existence of free will, and the power of unaided fallen man to know and to do good, insofar as these issues touch upon initial justification. The article will next address the Church's doctrine on the preparation for justification through faith and other good works, and the justification of the sinner as a transition from the state of sin to the state of justice, emphasizing its twofold dimension as both the forgiveness of sin and the renovation of man.

Sources for Understanding Catholic Teaching on Justification

The basis, of course, of all Catholic reflection on initial justification is revelation as found in Sacred Scripture and Apostolic Tradition. Cardinal Newman observed that "no doctrine is defined until it is challenged,"[3] and so it is no surprise that the magisterium did not begin to define the doctrine of initial justification until the Pelagian and Semi-Pelagian controversies of the fourth and fifth centuries. Catholic doctrine on initial justification was not again substantially challenged until the Protestant Reformation in the 16th century, and in response the magisterium solemnly defined a large number of doctrines surrounding this issue at the Council of Trent (1545-1563).[4] Shortly thereafter, the Catholic theologians Michael de Bay (1513-1589) and Cornelius Jansen (1585-1638) and their followers held several errors that touched upon our issue, and a number of popes felt obligated to warn the faithful by condemning these errors. So St. Pius V (r. 1566-1572), Pope Innocent X (r. 1644-1655), Pope Alexander VII (r. 1655-1667), and Pope Clement XI (r. 1700-1721) all issued documents condemning these errors. There the issue sat until the end of the 20th century when, in 1999, the Catholic Church's Pontifical Council for Promoting Christian Unity (PCPCU) and the Lutheran World Federation (LWF) came to substantial agreement on the issue of justification in the *Joint Declaration on the Doctrine of Justification* (JDDJ).[5] The JDDJ, however, did not resolve all the issues surrounding initial justification, nor was it accepted by all bodies descended from the Reformation.

Man in Original Justice

Pelagius (c. 390-418) and many Protestant theologians' theological anthropology was based in part on the principle that all of Adam's gifts were natural gifts that allowed him to know and to love God. This error was rejected not only by the Council of Trent but also in the condemnations of Michael de Bay by St. Pius V (r. 1566-1572) and Gregory XIII (r. 1572-1585).[6] The Catholic Church's basic thesis is that God created our first parents in His image and likeness and bestowed on them special gifts that supernaturally elevated their nature. Thus God endowed them with natural gifts (*dona naturalia*), such as the body and soul, and with supernatural gifts (*dona supernaturalia*), such as sanctifying grace.[7] These latter are classified as supernatural for a number of reasons. First, these gifts were both positively unowed (*indebita*) to Adam and were superadded (*superadditum*) to his nature. Second, these supernatural gifts were simply (not relatively) supernatural, as they were not part of man's nature, nor did they proceed from his nature, nor could they be claimed by another nature.[8] It is precisely this distinction between natural and supernatural goods in original justice that forms the fundamental basis of the disagreement on issues of justification between the Catholic Church and the Reformation. The importance of this distinction was not lost on the reformers. Luther rejected the distinction between natural and supernatural gifts as a "poison" and thought that any distinction in the order of gifts would entail a subsequent minimization of original sin.[9]

So what exactly was man's condition before the Fall? At Trent the magisterium *implicitly* defined, against the reformers, that our first parents were "constituted in" "holiness and justice."[10] Trent indicated that in original justice our first parents were endowed with the supernatural gift of sanctifying grace, making them not only holy but also just. Sanctifying grace is the cause that effects the other supernatural gifts. In this state, original justice was so joined to sanctifying grace that the integrity of the will, that is, the obedience of the lower part of the soul to the upper part, depended on that grace as its root and source.[11] Some Protestant theologians have objected that Catholic doctrine seems to make God into a monster who created man to be damned, since man's nature on its own was incapable of obtaining his end, heaven. Catholic theology, however, is clear that God gave man the supernatural and preternatural gifts precisely so that man would be able to obtain his supernatural end, the beatific vision.

God also bestowed on our first parents the *state of integrity,* which was intended to complete and elevate man's perfection so that man could live in a way consistent with his orientation toward God. That this state was supernatural is clear from the teaching of St. Pius V, who condemned the error that "the integrity of the first creation was not the undeserved exaltation of human nature, but its natural condition," and Clement XI, who condemned the error that "the grace of Adam" was "certainly due to integral nature."[12] There are four gifts that constituted this state. The first of these was infused knowledge; the second, immunity from concupiscence, i.e., from disorderly inclinations of the sense appetite. In the order of nature, conflict between our flesh and spirit is entirely natural, for man has an animal body endowed with sensibility and appetites and a rational soul that seeks the spiritual good. Since a rational soul and an animal body form a single nature, man has within himself diverse propensities, which is often described as a *languor naturae*.[13] This gift of immunity from concupiscence acted as a kind of "golden bridle," so that man's lower powers were subject to the higher and his higher powers were submissive to God.[14] The final two supernatural gifts were immortality and impassibility.

The Fall of Man

The most definitive statement on original sin to date by the extraordinary magisterium is the Council of Trent's *Decree on Original Sin* (17 June 1546), containing five canons. The first three canons, essentially a re-condemnation of Pelagianism, make liberal use of the language of the synods of Carthage (418) and II Orange (529), in part to combat Protestant theologians' insistence that the Catholic Church was teaching Pelagian doctrine. In Canon 1, the council taught that Adam broke God's law and was punished by God for this transgression. With this punishment, Adam was "transformed in body and soul for the worse" (*in deterius commutatum*), lost his "holiness and justice," earned the wrath of God and death, and fell "captive to the devil."[15] In Canons 2 and 3, the council reaffirmed that these punishments were transmitted to Adam's descendants by natural generation.[16]

What, then, is the nature of original sin? Although Trent did not formally define this, its nature was clearly implied where the council described original sin as the death of the soul (*mors animae*) and defined that baptism cleanses original sin by infusing sanctifying grace into the soul.[17]

Beyond this, different theological schools within Catholicism have tended to explain more precisely the nature of original sin. Prior to Trent, Aquinas, for example, saw not only a privation but also a positive element in original sin. He states, "As bodily sickness is partly a privation, in so far as it denotes the destruction of the equilibrium of health, and partly something positive, viz. the very humors that are inordinately disposed, so too original sin denotes the privation of original justice, and besides this, the inordinate disposition of the parts of the soul. Consequently it is not a pure privation, but a corrupt habit."[18] After Trent, Catholic theologians tended to see original sin as a loss of the supernatural gift of sanctifying grace and secondarily as the loss of the state of integrity.[19] In any case, this understanding of original sin as privation clearly implies that fallen human nature is not any different than it would have been had it originally been created in a state of pure nature without the supernatural gifts.[20] In losing this original justice, man has not lost his natural faculties. Bellarmine argues that

> the state of man, after the Fall of Adam, is no worse than the state of man in a purely natural state, any more than a man stripped of his clothes is worse than a naked man. Disregarding original sin, the present condition of human nature is second to nothing that it had been; it is not more ignorant or weak than he would have been if he had been placed in a condition of pure nature. Therefore the corruption of nature is not from the lack of some natural gift, nor from the addition of some evil quality, but it is only the absence of a supernatural gift, lost by the sin of Adam.[21]

Therefore, our nature is only said to be wounded and corrupt in comparison to that goodness in which the Creator had originally created man.[22]

What does it mean to say that the whole man, body and soul, was changed for the worse by the prevarication of Adam? The privation of grace results in a number of other eternal and temporal effects. First, by this privation man is no longer a friend of God: he is His enemy.[23] Consequently, those who die in the state of original sin are deprived of the beatific vision.[24]

For our purposes, the more important effects of the Fall are the "wounds of nature" (*vulnera naturae*), which directly affect man's ability to respond to God.²⁵ First, man has the wound of ignorance, whereby the intellect has great difficulty recognizing the truth, especially moral or practical truth, and he easily falls into error in these areas.²⁶ Moreover, man has great difficulty learning, knowing his last end, or understanding the means to this end.²⁷ Second, there is the wound of malice (ill will), so that man suffers from inordinate self-love, has difficulty overcoming vice and acquiring virtue, and neglects those goods necessary for a happy life in this world and the next.²⁸ Third, there is the wound of concupiscence, through which the concupiscible appetite moves inordinately to sensible goods contrary to reason. Fourth, there is the wound of infirmity, through which the irascible appetite labors under sluggishness when difficulties arise and man often becomes inordinately angry.²⁹ There are, of course, a number of other results of original sin,³⁰ but these need not detain us. What is clear is that man now has considerable problems that will affect his ability to respond to God's call by his own efforts.

Catholic doctrine does not see concupiscence as sin. St. Paul called concupiscence "sin" in Romans 7, but Catholic theologians see this as an instance of Paul's use of metonymy, whereby the cause stands for the effect or the effect for the cause. Since concupiscence is a cause of sin, Paul calls it sin.³¹ Catholic theologians insist that concupiscence cannot be sin for three main reasons. First, concupiscence, which remains in the justified even after baptism, is not original sin because it has nothing of the nature of sin since it is involuntary.³² Second, concupiscence is an effect and a punishment due to sin, and therefore it cannot be a sin itself.³³ Third, to identify sin as concupiscence detracts from Christ's redemptive work. If concupiscence remains in us, even when we are justified, then Christ did not really redeem us and deliver us from sin. Moreover, this suggests that the devil is stronger than Christ, since the devil could defile the soul while Christ could not really purify it.³⁴

STATE OF MAN'S POWERS AFTER THE FALL WITHOUT GRACE

The question remains: what are the powers of the fallen intellect and will without grace? Concerning the powers of the unaided intellect, the magisterium has maintained that man can know some moral truth without the assistance of grace. In *Unigenitus Dei Filius* (1713), Clement XI rejected the Jansenist proposition that without faith we are in darkness.³⁵

Later, Vatican I defined against both Traditionalism and atheism that the one true God, our Creator and Lord, can "be known with certainty with the natural light of reason through the things that are created."[36] Aware of the wound of ignorance, however, the council went on to affirm the need for Revelation, not only so that supernatural mysteries above human reason can be known, but also so that divine truths accessible to human reason can be known even after the Fall "by everyone with facility, with firm certitude, and with no admixture of error."[37]

Catholic theologians hold that man retained his ability to know natural and civil truths, which would include such things as the knowledge of God's existence or the knowledge of the moral obligation to honor God. For this type of knowledge man does not need a special grace from God; it is sufficient for man to have God's general help.[38] One may also know moral truths, such as it is good to give alms or it is evil to steal. Here what is intended is not simply knowledge about the virtue as such but primarily one's ability to know a moral truth considered together with all its moral circumstances.[39] Theologians generally hold that "in the state of fallen nature the light of practical reason was not so extinguished" in man that he could not know some moral truths with the general help of God, although he is often mistaken when divine guidance is absent.[40]

Concerning the powers of the unaided will, many Protestant theologians came to conclude, partly on the basis of their doctrine of original sin, that while man still has free will (in the sense of freedom from coercion), it can no longer operate in matters that pertain to salvation.[41] In response, the Council of Trent was clear that man's "free will, although weakened and inclined to evil, was by no means destroyed."[42] And it went on in Canon 5 to anathematize those who say that "after the sin of Adam, man's free will was lost and destroyed, or that it is a thing in name only, indeed a title without a reality, a fiction, moreover, brought into the Church by Satan."[43] This affirmation is in part based on scriptural passages that assert the existence of free will, such as in Sirach 15:14: "God made man from the beginning, and left him in the hand of his own counsel" and in part on the vain nature of scriptural counsels, exhortations, commands, prohibitions, rewards, and punishments, if free will is non-existent.[44] Freedom from coercion is not, however, an adequate definition of free will, for it also requires freedom from an intrinsic natural necessity (such as that based on one's essential constitution). Following St. Thomas, Bellarmine defines free will as "the power to choose freely between the means that may lead to an end, one over the other, or to accept or reject at will a single thing."[45]

The magisterium has also condemned the position that all the works of unbelievers, the unjustified, or one in the state of mortal sin, are sinful.[46] Moreover, neither actual grace nor habitual grace is necessary for the performance of a morally good work. The magisterium has repeatedly affirmed that man can do some good acts without any supernatural grace at all. Theologians have provided examples of the types of acts that one is able or unable to do after the Fall; these help to clarify exactly the issue at hand. Thus, for natural acts such as walking, one does not need a special grace from God; it is sufficient for man to have God's general help.[47] With respect to natural moral acts concerning virtue or vice, such as giving alms or stealing, man is able to perform these without grace. Nevertheless, he is still incapable of fulfilling all the precepts of the moral law, even *quoad substantiam tantum*.[48] Moreover, while man may do some morally good works without grace if no temptations are present, man cannot keep any commandment solely by the forces of his nature if temptation is pressing.[49]

The most important question, however, is not whether one can know and do good but whether one is able without grace to perform any supernatural or salvific act, and to this question the council gave a resounding no. Trent began its canons on justification, like its canons on original sin, with a condemnation of Pelagianism. Thus, Trent anathematized anyone who claims that "man can be justified before God by his own works, whether done by his own natural powers or through the teaching of the law, without divine grace through Jesus Christ."[50] The council went on to condemn those who say that "divine grace through Christ Jesus is given for this only, that man may be able more easily to live justly and to merit eternal life, as if by free will without grace he is able to do both, though with hardship and difficulty."[51] Finally, in Canon 3, the council condemned those who say "that without the predisposing inspiration of the Holy Ghost and without His help, man can believe, hope, love or be repentant as he ought, so that the grace of justification may be bestowed upon him."[52] What is clear from Trent's condemnation is that both Semi-Pelagianism and Pelagianism are formally excluded and that divine grace then is not merely a help but a *sine qua non* for living a properly Christian life.

Again, Catholic theologians have specified some types of ungraced acts as completely beyond man's capacity per se. For example, one cannot believe God's word or the mysteries of faith.[53] Nor can an unbeliever, by his own powers of natural reason alone, without a special grace, believe as he ought to believe even if he understands the value of the evidence concerning the Christian religion.[54] Concerning supernatural acts, Catholic theologians deny that man, by the power of the human will and without the special grace of God, is able to desire or do anything in matters affecting piety and salvation.[55] Nor is man able by his own strength to dispose himself to receive grace or to do something on account of which God would confer grace.[56] Finally, man is not able to love God either perfectly or imperfectly as the author of nature without the special grace of God.[57]

Given this last consideration, I think that the distinction between the natural and the supernatural led to a basic misunderstanding between Protestant theologians and the Catholic Church. It seems that the Reformers, in denying the unregenerate man's ability to know and to do good, are not denying that the acts as such are, in Catholic terms, naturally good; rather, these natural acts are simply displeasing to God because they always lack some quality that God requires for the act to be perfectly good. This seems clear in Calvin's claim that spiritual discernment is wholly lost until we are regenerated; he asserted that even the greatest geniuses are like a "traveler passing through a field at night who in a momentary lightning flash sees far and wide, but the sight vanishes so swiftly that he is plunged again into darkness before he can take another step."[58] Catholic theologians could agree with Reformed thought that a truly Christian spiritual discernment is not possible for the unregenerate. But here much depends on the meaning of the term "spiritual," and if by spiritual we think of that knowledge that comes from God alone and is absolutely perfect in all its dimensions, as in this last sense outlined above, then Catholics could agree that supernaturally perfecting knowledge is entirely gratuitous and absolutely above man's nature. On the other hand, some of the analogies used by Protestant theologians are both shocking and unacceptable to Catholic ears, such as likening the unregenerate men to "moles" or a "block of wood or a stone."[59] The analogies suggest that man cannot even respond to God *qua* man who was created by God with the capacity and the ability to know even when he is a sinner.

Graced Preparation for Initial Justification

We have just considered man's ungraced capacity after the Fall to know and to do the good, and now we turn to the capacity of fallen man to know and to do the good with grace. The Council of Trent affirmed that the sinner "is required to cooperate in order to obtain the grace of justification" and that "he be prepared and disposed by the action of his own will."[60] The council repeatedly spoke of the necessity of cooperation, disposition, and preparation.[61] The reason for this is in part because, as Aquinas explains,

> God moves everything in its own manner, just as we see that in natural things, what is heavy and what is light are moved differently, on account of their diverse natures. Hence He moves man to justice according to the condition of his human nature. But it is man's proper nature to have free-will. Hence in him who has the use of reason, God's motion to justice does not take place without a movement of the free-will; but He so infuses the gift of justifying grace that at the same time He moves the free-will to accept the gift of grace, in such as are capable of being moved thus.[62]

The way that God often moves man's free will is by grace, and this grace may be understood as either sanctifying grace or actual grace. In the case of sanctifying grace, some preparation is needed, "since a form can only be in disposed matter." In the case of actual grace, which moves the free will to do good or to accept habitual grace, however, no preparation is required for God to move the free will.[63] This movement of the will, effected by God's grace, may occur gradually, by small, imperfect steps, or it may happen in one perfect step in a flash, as in the case of St. Paul: "It is easy in the eyes of God on a sudden to make the poor man rich" (Sirach 11:23).[64] As Trent made clear, this preparation usually occurs in adults through a series of graces. Thus Trent declared that "in adults the beginning of that justification must proceed from the predisposing grace of God through Jesus Christ, that is, from His vocation, whereby, without any merits on their part, they are called." The unjustified

> may be disposed through His quickening and helping grace to convert themselves to their own justification by freely assenting to and cooperating with that grace; so that, while God touches the

heart of man through the illumination of the Holy Ghost, man himself neither does absolutely nothing while receiving that inspiration, since he can also reject it, nor yet is he able by his own free will and without the grace of God to move himself to justice in His sight.[65]

The first and most important way that one prepares for justification is through the act and habit of faith in the case of an adult. Trent declared that faith is "the beginning of human salvation, the basis and the root of all justice," and that without faith "no one can ever come to justification."[66] This faith is necessary not only because it is the beginning of salvation but because it is part of the perfective transformation of the entire person, by which "man is continually raised to greater things."[67] There are, however, two central points of contention between the Reformation and the Catholic Church: 1) the object of the faith that justifies, and 2) the necessity of other preparatory acts besides faith.

First, with respect to the object of justifying faith, classical Lutheran theology often trifurcated faith into: 1) historical faith (*fides historica*), 2) faith of miracles (*fides miraculorum*), 3) faith of the promise (*fides promissionum, justificans, apprehensiva*).[68] This division was intended to make clear that it is the faith of the promise alone that justifies. From a Catholic perspective, however, it must be said that each element in this tripartite division is part of the object of the faith that justifies. Faith is an absolutely firm assent to the totality of God's revealed word; to put it another way, the faith that justifies is principally a dogmatic faith.[69] This is clear from the teaching of the extraordinary magisterium. In Chapter 6 of its decree on justification, treating the manner of preparation, Trent noted that adults "are disposed unto the said justice, when, excited and assisted by divine grace, conceiving faith by hearing, they are freely moved towards God, believing those things to be true which God has revealed and promised...."[70] In Canon 12, the Fathers of Trent anathematized those who say that "justifying faith is nothing else than confidence in divine mercy, which remits sins for Christ's sake, or that it is this confidence alone that justifies us."[71] Later in the 19th century, the First Vatican Council made it clear that this justifying faith was a dogmatic faith when it affirmed, "This faith, which is the beginning of human salvation, the Catholic Church professes to be a supernatural virtue, by means of which, with the grace of God inspiring and assisting us, we believe to be true what He has revealed, not because we perceive its intrinsic truth by the natural light of reason, but because of the authority of God Himself, who makes the revelation and can neither deceive nor be deceived."[72]

Second, with respect to the necessity of other preparatory acts besides faith, the council was clear that they are necessary. Trent, in rejecting that faith alone justifies, affirmed that other acts and virtues are required in preparation for justification. Thus, Trent taught: "If anyone says that the sinner is justified by faith alone, meaning that nothing else is required to cooperate in order to obtain the grace of justification, and that it is not in any way necessary that he be prepared and disposed by the action of his own will, let him be anathema."[73] Thus, in Chapter 6 of the sixth session, Trent listed other dispositions present in the conversion of a sinner besides faith, such as fear, hope, love, penitence, desire for baptism, the determination to live a new life.[74] One must be clear that Trent did not intend either that each and every one of these acts was to be always found in the conversion of a sinner or that the list is exhaustive. The most important of these dispositions is love. Justifying faith necessarily includes the virtue of charity as faith's form, since without charity faith simply does not justify. Love is the perfecting virtue of faith, and so only faith that "worketh by charity"—i.e., the faith that is moved, formed, and vivified by charity—can justify.[75]

The question that remains is in what way do these acts of preparation contribute to justification? Trent is clear that initial justification is absolutely gratuitous and that preparatory works do not justify one. Thus, Trent states that "nothing that precedes justification, neither faith nor works, merits the grace of justification."[76] What value do they have then? Theologians have generally given different answers to this question. Bellarmine, for example, held that faith, like the other virtues, justifies *per modum dispositionis*;[77] thus, while faith and the other virtues are dispositive to initial justification, the act of faith, like other preparatory works, does not efficiently justify the sinner. In teaching this, Bellarmine reaffirmed the entirely gratuitous nature of initial justification, and in this he is followed by most theologians. A related question is whether initial justification can be merited, either condignly or congruously, through these works. Condign merit is merit in the proper sense of the term, and all orthodox Catholic theologians are in agreement that one cannot condignly merit (*ex condigno*) initial justification.[78] Nevertheless, it appears that Trent left as an open theological position the possibility that one can congruously merit initial justification.[79] Congruous merit, however, is only merit in the improper sense, since it is not based on any dignity or proportion of the work to the grace of justification and is instead based merely on the promise of God.[80] This view is now almost universally repudiated by Catholic theologians although the magisterium has not made any formal definition against it.[81]

What Is Initial Justification?

On 13 January 1547, in the sixth session, the Council of Trent promulgated its *Decree on Justification*. For the first time, the council introduced long doctrinal explanations in 16 chapters preceding its 32 canons anathematizing errors. The chapters are arranged according to the three states of justification. The first state (*primus status*) is a transition (*translatio*) from infidel to faithful (Chapters 1-9), i.e., man's initial justification. The second state (*secundus status*) finds the justified individual in a state of grace, living a life faithful to Christ and growing in justification in order to obtain the end, heaven, which Christ desires for him (Chapters 10-14). The third state (*tertius status*) is how man who has lost justification by mortal sin can restore this justification through the sacrament of penance (Chapters 15-16). This tripartite division allowed for conceptual clarity in dealing with the place of works and merit in the Christian life. It must be recalled that here we are only speaking of that first state (*primus status*), which is a transition (*translatio*) from infidel to faithful.

In Chapter 4 of its decree on justification, Trent defined initial justification as

> a transition from that state in which a person is born as a child of the first Adam to the state of grace and of adoption as children of God through the agency of the second Adam, Jesus Christ our savior; indeed, this transition, once the gospel has been promulgated, cannot take place without the waters of rebirth or the desire for them, as it is written: Unless a person is born again of water and the Holy Spirit, he cannot enter the kingdom of God.[82]

The justification of a sinner, whether an infant or an adult, must be understood in the sense of a transition from the state of sin to the state of grace. There are "two ends" or effects of one's initial justification: a remission of sins and the sanctification and renewal of the interior man through the voluntary reception of grace and gifts.[83] The *Catechism of the Catholic Church*, quoting St. Augustine, says that this "justification of the wicked is a greater work than the creation of heaven and earth."[84]

The first and negative end of this infusion of sanctifying grace in justification is the true remission of sins. Against Luther's insistence on the ongoing presence of sin in the justified sinners, Pope Leo X condemned the proposition: "To deny that in a child after baptism sin remains is to treat with contempt both Paul and Christ."[85] In Canon 5, the council completely rejected both Luther's doctrine of the ongoing presence of sin after baptism and Girolamo Seripando's (1493-1563) doctrine of the presence of something hateful to God in man after baptism. Instead, the council held that the guilt of original sin is remitted by baptism and anathematized anyone who says that "all that is sin in the true and proper sense" is not taken away by the grace conferred in baptism. Instead, baptism so transforms men that they are made "innocent, immaculate, pure, guiltless and beloved sons of God."[86] Therefore, after baptism, God hates nothing, and men are no longer under His wrath. The council also taught that concupiscence, i.e., an inclination to sin (*inclinatio ad peccatum*),[87] remains in the baptized and that concupiscence is not "truly and properly" sin in those born again. Lastly, the council stated that it did not intend to include in this decree on original sin the immaculate Virgin Mary.[88]

The second and positive end or element of justification is "the sanctification and renewal of the inner man" (*sanctificatio et renovatio interioris hominis*).[89] Both the Lutheran and Reformed traditions acknowledge a positive element, but in both cases it is extrinsic: in the case of Lutherans, it is an apprehension of the extrinsic justice of Christ; in the case of the Reformed, it is the right to life or the imputation of righteousness.[90] In contrast, the Council of Trent affirmed that grace and charity are "poured forth in their hearts by the Holy Ghost, and remains in them."[91]

The Catholic Church generally sees five effects of sanctifying grace in the interior renovation of man.[92] First, it makes one holy. Second, sanctifying grace bestows beauty on the soul. Thus the *Catechism of the Council of Trent* says that sanctifying grace is a "brilliant light that effaces all those stains which obscure the luster of the soul, investing it with increased brightness and beauty."[93] Third, sanctifying grace makes one a friend of God. Recall that original sin makes one an enemy of God. Thus, Trent taught that one is transformed in justification "from an enemy into a friend of God."[94] Fourth, sanctifying grace makes the just man a child of God through adoption. One may understand this sonship in three ways. Sonship may occur by reason of natural generation as the Word of God or a human son; by creation on account of an imperfect similitude to God; or by spiritual generation, whereby an infused spiritual gift grants similitude to the human. This adoption is unlike natural human adoption. In natural human adoption, a similitude of natures is almost always required. Moreover, natural human adoption is almost always a merely external reality. Instead, in divine adoption the one adopted is said to be born of God through spiritual regeneration and can call God his Father.[95] This spiritual regeneration is essentially supernatural, whereby we are elevated to a supernatural likeness to the Father. This is because God not only loves us as His children, "in His Son and through His Son," but He also "impresses on us the image of His Son and makes us like Him, that we may be truly His children."[96] Fifth, sanctifying grace makes the justified man a temple of the Holy Ghost.[97]

God in His generosity does not bestow on us only sanctifying grace with its effects but also a series of other supernatural gifts. Thus the *Catechism of the Council of Trent* asserted that sanctifying grace "is accompanied by a most splendid train of all virtues, which are divinely infused into the soul along with grace."[98] These include the three supernatural theological virtues. The Council of Trent stated that "in justification, man receives simultaneously with the remission of sins all the three virtues of faith, hope, and charity."[99] Theologians also generally hold that in justification one receives the supernaturally infused moral virtues and the gifts of the Holy Spirit.[100] The reason for the comity of these gifts is that they are understood to be necessary both to salvation and to the living of a life in Christ that is worthy of His name and eternal life.

The Causes of Initial Justification

The Council of Trent described initial justification in terms of Aristotelian causation, and the council is sometimes faulted for the imposition of these concepts onto an otherwise biblical presentation. The genius of the use of these concepts, however, is that they help to make clear both the theocentric and Christocentric orientation of justification as well as the relationship of each of God's actions with man's. The council specified that the final cause of justification of the ungodly is "the glory of God and of Christ" and the salvation of those who are justified. The principal efficient cause is the goodness and mercy of God. The meritorious cause is the passion and death of Christ, and baptism is the instrumental cause. Finally, the council defined that "the sole formal cause" (*unica causa formalis*) of justification is "the justice of God, not that by which He Himself is just, but by which He makes us just."[101] This identification of the single formal cause is perhaps the most important element in the *Decree on Justification,* and it has a number of important implications for understanding initial justification.

First, there is a striking lacuna in the Tridentine list of causes: the material cause, i.e., the human soul. Scholars have often overlooked this, and this is unfortunate, for the use of the concepts of material causation and formal causation, given their relation to one another, clearly implies that without the formal cause man is simply spiritually dead. I will draw an analogy between sanctifying grace as the formal cause of justification and the soul as the formal cause of the human person in order to explain in part the use of this term "formal cause." Just as, with regard to the human being's natural constitution, the disembodied soul is the form of a body merely potentially alive, so, with regard to the spiritual perfection of man, sanctifying grace is the form of the unjustified human being who is merely potentially alive spiritually. As the human body of a man without soul is nothing more than a heap and is no longer either living or human,[102] so a living man deprived of sanctifying grace is no longer spiritually alive or one with Christ.

Second, this formal cause, "the justice of God, not that by which He Himself is just, but by which He makes us just," was repeatedly described as both "inhering" and "infused."[103] The council intended to indicate that inhering sanctifying grace is that which makes us formally just. In this justice there is both an absolute forgiveness of sin and an intrinsic renewal. This of course was completely opposed to the Lutheran and Reformed understandings of a totally extrinsic justification, which is expressed in their doctrines of the non-imputation of sin and the imputation of justice.[104] It cannot be stressed enough, however, that neither the expression "inhering grace" nor Canons 10 and 11 exclude a theory of imputation; they only exclude such an imputation or a forensic declaration as a formal cause of justification.[105] A Catholic can and should affirm that there is some type of divine declaration in the process of justification, but it can be affirmed precisely because God is declaring what He has made man.[106]

Third, that which makes us justified is *a* created grace and not *the* uncreated grace. The council's use of Augustinian language was again studied and deliberate. St. Augustine had used this language, for example, in *On the Spirit and the Letter*, in which, commenting on Romans 3:21, he stated, "He said: *the righteousness of God*, not that by which God is righteous, but that with which He clothes a human being when He justifies a sinner."[107] Augustine had employed this language to make it clear that the justice that is given is not the justice by which God is just, which in the case of God is God Himself. If the justice by which God is just were the formal cause of our justification, then this justice would either be God Himself or at least the divine indwelling. It is therefore clear that what makes us justified is a created grace and not the uncreated grace. This helps to make it clear that this grace is proper to each justified person. Lastly, inasmuch as this grace is a created reality, by implication it inheres within each justified person as an accident, lest we are to make it a subsisting subject unto itself.[108]

Fourth, the addition of the word "sole" (*unica*) to formal cause was studied and deliberate,[109] and by this one word the council intended principally to repudiate the doctrine of double justification held by such eminent Catholic theologians as Cardinal Gasparo Contarini (1483-1542) and the General of the Hermits of St. Augustine, Girolamo Seripando. In an irenic attempt at rapprochement with Protestant theology, these theologians posited that there are two formal causes in justification (that is, two types of righteousness): inherent and imputed.[110] The position of Trent is also a repudiation of the Protestant view that the formal cause is anything, including the remission of sin or the imputation of righteousness, other than sanctifying grace.¹¹¹ With this inhering righteousness, one is truly made righteous, not with an imperfect righteousness but with an absolute and perfect righteousness.¹¹² The term "perfect" here is used in its classical sense and simply means that this righteousness is whole and complete and does not require the addition of some other righteousness.

Conclusion

Catholics hold that God endowed our first parents with natural gifts (*dona naturalia*), such as the body and soul, and with supernatural gifts (*dona supernaturalia*), such as sanctifying grace. It is precisely this distinction between natural and supernatural goods in original justice that forms the fundamental basis of the disagreement on issues of justification between the Catholic Church and the Reformation and informs the structure of each theological system. This distinction entails that after the Fall, the first parents did not lose their natural capacities and so were able to know and to do natural good but not supernatural good. Thus, if the gifts in the Garden are conceived of as "natural," then the loss of these gifts, at least to Catholic theology, suggests that after the Fall man is something less than a man, and of course something less than a man is incapable of doing any morally good works. So too the restoration of man in justification is simply a return to a natural state. Catholic theology, on the other hand, will see in the Fall a return to man's natural state, in which man still has all of his natural faculties; in the restoration through justification man is elevated beyond his natural state. Thus, while the unregenerate's ability to do good may be a point of dispute, it is a point of convergence that whatever they do unaided is not salutary. It is the case that for both Evangelicals and Catholics, initial justification is seen as entirely gratuitous, for none of the goods done prior to justification are able to cause or merit justification.

Notes

[1] Martin Luther, *Vorlesungen uber Mose*, WA 42, 124.4-6. John Theodore Mueller, *Christian Dogmatics: A Handbook of Doctrinal Theology for Pastors, Teachers, and Laymen* (St. Louis: Concordia Publishing House, 1934), 206; Francis Turretin, *Institutes of Elenctic Theology*, 3 vols., trans. George Musgrave Giger and ed. James T. Dennison (Phillipsburg, NJ: P & R Pub., 1992), 1:592; Charles Hodge, *Systematic Theology* (Grand Rapids: W.B. Eerdmans, 1981), 2:103; Robert Lewis Dabney, *Systematic Theology* (Edinburgh: Banner

of Truth Trust, 1985), 296-97; Louis Berkhof, *Systematic Theology* (Grand Rapids: W.B. Eerdmans, 1996), 208-09; William Greenough Thayer Shedd, *A History of Christian Doctrine* (New York: C. Scribner's Sons, 1894), 2:147-148; Herman Bavinck, *Reformed Dogmatics*, ed. John Bolt and trans. John Vriend (Grand Rapids, MI: Baker Academic, 2003), 2:539-541. Some Protestant theologians recognized a distinction between supernatural and natural gifts in the Garden but restricted the supernatural gifts to what Catholics would call uncreated grace, e.g., the indwelling of the Holy Ghost. Johann Gerhard, *Loci theologici cum pro adstruenda veritate ... opus praecilissimun novem tomis comprehensum denuo ... curavit adjectis notis ipsius Gerhardi posthumis a filio collectis paginis editionis Cottae in margine diligenter notatis* (Berolini: sumtibus Gust. Schlawitz, 1864), 2:116-118.

2   Quoted from Peter Hünermann, Helmut Hoping, Robert L. Fastiggi, Anne Englund Nash, and Heinrich Denzinger, eds., *Compendium of Creeds, Definitions, and Declarations on Matters of Faith and Morals*, 43rd edition (San Francisco: Ignatius Press, 2012) (Hereafter DH), DH 1528/799, 1529/799, 1535/803. The second number refers to the numbering of the 30th edition. Heinrich Denzinger and Roy J. Deferrari, *The Sources of Catholic Dogma* (St. Louis: Herder, 1957).

3   John Henry Newman, *An Essay on the Development of Christian Doctrine* (London: Pickering, 1878), 151.

4   It must be remembered that the Tridentine *Decrees on Original Sin and Justification* were directed at the Lutherans and not at the Reformed.

5   For an Evangelical assessment of the various dialogues on justification, see Anthony Lane, *Justification by Faith in Catholic-Protestant Dialogue: An Evangelical Assessment* (London: T & T Clark, 2006).

6   Two propositions condemned by Pius V in *Ex omnibus afflictionibus* (1567) are directly related to the issue at hand. Thus, Article 21 states, "Humanae naturae sublimatio et exaltatio in consortium divinae naturae, debita fuit integritati primae conditionis, ac proinde naturalis dicenda est, non supernaturalis." Article 26 states, "Integritas primae conditionis non fuit indebita humanae naturae exaltatio, sed naturalis eius conditio." DH 1921, 1926. Gregory XIII's Bull, *Provisionis nostrae* (1579), reconfirming Pius V's condemnation, is found in Aloysius Tomassetti and Francisco Gaude, *Bullarum diplomatum et privilegiorum sanctorum Romanorum pontificum Taurinensis editio locupletior facta collectione novissima plurium brevium...a S. Leone Magno usque ad praesens* (Naples: Henrico Caporaso Editore, 1883), 8: 316.

7   "Porrò CATHOLICI Doctores, qui multis supernaturalibus donis primum nostrum parentem initio creationis ornatum fuisse non dubitant, duos illos errores sine ulla difficultate declinant. Docent enim per Adae peccatum totum hominem verè deteriorem esse factum; tamen nec liberum arbitrium, neque alia naturalia dona, sed solùm supernaturalia perdidisse." Robert Bellarmine, *Disputationes Roberti Bellarmini Politiani Societatis Jesu, de controversiis Christianae fidei, adversus hujus temporis haereticos* (Paris: Triadelphorum, 1613), 13.1.1, vol. 4, 5. Historically, the preternatural gifts (*dona preternaturalia*) were generally classified as supernatural gifts. While these gifts are not considered above all created nature, since other natures can by nature possess these gifts as natural gifts, nevertheless they are classified as supernatural since they are supernaturally bestowed on man.

8   Iosepho F. Sagüés, S.J., *"De hominis elevatione,"* in Iosepho A. De Aldama, S.J., Richardo Franco, S.J., Severino Gonzalez, S.J., Francisco A. P. Sola, S.J., Iosepho F. Sagüés, S.J., *Sacrae Theologiae Summa*, 4th ed. (Matriti: Biblioteca De Autores Cristianos, 1967), 3: 743-749.

9   Luther was quite clear about the loss of these "natural" powers. Thus, in his *Commentary on Genesis* he wrote, "quin hoc statuamus, justiciam non fuisse quoddam donum, quod ab extra accederet, separatum a natura hominis: sed fuisse vere naturalem, ita ut natura Adae esset diligere Deum, credere Deo, cognoscere Deum, Haec tam naturalia fuere in Adamo, quam naturale est, quod oculi lumen recipient." *Vorlesungen uber Mose*, WA 42, 124.4-6. LW 1:164-165.

10   DH 1511. This is also implied by the Council of Orange: "human nature, even if it should remain in the integrity in which it was constituted, in no way preserves itself without the help of the Creator; hence since without the grace of God it cannot preserve the salvation that it accepted, how without the grace of God will it be able to restore what it has lost?" DH 389. By substituting the phrase "in iustitia constitutus" for "in iustitia creates," the Council of Trent intentionally avoided resolving the issue of whether Adam and Eve were created with sanctifying grace or whether Adam was created *in puris naturalibus* and only later given sanctifying grace and the friendship of God. Pietro Cardinal Sforza Pallavicino, *Vera concilii tridentini historia, contra falsam Petri Suavis Polani narrationem,.... primo italico idiomate in lucem edita; deinde ab ipso auctore aucta & revia; ac latine reddita a P. Johanne Baptista Giattino* (Antwerp: n.p., 1673), 1: 245. See also *Concilium Tridentinum. Diariorum, Actorum, Epistularum, Tractatuum nova collection*, Edidit Societas Goerresiana, ed. Stephanus Ehses (Freiburg im Br.: B. Herder, 1911), 5.218.19-21 (hereafter CT).

11   Bellarmine, *De Controversiis*, 13.1.3, vol. 4, 9-10. On Bellarmine's contribution to these issues, see Christian D. Washburn, "The Shaping of Modern Catholic Anthropology in the Context of the Counter-Reformation: St. Robert Bellarmine and the Transformative Power of Grace," in *Das Menschenbild der Konfessionen – Achillesferse der Ökumene?*, ed. Bertram Stubenrauch/Michael Seewald (Freiburg im Breisgau: Verlag Herder, 2015): 217-48; Cyril Vollert, S.J., "Saint Thomas on Sanctifying Grace and Original Justice: A Comparative Study of a Recent Controversy," *Theological Studies* 2 (1941): 369-87; Cyril Vollert, S.J., "Herveus Natalis and the Problem of Original Justice," *Theological Studies* 3 (1942): 231-51.

12   DH 1926/1026, 2435/1385.

13   Bellarmine, *De Controversiis*, 13.1.6, vol. 4, 23.

14   Ibid., 13.1.5, vol. 4, 15.

15   DH 371, DH 1511/788.

16   DH 1512/789, 1513 /790.

17   DH 1512/789, 1523/795. On the history of the question of the nature of original sin, see George Vandervelde, *Original Sin: Two Major Trends in Contemporary Roman-Catholic Reinterpretation* (Amsterdam [Keizersgracht 302-04]: Rodopi, 1975).

18   St. Thomas Aquinas, *Summa Theologiae*, trans. Fathers of the English Dominican Province (1948; reprint, Westminster, MD: Christian Classics, 1981), l-ll, q. 82, a. 1.

19   Bellarmine, *De Controversiis*, 14.5.17, vol. 4, 345; Joseph Hubert Busch, *Das Wesen der Erbsünde nach Bellarmin und Suarez: e. dogmengeschichtl. Studie* (Paderborn: Schöningh, 1909), 92-93; Julius Gross, *Geschichte des Erbsündendogmas: ein Beitrag zur Geschichte des Problems vom Ursprung des Übels* (München: E. Reinhardt, 1960), 4: 132-33.

20   Bellarmine, *De Controversiis*, 13.1.5, vol. 4, 16-17; "Per Adae peccatum totum hominem vere deteriorem esse factum; tamen nec liberum arbitrium, neque alia naturalia dona, sed solum supernaturalia perdidisse." Bellarmine, *De Controversiis*, 13.1.1, vol. 4, 5. Suarez held that "Communis et vera sententia est, naturales vires hominis vel liberi arbitrii, quoad gradum, seu perfectionem quam in statu purae naturae haberent, non

fuisse diminutas in natura lapsa ex vi solius peccati originalis sed solum quoad robur et integritatem quam a iustitia originali accipiebant. Haec sine dubio est sententia S. Thomae et communis antiquorum theologorum." Francisco Suarez, S.J., *Commentaria ac disputationes in primam secundae D. Thomae, de gratia*, in *Opera Omnia*, ed. Carolo Berton (Paris: Ludovicum Vivès, 1857), 7: 207. The issue is whether man has been affected intrinsically or extrinsically by the Fall. Both Bellarmine and Suarez rejected the view that man has been intrinsically affected.

21 Bellarmine, *De Controversiis*, 13.1.5, vol. 4, 16-17.

22 Ibid., 13.1.6, vol. 4, 21.

23 DH 1528/799, 1529/799.

24 Lyons II : "...The souls of those who die in mortal sin or with original sin only, however, immediately descend to hell, to be punished with different punishments..." (DS 464). Florence: "Moreover, the souls of those who depart in actual mortal sin or in original sin only, descend immediately into hell but to undergo punishments of different kinds." (DS 693).

25 Thomas Aquinas, *Summa Theologiae*, I-II q.85 a.3.

26 Ibid.

27 Bellarmine, *De Controversiis*, 14.6.9, vol. 4, 378-80.

28 Ibid., 14.6.10, vol. 4, 380-82.

29 Thomas Aquinas, *Summa Theologicae* I-II q.85 a.3.

30 Bellarmine, *De Controversiis*, 14.6.13, vol. 4, 384-86.

31 Ibid., 14.5.3, vol. 4, 279.

32 Ibid., 14.5.9, vol. 4, 306.

33 Ibid., 14.5.9, vol. 4, 305.

34 Ibid., 14.5.9, vol. 4, 307.

35 DH 2448/1398, 2441/1391.

36 DH 3026/1806.

37 DH 3005/1785, 1806, 2145.

38 Bellarmine, *De Controversiis*, 15.1.4.2, vol. 4, 549; 15.1.4.3, vol. 4, 553; Domingo de Soto, *De natura & gratia. Quod opus ab ipso authore denuo recognitum est, nonnullisque in locis emendatum, & apologia contra reverendum episcopum Catharinum auctum* (Paris: Apud Ioannem Foucher et excudebat Ioannes Gemet, 1549), 10.

39 Bellarmine, *De Controversiis*, 15.1.5.1, vol. 4, 585.

40 Ibid., 15.1.5.2, vol. 4, 586; 15.1.5.9, vol. 4, 605.

41 *Westminster Confession* (1646) teaches: "Man, by his fall into a state of sin, hath wholly lost all ability of will to any spiritual good accompanying salvation; so as a natural man, being altogether averse from that good, and dead in sin, is not able, by his own strength, to convert himself, or to prepare himself thereunto." Chapter IX, On Free-will, III.

42 DH 1521/793, 1525/797.

43 DH 1555/815.

44 Bellarmine, *De Controversiis*, 15.1.3.5, vol. 4, 508.

45 Ibid., 15.1.3.3, vol. 4, 506. Thomas Aquinas, *Summa Theologiae*, I, q. 83, a. 1. Ultimately, the root of the will's freedom lies within the faculty of reason, and the will depends in its determination on the final judgment of practical reason. The will is free because it is a rational appetite. In contrast, in animals the appetite is not free because it is not

rational: it cannot turn to an object perceived as good (or evil), conscious of its goodness as such or of its relation to a more universal good. This is why animals whose knowledge is purely sensitive are committed "instinctively" toward appetible objects. In men, however, the intellect is able to present the object to the will in varying manners, under a more or less universal good (or evil). The will is therefore free, because reason discerns the universal good in distinction from its particular expressions and can subordinate one good to another, whereby the will can opt for a variety of means to achieve its end or none of them at all.

46 DH 1557/817, 2499/1399. DH 1935/1035, 1940/1040.

47 Bellarmine, *De Controversiis*, 15.1.4.2, vol. 4, 549; 15.1.4.3, vol. 4, 553; Soto, *De natura & gratia*, 10.

48 Bellarmine, *De Controversiis*, 15.1.5.5, vol. 4, 595. This was a common teaching amongst the scholastics. Johann Auer, *Die Entwicklung der Gnadenlehre in der Hochscholastik: Das Wirken der Gnade* (Freiburg: Herder, 1951), 2: 43-44. See also Soto, *De natura & gratia*, 88ᵛ.

49 Bellarmine, *De Controversiis*, 15.1.5.7, vol. 4, 600; 15.1.5.9, vol. 4, 605.

50 DH 1551/811.

51 DH 1552/812.

52 DH 1553/813.

53 Bellarmine, *De Controversiis*, 15.1.4.1, vol. 4, 547.

54 Ibid., 15.1.6.2, vol. 4, 677; 15.1.6.3, vol. 4, 681.

55 Ibid., 15.1.6.4, vol. 4, 683.

56 Ibid., 15.1.6.5, vol. 4, 686.

57 This was a contested issue in the 16th century. Normally in the Scholastic Period, the issue was whether one could love God *super omnia* without grace, but the second question, whether one could love God with a perfect act of natural love, was not always denied. Aquinas denied that man can love God above all things in the state of fallen nature without the grace of God (*gratia sanans*). *Summa Theologicae*, Ia-IIae, q. 109, a. 3. See also Domingo Báñez, *Scholastica commentaria in secundam secundae angelici doctoris S. Thomae. Quibus, quae ad fidem, spem, & charitatem spectant; clarissimè explicantur* (Douai: Ex typographia Petri Borremans, 1615), 3: 345; Soto, *De natura & gratia*, 88; Bellarmine, *De Controversiis*, 15.1.6.7, vol. 4, 691.

58 John Calvin, *Institutes of the Christian Religion*, 2.2.18., ed. John T. McNeill, trans. Ford Lewis Battles, The Library of Christian Classics, vol. 20 (Philadelphia: The Westminster Press, 1960), 1:277.

59 (moles): Calvin, *Institutes of the Christian Religion*, 2.2.18. 1:277. (blocks of wood): Similarly, the Solid Declaration of the *Formula of Concord* (1580) quotes Luther: "In spiritual and divine matters, which concern the soul's salvation, the human being is like a pillar of salt, like Lot's wife, indeed like a block of wood or a stone, like a lifeless statue, which needs neither eyes nor mouth, neither senses nor heart, inasmuch as this human being neither sees nor recognizes the dreadful, fierce wrath of God against sin and death, but instead abides in a sense of security willingly and knowingly as a result runs into a thousand dangers and finally into eternal death and damnation....Indeed, every bit of teaching or preaching is wasted here, before the Holy Spirit enlightens, converts, and gives new birth to this creature." Solid Declaration, II, 20 in Robert Kolb, Timothy J. Wengert, and Charles P. Arand, *The Book of Concord: The Confessions of the Evangelical Lutheran Church* (Minneapolis: Fortress Press, 2000), 548.

60 DH 1559.
61 DH 1525, 1527, 1554, 1559.
62 Thomas Aquinas, *Summa Theologiae*, I-II, q. 113, a. 3.
63 Ibid., I-II, q. 112, a. 2.
64 Ibid.
65 DH 1525/797.
66 St. Thomas explained the necessity of faith this way: "a movement of free-will is required for the justification of the ungodly, inasmuch as man's mind is moved by God. Now God moves man's soul by turning it to Himself according to Psalm 84:7 (Septuagint): 'Thou wilt turn us, O God, and bring us to life.' Hence for the justification of the ungodly a movement of the mind is required, by which it is turned to God. Now the first turning to God is by faith, according to Hebrews 11:6: 'He that cometh to God must believe that He is.' Hence a movement of faith is required for the justification of the ungodly." *Summa Theologiae*, I-II, q. 113, a. 4.
67 Bellarmine, *De Controversiis*, 15.2.1.20, vol. 4, 786.
68 Martin Chemnitz, *Examen concilii Tridentini*, ed. Preuss (Leipzig: J.C. Hinrichs'sche Buchhandlung, 1915), 180, 192; John Theodore Mueller, *Christian Dogmatics: A Handbook of Doctrinal Theology for Pastors, Teachers, and Laymen* (St. Louis, MO: Concordia Pub. House, 1955), 322.
69 This is not intended to describe every aspect of faith.
70 DH 1526.
71 DH 1562.
72 DH 3008, 3032.
73 DH 1559.
74 DH 1526-1527.
75 Bellarmine, *De Controversiis*, 15.2.2.4, vol. 4, 812-813.
76 DH 1532.
77 Bellarmine, *De Controversiis*, 15.2.1.17, vol. 4, 777.
78 Christian D. Washburn, "Transformative Power of Grace and Condign Merit at the Council of Trent" *The Thomist* 79 (2015): 173-212.
79 See Heiko Oberman, "The Tridentine Decree on Justification in the Light of Late Medieval Theology," *Journal for Theology and the Church* 3 (1967): 28-54; "Duns Scotus, Nominalism, and the Council of Trent," in *The Dawn of the Reformation: Essays in Late Medieval and Early Reformation Thought* (Grand Rapids: W.B. Eerdmans, 1992), 204-233; Hanns Rückert, "Promereri. Eine Studie zum tridentinischen Recht-fertigungsdekret als Antwort an H. A. Oberman," *Zeitschrift fur Theologie und Kirche* 68 (1971), 162-94.
80 Bellarmine, *De Controversiis*, 15.2.21, vol. 4, 787; 15.2.5.21, vol. 4, 1020.
81 F.X. de Abarzuza, O.F.M. Cap., *Manuale Theologiae Dogmaticae*, 2nd ed. (Madrid: Ediciones Studium, 1956), 3: 521; Severino Gonzalez, S.J., "*De gratia*," in Iosepho A. De Aldama, S.J., Richardo Franco, S.J., Severino Gonzalez, S.J., Francisco A. P. Sola, S.J., Iosepho F. Sagues, S.J., *Sacrae Theologiae Summa*, 4th ed. (Matriti: Biblioteca De Autores Cristianos, 1967), 4: 694-695; Jean Herrmann, *Institutiones theologicae dogmaticae* 7th ed. (Lugduni: E. Vitte, 1937), 326; J. M. Hervé, *Manuale Theologiae Dogmaticae*, 16th ed. (Westminster, MD: The Newman Bookshop, 1943), 3: 243; H. Hurter, S.J., *Theologiae Dogmaticae Compendium*, 12th ed. (Oeniponte: Libraria Academica Wagneriana: 1908),

3: 204; Ludovico Lercher, S.J., *Institutiones Theologiae Dogmaticae*, 3rd ed. (Oeniponte: Feliciani Rauch, 1948), 4.1: 109; J. Riviere, "Mérite," *Dictionnaire de theologie catholique contenant l'exposé des doctrines de la théologie catholique, leurs preuves et leur histoire*, vol. 10-1, ed. E. Amann, E. Mangenot, A. Vacant (Paris: Letouzey et Ané, 1928), 757; Ludwig Ott, *Grundriss der katholischen Dogmatik* (Freiburg: Herder, 1959), 320; Christian Pesch, *Praelectiones Dogmaticae*, 4th ed. (Freiburg im Breisgau: B. Herder, 1916), 5: 247; Joseph Pohle and Arthur Preuss, *Grace, Actual and Habitual: A Dogmatic Treatise*, 6th ed. (St. Louis: B. Herder Book Co, 1929), 407; Adolphe Tanquerey, *Synopsis Theologiae Dogmaticae*, 27th ed. (Paris: Desclée et Socii, 1953), 3: 195-196.

[82] DH 1524/811.

[83] Bellarmine, *De Controversiis*, 15.2.2.6, vol. 4, 818.

[84] CCC 1994. St. Augustine: "Prosus maius hoc esse dixerim, quam est coelom et terra, et Quaecunque cernuntur in coelo et in terra." St. Augustine, *On the Gospel of John*, 72, 3. Like St. Augustine, St. Thomas Aquinas said, "The justification of the ungodly ... is greater than the creation of heaven and earth." St. Thomas Aquinas, *Summa Theologiae*, Ia IIae q. 113, a.9, vol. 2:1152.

[85] Leo X condemned the following proposition: "In puero post baptismum negare remanens esse peccatum, est Paulum et Christum simul conculcare." DH 1452.

[86] DH 1515. See also the Council of Trent: "Si quis per Iesu Christi Domini nostri gratiam, quæ in baptismate confertur, reatum originalis peccati remitti negat; aut etiam asserit, non tolli totum id, quod veram et propriam peccati rationem habet, sed illud dicit tantum radi aut non imputari: anathema sit." DH 1515. The ongoing presence of sin in the justified is perhaps one of the most contentious issues and one not fundamentally resolved with respect to the JDDJ. It is difficult to see in light of the clear and infallible teaching of the magisterium how this issue does not still remain as a church-dividing issue. See *Response of the Catholic Church to the Joint Declaration of the Catholic Church and the Lutheran World Federation on the Doctrine of Justification*, 1; Cardinal Avery Dulles, S.J., "Justification: The Joint Declaration," *Josephinum* 9 (2002): 113.

[87] DH 1515.

[88] DH 1516.

[89] DH 1528/799.

[90] John Theodore Mueller, *Christian Dogmatics: A Handbook of Doctrinal Theology for Pastors, Teachers, and Laymen* (St. Louis: Concordia Publishing House, 1934), 367. Calvin defined justification, "Acceptionem qua nos Deus in gratiam receptos pro iustis habet. Eamque in peccatorum remissione ac iustitiae Christi imputatione positam esse dicimus." Calvin, *Institutes*, 3.11.2; François Turrettini, *Institutes of Elenctic Theology*, 3 vols., trans. George Musgrave Giger and ed. James T. Dennison (Phillipsburg, N.J.: P & R Pub, 1992), 2: 657; Robert Lewis Dabney, *Systematic Theology* (Edinburgh: Banner of Truth Trust, 1985), 624.

[91] DH 1561.

[92] Ludovico Lercher, S.J., *Institutiones Theologiae Dogmaticae*, 4.1: 79-93.

[93] *Catechism of the Council of Trent for Parish Priests: Issued by Order of Pope Pius V*, 188.

[94] DH 1528/799, 1529/799, 1535/803.

[95] Iosepho F. Sagüés, S.J., "*De hominis elevatione*," 3: 627.

[96] Matthias Joseph Scheeben, *The Glories of Divine Grace* (Rockford, IL: TAN, 2000), 99.

[97] On the gift of the divine indwelling, see Daniel A. Keating, *Deification and Grace* (Naples, FL: Sapientia Press, 2007).

⁹⁸ *Catechism of the Council of Trent for Parish Priests: Issued by Order of Pope Pius V* (Rockford, IL: Tan Books, 1982), 188.

⁹⁹ DH 1530/800.

¹⁰⁰ Adolphe Tanquerey, *Synopsis Theologiae Dogmaticae*, 27th ed. (Paris: Desclée et Socii, 1953), 3: 85.

¹⁰¹ DH 1529.

¹⁰² In Catholic theology, natural or physical death is defined as the separation of the soul from the body. F.X. de Abarzuza, O.F.M. Cap., *Manuale Theologiae Dogmaticae*, 3:399; J. M. Hervé, *Manuale Theologiae Dogmaticae*, 3:552; H. Hurter, S.J., *Theologiae Dogmaticae Compendium*, 3: 606; Christian Pesch, *Praelectiones Dogmaticae*, 5:273; François Xavier Schouppe, *Elementa theologiae dogmaticae e probatis auctoribus collecta : et divini verbi ministerio accommodata* (Lyon; Paris: Delhomme et Briguet, 1867), 469. It might be added that this also seems to be the assumption both in Benedict XII's *Benedictus Deus* and in the Council of Florence's decree of union with the Greeks. See DS 530-531/1000 and 693/1304-1305.

¹⁰³ DH 1529, 1530.

¹⁰⁴ The *Catechism of the Catholic Church* defines sanctifying grace as "an habitual gift, a stable and supernatural disposition that perfects the soul itself to enable it to live with God, to act by his love. Habitual grace, the permanent disposition to live and act in keeping with God's call, is distinguished from actual graces which refer to God's interventions, whether at the beginning of conversion or in the course of the work of sanctification." CCC 2000.

¹⁰⁵ Bellarmine, *De Controversiis*, 15.2.2.9, vol. 4, 829.

¹⁰⁶ "Quando Deus iustificat impium, declarando iustum, facit etiam iustum; quoniam iudicium Dei secundùm veritatem est." Bellarmine, *De Controversiis*, 15.2.2.3, vol. 4, 805.

¹⁰⁷ Augustine, *On the Spirit and the Letter*, in *Answer to the Pelagians, I* (Hyde Park, NY: New City Press, 1997), 158. "*Iustitia Dei manifestata est* [Rom 3:21]; non dixit: iustitia hominis, vel iustitia propriae voluntatis; sed: *iustitia Dei*, non qua Deus iustus est, sed qua induit hominem, cum iustificat impium." Rouët de Journel, *Enchiridion patristicum: loci ss. patrum, doctorum, scriptorum ecclesiasticorum* (Barcinone: Herder, 1969), 1730.

¹⁰⁸ This is also made clear from Trent's repeated use of the term "inhaerere," which also suggests an accidental mode of being. DH 1530/800, 1547/809, 1561/821. This is also made clear in the use of the term "infundere." DH 1530/800, 1547/809 (2x).

¹⁰⁹ On the development and importance of the phrase "unica formalis causa," see Christopher J. Malloy, *Engrafted into Christ: A Critique of the Joint Declaration* (New York: Peter Lang, 2005), 69-78; Christopher J. Malloy, "The Nature of Justifying Grace: A Lacuna in the Joint Declaration," *The Thomist* 62 (2001): 93-120.

¹¹⁰ On double justification, see Stephan Ehses, "Johannes Groppers Rechtfertigungslehre auf dem Konzil von Trient," *Römische Quartalschrift für christliche Altertumskunde und für Kirchengeschichte* 20 (1906): 17588; Hubert Jedin, *Papal Legate at the Council of Trent, Cardinal Seripando*, trans. Frederic Eckhoff (St. Louis, London: B. Herder Book Co., 1947), 348-392; J.F. McCue, "Double Justification at the Council of Trent: Piety and Theology in Sixteenth Century Roman Catholicism," in Carter Lindberg and George W. Forell, eds., *Piety, Politics, and Ethics: Reformation Studies in Honor of George Wolfgang Forell* (Kirksville, MO: Sixteenth Century Journal Publ., Northeast Missouri State Univ, 1984), 39-56; Paul Pas, "La doctrine de la double justice au Concile de Trente," *Ephemerides theologicae Lovaniensis* 30 (1954): 553; E. Yarnold, "Duplex iustitia: The Sixteenth Century

and the Twentieth," in Henry Chadwick and G.R. Evans, *Christian Authority: Essays in Honour of Henry Chadwick* (Oxford: Clarendon Press, 1988), 213-22.

[111] On the formal cause in Protestant thought, see John Henry Newman, *Lectures on the Doctrine of Justification* (Westminster, MD: Christian Classics, 1966), 343-404. Johannes Wollebius considered that the form of justification "is expressed in two acts: the remission of sins and the imputation of righteousness, or the declaration that sin is not to be held against us, and the declaration that perfect righteousness is to be credited to us." J. Wollebius, G. Voetius, and F. Turretin, *Reformed Dogmatics*, ed. and trans. by J.W. Beardslee (Grand Rapids: Baker, 1977), 167.

[112] Bellarmine, *De Controversiis*, 15.2.2.3, vol. 4, 804.

Section 3

SANCTIFICATION AND JUSTIFICATION

The third of four dialogues on justification took place at the University of Mary, Bismarck, North Dakota, October 13 – 15, 2016. Catholics and Evangelicals examined the understanding of the relationship between justification and sanctification. All positions within the Evangelical tradition affirm a distinction between the two, with justification being permanent and unchanging as it largely resides in Jesus Christ and sanctification representing the interior growth that is a response to justification. For Catholics, the two are an identity, both of which grow in the redeemed. Justification is the interior state of sanctity as it justifies us before God. This interior state of sanctity itself grows in holiness through God's gifts and human merit.

Common Statement

Sanctification and Justification

1. Catholics and Evangelicals affirm that sanctification is essential to the Christian life. Sanctification is begun in us by the grace of God and is meant to grow in us over time.

2. Evangelicals and Catholics affirm that justification and sanctification occur simultaneously in the believer through living faith. God justifies no one whom he does not also sanctify. However...

    i. Catholics see justification and sanctification as two aspects of one work of God's grace. Both begin at the same time and continue to grow together under the action of God's grace.

    ii. Some Evangelicals believe that justification and sanctification must be distinguished as two essentially different works, yet never separated from each other. Justification consists of the imputation of Christ's alien righteousness while sanctification consists in God's progressive transformation of the believer into the image of Christ. Justification occurs once and for all and admits of neither increase nor diminution. Sanctification continues throughout the life of the believer.

iii. Some Evangelicals affirm justification and sanctification occur and grow simultaneously. However, justification is a distinguishable work of grace that refers to a right relationship with God that is not merely a legal declaration (imputation). Sanctification refers to the living dynamic reality of sharing in the divine life.

3. Catholics and Evangelicals affirm that the increase of sanctification, which is the will of God for us, comes about by our cooperation with the grace of God. However...

   i. Some Evangelicals believe that God ensures that everyone whom he justifies will cooperate with his sanctifying grace and certainly be saved.

   ii. Other Evangelicals believe that whereas sanctifying grace is provided for the church in general, individual believers may stop cooperating with it, fall away from Christ, and lose their salvation.

4. Evangelicals and Catholics affirm that sanctification is the work of God in us, accomplished by the Holy Spirit, by which we grow in the image and likeness of Christ. Sanctification necessarily includes communion with God and participation in his divine life.

5. Catholics and Evangelicals affirm that among the means of sanctification are Scripture, prayer, sacraments or ordinances, Christian community, and sacred music.

6. Evangelicals and Catholics affirm that good works—works of charity and mercy—flow from and contribute to our sanctification. However...

   i. Catholics affirm that after initial justification, the justified individual is able to cooperate with the grace of God in such a way that she or he is able to "merit" an increase in grace, eternal life, and an increase in glory.

   ii. Evangelicals deny any such cooperation with divine grace by which justified people may merit eternal life, either for themselves or for others.

7. **Catholics and Evangelicals affirm that evil works are injurious to sanctification. However...**

    i. Catholics and some Evangelicals affirm that both justification and sanctification are lost through sin that leads to death (which Catholics call "mortal sin").

    ii. Some Evangelicals affirm that justification and sanctification can be lost. Sanctification can be lost through willful disobedience to God. However, the loss of justification also requires the loss of believing faith.

    iii. Some Evangelicals believe that God allows no one whom he justifies to sin so gravely as to interrupt the process of sanctification and forfeit salvation entirely.

8. **Evangelicals and Catholics affirm that sanctification results in efforts to glorify God and spread the Gospel.**

Background Paper

An Evangelical Reformed Perspective on the Relation between Justification and Sanctification

Dr. Dennis W. Jowers

EVANGELICAL MONERGISTS BELIEVE the doctrine of justification taught in the Westminster Confession and kindred documents[1] to be true because they hold the Bible to be God's inerrant Word—and because the Bible at least implicitly teaches this doctrine. One can appreciate the cogency and attractiveness of Evangelical monergist views on justification, therefore, only insofar as one grasps how monergist Evangelicals derive their doctrine of justification from Scripture.

ΔΙΚΑΙΟΩ IN PASSAGES RELATED TO THE DOCTRINE OF JUSTIFICATION

A logical way to clarify this is to survey the usage of the term δικαιόω, "justify," in New Testament passages that relate directly to disputes about justification. The first such passage in which δικαιόω appears is Acts 13:38-9: "Let it be known to you, then, men, brethren, that through this man forgiveness of sins is proclaimed to you. From all those from which you cannot be justified through the Law of Moses, everyone who believes in him is justified." Here, Paul identifies the great boon that human beings receive from Jesus as forgiveness of sins and announces that all who believe in Jesus are justified from the offenses from which they cannot be justified through the Law of Moses. In this passage, Paul seems to equate justification with the forgiveness of sins.

The term δικαιόω surfaces next in Romans 2:13: "For not the hearers of the law are righteous before God, but the doers of the law shall be justified." One can grasp this passage's significance most easily if one views it in the context of Romans 2:6-13:

> Who will recompense to each according to his works: to those who by perseverance in doing good seek glory and honor and incorruption, life eternal, but to those who out of selfish ambition disobey the truth, but obey unrighteousness, wrath and fury, tribulation and distress upon the soul of every man who practices wickedness, on the Jew first and on the Greek; but glory and honor and peace to everyone who works the good, to the Jew first and to the Greek. For there is no respect of persons with God. For as many as have sinned apart from the law will perish apart from the law, and as many as have sinned in the law will be judged by the law. For not the hearers of the law are righteous before God, but the doers of the law will be justified.

In these words, Paul teaches that God will justify—i.e., acquit—those who obey the law. Christ teaches materially the same doctrine in Luke 10:25-28:

> And, behold, a certain lawyer arose and tested him, saying, "By doing what shall I inherit eternal life?" He said to him, "What is written in the law? How do you read it?" He said in response, "Love the Lord your God with all of your heart and all of your soul and all of your strength, and all of your mind, and your neighbor as yourself." He said to him, "You have replied well; do this, and you will live."

Moses teaches the same in Leviticus 18:5b, when, having just referred to God's statutes and judgments, he writes, "A man who does them will live by them"; many more biblical texts teach precisely the same doctrine. One who accepts Scripture's authority, therefore, cannot reasonably deny that God will judge every human being on the basis of his works.

The same Scripture, however, teaches no less clearly that, in humanity's present ruined state, no mere human being can attain justification by works performed in obedience to the law. Paul writes in Galatians 3:10, "As many as are under the works of the law are under a curse, for it is written, 'Cursed is every one who does not continue in all of the things written in the book of the law to do them.'" Likewise, one reads in Psalm 130:3: "If you regard [literally 'keep,' תִּשְׁמָר] iniquities, O Lord my God, who will stand?" "No one living," David confesses in Psalm 143:2, "is righteous before you." Both testaments of Scripture thus confirm that no one whom God favors, prescinding from God Incarnate, satisfies God's standard of righteousness.

David, after recounting his confession of sin and God's forgiveness of it in Psalm 32:5, writes, "For this [forgiveness] will every godly man pray to you in a time of finding."[2] Every godly man, David implies, everyone whom God favors, enjoys this favor because God forgives him. Any talk of justification on the basis of works *simpliciter* such as one finds in Romans 2:13, therefore, must refer to a hypothetical and, for human beings other than Christ, now foreclosed possibility.[3] Everyone, Christ alone excepted, needs forgiveness.

Such forgiveness would be unnecessary, however, if God failed to hold human beings accountable for their transgressions. Talk of divine forgiveness throughout Scripture presupposes the truth that "we shall all stand before the judgment seat of God."[4] In Romans 2:6-13, consequently, Paul scarcely denies that God will save his people on some basis other than their works. For it is precisely the looming threat of judgment that renders salvation on some other basis urgently necessary.

Paul next employs the term δικαιόω in a context directly related to controversies over justification in Romans 3:20. Here, after a litany of scriptural quotations calculated to impress upon the reader the depth of the human race's depravity, one reads: "We know that as many things as the law says, it speaks to those in the law, that every mouth might be stopped and the whole world become guilty before God. Therefore, by the works of the law no flesh will be justified before him, for through the law is the knowledge of sin."[5] Here, "justified" seems almost certainly to mean either "shown to be righteous" or, if Paul has the final judgment in view, "acquitted." The works by which no one will be justified, moreover, include all works whatsoever.[6]

Having established then that works will justify no one, Paul writes:

> But now without the law the righteousness of God has been manifested, being witnessed by the law and the prophets, the righteousness of God that is through faith in Jesus Christ for all who believe. For there is no distinction, for all have sinned and fallen short of the glory of God, being justified freely by his grace through the redemption that is in Christ Jesus.[7]

Inasmuch as Paul characterizes the righteousness of God as "through faith in Jesus Christ," the phrase "righteousness of God," in this context at least, must refer to a righteous status God bestows on human beings. For if by "the righteousness of God," Paul meant God's intrinsic righteousness, he would imply that this intrinsic righteousness in some way depended on human beings' faith in Christ. Unless one wishes to ascribe the notion that God justifies unbelievers to the apostle Paul, likewise, one must regard the "all" who, having sinned and fallen short of God's glory, have been justified freely by his grace, as identical with the "all who believe."

Paul proceeds to characterize "all who believe" as δικαιούμενοι δωρεάν: justified freely, i.e., gratuitously, without a meritorious cause on the side of the recipient. As David's enemies hated him δωρεάν,[8] and Jesus' opponents hated him δωρεάν,[9] God justifies us δωρεάν: i.e., without any cause on the side of the recipient that merits the gift he receives. Other senses of δωρεάν like "in vain" or "without cost to the provider" make little if any sense in this context.

Paul's characterization of the justification to which he refers in verse 24 as δωρεάν implies that in this instance δικαιόω can refer neither to a manifestation of the righteousness a believer already possesses nor a declaration that the believer is already righteous. If the believer was already righteous, this would constitute a basis in him for God's decision to justify him, which is precisely what the adverb δωρεάν excludes in verse 24. If the justification to which Paul refers in verse 24 is strictly gratuitous, it can consist only in 1) God's liberation of the believer from sin; 2) his transformation of the believer into one who is actually righteous; or, 3) his declaration that the believer is righteous on some basis other than actual righteousness that inheres within him. One may collapse the first two options into one inasmuch as one can free a human being of sin only by rendering him inherently righteous, and one can render him inherently righteous only by freeing him from sin.

The justification of which Paul writes in Romans 3:24, then, consists either in an infusion of righteousness or a declaration, on some basis other than a believer's intrinsic righteousness, that the believer is righteous. After declaring Christ a propitiatory sacrifice, which God sets forth to display his righteousness on account of his passing over, i.e., his failure to exact condign punishment for sins previously committed in verse 25, Paul employs the verb δικαιόω again in verse 26, in which he asserts that God's display of righteousness by means of his Son's propitiatory sacrifice occurred "so that he might be just and the justifier of him who is of faith in Jesus." By his remarks in verses 25-26, Paul seems to mean that God set forth his son as a propitiatory sacrifice to satisfy his retributive justice so that, without failing to exact the retribution his justice requires and his people's sins deserve, he might nonetheless receive his people into eternal, blissful communion with him.

These considerations, although sublime, do not suffice to resolve the question of whether God's justification of sinners consists in a transformation of previously unrighteous persons so that they become righteous or a declaration that justified persons are righteous in spite of their remaining corruption. A resolution of this dilemma begins to emerge in verse 28, in which Paul writes: "[W]e deem a man to be justified by faith without the works of the law." If in justification God bestows inherent righteousness on human beings in the process of time, those on whom God bestows this righteousness will presumably be capable of augmenting that righteousness through good works.

Certain passages of Scripture plainly presuppose that Christians can augment their inherent righteousness through their own works. The apostle Peter, for example, commands his addressees in 2 Peter 1:5-7 to "employ all diligence to add to your faith virtue and to virtue knowledge and to knowledge temperance and to temperance perseverance and to perseverance godliness." This text and others like it would make little sense if Christians were not both capable of augmenting and obliged to augment their inherent righteousness by performing good works. If justification consists in God's bestowal of inherent righteousness in the process of time, the righteousness that constitutes the sinner's justification will consist not merely in another's righteousness bestowed on account of another's obedience, but in one's own righteousness obtained, to a considerable extent, through one's own obedience.

Scripture plainly testifies in at least two instances that the righteousness on the basis of which God accepts us into his favor does not consist in our own righteousness. Paul writes, for instance, in Philippians 3:8-9:

> I consider all things to be loss because of the surpassing excellence of the knowledge of Christ Jesus my Lord, for whose sake I have suffered the loss of all things and consider them dung that I may gain Christ and be found in him, not having my own righteousness, which is of the law, but that which is through faith in Christ, the righteousness from God that is by faith.

One may observe with some justice, admittedly, that Paul renounces here only the spurious righteousness that he attained as a Pharisee. Nevertheless, Paul discusses in the same context the inherent righteousness he has gained since regeneration:

> Not that I have already obtained or already been perfected, but I pursue that I may seize that for which I also have been seized by Christ Jesus. Brethren, I do not consider myself to have seized it, but this one thing I do: forgetting the things that are behind, but stretching forth toward what is before me, I pursue the mark for the prize of the upward calling of God in Christ Jesus.[10]

Quite soon after Paul expresses his desire to be found in a righteousness that is not his own, he expresses his determination to acquire a righteousness of his own, which he seems to consider requisite to the achievement of ultimate beatitude. Paul's beliefs on this score in no way conflict with the convictions of conventional Evangelical monergists about justification by faith alone or the utter gratuity of salvation, for Evangelical monergists typically hold that inherent righteousness, although not an antecedent condition of justification, is a consequent condition. Inherent righteousness, however, neither is nor can be a prerequisite of justification—that is to say, inherent righteousness is justification's inevitable concomitant so that one may and ought to pursue "the holiness, without which no one will see the Lord."[11]

One might regard the juxtaposition of Philippians 3:8, 9 with verses 10-14 as evidence that Paul sees no inconsistency in characterizing the righteousness on which he relies for his salvation as another's and stating that he actively seeks to augment precisely the same righteousness by his own efforts. This hardly seems plausible. Paul composed the Epistle to the Philippians many years after God regenerated him and he began his extraordinary labors for Christ.[12] While Paul might well have characterized the inherent righteousness he received in regeneration as another's shortly after he received it, he could not credibly have characterized his inherent righteousness, which he had molded over decades of indefatigable obedience, as another's when he authored his Epistle to the Philippians.

It seems more likely that Paul distinguishes radically between the righteousness God imputes to him, which constitutes the sole ground of his hope for salvation, and the righteousness he himself builds through the Spirit's cooperation with his own efforts. All of this implies that when Paul writes in Romans 3:28, "[W]e deem a man to be justified by faith without the works of the law," he probably means not only that human beings' good works in no way contribute to their initial justification, but that human beings' good works never contribute to their justification at all. For the righteousness one receives in justification is not one's own, but another's: a righteousness already complete and in no way subject to increase or diminution.

Paul's remarks in Romans 9:30-10:4 confirm this conclusion's accuracy:

> What then shall we say? That the Gentiles who pursued not righteousness have obtained righteousness, the righteousness that is by faith, but Israel who pursued the law of righteousness has not arrived at the law. Why? Because they sought it not of faith, but as if it were of works; they stumbled at the stone of stumbling as it is written, "Behold, I lay in Zion a stone of stumbling and a rock of offense, and he who believes in him will not be put to shame." Brethren, my heart's desire and petition to God for them is for salvation. For I bear them witness that they have a zeal for God, but not according to knowledge. For, being ignorant of the righteousness of God and seeking to set up their own righteousness, they have not been subject to the righteousness of God. For Christ is the end of the law for righteousness to everyone who believes.

Unbelieving Jews fall short of God's righteousness, the righteousness that is of faith, precisely because they seek their own. Whatever Paul means by the phrase "the righteousness of God," he cannot mean a righteousness that fallen human beings can in any straightforward sense call their own, and he cannot mean a righteousness that one can obtain or increase by obeying the law. When Paul writes, "we deem a man to be justified by faith without the works of the law,"[13] accordingly, he identifies the righteousness one receives in justification as another's righteousness, which one cannot augment by one's own deeds.

Paul's next use of δικαιόω that bears directly on the questions under consideration here occurs in Romans 4:5. In Romans 4:3-5 Paul writes: "For what says the Scripture? 'Abraham believed God and it was counted to him for righteousness.' To him who works the reward is counted not according to grace, but according to debt, but to him who works not, but believes in him who justifies the ungodly, his faith is counted for righteousness." The term "counted" here, ἐλογίσθη, might also be translated as "accounted," "credited," or "imputed." Each of these terms denotes a thought that one might express through a declaration such as "this man is righteous." It seems difficult, however, to conceive of why anyone who desired to express the thought, "God infused righteousness into Abraham," would attempt so to do by saying, "God counted Abraham righteous." One might recoil, admittedly, at the thought that an omniscient God who cannot lie would declare anyone righteous who is not intrinsically righteous. One might recoil for much the same reason, however, at the notion that the unfailingly just God would fail to exact a condign punishment of each human being for his sins. As Christ's obedience and suffering render the latter failure conceivable, however, the same obedience and suffering render a divine declaration that unrighteous persons are righteous conceivable on one condition: that the declaration constitutes not a statement of fact, but a judicial verdict warranted by Christ's obedience and suffering.

It appears, then, that justification, in the primary sense in which Paul employs the term, consists in a divine imputation of righteousness to sinners, warranted by Christ's saving life, death, and resurrection on their behalf, which entails the cancelling of the punishments they deserve and their provision with eternal life. Paul's subsequent uses of the term δικαιόω consistently confirm this verdict.

In Romans 8:33, for instance, Paul plainly uses δικαιόω in the sense of "acquit." Here, alluding to Isaiah 50:8-9, Paul writes, "Who will bring a charge against the elect of God? It is God who justifies." Reforming a criminal does not suffice to discharge him from liability to punishment for his crimes. Acquitting a criminal does. One who takes δικαιόω in Romans 8:33 to mean "acquit," therefore, will find Paul's meaning easily comprehensible. One who takes δικαιόω here to mean "make righteous" will struggle to extract a plausible meaning from Romans 8:33.

Paul employs the term δικαιόω again in his rebuke of Peter in Galatians 2:14-21:

> If you, although you are a Jew, live as a Gentile and not as a Jew, why do you compel the Gentiles to Judaize? We, who are by nature Jews and not sinners of the Gentiles, because we know that a man is not justified by works of the law, but through faith in Jesus Christ, even we have believed in Christ that we may be justified by faith in Christ and not by the works of the law, because by the works of the law, no flesh will be justified. But if, while we seek to be justified in Christ, we ourselves are also found to be sinners, is Christ, therefore, a minister of sin? Let it not be. For if I build again these things that I destroyed, I make myself a transgressor. For I through the law died to the law that I might live to God. I have been crucified together with Christ. I no longer live, but Christ lives in me; that which I now live in the flesh, I live by faith in the Son of God who loved me and gave himself up for me. I do not nullify the grace of God; for if righteousness is through the law, then Christ died in vain.

A few observations should suffice to clarify the sense in which Paul here employs the term δικαιόω. First, by δικαιόω in this context, Paul evidently does not mean "sustain in righteousness," "manifest righteousness," "dispense justice," "secure justice for," or "deserve." For Paul's remark, "I live by faith in the Son of God," indicates that the justification by faith without the works of the law of which he speaks constitutes a prerequisite of spiritual life. Remarks elsewhere in the Pauline corpus, moreover, indicate that Paul regards all those who lack saving faith as profoundly unrighteous:[14] enemies of God, who cannot please him.[15]

The justification of which Paul speaks in Galatians 2:14-21, therefore, must be a justification of persons bereft of righteousness,[16] who need both acquittal before God's tribunal and transformation into actually righteous persons. When Paul speaks of God's justifying persons in Galatians 2, consequently, he may mean 1) God's acquittal of human beings; 2) God's infusion of righteousness into human beings, whereby he makes them actually righteous; or, 3) some combination of the two.

Second, Paul's opponents in Galatians appear to be Judaizing Christians.[17] The apostle does not argue against persons who deny the indispensability of faith in Jesus for salvation and advocate salvation on the basis of works instead. If Paul's opponents are Judaizing Christians, he and his opponents agree that everyone must believe in Jesus to be saved. The principal error Paul combats in Galatians, therefore, is not the idea that human beings can achieve salvation simply by performing righteous works. The principal error, rather, consists in the belief that authentic Christian faith is insufficient to secure salvation: the notion that, in order to attain salvation, human beings must supplement the righteousness that comes through faith with a righteousness that comes through works performed in obedience to the law.

Third, various remarks in Paul's letters suggest that he himself embraces the teaching he criticizes in Galatians 2:14-5:12 and 6:12-15: the teaching that one must complement faith in Christ with good works to attain salvation. In Galatians 6:8, for instance, Paul writes: "He who sows to his flesh will of the flesh reap corruption, but he who sows to the Spirit will of the Spirit reap life eternal." Paul writes in Romans 8:13: "If you live according to the flesh, you will die; but if through the Spirit you put to death the deeds of the body, you will live." Paul commands the Philippians, "With fear and trembling work out your salvation,"[18] and he implies that only doers of good works will attain final salvation when he asserts that the unrighteous will not inherit God's kingdom.[19]

Fourth, only two paths appear to be open to one who seeks a plausible means of resolving the apparent contradiction between Paul's acceptance of the necessity of a kind of works-righteousness for salvation and his insistence on the sufficiency of faith for justification. One could hold that when Paul says things like "a man is not justified by the works of the law, but by faith in Jesus Christ"[20] and "by the works of the law no flesh will be justified,"[21] he means only to exclude works from playing a role in initial justification. Alternatively, one could distinguish between the imputed righteousness one receives in justification, which suffices by itself to secure everlasting life, and the inherent righteousness, which one may augment by one's works and which invariably accompanies the imputed righteousness received in justification but plays no role in securing the sinner's right to eternal life.

Two reasons for drawing the latter distinction have already emerged in our previous discussions. First, Paul insists that the only righteousness whereby one may secure acceptance with God is a righteousness that is not one's own.[22] Second, Paul identifies this righteousness as imputed when he identifies justification with God's act recorded in Genesis 15:6:[23] "Abraham believed God, and it was counted to him for righteousness."

From Paul's remarks in Galatians one may derive an additional, quite powerful reason to distinguish sharply between inherent righteousness and the righteousness that secures the Christian's acceptance by a holy God. Paul conceives of seeking God's favor through faith and seeking his favor through works as two distinct and radically opposed paths to salvation. As Paul explains in Galatians 3:7-13:

> Know then that those who are of faith, these are the sons of Abraham. Scripture, foreseeing that God would justify the nations by faith, promised Abraham beforehand, "In you all nations will be blessed." Therefore, those who are of faith are blessed with faithful Abraham. For as many as are of the works of the law are under a curse. For it is written, "Cursed is everyone who does not stand fast by all the things written in the book of the law to do them." That by the law no one will be justified before God is manifest, because "the righteous will live by faith." The law is not of faith, but "he who does these things will live by them." Christ has redeemed us from the curse of the law by becoming a curse for us, as it is written, "Cursed is everyone who is hanged on a tree."

In Paul's view, one must choose between seeking God's favor by faith and seeking his favor by works. One is either "of the law" and therefore doomed or "of faith" and therefore "blessed with faithful Abraham." Paul does not envision a third way of obtaining God's favor by some combination of the two. In fact, he denies that such a combination is possible. "If the inheritance is of the law," he writes in Galatians 3:18, "it is no longer of promise; but God gave it to Abraham by promise." One can receive the blessing of Abraham as a divinely promised benefit, that is to say, or as compensation for obedience to the law. One cannot have both simultaneously.

Elsewhere Paul states more fully his belief that one cannot receive the inheritance of Abraham's offspring through both faith and works. Paul writes:

> For not by law was the promise to Abraham or to his seed that he would be the heir of the world, but through the righteousness of faith. For if those who are of the law are heirs, faith is made void, and the promise is cancelled. For the law works wrath; but where there is no law, neither is there transgression. Therefore, it is by faith that it might be by grace, that the promise might be sure to all the seed, not to that of the law only, but also to that of the faith of Abraham, who is the father of us all.[24]

If those who seek justification by obedience to the law are heirs, Paul asserts, "faith is made void, and the promise is cancelled." One cannot plausibly reconcile such condemnation of any reliance on one's works for salvation with the notion that Paul acknowledges the possibility of justification by works, provided only that works do not contribute to initial justification. If works contributed anything to justification, in Paul's view, justification would no longer constitute a gift of divine grace. "If it is of grace, it is no longer of works; otherwise, grace would no longer be grace."[25]

Paul explicitly states, in fact, that to seek divine acceptance on the basis of one's works is to forfeit whatever acceptance one might have enjoyed by grace through faith. Hence, Paul warns the Galatians: "Behold, I Paul say to you that if you are circumcised, Christ will profit you nothing. For I bear witness again to every circumcised man that he is a debtor to do the whole law. You have been separated from Christ, you who are justified by the law, you have fallen from grace."[26] Salvation, as Paul understands it, cannot constitute both a gift of grace and compensation for human merits.

James might appear to contradict this verdict:

> What does it profit, my brothers, if someone says he has faith, but does not have works? Is faith able to save him? If a brother or sister

is naked and lacks daily food, and one of you says to him, "Go in peace; be warmed and filled," but you give him not the things necessary to the body, what profit is it? So also faith, if it has not works, is dead, being alone. But someone will say, "You have faith, and I have works; show me your faith without works, and I will show you my faith by my works. Do you believe there is one God? You do well; the demons also believe and shudder. Do you want to know, vain man, that faith without works is useless? Was not Abraham our father justified when he offered up Isaac his son on the altar? You see that faith cooperated with his works, and by works faith was perfected, and the Scripture was fulfilled, which says, "Abraham believed God, and it was imputed to him for righteousness," and he was called the friend of God. You see that by works a man is justified and not by faith only. Likewise, was not also Rahab the prostitute justified by works when she received the messengers and sent them out another way? For as the body without the spirit is dead, so faith without works is dead.[27]

In these verses, James remonstrates against an understanding of salvation by faith against which Paul also protests, for instance, when he enumerates the works of the flesh in Galatians 5:19-23 and declares, "those who practice such things will not inherit the kingdom of God."[28] The faith James declares insufficient for salvation is the kind of faith demons might have,[29] not the thoroughgoing renunciation of self-reliance and resting upon Christ alone for salvation that Paul identifies as the sole means whereby sinners may attain salvation. This latter, Pauline species of faith, which issues necessarily in gratitude and obedience, thus differs *toto coelo* from the bare, cognitive assent of which James speaks.

This consideration alone would suffice to resolve any seeming conflict between James and Paul if Paul's understanding of the faith by means of which God justifies believers were sufficiently broad to encompass good works. One might think that this must be the case, because the act of faith itself is a good work. Scripture identifies it as such. One reads in John 6:28-29 of the crowds asking Jesus: "What must we do to work the works of God?" And, receiving the answer from Jesus' lips: "This is the work of God, that you believe in him whom he has sent."

Manifestly, Paul does not consider faith *qua* instrument of justification a work. Otherwise, he would not make statements like "We deem a man to be justified by faith without the works of the law,"[30] "A man is not justified by the works of the law, but by faith in Jesus Christ,"[31] and "By grace you are saved by faith...not of works so that no one may boast."[32] One may resolve the seeming conflict between Scripture's testimonies that the act of faith constitutes a work and that human beings are justified by faith rather than works most readily, it seems, by distinguishing between faith as the disposition to believe, on the one hand, and faith as the act of believing, on the other. Many Evangelical monergists, accordingly, identify the instrumental cause of justification not as faith *qua* act, but as faith *qua* disposition.[33]

Armed with this distinction, one may reconcile Paul's teaching on justification with that of James by distinguishing what Paul designates by the word δικαιόω from that which James designates by the same term. Paul uses δικαιόω primarily (Romans 2:13 is an exception) to refer to God's declaration that believers are judicially righteous and therefore not only inculpable but entitled to reward. Believers receive the justification of which Paul writes through faith alone—not on the basis of anything they have done, but solely on the basis of Christ's sacrificial obedience on their behalf.

The justification of which James writes, by contrast,[34] occurs when God declares Abraham, Rahab, and other saints intrinsically righteous by working in them righteous deeds, which outwardly manifest their divinely bestowed intrinsic righteousness. The two species of justification concern two distinct varieties of righteousness: the righteousness imputed to the saints in what monergist Evangelicals ordinarily refer to as justification (Paul) and the righteousness imparted to Christians in what Evangelical monergists typically refer to as sanctification (James).

The Righteousness Imputed in Justification Is That of Christ

The justification of which Paul speaks, as noted above, consists in the imputation of another's righteousness. It remains now to identify this other as the Lord Jesus Christ. As Paul explains in 2 Corinthians 5:21, "[H]e [God] made him who knew no sin to be sin for us that we might become the righteousness of God in him." Manifestly, Christ never became substantially sin.[35] Christians, likewise, never become the divine attribute of righteousness. In 2 Corinthians 5:21, therefore, the words "make" and "become" cannot refer to any substantial transformation.

Three considerations suggest that 2 Corinthians 5:21 may refer to a double imputation of Christ's righteousness to Christians, who without it possess no record of obedience sufficient to avoid divine condemnation, and to Christians' sins to Christ, who alone can offer a sacrifice sufficiently valuable to pay the debt of punishment his people owe God for their sins.

First, Scripture teaches that Christ bore his people's sins.[36] That God, by an imputation of those sins to Christ, might have rendered him, rather than his people, liable to punishment for them thus seems highly plausible. Second, Rom 5:12-21 seems to teach that God imputes Adam's first sin to all whom he represents before God—that is, all humanity except Christ—and that God likewise imputes Christ's obedience to his people, whom he represents.[37]

Third, and most importantly, the righteousness that God imputed to Abraham and that he imputes to all saints, the basis on which he accepts them as righteous, must be real and perfect. Only Christ's righteousness fulfills these conditions. The righteousness God imputes to his children when he grants them faith, therefore, can only be that of Christ.

Conclusion

While both justification and sanctification originate in God and constitute benefits Christ purchased for the elect by his obedience and suffering, then, the words "justification" and "sanctification," as monergist Evangelicals employ them, refer to quite distinct realities. The radical distinction monergist Evangelicals draw between justification and sanctification seems to be incompatible with the Catholic Church's official teaching on these subjects.

Notes

[1] For statements of the doctrine of justification in Reformed confessional documents, see, e.g., chapter 11 of the *Westminster Confession of Faith*, article 22 of the *Belgic Confession*, chapter 15 of the *Second Helvetic Confession*, and articles 18 and 20 of the *Gallican Confession*.

[2] Ps. 32:6a.

[3] Others who consider the justification by works of which Paul speaks in Rom. 2 as a hypothetical possibility that is unavailable to actual, fallen human beings include

Otfried Hofius, "Rechfertigung des Gottlosen als Thema biblischer Theologie" in idem, *Paulusstudien*, WUNT 51, 143 (Tübingen: Mohr Siebeck, 1989-2002) 1:121-47 at 127; Ulrich Wilckens, *Der Brief an die Römer*, 3 vols., EKT VI (Einsiedeln and Neukirchen-Vluyn: Benziger and Neukirchener, 1978-83) 1:132-3; and Doug Moo, *The Epistle to the Romans*, NICNT (Grand Rapids: W.B. Eerdmans, 1996), 155.

4   Rom. 14:10.

5   Rom. 3:19-20.

6   Some contend, admittedly: 1) that Paul intends to declare only obedience to ritual laws, adherence to which distinguishes Jews from Gentiles, incapable of justifying human beings (see, for example, Peter Abelard, *Commentarius in Epistolam ad Romanos* 3:20); or, 2) that, though Paul refers to the whole law, he is primarily concerned with distinctively Jewish observances (see N.T. Wright, *Paul and His Recent Interpreters* [Minneapolis: Fortress, 2015], 92-94). Since the offenses Paul catalogs in verses 10-18 all constitute violations of the moral rather than the ceremonial law, neither of these views can be correct.

7   Rom. 3:21-24.

8   *LXX* Ps 68:5.

9   John 15:25.

10 Phil. 3:12-14

11 Heb. 12:14. Daniel Chamier introduced the terms "antecedent condition" and "consequent condition" from contemporary commercial practice into Reformed theology in his *Panstratiae catholicae*, 3 vols. (Geneva: Typis Roverianis, 1626), vol. 3, § 3.15.26-9, 518a.

12 Rom. 3:28. Scholarly opinion is divided as to whether Paul composed Philippians in Rome, Ceasarea, or Ephesus; cf. the discussions of Philippians' provenance in Christoph Schluep-Meier, *Philipperbrief/Philemonbrief* (Neukirchener-Vluyn: Neukirchener, 2014), 14-16 and Ben Witherington, *Paul's Letter to the Philippians: A Socio-Rhetorical Commentary* (Grand Rapids: W.B. Eerdmans, 2011), 9-11. Virtually all agree that Paul composed Philippians, at the earliest, in the final stage of his third missionary journey.

13 Rom. 3:28.

14 Rom. 3:9-20; Eph. 2:1-3.

15 Rom. 8:7-8.

16 Rom. 4:5.

17 For a thorough defense of the view that Paul's Galatian opponents were Judaizing Christians, i.e., the view of almost all commentators on Galatians before the second half of the 20th century, see Walt Russell, "Who Were Paul's Opponents in Galatia?" *Bibliotheca Sacra* 147 (1990), 329-50.

18 Phil. 2:12.

19 1 Cor. 6:9-10; Gal. 5:19-21; Eph. 5:5.

20 Gal. 2:16a.

21 Gal. 2:16c.

22 Rom. 10:3-4.

23 cf. Rom. 4:3, Rom. 4:9; Gal. 3:6.

24 Rom. 4:13-16.

25 Rom. 11:6.

26 Gal. 5:2-4.
27 James 2:14-26.
28 Gal. 5:23.
29 James 2:19.
30 Rom. 3:28.
31 Gal. 2:16.
32 Eph. 3:8-9.
33 Reformed theologians refer to this infused disposition as a disposition (e.g., Louis le Blanc de Beaulieu, *Theses theologicae*, 3rd ed. [London: Moses Pitt, 1683], thesis 1, c. 32, 6), a virtue (e.g., Franciscus Gomarus, "Illustrium ac selectorum ex Euangelio Matthaei locorum explicatio" at Matt 23:37 in *Opera theologica omnia: pars prima* [Amsterdam: Ex officina Joannis Jansonii, 1644, 114]), a root (Bernhard de Moor, *Commentarius perpetuus in Johannis Marckii Compendium theologiae Christianae didactico-polemicae: pars quarta*, c. 22.12 [Leiden: Johannes Hasebroer, 1756], 324), a seed (Gerhard Johann Vossius, *Disputatio de sacramentorum*, thesis 1, c. 47 in idem, *Opera omnia* [Amsterdam: P. & J. Blaev, 1701] 6:252), and/or a *habitus* (Johann Heinrich Heidegger, *Medulla theologiae Christianae* [Zurich: Ex typis Henrici Bodmeri] lib. 2, loc. 21, c. 35, 153). If justifying faith consists in the disposition for faith, incidentally, God may justify by faith infants or mentally disabled persons simply by infusing into them the disposition for faith, which fails to blossom into the act of faith only because they lack the requisite cognitive apparatus.
34 James 2:21-25.
35 Heb. 4:15; 1 Pet. 2:22; 1 John 3:5.
36 Isa. 53:5-12; 1 Cor. 15:3; Gal. 1:4.
37 See the defense of this claim in the monergist paper on original sin.

Background Paper

Life in the New Creation: Justification and Sanctification Revisited

Dr. Jackie David Johns & Dr. Cheryl Bridges Johns

Salvation as Deliverance and Transformation into Divine Life

THE WESLEYAN-PENTECOSTAL UNDERSTANDING of the relationship between justification and sanctification flows out of a synergist theological model of salvation as both deliverance from sin and participation in the Divine life. Evangelical synergists understand salvation as the healing and restoration of creation in and through persons regenerated and empowered by God. In this model, salvation is thus deeply personal and cosmic in orientation.

Too often, Evangelical soteriological formulations have been developed within a worldview based upon a stark separation between spiritual and material realities. Wesleyan theologian Howard Synder describes this worldview as one that "inverts the direction of salvation, enabling people to go to heaven rather than bringing heaven to earth."[1] To put this vision in simple lay terms, salvation is too often viewed as granting those who are saved a "ticket to heaven." Added to this worldview is an overemphasis on individual human reason as a means of knowing God and the world. In lay terms, the person who is saved "accepts Jesus as personal savior" and that becomes the completion of salvation. Such a view is a spiritualizing of salvation, an individualizing of the cosmic work of the salvation offered by God.

Collapsing the *oikonomia* into individualistic, spiritual salvation does not do justice to the plan of God to reconcile all things in Jesus Christ. All creation is groaning for this reconciliation, when it will be liberated from its bondage to decay and brought into the freedom and glory of the children of God.[2] Christ's birth, life, death, resurrection, ongoing ministry by the Holy Spirit, and return is a narrative of salvation history with both personal and cosmic implications. This narrative demands a holistic soteriology in which Christ's atonement is a "cosmic historical act through which all creation is redeemed—potentially and partially now, and fully when the kingdom comes in fullness."[3]

Pentecostal Worldview and Salvation

This essay focuses on a particular Pentecostal paradigm of understanding the Evangelical synergist approach to the doctrine and work of salvation. While Pentecostals have inherited the inherent dualism found in much of Evangelical soteriology, their understanding of salvation operates out of a worldview containing robust synergy between the spiritual and material dimensions. Jackie Johns lists several characteristics of a Pentecostal worldview. First, it is God-centered. "All things relate to God and God relates to all things."[4] In this fusion God is not collapsed into creation. Instead, God is seen at work in, with, through, above, and beyond all events. This fusion holds all things and particularly what occurs within salvation in a dialectic tension between the "already" and the "not yet."

Second, Pentecostals are inclined to think systemically. The world is held together in a unified field. The Holy Spirit serves as agent, bringing all things together. Even time is viewed as a whole. Eschatologically, the past is made real in the present, and the future bends backward into the present.

Third, a Pentecostal worldview is trans-rational. Truth is not limited to reason. Knowledge includes a full spectrum of cognition, affection, and behavior, each of which is fused into the other two. The epistemology flowing out of this construct is eschatological as well as comprehensive. It is one "in which all of creation which flows out of God is on the threshold of returning unto God."[5]

Given the above worldview, "a Pentecostal vision of salvation understands the need for total transformation of the believer as a down payment on the total transformation of creation."[6] This emphasis is reflected in the early fivefold gospel: Jesus is Savior, Sanctifier, Spirit Baptizer, Healer, and Coming King. This pattern is a narrative-based understanding of soteriology arising out of the Divine life and thoroughly integrating what Pentecostals believe in the ministry of Jesus to all creation.[7]

Salvation as Deliverance

The above fivefold gospel, sometimes called the "full-gospel," is based upon an understanding of sin as the poisoning of creation, creating alienation between God and humanity and within the human family. Sin is the absence of *shalom*, or the peace of Christ, destroying the interconnections in the web of life. Sin is the bondage of creation to decay. It is slavery. It is death.

For creation to be healed, it must be delivered from the powers of darkness. This deliverance is found in the atoning work of Christ. For Pentecostals, the atoning work of Christ involves what early Pentecostal leader J.H. King described as "complete deliverance from death, spiritual, mental, and physical, and all decay in the world around us."[8] Pentecostal theologian Dale Coulter echoes this sentiment in his description of a Pentecostal understanding of salvation as "the ongoing deliverance from sin in all of its permutations."[9]

Further, this has led Pentecostals to an understanding of Justification based on this paradigm. Richard Shaull, after years of research in Latin American Pentecostalism, concluded that among Pentecostals in Latin America, a "post-Reformation" paradigm of salvation was emerging.[10] This paradigm differs from classical Reformation categories in two key ways. First, the human problem is not seen in light of original sin, making people guilty before God and under God's judgment. Instead, human beings are impotent, condemned to insignificance and desperate for survival. They and their world are "possessed," dominated by supernatural forces who are agents of chaos and destruction.[11] Second, in the emerging paradigm salvation is not so much "forgiveness and justification as an experience of the presence and power of the resurrected Christ and of the Holy Spirit as the source of life and hope, the power to make it through each new day, and the guarantee of victory over demonic forces." Shaull describes this paradigm of salvation as "the reconstruction of life in the face of death."[12]

Implications of the above for discussions on justification and sanctification reflect the complexity and totality of sin's impact on humanity. As Coulter aptly states, at "a minimum it would imply that *total* depravity cannot be reduced to a thorough warping of the interior life of the person by means of inherited evil desires. To ground sinful existence in an inherited sinful condition not only leads to unhealthy views of the person...but fails to deal adequately with the political, social and cosmic forms of sinful existence from which one must be delivered."[13] Pentecostals' use of images of holistic deliverance indicates an awareness of the need for God's power to confront the totality of sinful existence.

SALVATION AS PARTICIPATION IN THE DIVINE LIFE

As Pentecostalism is flourishing in places where sin has ravaged the very structures of human existence, this understanding of Salvation is bearing new fruit. In these cultures of death, millions of believers find salvation as participation in the Divine Life to be more than an abstract idea: the entrance of eternity into temporal existence is their only hope.

Salvation as participation in the Divine Life is not new to Christianity. It has been an integrating center for understanding salvation throughout the history of Christianity. Eastern Christianity understands deification, or participation in the Divine life, as the defining doctrine around which everything else revolves. In his comparison of Eastern Orthodoxy and Pentecostalism, Edmund Rybarczyk points to a common theological anthropology that allows for a synergistic transformation of persons.[14] Likewise, Stephen Land, in his text on Pentecostal spirituality, states, "God is a communion who creates us for communion and moves us toward ultimate full participation in the divine life."[15]

Coulter observes: "Pentecostalism offers a holistic soteriology in which the liberating power of divine life progressively frees the individual from internal and external hostile forces."[16] In this freedom, human beings, through greater degrees of cooperation with the Spirit, are enabled to grow ever deeper in grace, aligning their affections with the heart of God.

Spirit-Empowered *Via Salutis*

The Wesleyan-Pentecostal understanding of salvation as a cosmic and personal participation in the Divine life has broad implications for the relationship between justification and sanctification within that broader schema of salvation. Given that this understanding of salvation is less forensic and more dynamic and organic, it follows that this understanding of justification is more relational and less positional, more imparted conformity and less imputed possibility. While holding steadfastly to the position that justification and sanctification are received by grace through faith and that faith itself is a gift from God, the Wesleyan-Pentecostal theological worldview views all dimensions of salvation as sharing in the divine life and inclusive of participation through the redeemed free-will of believers.

Righteousness and Holiness

Any consideration of the relationship between justification and sanctification includes the distinctiveness between the primal concepts of righteousness and holiness. Both in Hebrew and in Greek the concept of righteousness weaves together the desires of the heart with the actions of the individual. As such, "righteousness" is an antonym for "sin." There is an underlying theme of justice within the Biblical concept of righteousness.[17] Further, all righteousness is grounded in God; God alone is righteous and personal righteousness is both required by Him and derived only from Him. Thus, righteousness is always a relational term; righteousness is before and with God, before and with His creation. In reference to the Old Testament usage, A.H. Leitch expressed it this way: "Righteousness has to do with the fulfillment of the demands of relationships, whether with men or with God."[18] To be righteous is to be in right relationships with others and with God as defined by God.

Holiness is an attribute of God and yet it is more: it represents His essential nature. Given the paradigm of participation in the Divine life, salvation holistically conceived is a participation in the Divine nature. God and God alone is holy, and only that which is in communion with Him shares in His holiness. Following the trajectory of "holy" from the Pentateuch forward into the New Testament, we see its careful expansion in application from God alone to God and the things dedicated to his service in the Tabernacle and Temple, to His Spirit, the Scriptures, those few whose lives conform to the Scriptures, and finally in Paul, the saints who comprise the church. In brief: holiness is a descriptor of the essential nature of God, and it is an aspect of His existence that He can share with His creation. In His holiness He cannot know sin, and yet humanity is marred by sin. Sin is the central enemy of the human being.

JOHN WESLEY

With these two concepts briefly sketched, a distinctive Wesleyan-Pentecostal view on the relationship between justification and sanctification can be understood more fully. The foundations of this view begin with John Wesley's critique of that relationship. Wesley (1703-1791) is the fountainhead of Evangelical synergist theology. Wesley lived his life and worked out his theology as a minister in the Church of England and was particularly devoted to the Anglican faith. As such, he was a child of and contributor to the Protestant Reformation in England. While much has been written about the influences of early Christianity and Eastern Christianity on his thought and spirituality, it must not be glossed over that he was primarily a product of the Reformation, and his experiential faith was but one lens by which he addressed the theological issues of his context. Relative to this discussion, Wesley took as his foundation for the *via salutis* (life of salvation) the forensic model of the *ordo salutis* (order of salvation). He repeatedly stressed the Protestant ideal of salvation by faith alone and also insisted on an essential distinction between justification and sanctification. One of his oft repeated phrases was that "justification is what God does for us while sanctification is what God does in us."

Yet, there is in Wesley a recurring hint that justification is more than a forensic declaration or imputation of the righteousness of Christ. At times he implies that justification encompasses actualized changes in the believer's relationship with God, i.e., an imparted righteousness. Consider his statement that justification "changes our outward relation to God, so that of enemies we become children [of God]." [19] While justification is for Wesley a forensic act, it is also an actualized act; God does not think the justified "to be what in fact they are not." Neither does He believe them to be righteous when they are unrighteous.[20]

The judgment of the all-wise God is always according to truth. Neither can it ever consist with his unerring wisdom to think that I am innocent, to judge that I am righteous or holy, because another is so. He can no more in this manner confound me with Christ than with David or Abraham.[21]

Kenneth Collins elaborates on Wesley's views, saying, "justification restores the sinner to a right relationship with God—a relationship no longer marked by alienation and excessive fear."[22] He adds that for Wesley this is a genuine healing of the soul as well as a quickening of the spiritual senses. In Wesley's words, in justification "the atonement of Christ [is] actually applied to the soul."[23] In summation, while Wesley insists that justification is what God does for the believer, he considers justification an actual transformation of the human soul, casting the transformation in terms of warfare or deliverance (enemies to children) and a healing of the soul resulting in a quickening of the spiritual senses. This ideal was often a struggle for Wesley. Yet despite his own objections, these effects are clearly works of grace within the believer.

It follows that for Wesley, sanctification is an act of grace logically subsequent to the grace of justification, whereby the justified believer begins to share in God's holiness. He refers to this as "the renewing of our fallen nature." This is a process whereby the nature toward sin is excised and the nature of God first imparted at regeneration is strengthened within a person. It is a process, but the believer can achieve perfection in Christian love while still in this life. By this process, sinners become saints. If justification removes the guilt of sin, sanctification removes the power of sin. His well-known emphasis in relation to sanctification is of course on the perfection of the heart in Christian love. This sanctified heart in the believer is the essence of holiness and the expression of union with God. Thus, sanctification is the way to *theosis,* the sharing in the Divine life.

A Wesleyan-Pentecostal Perspective on Justification and Sanctification

Wesleyan-Pentecostals, then, are Evangelical synergists who understand the dynamic of justification-sanctification as existing on a trajectory that flows out of the teachings of Wesley without being confined to his theological context. With him we see the promise of sanctification as a central doctrine of the Scriptures. We believe in "sanctification subsequent to the new birth, through faith in the blood of Christ; through the Word, and by the Holy Ghost," and we believe "holiness to be God's standard of living for His people."[24] However, Pentecostals interpret the doctrines of justification and sanctification through a different lens than that of the Reformation. Our primary lens for reading life and the Scriptures is that of Spirit Baptism: the grace of sanctification experienced as participation in the Divine life and freed from the power of sin.

There are subtleties to this understanding that allow for points of dialogue within this position. Frank Macchia, a Pentecostal but not a Wesleyan, has suggested that Pentecostals read the *via salutis* through the lens of Spirit fullness. For him, justification and sanctification should not be construed as stages of salvation but rather as "two overlapping metaphors."[25] In this soteriology, Pentecostals see the entire way of salvation as a process of sharing in the eternal life of God. Salvation is to possess (and be possessed by) the Spirit. Justification includes the imputation of the righteousness of Christ, but it also inaugurates life in the Spirit.[26] It follows that what was for Wesley a healing of the spiritual senses is for Pentecostals the inauguration of communion with the Holy Spirit. Justification encompasses our righteous standing before God and our righteous life in God. It is to be transformed by God's grace so that the righteousness of Christ is both imputed and imparted. The righteousness expressed within the Three-Person God is imprinted on the believer.

The central point here is that, first, justification is the inauguration and continuation by grace of a right relation with God. It is what God does for us and connectively with us as He, by the Spirit, begins His abode within us and we, by the Spirit, begin our abode within Him. To be justified is to exist in right relationship with God as is defined by God and is appropriate to our maturing standing in Christ. Adoption and regeneration are thus descriptive components of justification.

Sanctification, on the other hand, while inextricably tied to justification, is for Wesleyan-Pentecostals the process of sharing the Divine life. It is participation in the holiness of God. Sanctification is inaugurated in justification but remains logically distinct as another work of grace. By grace, it is what God does in us to transform our natures from sinners to saints and what he does with us through union with Him and the sharing of His life and nature. If justification inaugurates a mutual indwelling, sanctification is a process that initiates and perfects union with God. There is a purgative element to sanctification, both the crucifixion of residual inclination to sin and an ever-increasing consciousness of sin and righteousness. Sanctification increasingly gives us eyes to see our own sins and the effects of sin on all of creation so that we may live in God, freed from the power of sin. With Wesley, we affirm that the inclination to sin is not in and of itself sin from which we need forgiveness. And so we think of this purgation as healing and the removal of the marks of sin that entangle us with our old lives and disjoin us from others and all of creation.

In addition to healing, sanctification is generative. By it we come to flourish in the new order of creation. The life of God is a fruitful life, a sharing in God's Divine life. With Wesley we affirm that there is no holiness that is not social holiness. The sanctifying grace of God is communicative. Those being sanctified are themselves agents of God's sanctifying grace within creation. This is more than good works; it is participation in the sanctifying presence of God within creation. Believers are to be agents of the new creation within creation.

Sanctification and Eschatology: Corporate and Personal

In conclusion, a Wesleyan-Pentecostal understanding of sanctification is eschatological in orientation, personal in its appropriation, and corporate in its manifestation. Sanctification is eschatological in orientation, pointing toward the completed or perfected life of the entire creation. Life in Christ is oriented toward His return and the fullness of all things in Him. To share in the divine life is, in part, to hunger for the eschaton, that day of unencumbered union and communion with God.

Having stated that sanctification is social and by implication corporate, it must be noted that it is always personal in appropriation. Personal maturity and completion in Christ are the promises of God joined to the promise of the perfection of all things. Personal holiness is always manifested within the communion of the saints.

Notes

1. Howard Snyder and Joel Scandrett, *Salvation Means the Healing of Creation: The Ecology of Sin and Grace* (Eugene, OR: Cascade Books, 2011), 61.
2. Rom. 8:19-21.
3. Snyder and Scandrett, *Healing of Creation*, 103.
4. Jackie David Johns, "Pentecostalism and the Postmodern Worldview," *Journal of Pentecostal Theology* 7 (1995).
5. Ibid., 92.
6. Ibid.
7. Christopher John Thomas, "Pentecostal Theology in the Twenty-First Century," *Pneuma* 203 (Spring 1998): 3-19.
8. J.H. King, *From Passover to Pentecost*, 4th ed., revised and enlarged (Franklin Springs, GA: Advocate Press, 1976), 103.
9. Dale Coulter, "Delivered by the Power of God: Toward a Pentecostal Understanding of Salvation," *International Journal of Systematic Theology* 10 (Oct. 2008).
10. Richard Shaull, *Pentecostalism and the Future of the Christian Churches* (Grand Rapids: W.B. Eerdmans, 2000), 145.
11. Shaull, *Pentecostalism*, 144-45.
12. Ibid.
13. Coulter, 461.
14. Edmund Rybarczyk, *Beyond Salvation: Eastern Orthodoxy and Classical Pentecostalism on Becoming Like Christ* (Milton Keynes: Paternoster Press, 2004), 116.
15. Stephen Land, *Pentecostal Spirituality: A Passion for the Kingdom*, JPT supplement 1 (Sheffield: Sheffield Academic Press, 1993), 197.
16. Coulter.
17. Mic. 6:8.
18. A.H. Leitch, "Righteousness," *Zondervan Pictorial Encyclopedia of the Bible: Q-Z* (Grand Rapids: Zondervan, 1977), 5:107.
19. John Wesley's *Sermons* in Albert C. Outler, *The Works of John Wesley*. 1:431-32.
20. Ibid., 1:188.
21. Ibid.
22. Kenneth Collins, "The Doctrine of Justification: Historic Wesleyan and Contemporary Understandings," in *Justification*, eds. Mark Husbands and Daniel J. Treier (Downers Grove, IL: InterVarsity Press, 2004), 186.
23. Ibid.
24. Church of God Declaration of Faith: Items 5 & 6.
25. Baptized in the Spirit, 129, 140.
26. Frank D. Macchia, *Justified by the Spirit* (Grand Rapids: W.B. Eerdmans, 2010), 75-99.

Background Paper

Justification and Sanctification in Scripture and the Church Fathers

Dr. Daniel Keating

THE TOPIC OF JUSTIFICATION and sanctification in Scripture and the Fathers is like a vast forest, enormous in extent and tangled in its pathways. As I searched through primary and secondary sources, I found myself wandering around in this deep forest, needing to reconnoiter where I was and where I hoped to go. To be of service to our dialogue on the relationship between justification and sanctification, I have attempted to narrow my focus considerably.

The first line of investigation explores a select number of biblical texts: Where do the biblical texts speak of justification or righteousness as the actual *reality* of righteousness in the believer? Do they ever point to the idea of righteousness as something that grows and progresses? And further, are there links to what is commonly understood by the term "sanctification"?[1] My discussion of these texts is plainly incomplete in terms of a full exegesis; my hope is simply to indicate where in the Scripture certain understandings of justification may find their root. The second line of investigation concerns how the understanding of justification/righteousness developed in the early Church, especially as found in two representative and paradigmatic Church Fathers: Augustine and Cyril .

of Alexandria. How do Augustine and Cyril view justification, and how is this related to ongoing sanctification?[2]

There is obviously a high degree of selectivity in which biblical texts I have chosen to investigate and in my choice of these two early church authors. I am approaching both the biblical and patristic material with a desire to hear and understand what is being said about justification and its relationship to sanctification, but plainly I do so as someone interested in seeing where the texts point (either brightly or dimly) to a Catholic understanding of the meaning of justification in the believer.

I am assuming that many of the New Testament texts, in Paul especially, *include* the notion of justification as a declaration of righteousness and of the forgiveness of sins, akin to Jesus saying to the paralytic, "My son, your sins are forgiven."[3] The crucial question I want to explore is whether in some passages at least "justification" and especially "justification through faith" entails more than this; that is, whether it includes the sense of "making just" and whether there is ever any indication of an *increase* or *progress* in the righteousness given.

INVESTIGATION OF SELECT NEW TESTAMENT TEXTS

As a backdrop to the New Testament texts, the summary statement by John Reumann concerning the Old Testament notion of righteousness is significant: "This lengthy survey of but a part of the OT evidence makes it clear that 'righteousness/justice/justification' terminology in the Hebrew scriptures is 'action-oriented,' and not just 'status' or 'being' language, and binds together forensic, ethical and other aspects."[4] Reumann then makes use of these senses of righteousness in the Old Testament to help identify various uses in the New Testament.

We will begin with the meaning of "righteousness" in the Sermon on the Mount.[5] Here the term functions as an important criterion: it is what we are to hunger and thirst for and to seek; it is what must surpass in us that of the scribes and Pharisees. But what specially marks out this idea of "righteousness" is that it can be *practiced* and functions as a synonym for "piety." It is an inward quality that manifests itself in outward acts, and it imitates the uprightness of God himself.[6]

Two passages in Luke and Acts are relevant to our topic. The first, Luke 1:74-75, is found in Zechariah's hymn of praise and puts the terms "righteousness" and "holiness" in synonymous parallelism: "...to grant us that we, being delivered from the hand of our enemies, might serve him without fear, in holiness and righteousness before him all the days of our life." The two terms appear to be similar in meaning and point to a right way of living according to God's ways.[7] It is instructive that Ephesians 4:24 contains the exact pair of terms in reverse order: "And put on the new nature, created after the likeness of God in true righteousness and holiness." Here again righteousness and holiness are paired together and characterize the *quality* of the new nature we have in Christ.

The second relevant text is Acts 13:38-39. Paul is speaking in the synagogue in Pisidian Antioch and sums up his message in this way: "Let it be known to you therefore, brethren, that through this man forgiveness of sins is proclaimed to you, and by him every one that believes is freed from everything from which you could not be freed by the law of Moses." It is noteworthy that the verb "freed from/freed by" is *dikaioō*, to justify (used in the passive voice). The meaning seems to be equivalent to forgiveness of sins but in the context carries the sense of actual freedom from these sins, not just a declaration of non-imputation.[8]

Two passages in 1 Corinthians correlate righteousness and sanctification but without clearly identifying the content of each or their relationship to each other. In 1 Corinthians 1:30, Paul writes: "He is the source of your life in Christ Jesus, whom God made our wisdom, our righteousness and sanctification and redemption." This is Paul's way of summing up what *Christ* is for us. The four aspects are neither equated nor distinguished, but together they sum up what Christ is for us. This passage seems to have had an impact on the characteristic patristic pattern of "piling up" without clear distinction a set of related terms that together function to encompass what Christ has done. They are *distinguishable* qualities but function as a *compound expression* of a single work.

Later in the letter, Paul applies a similar set of terms to the work of God in us: "And such were some of you. But you were washed, you were sanctified, you were justified in the name of the Lord Jesus Christ and by the Spirit of our God."[9] Once again we are presented with a collection of terms denoting what the faithful have received in Christ. "Washed" is almost certainly a reference to baptism and probably has both a physical and spiritual connotation. The terms "sanctified" and "justified" follow in turn, and notably here justification is named *after* sanctification. Does the adverbial phrase ("in the name of") modify only the last item or all three? The latter is more likely given the perfect parallelism of the three phrases. The three consequences ("washed," "sanctified," "justified") all occur together and are grouped together as portraying the result of initiation into Christ.

The Letter to the Romans contains the densest concentration of the term "righteousness" within the New Testament. For our purposes, I propose to look at texts from Chapters 5 and 6. In Romans 5:19, after a set of parallel phrases describing the inverse relationship between Christ and Adam, Paul says: "For as by one man's disobedience many were made sinners, so by one man's obedience many *will be made righteous*."[10] Employing the verb *kathistēmi* in both terms of this parallel statement, Paul seems to be saying that in the first case many were made *to be* sinners, while in the second many are made *to be* righteous. This seems to indicate a *transformative* understanding of justification, at least in this case, but leaves open the question of the relation between being "made righteous" and receiving "sanctification" found elsewhere in Paul (for example, in Romans 6:19, 22).

Turning to Romans Chapter 6, Paul writes: "We know that our old self was crucified with him so that the sinful body might be destroyed, and we might no longer be enslaved to sin. For he who has died is freed from sin."[11] The phrase translated "is freed from" is literally "is justified from" (*dedikaiōtai*). Here again (as in Acts 13) we have the verb *dikaioō* used in the sense of "freed from." This would seem to imply a genuine change in the person, a genuine freedom from sin gained. The verb tense is also worthy of notice: it is in the perfect tense, indicating an ongoing condition, not a simple past action. This lends itself to the idea of a freedom given internally that then becomes the ongoing reality of the person—freedom from sin's dominion in Christ.

A few verses later, Paul writes, "For just as you once yielded your members to impurity and to greater and greater iniquity, so now yield your members to righteousness for sanctification.... But now that you have been set free from sin and have become slaves of God, the return you get is sanctification and its end, eternal life."[12] Here "righteousness" appears to have a moral quality: Paul is speaking of ongoing life and uses the term "righteousness" to describe how we are to present or orientate our "members" (our bodies, our lives). This yielding to righteousness accomplishes the end or goal, which is the actual sanctification of the person. The logic of the passage points to "process," with the believer yielding more and more to what God has already done, and the result is our sanctification.[13]

The Letter to the Hebrews appears to conceive of righteousness as *faith in action*: the examples of the renowned figures in Chapter 11 portray those who heard the word of God and acted upon it. Noah provides a clear example: "By faith Noah, being warned by God concerning events as yet unseen, took heed and constructed an ark for the saving of his household; by this he condemned the world and became an heir of the righteousness which comes by faith."[14] Righteousness in Hebrews is the peaceful fruit that we obtain as we endure the Lord's discipline.[15] The author does not enter into the debate on faith and works but would appear to hold a view closest to James.

The First Letter of John plainly takes a view of "righteousness" that entails a moral quality that we act upon: "If you know that he is righteous, you may be sure that everyone who practices righteousness has been born of him.... Little children, let no one deceive you. Whoever practices righteousness is righteous, as he is righteous."[16] The phrase "do/practice righteousness" clearly indicates the moral quality of righteousness in John's eyes.

We come last of all to James 2:14-26. Much can and has been said about these verses. For our purposes, I wish only to make a few observations. First, for James, a claim to "faith" without the proof of good works only shows that such faith is dead. Second, the crucial step that James takes is to use Abraham as his example (as Paul does in Romans 4), concluding that Abraham was justified by his faith and his works: "Was not Abraham our father justified by works, when he offered his son Isaac upon the altar? You see that faith was active along with his works, and faith was completed by works.... You see that a man is justified by works and not by faith alone."[17]

Abraham, as viewed by James, is the pivotal figure for the idea of a righteousness that progresses or comes in stages. Abraham believed God when the word came to him. But for James, he was only fully justified and his faith proved to be real faith when he acted on the word of God and obeyed. There is at work here a sense of chronological (and textual) succession: the testing of obedience cannot be simultaneous with the hearing (and in Abraham's case, it comes seven chapters later). The crucial step made by James is that he characterizes both "hearing in faith" and "obedience in response to faith" in terms of "righteousness" and being "justified." As I will indicate below, I believe that James, along with the evidence of these other New Testament texts, was decisive for this idea that arose in the early church: that righteousness is an inherent attribute that grows and progresses over time, and so is a quality of who we are in Christ.

INVESTIGATIONS OF JUSTIFICATION IN AUGUSTINE AND CYRIL

Augustine (354-430 AD)

In his two-volume history on the meaning of "justification," Alister McGrath sums up the lack of attention to this concept in the period prior to Augustine: "Justification was simply not a theological issue in the pre-Augustinian tradition.... For the first three hundred and fifty years of the history of the church, her teaching on justification was inchoate and ill-defined."[18] He judges this to be the forgetting of Paul's great insight. But this changed with Augustine: "Augustine's doctrine of deification is the first discussion of the matter of major significance to emerge from the twilight of the western theological tradition, establishing the framework within which the future discussion of the justification of man before God would be conducted."[19]

What then are the marks of Augustine's doctrine of justification? The first is the most obvious and well known: the priority of grace. Justification is not the reward for our works but the free gift of grace through Jesus Christ. The second mark is the activity of our own free will in our justification. This activity of the will is due to the grace of God, who frees the will to freely assent to justification:

> Now they to whom this is not given either are unwilling or do not fulfil what they will; whereas they to whom it is given so will as to accomplish what they will. In order, therefore, that this saying, which is not received by all men, may yet be received by some, there are both the gift of God and free will.[20]

A selection from Augustine's Sermon 169 states in a striking way how he conceives of human participation in the act of justification:

> But the whole thing is from God; not however as though we were asleep, as though we didn't have to make an effort, as though we didn't have to be willing. Without your will there will be no justice of God in you. The will, indeed, is only yours, the justice is only God's. There can be such a thing as God's justice without your will, but it cannot be in you apart from your will. God made you without you. You didn't, after all, give any consent to God making you. How were you to consent, if you didn't yet exist? So while he made you without you, he doesn't justify you without you. So he made you without your knowing it, he justifies you with your willing consent to it. Yet it's he that does the justifying.[21]

The third mark of Augustinian justification is that the believer is made to be just, what McGrath calls *inherent* justification:

> Man's righteousness, effected in justification, is regarded by Augustine as *inherent* rather than *imputed*, to use the vocabulary of the sixteenth century. A concept of "imputed righteousness," in the later Protestant sense of the term, would be quite redundant within Augustine's doctrine of justification, in that man is *made righteous* in justification. The righteousness which man thus receives, although originating from God, is nevertheless located within man, and can be said to be *his*, part of his being and intrinsic to his person.[22]

For McGrath, this amounts to a theology of *deification* in Augustine, a conclusion that my own studies on Augustine would confirm.

A fourth mark is that, for Augustine, justification is both *an event and a process*; it has a beginning but progresses in us through our active cooperation. In the words of Augustine:

> What about being justified? What does it mean, being justified?... Have we no justice at all? Or do we have some, but not the whole of it?... So if there's something we have, and something we haven't

got, we must let what we have grow, and what we haven't got will be completed.... We have been justified; but this justice can grow, as we make progress. And how it can grow I will tell you, and after a fashion compare notes with you, so that you may all, each and every one of you, already established in the condition of justification, namely by receiving the forgiveness of sins in the washing of regeneration, by receiving the Holy Spirit, by making progress day by day; so that you may all see where you are, put your best foot forward, make progress and grow, until you are finalized, in the sense of not being finished off, but of being perfected.[23]

Augustine locates justification, it would seem, within baptism and as part of the regeneration of the believer through the Holy Spirit. As we shall see, Cyril adopts a similar position.

A fifth mark of Augustine's understanding of justification by faith is that this faith must be characterized by love. Here is where James Chapter 2 comes into play (as well as 1 Corinthians 13). Faith without love, for Augustine, is the "dead faith" of the devils:

> It is such faith which severs God's faithful from unclean demons—for even these "believe and tremble," as the Apostle James says; but they do not do well. Therefore they possess not the faith by which the just man lives...the faith which works by love in such wise, that God recompenses it according to its works with eternal life. But inasmuch as we have even our good works from God, from whom likewise comes our faith and our love, therefore the selfsame great teacher of the Gentiles has designated "eternal life" itself as his gracious "gift."[24]

For Augustine, "Faith is mighty, but without charity it profits nothing."[25] He effectively interprets "faith without *works* is dead"[26] as being equivalent to "faith without *love* is dead." McGrath goes so far as to say that "it is for this reason that it is unacceptable to summarize Augustine's doctrine of justification as *sola fide iustificamur*—if any such summary is acceptable, it is *sola caritate iustificamur*."[27]

A sixth and final mark of Augustine's understanding of justification is that though we cannot merit the initial gift of justification, we can and are called to merit our progress in justification—though all our merit is really nothing other than God crowning his own gifts: "When God crowns our merits, he crowns nothing but his own gifts."[28] McGrath concisely sums up Augustine's nuanced understanding of justification and merit:

> God *operates* upon man in the *act* of justification, and *cooperates* with him in the *process* of justification. Once justified, the sinner may begin to acquire merit—but only on account of God's grace. Thus it is clearly wrong to suggest that Augustine excludes or denies merit; while merit *before* justification is indeed denied, its reality and necessity *after* justification is equally strongly affirmed. It must be noted, however, that Augustine understands merit as a gift from God to the justified sinner, and does not adopt Tertullian's somewhat legalistic approach to the matter.[29]

McGrath's conclusion regarding Augustine's concept of justification and its relation to sanctification speaks directly to our topic: "For Augustine, justification includes both the beginnings of man's righteousness before God and its subsequent perfection, the event and the process, so that what later became the Reformation concept of 'sanctification' is effectively subsumed under the aegis of justification."[30]

Cyril of Alexandria (378-444 AD)

Cyril of Alexandria was a younger contemporary of Augustine. By virtue of a newly discovered letter found within a wider collection in 1969 (published in 1981), we now know that Augustine corresponded with Cyril specifically about the unfolding of the Pelagian controversy in the East.[31] It appears that Cyril was supplying Augustine with information about events in the East. In addition, Cyril probably had access, in Greek translation, to one of Augustine's shorter anti-Pelagian treatises, *De Gestis Pelagii*. The communication between Augustine and Cyril sheds new light on the condemnation of Pelagian teaching at the Council of Ephesus in 431 AD, a council in which Cyril presided, and indicates that Cyril understood and rejected what the Pelagians were teaching.[32]

Throughout his vast corpus, Cyril emphasizes Paul's teaching on justification by faith. He frequently refers to Paul's teaching (found in Romans 4) that, even according to the record of the law, faith *preceded* the law, and so the keeping of the commandments is grounded in a prior response of faith. For Cyril, then, justification by faith in Christ is not something novel but the fulfillment of what is already sketched in the example of Abraham, whose "faith was reckoned to him as righteousness, and the righteousness of faith has become his basis for freedom before God."[33] For Cyril, then, faith plays a decisive role in Christ's saving economy. By faith we freely receive the gift of God's grace—his righteousness—that we did not (and cannot) earn.

Cyril nowhere defines what he means by "justification" or by "righteousness," but when his writings are examined in context it appears that justification by faith is roughly equivalent to the remission of sins: "For we have been justified 'not by works of the law' but by his grace and the forgiveness granted to us from above."[34] Passages like this can be multiplied in his commentaries on Luke and John.

When we look more deeply, however, James proves decisive for Cyril's formulation of justification and for his view of Abraham as a model:

> We must realize, then, that if we are united to him by faith and we practice the form of our connection with only barren confessions of faith, and we do not clench the bond of union with works of love, we will indeed be branches, but dead and unfruitful ones. For without works faith is dead, as the saint says.[35]

When reviewing the story of Abraham as a type of justifying faith, Cyril speaks explicitly about the inseverable connection of faith and obedience: "Therefore, because of his obedience and sacrifice the divinely inspired Abraham was called a friend of God, and he was clothed with the boast of righteousness."[36] In Cyril's view, "the blessed Abraham then was justified by obedience and faith."[37] And he concludes that "much, therefore, at once was taught [Abraham] by this event. For, in the first place, he learnt that ready obedience leads on to every blessing, and is the pathway to justification, and the pledge of friendship with God."[38] The fact that Cyril can speak elsewhere about "the beginning of righteousness" in the believer indicates that he sees "righteousness" as something that can progress and increase.[39]

Cyril is a theologian of the divine indwelling, and for him this indwelling through the Spirit is the source of all the good that comes to us. He speaks at one point of righteousness being the *result* of the divine indwelling: Christ underwent suffering and death for us so that "nothing may stand in the way of our ability to draw near to God and have fellowship with him, namely, through participation in the Holy Spirit, who reshapes us into righteousness and holiness and into our original image."[40]

In summary, Cyril appears to view salvation in Christ as *one* event with *several* aspects. Justification by faith marks the new dispensation in Christ in contrast to "the works of the law" under the old covenant. Cyril interprets justification firmly through the lens of a new covenant dispensation. But crucially, the event of baptism itself is normally the context for Cyril's account of justification, sanctification, and the divine indwelling. Justification appears to be that part of Christ's work in us especially concerned with the remission of sins, but it is also capable of growth through good works that follow from love. Abraham seen through the lens of Paul and James is the exemplar *par excellence* for Cyril's conception of justification.

Conclusion

This brief and selective treatment of the biblical and patristic evidence is intended to provide pointers toward the roots of a Catholic understanding of justification and its integral link with the notions of sanctification and regeneration. The texts from the New Testament show that the terms "righteousness" and "justification" span a wide semantic range; even in Paul justification can refer to "making righteous." Against the backdrop of this wider biblical testimony, the early (and medieval) church adopted a view of justification that was pointedly anti-Pelagian (expressly so for Augustine and Cyril) but that included free human assent to justification and viewed justification as something that was actually accomplished in the life of the believer and should progress over time.

For Augustine and Cyril, it is not a matter of Paul vs. James, but rather Paul read within the context of the wider New Testament witness, with James providing the clearest statement that justification occurs not by bare confession but by the accompaniment of good works. The logic of James' statement leads to the conclusion that justification is not a onetime event or a simple declaration, but something that is capable of being advanced through good works over time. If Paul ensured for the early church that justification could not be understood in a Pelagian sense, James ensured that justification was not simply a matter of belief/confession but a work of God that demanded free assent and ongoing cooperation for its accomplishment.

Alister McGrath states with particular lucidity the crucial distinction between the early church and medieval approach to justification and sanctification on the one hand and the Reformers on the other, and sets the stage for our dialogue:

> The medieval statements concerning the nature of justification demonstrate that justification is universally understood to involve a real change in its subject, so that regeneration is subsumed under justification.... The notional distinction between *iustificatio* and *regeneration* provides one of the best *differentiae* between Catholic and Protestant understandings of justification, marking the Reformers' complete discontinuity with the earlier western theological tradition.[41]

Notes

[1] Here I have made use of *Righteousness in the New Testament* (Philadelphia: Fortress Press, 1982) by John Reumann (a Lutheran), with responses by Joseph Fitzmyer and Jerome Quinn (both Catholic). Further, I have drawn on the summary of their conclusions as embedded in the published findings of *Justification by Faith: Lutherans and Catholics in Dialogue VII*, eds. H. George Anderson, T. Austin Murphy, and Joseph A. Burgess (Minneapolis: Augsburg, 1985).

[2] Here I am especially indebted to Alister E. McGrath's two-volume work, *Iustitia Dei: A History of the Christian Doctrine of Justification*, vol. 1, *The Beginnings to the Reformation*; vol. 2, *From 1500 to the Present Day* (Cambridge: Cambridge University Press, 1986).

[3] Mark 2:5. Scripture texts are taken from the Revised Standard Version unless otherwise noted.

[4] Reumann, *Righteousness*, 15-16.

[5] Matt. 5:6, 10, 20; 6:1, 33.

[6] For Reumann, *Righteousness*, 135, "righteousness" in Matthew has first the sense of human response to the kingdom, but also has the quality of a gift of God and is not without an emphasis on faith: "The theology of Matthew is thus different from, but not contrary to, that of Paul."

[7] Reumann, *Righteousness*, 136, identifies this as the Old Testament sense of righteousness as a moral quality.

[8] Ibid., 142-43, sees Acts as representing "not Paul's view, but a different sort developed in Gentile Christianity, from the gospel and OT traditions, but in light of the Christ-event."

9 1 Cor. 6:11.

10 The translation "will be made righteous" is adopted by the RSV, NRSV, ESV, and NAB. Italics added.

11 Rom. 6:7.

12 Rom. 6:19b, 22.

13 Michael Gorman, *Reading Paul* (Eugene, OR: Cascade Books, 2008), 118, draws a similar conclusion regarding Paul's teaching on justification in chapters 5-6: "Rom 5:1-11, about justification by God's grace as reconciliation, is soon followed by Romans 6, about baptism as co-crucifixion and co-resurrection with Christ. As we will see below, the two experiences are actually one and the same, viewed from different perspectives."

14 Heb. 11:7.

15 Heb. 12:7.

16 1 John 2:29; 3:7, ESV.

17 James 2:21-22, 24.

18 McGrath, *Iustitia Dei*, vol. 1, 19, 23.

19 Ibid., 24.

20 *De gratia et libero arbitrio*, 7; in *Saint Augustin: Anti-Pelagian Writings*, ed. P. Schaff, trans. P. Holmes, *Nicene and Post-Nicene Fathers of the Church* (*NPNF*), series 1, vol. 5 (Grand Rapids: W.B. Eerdmans, 1978), 447.

21 *Serm.* 169.13, in *Sermons*, trans. Edmund Hill, *The Works of St. Augustine: A Translation for the 21st Century*, III/5 (New York: New City Press, 1992), 230-31.

22 McGrath, *Iustitia Dei*, vol. 1, 31.

23 *Serm.* 158.4-5, in *Sermons*, trans. Edmund Hill, 116-17.

24 *De gratia et libero arbitrio*, 18, in *Saint Augustin: Anti-Pelagian Writings*, ed. P. Schaff, trans. P. Holmes, *NPNF*, series 1, vol. 5 (Grand Rapids: W.B. Eerdmans, 1978), 451.

25 *Tract. In Io.* 6.21, in *St. Augustin: Homilies on the Gospel of John, Homilies on the First Epistle of John, Soliloquies*, ed. P. Schaff, trans. J. Gibb & J. Innes, *NPNF*, series 1, vol. 7 (Grand Rapids: W.B. Eerdmans, 1978), 46.

26 James 2:26.

27 McGrath, *Iustitia Dei*, vol. 1, 30.

28 *Serm.* 194.5.19, cited in McGrath, *Iustitia Dei*, vol. 1, 28.

29 McGrath, *Iustitia Dei*, vol. 1, 28.

30 Ibid., vol. 1, 32.

31 Johannes Divjak, *Sancti Aureli Augustini Opera: Epistulae ex duobus codicibus nuper in lucem prolatae*, *CSEL* 88 (1981).

32 For commentary on Augustine's letter to Cyril, see Gerald Bonner, "Some Remarks on Letters 4* and 6*," in J. Divjak, ed., *Les lettres de saint Augustine* (Paris: Études Augustiniennes, 1983), 155-64.

33 Cyril of Alexandria, "Comm. on Jn. 8:33," in *Commentary on John*, vol. 1 of *Ancient Christian Texts*, trans. David R. Maxwell (Downer's Grove, IL: IVP Academic, 2015), 354.

34 *Comm. Jn.* 6:64-65 (Maxwell, vol. 1, 248).

35 *Comm. Jn.* 15:2 (Maxwell, vol. 2, 217).

36 *Comm. Jn.* 15:14-15 (Maxwell, vol. 2, 232).

37 *Comm. Lk. 8:49-56, Homily* 46, in St. Cyril of Alexandria, *Commentary on the Gospel of Saint Luke*, trans. R. Payne Smith (New York: Studion, 1983), 202. It is worth notice that in Romans Paul himself closely links "faith" and "obedience" through the phrase "obedience of faith" (1:5; 16:26), which acts like bookends for the letter. Michael Gorman summarizes this in *Reading Paul*, 123: "Scripturally speaking, faith and obedience are two sides of one coin."

38 *Comm. Lk. 9:59-60, Homily* 58 (Payne Smith, 251).

39 *Comm. Jn. 6:68* (Maxwell, vol. 1, 253).

40 *Comm. Jn. 17:18-19* (Maxwell, vol. 2, 298).

41 McGrath, *Iustitia Dei*, vol. 1, 48, 51.

Background Paper

Justification and Sanctification in the *Catechism of the Catholic Church*[1]

Dr. David P. Fleischacker

Justification and Sanctification are One

Justification is not only the remission of sins, but also the sanctification and renewal of the interior man.[2]

Catholic Tradition and dogma hold that justification and sanctification are intimately united in an identity that is the same as that found in justifying grace and sanctifying grace. Justification refers to making right, just, or properly ordered. In the human being, this includes more often than not a turning away from sin. However, it can be something that grows and deepens in the same way and for the same reason that love of God can grow and deepen. This kind of love is that which is the alpha and the omega of all facets, faculties, and operations of a human person. Sanctification refers to the making of a soul pure and holy. As with justification, it grows, and it usually does so with a repudiation of sin in a conversion.

One glimpses the unity of the two in an identity when one begins to attend to the language that formulates what each means. Justification makes one right with God. This means that one gives what is due to God.[3] To account for what is due requires that we turn to the meaning of the human person and what God created us to be. The *Catechism of the Catholic Church* (*CCC*) points to our rich Tradition, which has developed and deepened our understanding of the human person over the millennia. It begins with Genesis, of course, and the affirmation that we are made in the image of God.

Reflection on this image has a long history. One sees St. Augustine pursuing its meaning from some of his earliest years (in the Soliloquies, for example) after his conversion in 384.[4] This reflection reaches its height in Augustine's mature years, as he wrote *De Trinitate*.[5] The image does not refer to the material facets of the human person, but to those that are spiritual, and in general, this had been codified over the centuries and is expressed in the *Catechism* as knowing and loving.

Being a creature that is knowing and loving is central to the meaning of being human. However, there is a deeper aspect to this personhood than the standard account of knowing and loving: one's knowing and loving are not complete and fulfilled in beatitude by any limited, finite creature, even though it has the potential to be a spiritual home to all of creation.[6] Rather, our knowing and loving are in a potency that is without bounds, and thus could only be completed in that which is a boundless being of truth and goodness and beauty. We are created for God, to know and to love God with our entire being.[7] Thus we do not have merely a mind and a will, but a mind that thirsts for Truth that has no conditions and a will that yearns for the good without bounds.[8]

Augustine and others have held that this image is a Trinitarian one. The *CCC* does not state this explicitly, but it does proclaim that our souls thirst an intimate, indwelling relationship with the Father, the Son, and the Holy Spirit.[9]

At the same time, we are not angels, but spiritual creatures that are embodied. We share with the animals sensory and motor capabilities, along with emotions and passions that constitute our sensitive life. Our sensate being too yearns for God and has a relation to God. Our hungers and thirsts for food, peace, and procreation faintly image God, and these have vertical relationships that come alive in the human world of reason and good will. Thus, these come to be explicitly a part of the thirst we have for God. One sees this in the dual meanings of hunger and thirst that permeate so many stories in the Gospels.

Purification and Perfection of the "Inner Man"

The Holy Spirit is the master of the interior life. By giving birth to the 'inner man,' justification entails sanctification of his whole being.[10]

The human person being both material and spiritual is fulfilled only when both are brought into perfection and beatitude, when both are in right relation to God, hence justified. Another way to identify this justice is to quote the famous passage of Augustine, namely that "our hearts are restless until they rest in you, Lord."[11] In being made for God, one symbol above all others points us to the core of this image or, in other words, the essence of the human person. That symbol is the heart. The heart reveals that our souls are intimately linked to love, which really is agapic love. Thus, at the root of all our being, at the root of being in the image of God, Who is love, is a soul that is made in and for love. The desire of all desiring, then, is that of love. It too has no bounds, and thus will be restless until it rests in boundless love, an infinite exchange of being and truth and wisdom between the Father, the Son, and the Holy Spirit.

God Made Us to Love and to Know Him

Thus, at the crux of justice, of giving what is right to God, is the reality that we were made for God, to know and to love him with our whole heart, mind, soul, and body. To love him is to be a free slave, to be bound to him in freedom, to dwell in Him and He in us. Our minds do this when we know him. Our wills do this when they are good. Our bodies do this by participating in a rightly ordered soul. This is interior justice.

One should be able to see why sanctifying grace for a Catholic is the same thing as justifying grace, and thus likewise why sanctification is also justification. The same reality, the same state of soul, is the key to both. It is a likeness to God that is the realization and perfection of the image of God in us.

Hence, as with justice and justification, the language of sanctification points to this same reality. To become holy means to become a saint, a lover of God. To love in this manner means that an indwelling of another's being and goodness is taking place in one's soul. When one knows

God and does God's will, then the being and goodness of God are dwelling in one's heart. The more that all of the facets of the human person become like God, the holier the soul becomes. This is sanctification and ongoing sanctification.

Last year, as we touched on initial justification, we as Catholics also held to initial sanctification as being the same. What needs to be in place for both initial sanctification and justification—as well as for a deepening and broadening of sanctification and justification—is that the human heart, the essence of the soul, has been converted into a heart of flesh, a heart that loves God as God, that loves the Father as a son or daughter.[12] Receiving the heart of flesh for the first time is initial sanctification. It sets our hearts on God and allows us to return our hearts to God in love as God wants us to do. God makes us right with God at our core, the essence, of our beings by giving us a heart of flesh so that we can love him in return with our whole heart, mind, and soul. This is initial justification.

Both sanctification and justification can deepen and broaden. Every time we expand in our virtues, increase the good and range of good of our wills, increase our understanding, knowledge, and wisdom of creation, and reorient our desires to God, the more that our entire being comes to dwell in God and God in us.

Fall, Sin, Sanctification, Justification

Before we proceed, we must introduce a criminal element that conditions the manner by which justification and sanctification take place in us. We are fallen, and we perpetuate and deepen that fall in our own personal sin. Because of our sin, the image of God in us is wounded.[13] We have marred the image,[14] and though it is restored in a profound way with sanctifying grace, the propensity to sin remains.[15] Adam and Eve, as was discussed two years ago, were created in a just and right state of love for God and each other and the whole of creation.[16] But they abandoned that life at the beginning with a turning away from God. This turning away, this act of disobedience out of pride brought on by listening to the fallen serpent, resulted in interior injustice.[17] The desires turned against the mind and will.[18] This was the immediate cause of a disordered relationship between the man and the woman, and it had consequences.[19] They were no longer able to live in the Garden, and their children would be born outside of its realm, conceived in sin.[20]

This state of original sin would grow into the murder of a righteous brother: Abel.[21] Cain would become the father of cities on earth, and cities would be born of thirsts for domination, greed, and lust, and filled with envy and anger.[22] The sin of the world would grow with the growth of the human race, even after the flood; it would grow into the tower of Babel.[23] Mankind was enslaved in sin.[24] Interiorly, man, woman, and child were weakened in their wills, darkened in their minds, torn by disordered desires, and doomed to sickness and death.[25] It was impossible to love God. Man, woman, and child were incapable of receiving the only one who could bring beatitude. Injustice and unholiness ruled the day, the century, the millennia.

But God did not leave the human race in a state of hopelessness.[26] He came looking for Adam and Eve in haste. He received their confession. He indicated and effected their penance. He could restore the fallen into a right relationship with him as his prerogative revealed over and over again in the Old Testament. He made Abel and Seth, Abraham, Moses, David, and the prophets. He could reconcile and restore. The Old Testament covenant reveals a God of mercy who did not have to call after Adam and Eve, or bestow Seth, or form a people under Moses, or a kingdom of priests and prophets under David, yet did so. His abundant mercy shouts from the psalms and from all of the stories that one finds, one of my personal favorites being that of Joseph and his brothers in Egypt.

God Using Mediators for Salvation

The Old Covenant reveals God working his mercy and love and truth through human beings. He revealed what was just via the prophets who, even if God needed to toss them into a whale, brought the message to others. One of the first prophets was Moses, and the Commandments of course summarize this love of God and neighbor in its most succinct and abiding manner.[27] And it continued to grow. As God opened the gates of the promised land, he did so through the efforts of Joshua by bringing him into a deeper and more abiding trust in his Lord. As the people of God grew into a nation, and then a kingdom, the key was that God would continue to bring blessings to them if they grew in justice and mercy themselves, if they grew in trust and obedience. God wanted them to do so, so that He could give them even more, a point to which so many of the prophets give testimony.

However, in the Old Covenant, if one was made righteous by virtue of God's grace, it was just that: by virtue of God's grace. In the Old, God did not make us like Him in this aspect. God did not ordain specific created mediations of that grace.[28] Adam and Eve were, in their procreative love, arguably supposed to be the vehicles who would conceive children in grace, to give birth to children in the Garden. God would make their children right and holy from conception because that was the right thing to do for a couple who would be rightly ordered. It would be unjust for the just to conceive an unjust child. God made this couple co-creators of His children. They lost this, of course. Their children and their children's children were to be conceived and born in original sin.

But with the Incarnation of the Son of God, this mediational role was to change.[29] God himself was to become man, one of us, to return and even elevate the way that we would participate in the economy of salvation.[30] He would give gifts by which we could participate in the incarnate Son's mediational role.[31] Christ Jesus became the mediator to reconcile us to His Father in His Spirit.

The outcome? "O Happy Fall..."[32] The grace and sanctity of Adam and Eve has returned, but it is now mediated in the most fantastic manner: the Son of God is the mediator, and because of his hypostatic union, we suddenly are to be made into sons and daughters with Him, because of Him, because of His Father, and because of their Holy Spirit.[33] He gives to us gifts that raise us into the very inner life of the most Holy Trinity.[34] These gifts are the Church and the sacraments.

These gifts have their power in the Holy Trinity, through the incarnate Son. God the Son in His humanity is now the mediator and, because of the unity of the human race, the new Adam. This raises us into a new unity with Him. Because of the social and historical nature of the human race, we have always mediated each other, and one generation to the next. It is why original sin is transmitted.[35] It is how tradition comes to be, both its good and evil elements. It is how language and culture passes from one generation to the next. When our Lord became one of us, he entered our history, becoming consubstantial with us through His mother.[36] On the mediational plateau of the human race, where sin had reigned and where Satan was its prince, the trend was broken in Christ.[37] The slaves to the Evil One could now be set free. Justice and sanctity could be mediated once again and returned to the human race through Christ made man.

It is of course a freedom that itself can be ignored or rejected. God wants to return us to His likeness, in an even higher way than was found in Adam and Eve. This new likeness constitutes a new justice, and a new religion, and a higher sanctity. A new justice because the relationship to God that is innate in our natures is now elevated to be one alongside of the Son, as an adopted son or daughter. A new religion because now what we owe to God is a participation in this higher order of salvation that He has made possible.[38] We are to worship Him in freedom and love that brings alive the real possibility of living out the Commandments by abiding in His body.[39] God is so gracious that He wants to owe us His eternal life because of what He has made and restored us to be. This restoration is the higher sanctity. Our renewal in the inner man is a new ordering as brothers and sisters to the Son, as sons and daughters to His Father and His mother.

THE SACRAMENTS AND THE CHURCH IN SANCTIFICATION AND JUSTIFICATION

Where is this new mediational role prominently found? The sacraments. Baptism is the initial justification and sanctification of the soul.[40] However, it does not remove the trials of faith, nor does it guarantee salvation.[41] It is salvific. It is a permanent mark as sons and daughters of God the Father, as members of the Son's bride.[42] But He wants to bring even higher goods in us that overcome our ongoing propensity to sin, that crushes the head of the prideful serpent in our souls through ongoing acts of contrition and reconciliation that recover the grace of justification and God's friendship.[43] Subsequently, a greater good arises, namely our thankfulness in being sons and daughters because we have been forgiven. To create an intimate union with us, He wants to feed us his body and blood, soul and divinity in the Eucharist, to strengthen us against the continuous pummeling of our wills, the regular temptations to turn from the light to darkness, to give us strength of will against the never-ending trials of the flesh that warp our desires into their own self-destructive lusts.[44] He wants to crush cowardice in us by sealing us in Confirmation via his Holy Spirit.[45]

In the anointing of the sick, He wants to lift us from the dregs of sickness and death through a sanctification that weds us to him when He hung on the Cross.[46] At the last moments of our life, He gives us the hope He never lost at the last moments of His life.[47] He wants to give us a home, a place to belong, an ark, where we can grow and live as His brothers and sisters through the storms of life.[48] He does so in the first home of husband and wife, but in the New Covenant that becomes the domestic Church.[49] In the Old Covenant, the original home was graced many times from the beginning—in Adam and Eve, in Abraham and Sarah, and even in the sketchy marriage of David and Bathsheba. At the beginning of the new, it was graced most fully in Joseph and Mary. Revelation was given to the domestic church both in the Old and New Covenants. Justice became a possibility. Sanctity was called forth. And then there was the larger home, the people of God. In the Old Covenant, this grew from Abraham, Isaac, and Jacob into the ecclesia at the foot of the Mount under Moses, and then into a kingdom of priests and prophets under David.[50] Under the New Covenant, the incarnation elevated this to the body and bride of our Lord, the son of God, the mystical body of Christ.[51]

Once again, you can see why the Church and the sacraments are so crucial for Catholics. She is the place where the sacred gifts from her head flow because of the protection and guidance of His Holy Spirit.

The *Catechism of the Catholic Church* itself expresses the deposit of the faith as it has been transmitted down through the ages.[52] Our understanding of justification and sanctification comes from our Lord's mediation through His Church, guided by the Holy Spirit.

A New Kind of Merit

Since the initiative belongs to God in the order of grace, no one can merit the initial grace of forgiveness and justification, at the beginning of conversion. Moved by the Holy Spirit and by charity, we can then merit for ourselves and for others the graces needed for our sanctification, for the increase of grace and charity, and for the attainment of eternal life. Even temporal goods like health and friendship can be merited in accordance with God's wisdom. These graces and goods are the object of Christian prayer. Prayer attends to the grace we need for meritorious actions.[53]

As found in above, initial forgiveness and justification are entirely God's work. The Holy Spirit graces us to be bonded to the Son as His brothers and sisters, thus adopting us into a filial relationship with His Father. Our Father dwells in us with His Son and their Holy Spirit, gracing us to love Him as a child in the likeness of His Son. Forgiveness and filiation make this possible. We are made holy like the Son is holy, so that we dwell rightly, justly, in His Father. When we live and move and have our being reborn in this state of sanctity and justice, what we do then is itself a gift that God further sanctifies and justifies. Grace flows upon grace, increasing our love for him. He increases the good in us. He is so good that He makes it happen in such a way interiorly, that He can then "owe" it to us as a recompense.[54] God is generous in His love.

God has chosen to redeem us as sinners, both before and after our initial justification and sanctification.[55] God has chosen to give not only when it has no regard to our action, but even when it does. When God chooses to give gifts to us because of something we have done, it still is a result of God's giving, even though God chooses to make it a gift He owes as a result of our action.[56]

What Catholics would claim is that God not only could give and does give in response to our responses, but promises to do so in key areas. God will give gifts both to us and to others for actions that we perform. And God gives these gifts in such a manner as to recreate us in His Son's likeness, such that then He owes us further gifts. This goes so far as to include eternal life itself.

Why does God do this? Essentially it is rooted in the same reason as that of the Incarnation.[57] God the Son becomes one of us because this is the way that God wanted to reconcile each of us to the Father. He wants salvation to be mediated, as was discussed above. This human mediational element was lost in the Fall. It was restored in Christ. And this mediational role did not end when He ascended. Rather, He associated others by ordaining them to continue his mission to the ends of the earth. God wanted to associate us and does associate us with His work of salvation.[58] This is why He has chosen to give gifts to us. These include gifts through us and for others. God wants to grace others in response to our prayers, our sacrifices, our sanctified actions. God became incarnate so that He could mediate salvation not merely to us, but through us. In doing so, he bonds us to Him in likeness.

One could ask, why call this merit? The term merit sounds like we do it without any fundamental dependence on God. It is a valid question. Much of the confusion, I think, is rooted in understanding what is meant by merit, and with the incredible proposal that God wants to associate us in his work of salvation. The Catechism lays out the meaning of merit, which will help to brush away at least some of the confusion:

> The term "merit" refers in general to the recompense owed by a community or a society for the action of one of its members, experienced either as beneficial or harmful, deserving reward or punishment. Merit is relative to the virtue of justice, in conformity with the principle of equality which governs it.[59]

God giving a recompense, especially in a manner in which He created or caused it to be owed, in response to an action, allows that action to be called meritorious. Notice that recompense is related to the action, but not to the source and power of the action. It may be due to the immediate power of the subject of the action. It may be due to the special power of action given to the actor. Also, it does not specify how the action is related to the recompense. Rather, it is a recompense given because a certain action has taken place. It does not say that the action causes the recompense. In fact, it is clearer that the recompense is a power of the community or society. Furthermore, it does not say whether there is an intrinsic link between the nature of the action and that of the recompense. It could be a link that is fitting, or it could be one that is owed. Finally, it could be a recompense that is beneficial or harmful.

So when we speak of merit in Catholic circles, the society that bestows the recompense is that centered first and foremost in the Holy Trinity, then surrounded by the company of angels and saints, and by the pilgrim Church on earth. The center of that society—namely the Holy Trinity—is the cause of the recompense. It also is the cause of the state of the soul of the individual who acts. It is the cause that constitutes an individual as a son or daughter of God the Father. It is the cause of the interior sanctity that allows one to be rightly ordered to God. Likewise, if God wants to sanctify and justify these individuals in such a manner as to then include them in the work of salvation, then it is so. And if God promises such a manner, then it will happen. Thus, God can make individuals and even communities into actors whose actions become meritorious in justice. All of this fits with the meaning of merit. Thus, a prayer is meritorious. Sacraments are meritorious. Works of faith are meritorious. Living a moral life in Christ is meritorious. God has promised recompense to certain human actions, and certain human actions, especially those elevated in sanctity, are owed the recompense. The sacraments are the principal examples. The beatitudes promise eternal life. Of course, harmful actions are also meritorious, and God makes promises about these as well. Dying in mortal sin merits eternal damnation. But dying in his love merits eternal salvation.

Summary

The Catholic account of the unity of sanctification and justification, both initially and as both grow throughout one's life, is central to our understanding of how God is uniting us to him. He wants us to be like Him, to be divinized. He wants us to be brothers and sisters to His Son. With His Son, He sends the Holy Spirit to awaken us, to give us a heart of flesh, to convert and transform us so that we might become His sons and daughters by adoption. And then He associates us in this work of salvation. Just as His Son was born of a woman, so we are born of His bride. Just as his Son suffered severely, so we must pick up His cross. Just as the Father sent His Son into the world with their Holy Spirit to justify and sanctify, so He wants us to become like them, associates in the work of His salvation. All of this is so that we might become like the Son, so that we might become His and He ours.

Notes

1   The *Catechism of the Catholic Church* (*CCC*) has a rich account of sanctification and justification because it permeates nearly every facet of the text. The reason for this, of course, is that sanctification and justification are central to understanding the mystery of the human person and the destiny that God has for the whole of history. Though nearly all of the references in this essay point to the *CCC*, it is important to remember that these in turn are usually based upon Scripture and Tradition. In some of the other pieces that will be presented by Catholics at this dialogue, you will encounter some of the explicit scriptural and traditional sources of the Catholic understanding of sanctification and justification.

2   Council of Trent, DS 1528.

3 *Catechism of the Catholic Church* (CCC), 1806.
4 Augustine, *The Soliloquies*, l, 4.
5 Augustine, *De Trinitate*, books 8 – 10.
6 As St. Thomas notes, we are potentially the entire universe of being (ST Q. 79, a.2). Combine this with a formulation of indwelling along the lines of the known dwelling in the knower and the beloved dwelling in the lover, then one can understand how when we know something it can dwell in us both as known and as loved, and when loved properly, then it dwells in a spiritual home. Some theologies of creation draw this out, especially when reflecting upon the creation psalms.
7 *CCC* 358.
8 *CCC* 27.
9 *CCC* 50.
10 *CCC* 1995.
11 Augustine, *Confessions*, book 1, chapter 1.
12 Mortal sin destroys the graced heart and venial sin harms it and leads to its destruction.
13 *CCC* 407.
14 *CCC* 2566.
15 *CCC* 1264, 1426.
16 *CCC* 375.
17 *CCC* 400.
18 *CCC* 37.
19 *CCC* 400-401.
20 Ps. 51:5; *CCC* 404.
21 Gen. 4; *CCC* 401, 2259.
22 Augustine, *City of God*, book 15, chapters 1-17.
23 Gen. 11; *CCC* 57.
24 *CCC* 1739.
25 *CCC* 37.
26 *CCC* 410.
27 *CCC* 1962, 2072.
28 *CCC* 1963.
29 *CCC* 1965.
30 *CCC* 422.
31 *CCC* 1476.
32 *CCC* 412.
33 *CCC* 1701-1708.
34 *CCC* 1020, 1023-1025.
35 *CCC* 404.
36 Council of Chalcedon (A.D. 451). DS, 301.
37 *CCC* 2853.
38 *CCC* 1742.
39 *CCC* 1972.

40 *CCC* 1265-66.
41 *CCC* 978.
42 *CCC* 1272-74.
43 *CCC* 1446, 1468.
44 *CCC* 1391-95.
45 *CCC* 1303.
46 *CCC* 1521.
47 *CCC* 1523.
48 *CCC* 759.
49 *CCC* 1655-57.
50 *CCC* 761-62.
51 *CCC* 772-73.
52 John Paul II, *Apostolic Constitution Fidei Depositum*, sec. 3. This document, found at the beginning of the *CCC*, formally introduces the *CCC*.
53 *CCC* 2010.
54 *CCC* 2009.
55 *CCC* 1996.
56 *CCC* 2008.
57 *CCC* 2011.
58 *CCC* 2008.
59 *CCC* 2006.

Background Paper

Engrafted into Christ: Sanctification and the Transformative Power of Grace in the Catholic Tradition

Dr. Christian D. Washburn

MANY OF THE COMMUNIONS that are a result of the Protestant Reformation draw a rather sharp distinction, without separation, between justification and sanctification,[1] with justification seen as a discrete and completed act and sanctification seen as a progressive process in which one is more conformed to God's will. This sharp distinction was intended in part to protect the absolute gratuity of justification. Catholic doctrine, on the other hand, sees justification as a process in which one is initially sanctified through the infusion of grace that can be increased and even lost. In sanctification, one not only has grace infused into him but also is "engrafted" into Christ, becoming a living member of Him.[2] This engrafting and sanctification are a radical transformation of the whole human person and make possible a whole range of activities, including fulfilling the law and meriting heaven.[3] This essay will explain the nature of justification as an ongoing process capable of increase. It will then discuss the possibility of good works, Christ as a lawgiver, the relationship between law and Gospel, and man's ability to fulfill the law. Finally, this essay will address the notion of merit, its objects, and its conditions.

The Relationship between Justification and Sanctification and the Inequality of Justification

In its broad outlines Lutheran and Reformed theology of justification is consistent with the Catholic doctrine of initial justification as described by the magisterium. For both traditions, initial justification is entirely gratuitous and not dependent in any way on those works, including faith, that precede justification; however, the difference between the Catholic doctrine of an inhering habitual righteousness and the Protestant insistence on a merely imputed righteousness in initial justification leads to very divergent views about the distinction between justification and sanctification. The Council of Trent described initial justification as

> a transition from that state in which a person is born as a child of the first Adam to the state of grace and of adoption as children of God through the agency of the second Adam, Jesus Christ our savior; indeed, this transition, once the gospel has been promulgated, cannot take place without the waters of rebirth or the desire for them, as it is written: Unless a person is born again of water and the Holy Spirit, he cannot enter the kingdom of God.[4]

It should be recalled from my last essay that this initial justification has two aspects. The first aspect is the forgiveness of sins, which entails that men are made, not merely imputed, "innocent, immaculate, pure, guiltless and beloved sons of God."[5] The second aspect is "the sanctification and renewal of the inner man" (*sanctificatio et renovatio interioris hominis*).[6] Sanctification, then, is simply that part of justification in which God transforms the sinner internally, constantly sustaining him so that the justified man is a new creation who is both gifted and, by living the life that Christ wills for all men, able to obtain the reward of eternal life. Trent is clear that this transformation in man occurs through the infusion of inhering righteousness or sanctifying grace, which it holds is the "sole formal cause of justification."[7]

Lutheran and Reformed theologians have generally argued that the grace of justification is given in equal measure to all the justified. This is based on the teaching that all men are justified by faith alone through the external justice of Christ, which is the same in all Christians.[8] The Catholic Church, on the other hand, has explicitly and dogmatically taught that one's justification and sanctifying grace admit of degrees.[9] Thus the Council of Trent solemnly taught in its *Decree on Justification* that even our initial justification is unequal: "we are truly called and are just, receiving justice within us, each one according to his own measure,...and according to each one's own disposition and cooperation."[10] Trent went on in Chapter 10, entitled "Concerning the Increase of Justification Received," to affirm that the justified can increase their justification.[11] In Canon 24, the council condemned those who say "justice received is not preserved and also not increased in the sight of God through good works but that those same works are only the fruits and signs of justification received, but not a cause of its increase."[12]

Why does the Catholic Church see an unequal distribution of grace as possible? Catholic theology has generally found the basis for this teaching in five things. First, the Scriptures repeatedly affirm that grace either may be increased or is greater in one than in another. The Scriptures are clear that grace can be increased: "But the path of the righteous is like the light of dawn, which shines brighter and brighter until full day"[13]; "But grow in the grace and knowledge of our Lord and Savior Jesus Christ. To him is the glory both now and to the day of eternity"[14]; "Truly, I say to you, among those born of women there has risen no one greater than John the Baptist; yet he who is least in the kingdom of heaven is greater than he."[15] Other Scriptures affirm that love may be increased and is greater in one than another: Christ affirmed that Peter had a greater love than others[16]; so, too, the woman who anointed Christ's feet: "Therefore I tell you, her sins, which are many, are forgiven, for she loved much; but he who is forgiven little, loves little."[17]

Second, God is free to distribute grace to whom He wants and in the measure He wishes.[18] The Scriptures affirm that the Holy Spirit "distributes to everyone as he wills"[19]. Elsewhere, Paul wrote, "But to every one of us is given grace, according to the measure of the giving of Christ."[20] Aquinas commented on this verse, saying, "This grace, however, is certainly not bestowed on everyone uniformly and equally but *according to the measure of the giving of Christ.*"[21] In order to illustrate the absolute sovereignty of God with respect to the distribution of grace, Aquinas used a rather startling analogy in which God is compared to a potter and man to clay: "However much the clay is prepared, it does not necessarily receive its shape from the potter. Hence, however much a man prepares himself, he does not necessarily receive grace from God."[22]

Third, grace is received according to the disposition of the individual.[23] According to Aquinas, "adults, who approach Baptism in their own faith, are not equally disposed to Baptism; for some approach thereto with greater, some with less, devotion."[24]

Fourth, Catholic theology sees grace as a *superadditum* that is accidental to man's nature, and an accidental feature may be increased or decreased.[25] Substantial natures such as man cannot be more or less, since they define what a thing is. Any addition or subtraction with regard to substantial nature entails a change of species. Subtracting a rational soul from man entails that that animal is changed into another type of creature, in this case a primate, and adding a soul to a primate changes it into a man. Adding or subtracting accidents from a substantial nature does not entail a change in species but only changes the disposition of a substance in which they inhere. Virtues are a type of accident, and whether one has more or less of a particular virtue—take bravery, for example—only entails that one is more or less brave. If one is not brave at all but instead timorous, one does not cease to be a man. So too is it with grace: an increase or decrease in grace only makes better men or worse men; even without supernatural grace one is still a true man.[26]

Fifth and lastly, the inequality of justification is further confirmed by the fact that the Church teaches that the sacraments of the New Law, unlike those of the Old Law, can be the instrumental causes (*causae instrumentales*) of both our initial justification and an increase in this justification; the Church teaches further that the sacraments both contain and confer grace.[27] In describing the sacraments as causes, the Church is not committing herself to a particular school of thought on causality, but she wishes to make it clear that sacraments are neither merely occasions nor conditions for the conferral of grace;[28] instead they are proper causes so that grace is conferred "in virtue of the act performed" (*ex opera operato*). So baptism confers justification, the sacrament of confirmation increases one's grace and strengthens one in faith, and the Eucharist increases grace "among those who receive it worthily."[29] Clearly then, if the sacraments can increase the grace of justification already received, then the grace of justification must be unequal in at least some of the justified.

The Necessity of Good Works: Law and Gospel

The difference between Catholic theology and Reformed and Lutheran theology concerning justification is not only an anthropological one, as is sometimes maintained;[30] it is more fundamentally the difference of two competing views of the nature of Christianity itself. Luther introduced into Reformation thought a radical separation of law and Gospel that was subsequently advanced as doctrine in the Lutheran confessional documents[31] and taken up in a modified form by the Reformed tradition.[32] For these theologians, law and Gospel (*stricte dicta*) are not just distinct concepts but also antithetical.[33] The Gospel, understood in the strict sense, does not demand one's works or command one to do anything; it bids one simply receive the offered grace of the forgiveness of sins and eternal salvation.[34] Therefore, these theologians have been reluctant to see Christ as a lawgiver and a new Moses who perfects the Old Law.[35]

In response, the Council of Trent defined that Christ was a "lawgiver" and anathematized those who taught that the Gospel is "a mere absolute promise of eternal life, without the condition of observing the commandments."[36] Furthermore, it presented law and Gospel as not antithetical, for the Gospel contains within itself the law of Christ, which reveals the divine will for man. For Catholic theology the Gospel is the totality of the preaching of Christ and the Apostles. In the Gospel, Bellarmine writes, "one can find everything that opponents reserve only to the law, that is to say...laws in the proper sense, threats made to those who disobey them, and promises to those who obey them."[37]

Christ acted as a lawgiver in several different ways. First, he acted as a lawgiver by authoritatively confirming the law. Thus St. John Paul II affirmed that "from the very lips of Jesus, the new Moses, man is once again given the commandments of the Decalogue. Jesus himself definitively confirms them and proposes them to us as the way and condition of salvation. The commandments are linked to a promise."[38] Second, Christ perfected the Old Law with respect to three elements: mysteries which must be believed, promises in which to hope, and precepts to be obeyed.[39] Thus Christ in His Gospel gave us, for example, not only a more perfect understanding of the Trinity but also a whole new series of beliefs. Thus Christ ordained that the Christian must believe with an act of faith certain teachings, including: 1) the articles of faith found in the Creed; 2) the various

Christological dogmas; 3) the Marian dogmas; 4) the doctrine of the institution of the sacraments by Christ and their efficacy with regard to grace; 5) the real and substantial presence of Christ in the Eucharist; 6) the sacrificial nature of the Eucharistic celebration; 7) the foundation of the Church by the will of Christ; 8) the primacy and infallibility of the Roman Pontiff; 9) the existence of original sin; 10) the immortality of the spiritual soul; 11) the immediate recompense after death; and 12) the absence of error in the inspired sacred texts.[40] Furthermore, Christ replaced the promise of earthly goods with the promise of spiritual goods such as eternal life to the obedient.[41] It is true that Christ made the observation of the ceremonial law easier and its signification clearer,[42] for example by abolishing the ceremonial law. He also then added new ceremonies to be followed, such as the seven sacraments. Finally, Christ acted as a lawgiver when He corrected the Old Law. Thus Our Lord corrected the Mosaic Law[43], for example, when He unequivocally forbade an absolute divorce (*divortium perfectum*).[44] For Christ, death alone can sever the marriage bond, and adultery and willful desertion are not grounds for an absolute divorce, though they are accepted by some Protestant theologians.[45]

Christ also repeatedly offered both promises of reward as well as threats of punishment to all those who either obey or disobey His perfected laws respectively. He stated, for example, that "every tree that bringeth not forth good fruit, shall be cut down, and shall be cast into the fire."[46] Christ insisted, for example, upon the necessity of obedience ("if thou wilt enter into life, keep the commandments") and the necessity of faith ("He who believes and is baptized will be saved; but he who does not believe will be condemned").[47]

Most importantly, the new Moses, Christ, was not only a lawgiver but also the Redeemer who gave the New Law the power to justify.[48] Fundamentally, the Old Law in itself does not have the power to justify; it only helps us understand human misery and makes us desire our physician, Christ, and His Gospel.[49] The Old Law came without the means to accomplish it, but the New Law comes with the grace to accomplish it. The Mosaic Law, for example, merely instructed the Jews how to distinguish between vices and virtues; but the Gospel both contains correct teaching with respect to virtue and vice and also provides the grace to become virtuous. In this way Christ made Christian marriage indissoluble, but He also made it a sacrament that instrumentally confers both sanctifying grace and those sacramental graces necessary to live this Christian marriage. For Catholic theology, then, Christ is more than a lawgiver, but He is nevertheless a lawgiver; this is a salutary reminder that Christ's kingly office of lawgiver cannot be collapsed simply into His priestly office of propitiator or savior.

There are two fundamental elements that lead to the possibility of the justified Christian actually fulfilling the law. First, as St. Augustine wrote in a beautiful sentence that was adopted by the Council of Trent: "For God does not command impossibilities, but by commanding admonishes you both to do what you can do, and to pray for what you cannot do, and assists you that you may be able."[50] Since God does not command the impossible, one can conclude that the just can and must fulfill the law. Second, the justified man is a new creation, and this new objective condition, accomplished by the infusion of sanctifying grace, leads not only to the possibility but even to the necessity of observing the commandments for salvation. Indeed, Trent anathematized those who teach that "the commandments of God are impossible to observe even for the man who is justified."[51] Thus Bellarmine, for example, held that it is

> absolutely possible for a just man to observe the law of God, not, as the heretics falsely allege against us, by the mere strength of our free will, but by the help of the grace of God, of the spirit of faith, and of charity infused into us with justification.[52]

Although the unregenerate cannot be justified by works, the justified Christian can be further justified by good works so that he may be made "more righteous."[53] The just are able to grow toward perfection, and although at times the good works of the just are mixed with venially sinful works, this does not hinder them from attaining greater justification. Moreover, Catholic theologians hold that with the help of God's grace, not only is it possible to observe the law, it is also easy. They draw upon the Scriptures to support Christ's teaching, highlighting those places in the New Testament where He repeatedly testified to this point: "For my yoke is easy, and my burden is light" and "His commandments are not grievous."⁵⁴ Moreover, the Scriptures teach that "many" have kept the commandments, especially the command to love God with the whole heart and the command not to covet.⁵⁵ Yet another argument presented by theologians is that since man is able to do more than what God commands him—for example, observing the beatitudes—*a fortiori* he can fulfill the commandments.⁵⁶ Finally, Christ has taught us to pray: "Thy will be done, on earth as in heaven."⁵⁷ To insist that the law cannot be fulfilled is to say that Christ failed to obtain what He wanted, so that we pray daily in vain. If this were the case, God's will would never actually be done on earth as it is in heaven.⁵⁸

The Catholic Concept of Merit

Given the aforesaid, it is clear that the Lutheran and Reformed theologians could hardly affirm a doctrine of merit. Luther, in his more colorful moments, called the doctrine of merit "the theology of the antichristian kingdom"⁵⁹ and the "tricks of Satan."⁶⁰ These theologians argued that merit, understood as a right to a reward, presupposes that man can make a claim on God in justice, and they object that God is not a debtor to any person.⁶¹ In response, the Council of Trent defined that

> If anyone shall say that the good works of the man justified are in such a way the gifts of God that they are not also the good merits of him who is justified, or that the one justified by the good works, which are done by him through the grace of God and the merit of Jesus Christ (whose living member he is), does not truly merit increase of grace, eternal life, and the attainment of that eternal life (if he should die in grace), and also an increase of glory: let him be anathema [cf. n. 803 and 809].⁶²

It will be helpful to break this canon down into its constituent pieces to understand what the council intended.⁶³ First, the subject of the canon is the "justified man" who, by his justification, has become a member of Christ. Trent rejected any view that simply reduces our justice to the justice of Christ; however, the council was clear that "our justice" is not "considered as coming from us." It is precisely the infusion of sanctifying grace and the engrafting into Christ that makes one able to merit. Moreover, aside from sanctifying grace, the decree makes it clear that Christ's influence always "precedes, accompanies, and follows" the good actions of a justified man.[64]

Second, the Council Fathers anathematized those who say that merits are understood merely as the gift of God. The Fathers deliberately phrased this canon in Augustinian terminology.[65] Both Luther and Seripando had suggested that merits were not properly the merits of the one justified but rather were imputed to him from Christ. Canon 32 is quite clear that each merit is truly and properly "the good merits of him (*ipsius*) who is justified" and thus the result of the activity of the agent. This teaching is a corollary to Chapter 16's assertion that even the justice one receives in justification is not only "called ours" but is even "our own personal justice" since it inheres in us.[66]

Third, one should note the use of the phrase "truly merit," *vere mereri*. The Fathers of Trent almost without exception were convinced that the merit inherent in good works is a true *meritum*, based upon divine justice. They purposely employed the term *vere* to exclude the *quasi* merit, which, in the technical terminology of the Schools, is called *meritum de congruo*. They simply refrained from using the term *meritum de condigno* because *meritum verum* is "a plain and adequate term," and they thereby avoided certain theological controversies regarding the nature of *meritum de condigno* and its requisites.[67] This phrase is even more significant when one recalls that it was used prior to the Reformation against the Scotists, whose "*mereri* was not *vere mereri*."[68]

Some Catholic ecumenists, such as Pesch, have argued that the Tridentine doctrine of merit can be done away with and replaced with the original biblical concept of reward. Merit for Pesch is simply a concept that was introduced into theology in the post-biblical period.[69] The Tridentine concept of merit, however, cannot simply be collapsed into the concept of reward without making the council say something that it certainly did not intend to say. The concepts are not univocal but correlative, for as Bellarmine explained, a reward is that which is rendered to merit.[70] Reward and merit cannot be read as synonyms in the conciliar text. The council used the term "merit" in four crucial places: twice as a noun and twice as a verb. If we were to conflate the two concepts, then Chapter 16 would absurdly read, the justified "can also be regarded as having truly rewarded eternal life." And Canon 32 would read, "The justified truly rewards an increase of grace, eternal life." One can immediately see the absurd and Pelagian reading of Trent that one would be forced into, whereby man now is the agent rewarding some unknown subject.

In order to clarify what Trent was attempting to define, it is useful to compare it to the Council of Nicaea. The use of the term "merit" is analogous to the Council of Nicaea's use of the non-biblical term consubstantial (*homoousios*) for Christ in order to explain precisely the correct meaning of revelation. What was being disputed in the controversy over merit was in part the meaning of the term "reward" as used in the Scriptures. All parties in the dispute, whether Protestants, adherents of double justice, or opponents of double justice, used the term "reward" but without any agreement as to the meaning of the substance of the doctrine. So Trent used the extra-biblical term "merit" not simply because it had come to be used in the Schools but also because it wanted to define more precisely what was meant by the biblical concept of "reward."

Moreover, the Council of Nicaea added the term "true" in the phrase "true God from true God," just as Trent added "true" to merit. At Nicaea, the Council Fathers deemed this necessary in order to ensure that the Arian interpretation of the phrase "God from God" would be rejected. By adding "true" to God, the council ensured that the term "God" was not only being used univocally but being used in the strict sense. As in the Arian controversy, where all parties could happily call Jesus God as long as the sense of the term God was left ambiguous, so both Protestants and the adherents of double justice could equally use the term "merit" as long as it was not a merit grounded at least in part in justice.[71] Like Nicaea, Trent added the term "true" as a modifier of merit in an attempt to ensure that the term merit would be used in the strict sense.

This usage of the term is not merely by way of comparison to another council but is also clear from the debates above and is confirmed by the council's other and frequent usages of *verum*. The council, for example, in its *Decree on Original Sin*, denied that concupiscence is truly and properly (*vere et proprie*) sin.[72] Man is described as "truly (*vere*) justified" in contradiction to a merely imputed justification.[73] The seven sacraments are "truly and properly (*vere et proprie*)" sacraments, to distinguish Catholic doctrine from that of many Protestants, who were willing to call sacraments those things that they did not recognize in a broad sense.[74] "True" water must be used in baptism against those who thought that John 3 was to be understood metaphorically.[75] In the Eucharist are contained "truly (*vere*), really and substantially" the body and blood together with the soul and divinity of Jesus.[76]

Certain Catholic ecumenists have suggested that Trent's doctrine of merit is an "eschatological statement about grace" rather than a "practical-ethical thought."[77] This is clearly a false dichotomy. It is true that the reward for merit is beatitude, but this eschatological reality is the end of merit rather than merit as such. This is clear from the fact that merit is not merely an "eschatological statement about grace" since it occurs *in this life*. Second, merit occurs through the conformity of the justified's life to the law of Christ, in whom the justified has been engrafted. Merit therefore has a decidedly practical-ethical dimension, since, according to the council, heaven is rewarded in part on account of one's obedience to the commandments.

In Canon 32 Trent specified the true and proper objects of merit. First, one may merit an increase in grace; second, one may merit eternal life; and finally, one may merit an increase in glory.[78] Catholic theologians often look to biblical passages, such as this claim from Paul, to support this understanding: "I have fought the good fight, I have finished the race, I have kept the faith. Now there is in store for me the crown of righteousness, which the Lord, the righteous Judge, will award to me on that day—and not only to me, but also to all who have longed for His appearing."[79] Here we see the actual eschatological significance of merit, which has as its end not merely a good work but a good work that is ordered to attaining eternal beatitude. It must be recalled that according to Catholic doctrine, one may not merit the initial actual grace, initial justification, restoration from a fall due to mortal sin, or final perseverance. God's activity always precedes that of man's.

Catholic theologians generally enumerate seven conditions necessary to accomplish a meritorious work. Four of these have reference to the meritorious work itself, two to the agent who performs it, and one to God, who gives the reward.[80] The first four, namely, that the work must be morally good, done with a free will, done to honor and serve God, and be accompanied by actual grace, are obvious and universally admitted by Catholic theologians. For an act to be morally good, the following three conditions must obtain. First, the object of the act must be good.[81] Second, the end or the intention of the agent must be good. Third, its circumstances must be good. For an action to be good, it must be good in every respect, and if any of these three are evil, the act as such is evil, thus the expression, "A thing to be good must be wholly so; it is vitiated by any defect" (*Bonum ex integra causa, malum ex quocumque defectu*). Thus some acts are always intrinsically evil; these include abortion, homosexual acts, contraceptive acts, adultery, fornication, lying, and drunkenness.[82] Neither a good intention nor a good set of circumstances can ever render these intrinsically evil acts good, and as such there is no set of circumstances under which they would be meritorious before God. These acts always "remain 'irremediably' evil acts; per se and in themselves they are not capable of being ordered to God and to the good of the person.... Consequently, circumstances or intentions can never transform an act intrinsically evil by virtue of its object into an act 'subjectively' good or defensible as a choice."[83] So too a bad intention or bad circumstance always renders even an intrinsically good act evil.

Second, the act must be a human act (*actus humanus*) done with free will. The act must be free from natural necessity arising from an intrinsic principle or from an extrinsic principle. If an act is done without a free will, then it cannot be described as a moral act. That free will is necessary for a reward is clear from biblical texts regarding merit, which assume that works do not have to be done and are therefore voluntary.[84] For example, many things, such as the sun, vineyards, gardens, and beasts of burden, all actively provide goods to man; none of these, however, merit a reward from man because they act without freedom. So too an act of man that is not a human act, such as digesting or breathing, cannot be meritorious because one does not usually choose to breathe or digest food. Equally, evil acts, if they are done without freedom, deserve no punishment, since they would not be morally evil acts; for the same reason, good works done without freedom do not deserve a reward.[85]

Third, the meritorious act must not only be done with a morally good intention, but must be done with the intention to honor and serve God. Fourth, the work must be accomplished with the help of actual grace.[86] Actual grace is simply a transient divine assistance that enables man to enlighten the mind or strengthen the will to perform supernaturally good works that lead to heaven. This grace must also precede, accompany, and follow a good work for it to be a meritorious work.

There are two conditions for merit that pertain to the agent who performs it. First, the act must be accomplished by a man who is a wayfarer. Catholic doctrine is clear in teaching that death is the end of the probationary period in which one can either merit or demerit. Theologians have generally argued that this must be the end of the probationary period, since the human soul undergoes judgment immediately after death.[87] Second, Catholics understand that being in the state of grace is absolutely necessary for merit. By the state of grace Catholics mean that only those who are justified may merit. This was affirmed dogmatically at Trent, and as we saw above, is taken to be based on scriptural texts such as in John 15:4: "No branch can bear fruit by itself; it must remain in the vine. Neither can you bear fruit unless you remain in me. I am the vine; you are the branches. If you remain in me and I in you, you will bear much fruit; apart from me you can do nothing." This engrafting into Christ is considered in part the *sine qua non* of merit.

Lastly, and most importantly, there must be a promise from God to accept good acts as worthy of heaven. The Council of Trent described eternal life "as a reward promised by God Himself."[88] St. Pius V explicitly condemned Baius' proposition that denied that a special promise of God was necessary for the works of the righteous to deserve eternal life: for him, "Just as an evil work by its nature is deserving of eternal death, so a good work by its own nature is meritorious of eternal life."[89] In the Scriptures God often promises man an eternal reward for his works and eternal punishment for his mortal sins. Moreover, good works, if we consider only their nature, have no proportion to the supernatural beatitude. As St. Thomas explained, "If it is considered as regards the substance of the work, and inasmuch as it springs from the free-will, there can be no condignity because of the very great inequality."[90] This beatitude cannot therefore be due in justice to morally good works. God has no need of our works, and all good works are due to Him by virtue of His right of creation. He is not therefore obliged to grant them a reward.[91] Nonetheless, God can and does bind Himself to His own promises.

Loss of One's Justification

For the Christian, one's justification and sanctification are not only capable of growth, they can also be lost through mortal sin.[92] The Council of Trent defined "that the grace of justification, once received, is lost not only by unbelief, which causes the loss of faith, but also by any other mortal sin, even though faith is not lost."[93] It went on to anathematize those who "say that a man once justified can sin no more, nor lose grace, and that therefore he who falls and sins was never truly justified."[94] Mortal sin is simply a type of actual sin denominated according to its effects, i.e., the loss of friendship with God. This teaching is based on biblical texts such as 1 John, which clearly teaches, "If anyone sees his brother commit a sin that does not lead to death, he should pray and God will give him life. I refer to those whose sin does not lead to death. There is sin that leads to death. I am not saying that he should pray about that. All wrongdoing is sin, and *there is sin that does not lead to death.*"[95] John clearly taught that some sin does not lead to death. For a sin to be mortal, the matter must be grave, the sinner must exercise full consent to the sinful act, and he must understand that the act is sinful.

Venial sin, on the other hand, is an offense against God that does not cause the soul to lose friendship with God but that merits some sort of temporal punishment. Nonetheless, venial sin does not decrease the amount of sanctifying grace that one has. If it could, one would be in the position of saying that a sufficient number of venial sins would gradually diminish grace until it disappears. Instead, the evil effect of venial sin is indirect. By committing venial sins, man weakens his willpower, and temptation eventually grows so strong as to make mortal sin inevitable.[96]

Knowledge of One's Justification

The Church dogmatically teaches that no man knows with the certainty of faith whether or not he has sanctifying grace unless he has received a special private revelation from God. The Council of Trent therefore rejected the "vain confidence" of the Protestants, asserting that "just as no pious person should doubt the mercy of God, the merit of Christ, and the virtue and efficacy of the sacraments, so every one, when he considers himself and his own weakness and indisposition, may entertain fear and apprehension as to his own grace, since no one can know with the certainty of faith, which cannot be subject to error, that he has obtained the grace of God."[97] Generally, Catholic theologians have understood Scripture to affirm this. Thus, even St. Paul could say, "I am not aware of anything against myself, but I am not thereby acquitted. It is the Lord who judges me," and "Well, I do not run aimlessly, I do not box as one beating the air; but I pommel my body and subdue it, lest after preaching to others I myself should be disqualified."[98] This lack of certitude is true even of sacramentally baptized infants since it is possible that the infant's baptism was sacramentally invalid.

Nevertheless, the justified Christian can come to a broad moral certainty or the certainty of hope that the grace of justification has been received and continues in him. Catholic theologians have generally offered a number of signs by which we may know with the certainty of hope whether we are justified or not. These include love of spiritual things, contempt for earthly pleasures, zeal and perseverance in doing good, love of good, love of prayer and pious meditation, patience in suffering and adversity, a fervent devotion to the Blessed Virgin, and a frequent reception of the sacraments.[99]

Conclusion

For the Catholic Church, God not only mercifully forgives sins so that sinners become "innocent, immaculate, pure, guiltless and beloved sons of God," but He also transforms sinners internally through the infusion of sanctifying grace, which constantly sustains the justified as a new creation. This transformation of the sinner moreover transforms his acts, so that they may be pleasing to God, thereby allowing for an increase in justification and an increase in grace. That the justified man can act in a way pleasing to God necessarily requires of him obedience to God's laws, as evidenced by Christ's kingly work as lawgiver. This obedience, founded upon the sanctifying grace within his soul and the new relationship with God, who has promised a reward to those who work upon His grace, then merits truly an increase of grace, eternal life, and an increase of glory. Thus the process of justification, with sanctification, comes to perfection.

Notes

[1] The Lutheran formulation of this doctrine is seemingly starker than the Reformed, and this has given Reformed theologians some pause. Nevertheless, Reformed theology has in essence preserved Luther's distinction. Calvin wrote, "Yet we must bear in mind what I have already said, that the grace of justification is not separated from regeneration, although they are things distinct. But because it is very well known by experience that the traces of sin always remain in the righteous, their justification must be very different from reformation into newness of life (cf. Rom 6:4)." John Calvin, *Institutes of the Christian Religion*, 3.21.11, ed. John T. McNeill, trans. Ford Lewis Battles, The Library of Christian Classics, vol. 20 (Philadelphia: The Westminster Press, 1960), 1:739. Calvin, in response to the Council of Trent, was clear that while justification and sanctification are distinct, the one flows from the other. He explains the relationship between the two with the following example: "The light of the sun, though never unaccompanied with heat, is not to be considered heat. Where is the man so undiscerning as not to distinguish the one from the other? We acknowledge, then, that as soon as any one is justified, renewal also necessarily follows: and there is no dispute as to whether or not Christ sanctifies all whom he justifies. It were to rend the gospel, and divide Christ himself, to attempt to separate the righteousness which we obtain by faith from repentance." Calvin, *Antidote of the Council of Trent*, in *Tracts and Treatises* (Grand Rapids: W.B. Eerdmans, 1958), 3:115-116; Charles Hodge, *Systematic Theology* (Grand Rapids: W.B. Eerdmans, 1981), 3:213; Francis Turretin, *Institutes of Elenctic Theology* (Phillipsburg, NJ: P & R Pub., 1992), 2:690; Herman Bavinck, *Reformed Dogmatics*, ed. John Bolt, trans. John Vriend (Grand Rapids: Baker Academic, 2003), 4:249.

[2] Peter Hünermann, Helmut Hoping, Robert L. Fastiggi, Anne Englund Nash, and Heinrich Denzinger, eds., *Compendium of Creeds, Definitions, and Declarations on Matters of Faith and Morals*, 43rd edition (San Francisco: Ignatius Press, 2012) (Hereafter DH), DH 1530. The English edition of Hünermann's Denzinger follows the Neuner Depuis translation of Trent and translates "cui inseritur" as "into whom he is inserted." One wonders what it could mean to be "inserted into Christ." It is true that *inserere* can be rendered as "to insert"; however, Trent was making a biblical point about being engrafted into Christ. For other curious aspects of Hünermann's Denzinger, see Christian D. Washburn, Review of Compendium of Creeds, Definitions, and Declarations on Matters of Faith and Morals. By Hünermann *Nova et Vetera* 12 (2014): 597-600.

[3] This paper seeks to explain the Catholic doctrine on the nature of the process of justification, and it assumes the content of my previous paper, entitled "*Ex inimico amicus*: Catholic Teaching on Initial Justification."

[4] DH 1524/811.

[5] DH 1515. See also the Council of Trent: "Si quis per Iesu Christi Domini nostri gratiam, quæ in baptismate confertur, reatum originalis peccati remitti negat; aut etiam asserit, non tolli totum id, quod veram et propriam peccati rationem habet, sed illud dicit tantum radi aut non imputari: anathema sit." DH 1515. The ongoing presence of sin in the justified is perhaps one of the most contentious issues and one not fundamentally resolved with respect to the JDDJ. It is difficult to see, in light of the clear and infallible teaching of the magisterium, how this issue does not still remain as a church-dividing issue. See *Response of the Catholic Church to the Joint Declaration of the Catholic Church and the Lutheran World Federation on the Doctrine of Justification*, 1; Cardinal Avery Dulles, S.J., "Justification: The Joint Declaration," *Josephinum* 9 (2002): 113.

[6] DH 1528/799. In Canon 11, the Council of Trent anathematized those who claim that initial justification consists in "the remission of sin alone." DH 1561.

7   DH 1530. Christopher J. Malloy, "The Nature of Justifying Grace: A Lacuna in the Joint Declaration," *The Thomist* 62 (2001): 93-120.

8   In his sermon on the nativity of the Blessed Virgin, Luther affirmed, for example, that "all we who are Christians are equally great and holy with the Mother of God." Joseph Pohle, *Grace Actual and Habitual*, adapt. and ed. Arthur Preuss (St. Louis: B. Herder Book Co., 1929), 384. "At remissio peccatorum, similis et sequalis est omnium, sicut unus est Christus et offertur gratis omnibus, qui credunt, sibi propter Christum remissa esse peccata." *Apologia Confessionis Augustanae*, 4:195-196 in *Die Bekenntnischriften der evangelisch-lutherischen Kirche* (Göttingen: Vandehoeck und Rupprecht, 1986), 198. See also, John Theodore Mueller, *Christian Dogmatics: A Handbook of Doctrinal Theology for Pastors, Teachers, and Laymen* (St. Louis: Concordia Publishing House, 1934), 377; Turretin, *Institutes of Elenctic Theology*, 2:686; Robert Lewis Dabney, *Systematic Theology* (Edinburgh: Banner of Truth Trust, 1985), 644; Westminster Assembly, *The Larger Catechism of the Westminster Assembly: With Proofs from the Scripture* (Philadelphia: Presbyterian Board of Publication, 1841), 223.

9   To Catholic theologians, Protestant theology sounds remarkably like the error of Jovian, who attempted to revive the Stoic theory of the absolute equality of all virtue and vice. This is of some significance since Catholic theology has seen sanctifying grace as an entitative habit.

10 DH 1529/799. In response, St. Jerome affirmed that "we read (Ephesians 4:7) 'Unto each one of us was the grace given according to the measure of the grace of Christ': not that Christ's measure varies, but only that so much of His grace is poured out as we can receive." St. Jerome, *Contra Iovinianum*, 2:23 (NPNF-2 6:406).

11 DH 1535.

12 DH 1574.

13 Proverbs 4:18. All biblical quotations taken from the RSVCE.

14 2 Peter 3:18.

15 Matthew 11:11.

16 John 21:15.

17 Luke 7:47.

18 DH 1529/799.

19 1 Cor. 12:11.

20 Eph. 4:7.

21 St. Thomas Aquinas, *Commentary on the Letters of Saint Paul to the Galatians and Ephesians* (Lander, WY: The Aquinas Institute for the Study of Sacred Doctrine, 2012), 272.

22 St. Thomas, *Summa Theologiae*, I-II, q. 112, a. 4, ad 3.

23 DH 1529/799. St. Thomas, *Summa Theologiae*, III, q.68, a.4, co.

24 St. Thomas, *Summa Theologiae*, III, q.69, a.8, co.

25 See my previous paper on this point. Aquinas argued that man's "natural life pertains to man's substance, and hence cannot be more or less; but man partakes of the life of grace accidentally, and hence man may possess it more or less." St. Thomas, *Summa Theologiae*, I-II, q. 112, a. 4, ad 3.

26 It must be stated, however, that graced men (i.e., justified men) are infinitely better men than the non-graced (i.e., unjustified men).

27 DH 1311/695, 1606/849. DH 1529. Calvin rejected the notion of the sacraments as causing grace. He wrote, "The schools of the Sophists have taught with remarkable

agreement that the sacraments of the new law (those now in use in the Christian Church) justify, and confer grace provided that we do not set up a barrier of mortal sin. How deadly and pestilential this notion is cannot be expressed--and the more so because for many centuries it has been a current claim in a good part of the world, to the great loss of the church. Of a certain it is diabolical." *Institutes of the Christian Religion*, 4.16.14, 2:1289.

[28] On the various schools on the nature of sacramental causality, see P. Pourrat, *Theology of the Sacraments; A Study in Positive Theology* (St. Louis: B. Herder, 1910), 93-203; Bernard Leeming, *Principles of Sacramental Theology* (London: Longmans, 1960), 283-383.

[29] DH 695. The council also affirmed that just as "material food and drink" help us to sustain, increase, and restore corporal life, so too the Eucharist greatly strengthens goodness and increases the virtues and the graces of the spiritual life. DH 698. The effect of the sacrament of ordination is also an increase in grace, so that the one ordained may be a worthy minister. DH 701.

[30] Charles Hodge, *Systematic Theology*, 3:242.

[31] "Evangelion vero proprie doctrinam esse censemus, quæ doceat, quid homo credere debeat, qui legi Dei non satisfecit et idcirco per eandem damnatur, videlicet quod illum credere oporteat, Iesum Christum omnia peccata expiasse atque pro iis satisfecisse et remissionem peccatorum, iustitiam coram Deo consistentem et vitam æternam, nullo interveniente peccatoris illius merito, impetrasse." *Epitome* 5, 5, in *Die Bekenntnischriften der evangelisch-lutherischen Kirche*, 790-91.

[32] Andrew J. Bandstra, "Law and Gospel in Calvin and in Paul," in David E. Holwerda and John H. Bratt, *Exploring the Heritage of John Calvin* (Grand Rapids: Baker Book House, 1976), 11-39; Michael Horton, "Calvin on Law and Gospel," *Evangelium* 7 (2009): 16-21; Michael Horton, "Calvin and the Law Gospel Hermeneutic," *Pro Ecclesia* 6 (1997): 27-42; I. John Hesselink, *Calvin's Concept of the Law* (Allison Park, PA: Pickwick Publications, 1992). Hesselink wrote, "Here I can only try to demonstrate that Calvin recognizes as sharp an antithesis between law and gospel as Luther, despite his emphasis on the fundamental unity of the various covenants." I. John Hesselink, "Law and Gospel or Gospel and Law? – Karl Barth, Martin Luther, and John Calvin," *Reformation & Revival Journal* 14 (2005): 153.

[33] Luther wrote, "lex est negatio Christi." WA 40-2, 18.4-5. "Hic iterum videmus Legem et Evangelium quae inter se longissime distincta et plus quam contradictoria separata sunt, affectu coniunctissima esse." *In Epistolam S. Pauli ad Galatas Commentarius*, WA 40-1, 520.25-26. On the issue of law and Gospel, see G. Söhngen, "Gesetz und Evangelium," *Catholica* 14 (1960): 81-105; F. Böckle, *Gesetz und Gewissen: Grundfragen theologischer Ethik in ökumenischer Sicht* (Luzern: Räber Verlag, 1965); Otto Hermann Pesch, "Law and Gospel: Luther's Teaching in the Light of the Disintegration of Normative Morality," *The Thomist* 34 (1970): 84-113.

[34] Luther, WA 36:30–31.

[35] Turretin, *Institutes of Elenctic Theology*, 2:21. Luther WA TR 2:35-37.

[36] DH 1570 and 1571. The issue of law and Gospel has been largely ignored in ecumenical discussions. Dietz Lange, *Überholte Verurteilungen?: die Gegensätze in der Lehre von Rechtfertigung, Abendmahl und Amt zwischen dem Konzil von Trient und der Reformation, damals und heute* (Göttingen: Vandenhoeck & Ruprecht, 1991), 38.

[37] "Nos verò contendimus Evangelio contineri illa omnia, quae adversarii soli legi tribuunt, quae sunt praecipue tria, leges propriè dictae, communicationes, & promissiones cum conditione obedientiae." Robert Bellarmine, *Disputationes Roberti*

Bellarmini Politiani Societatis Jesu, de controversiis Christianae fidei, adversus hujus temporis haereticos (Paris: Triadelphorum, 1613), 15.4.2, vol. 4, 911. On the varied use of the term "gospel," one should consult J.A. Fitzmyer, "The Kerygmatic and Normative Character of the Gospel," in Harding Meyer, ed., *Evangelium, Welt, Kirche: Schlussbericht und Referate der Römisch-katholisch/evangelisch-lutherischen Studienkommission "Das Evangelium und die Kirche", 1967-1971* (Frankfurt am Main: O. Lembeck, 1975), 122-25.

38 John Paul II, *Veritatis splendor* 12. In John Paul II's general audience of October 14, 1987, he stated that Christ "conducted himself as a lawgiver" but not merely with "the authority of a divine envoy or legate, as in the case of Moses." John Paul II, *Jesus, Son, and Savior: A Catechesis on the Creed* (Boston: Pauline Books & Media, 1996), 231-32.

39 The *Catechism* states, "The New Law or the Law of the Gospel is the perfection here on earth of the divine law, natural and revealed....The Law of the Gospel 'fulfills,' refines, surpasses, and leads the Old Law to its perfection." CCC 1965, 1967. Aquinas wrote, "I answer that, as stated above (Article 1), the New Law is compared to the Old as the perfect to the imperfect. Now everything perfect fulfils that which is lacking in the imperfect. And accordingly the New Law fulfills the Old by supplying that which was lacking in the Old Law." *Summa Theologiae*, I-II, q. 107, a. 2; Bellarmine, *De Controversiis*, 15.2.4.3, vol. 4, 916; Gregory of Valencia, *De vera et falsa Differentia verteris et novae legis*, in Gregorio de Valencia, *De rebus fidei hoc tempore controversis libri: qui hactenus extant omnes, cum nonnullis aliis nondum antea editis, ab ipso auctore recogniti, & certa ratione ac methodo distributi, eodemque volumine comprehensi. Catalogum librorum pagina quinta tibi indicabit: additi autem sunt indices duo copiosissimi ; unus locorum Sanctae Scripturae expositorum, alter rerum omnium, quae in opere universo continentur* (Paris: È typographia Rolini Theoderici & Petri Chevalerii, 1610), 174 (1102).

40 CDF, *Doctrinal Commentary on the Concluding Formula of the Professio Fidei*, 11.

41 Bellarmine, *De Controversiis*, 15.2.4.3, vol. 4, 916-17.

42 Ibid., 15.2.4.3, vol. 4, 918.

43 cf Deut. 24:1-4.

44 Mark 10:1-12, Luke 16:18. John Paul II asserted that "the marriage bond has been established by God himself in such a way that a marriage concluded and consummated between baptized persons can never be dissolved. This bond, which results from the free human act of the spouses and their consummation of the marriage, is a reality, henceforth irrevocable, and gives rise to a covenant guaranteed by God's fidelity. The Church does not have the power to contravene this disposition of divine wisdom." Pope John Paul II, "Address to the Roman Rota" (Jan. 21, 2000). St. John Paul added: "[A] ratified and consummated sacramental marriage can never be dissolved, not even by the power of the Roman Pontiff....[Pius XII] presented this doctrine as being peacefully held by all experts in the matter." See John Corbett, O.P. et al., "Recent Proposals for the Pastoral Care of the Divorced and Remarried: A Theological Assessment," *Nova et Vetera* 12 (2014): 601-630.

45 Charles Hodge, *Systematic Theology*, 3:401. With respect to Matthew 19:9, *The Catholic Encyclopedia* explains that "the Catholic Church and Catholic theology have always maintained that by such an explanation St. Matthew would be made to contradict Sts. Mark, Luke, and Paul, and the converts instructed by these latter would have been brought into error in regard to the real doctrine in Christ. As this is inconsistent both with the infallibility of the Apostolic teaching and the inerrancy of Sacred Scripture, the clause in Matthew must be explained as the mere dismissal of the unfaithful wife without the dissolution of the marriage bond." Walter George Smith, "Divorce," *The Catholic Encyclopedia* (New York: The Encyclopedia Press, Inc., 1913), 5:56.

46 Matt. 7:19. Bellarmine, *De Controversiis*, 15.2.4.2, vol. 4, 911-12.

47 Matt. 19:17. Mark 16:16. Bellarmine, *De Controversiis*, 15.2.4.2, vol. 4, 913.

48 Bellarmine, *De Controversiis*, 15.2.4.4, vol. 4, 919.

49 Ibid., 15.2.4.4, vol. 4, 921.

50 DH 1536/804. Augustine, *De natura et gratia*, 43 (PL 44:271).

51 DH 1536. "Dei praecepta homini iustificato ad observandum esse impossibilia." DH 1568.

52 "Fatentur enim PRIMO, legem Dei iustis hominibus absolutè esse possibilem, non quidem per solas vires liberi arbitrii, ut haeretici calumniantur nos dicere, sed per auxilium gratiae Dei, & spiritum fidei, & charitatis in ipsa iustificatione nobis infusum." Bellarmine, *De Controversiis*, 15.2.4.10, vol. 4, 938.

53 Bellarmine, *De Controversiis*, 15.2.4.10, vol. 4, 939.

54 Matt. 11:30. 1 John 2:5. Bellarmine, *De Controversiis*, 15.2.4.11, vol. 4, 939.

55 Bellarmine, *De Controversiis*, 15.2.4.11, vol. 4, 939.

56 Ibid., 15.2.4.13, vol. 4, 943. Here it must be remembered that in Catholic theology the beatitudes are counsels, not commands. *The Catholic Encyclopedia* explains the difference in this way, "Christ in the Gospels laid down certain rules of life and conduct which must be practiced by every one of His followers as the necessary condition for attaining to everlasting life. These precepts of the Gospel practically consist of the Decalogue, or Ten Commandments, of the Old Law, interpreted in the sense of the New. Besides these precepts which must be observed by all under pain of eternal damnation, He also taught certain principles which He expressly stated were not to be considered as binding upon all, or as necessary conditions without which heaven could not be attained, but rather as counsels for those who desired to do more than the minimum and to aim at Christian perfection, so far as that can be obtained here upon earth."Arthur S. Barnes, "Counsels, Evangelical," *The Catholic Encyclopedia*, 4:435. See also Servais Pinckaers, *The Sources of Christian Ethics* (Washington, DC: Catholic University of America Press, 1995), 232.

57 Matt. 6:10.

58 Bellarmine, *De Controversiis*, 15.2.4.13, vol. 4, 944.

59 Luther, *Commentary on the Galatians* (1535), LW 27, 124.

60 Ibid., LW 27, 125.

61 "We cannot by our best works merit pardon of sin, or eternal life at the hand of God, by reason of the great disproportion that is between them and the glory to come; and the infinite distance that is between us and God, whom, by them, we can neither profit, nor satisfy for the debt of our former sins, but when we have done all we can, we have done but our duty, and are unprofitable servants: and because, as they are good, they proceed from His Spirit, and as they are wrought by us, they are defiled, and mixed with so much weakness and imperfection, that they cannot endure the severity of God's judgment." *Westminster Confession* XVI.5. Strikingly, Calvin held that not even Christ's humanity had the capacity to merit, since there "cannot be found in man a worth which could make God a debtor." Calvin, *Institutes*, 2.17.1.

62 "Si quis dixerit hominis iustifati bona opera ita esse dona Dei, ut non sint etiam bona ipsius iustificati merita, aut ipsum iustificatum bonis operibus, quae ab eo per Dei gratiam et Iesu Christi meritum (cuius vivum membrum est) fiunt, non vere mereri augmentum gratiae, vitam aeternam et ipsius vitae aeternae (si tamen in gratia decesserit) consecutionem, atque etiam gloriae augmentum: a.s." DH 1582.

⁶³ On the historical development of Canon 32 at the council, see Christian D. Washburn, "Transformative Power of Grace and Condign Merit at the Council of Trent," *The Thomist* 79 (2015): 173-212.

⁶⁴ DH 1546.

⁶⁵ *DTC*, s.v. "mérite." 759. Augustine on this point is frequently abused on account of a number of statements, usually taken out of context, particularly from his Letter 194. Augustine wrote: "When God crowns our merits, He crowns His own gifts." "Quod est ergo meritum hominis ante gratiam, quo merito percipiat gratiam, cum omne bonum meritum nostrum non in nobis faciat nisi gratia et cum Deus coronat merita nostra, nihil aliud coronet quam munera sua?" (Letter 194, 5.19; CSEL 57.176-214). Some argue that Augustine was quite clear with respect to that merit... "how is eternal life a grace since grace is not repayment for works,...It seems to me, then, that this question can only be resolved if we understand that our good works themselves for which eternal life is our recompense also pertain to the grace of God...." (WSA I/26, 83). Augustine also wrote, "If they understood our merits so that they recognized that they were also gifts of God, this view would not have to be rejected." *On Grace and Free Choice* (426, *De gratia et libero arbitrio*), 6.15. (WSA I/26, 81). Here Augustine was really describing the dual agency that takes place in merit. By affirming that "our merits" are "also" the gifts of God, he did not say that they are exclusively the "gifts of God."

⁶⁶ "Propria nostra iustitia" and "iustitia nostra dicitur." DH 1547.

⁶⁷ Pohle, *Grace, Actual and Habitual: A Dogmatic Treatise*, 407. The various pre-Tridentine theories of condign merit were often quite elaborate and had elements that were distinctive to particular schools of thought. Some emphasized the divine pact and others the good works themselves. Trent sought to avoid resolving questions that were freely debated by the schools. On the various schools prior to Trent, see Bellarmine, *De Controversiis*, 15.2.5.16-22, vol. 4, 1009-22.

⁶⁸ C. Feckes, *Die Rechtfertigungslehre des Gabriel Biel und ihre Stellung innerhalb der nominalistischen Schule* (Münster i.W.: Verlag der Aschendorffschen Verlagsbuchh, 1925), 84, note 251, cited in Hubert Jedin, *Papal Legate at the Council of Trent, Cardinal Seripando*, trans. Frederic Eckhoff (St. Louis, London: B. Herder Book Co., 1947), 364.

⁶⁹ Otto Hermann Pesch, "The Canons of the Tridentine Decree on Justification: To Whom Did They Apply? To Whom Do They Apply Today?" in *Justification by Faith: Do the Sixteenth-Century Condemnations Still Apply?*, 190f; Pesch, "Die Lehre vom 'Verdienst' als Problem fur Theologie und Verkündigung," in *Wahrheit und Verkündigung. Michael Schmaus zum 70. Geburtstag* (München: Schöningh, 1967), 2: 1865-907.

⁷⁰ "At merces, & meritum, relativa sunt: merces enim meritis redditur, sicut gratia gratis datur. Igitur cùm tam saepè, & tam perspicuè praemium operum dicatur merces, dubium esse non debet, quin ipsa opera secundùm morem loquendi Scripturae, rectè dicantur merita." Bellarmine, *De Controversiis*, 15.2.5.2, vol. 4, 970. The *Joint Declaration on the Doctrine of Justification* (1999) must be praised for its preservation of the distinction between merit and reward when it states: "When Catholics affirm the 'meritorious' character of good works, they wish to say that, according to the biblical witness, a reward in heaven is promised to these works." The consensus on the preservation of this distinction is a true ecumenical advancement toward more perfect communion. Dulles noted, however, in his discussion of the JDDJ that "the Joint Declaration softens the opposition by teaching that when Catholics speak of merit they mean that 'a reward in heaven is promised.' This is true enough, but it is incomplete because it fails to say that the reward is a just one. Without reference to justice, the true notion of merit would be

232 | Justified in Jesus Christ

absent." Dulles, "Justification: The Joint Declaration," 115. As the JDDJ acknowledges, it does not "cover all that each church teaches about justification," and my analysis of the Tridentine decree shows that there is more ecumenical work to be done on the doctrine of merit.

71 See footnote 18 above.

72 "Si quis per Iesu Christi Domini nostri gratiam, quae in baptismate confertur, reatum originans peccati remitti negat, aut etiam asserit, non tolli totum id, quod veram et propriam peccati rationem habet, sed illud dicit tantum radi aut non imputari: anathema sit." DH 1515.

73 "Sed neque illud asserendum est, oportere eos, qui vere iustificati sunt," DH 1534.

74 "Si quis dixerit, sacramenta novae legis non fuisse omnia a Iesu Christo Domino nostro instituta; aut esse plura, vel pauciora, quam septem, videlicet baptismum, confirmationem, Eucharistiam, poenitentiam, extremam unctionem, ordinem et matrimonium; aut etiam aliquod horum septem non esse vere et proprie sacramentum: anathema sit." DH 1601.

75 "Si quis dixerit, aquam veram et naturalem non esse de necessitate baptismi, atque ideo verba illa Domini nostri Iesu Christi...: anathema sit." DH 1615.

76 "Si quis negaverit, in sanctissimae Eucharistiae sacramento contineri vere, realiter et substantialiter Corpus et Sanguinem una cum anima et divinitate Domini nostri Iesu Christi, ac proinde totum Christum; sed dixerit, tantummodo esse in eo ut in signo vel figura, aut virtute: anathema sit." DH 1651.

77 Pesch, "The Canons of the Tridentine Decree on Justification," 190.

78 Ibid., 190f.

79 2 Tim. 4:7-8.

80 Joseph Pohle, *Grace: Actual and Habitual: A Dogmatic Treatise*, 410.

81 John Paul II affirmed the fundamental importance of the object of the act when he wrote, "The morality of the human act depends primarily and fundamentally on the 'object' rationally chosen by the deliberate will, as is borne out by the insightful analysis, still valid today, made by Saint Thomas." St. John Paul II, *Veritatis splendor*, n. 78. And Saint Thomas observed that "it often happens that man acts with a good intention, but without spiritual gain, because he lacks a good will. Let us say that someone robs in order to feed the poor: in this case, even though the intention is good, the uprightness of the will is lacking. Consequently, no evil done with a good intention can be excused. 'There are those who say: And why not do evil that good may come? Their condemnation is just' (*Rom* 3:8)." St. John Paul II, *Veritatis splendor*, n. 78.

82 Catholics consider the acts listed by Paul in 1 Cor. 6:9-10 as all intrinsically evil: "⁹ Do you not know that the unrighteous will not inherit the kingdom of God? Do not be deceived; neither the immoral, nor idolaters, nor adulterers, nor sexual perverts, ¹⁰ nor thieves, nor the greedy, nor drunkards, nor revilers, nor robbers will inherit the kingdom of God."

83 St. John Paul II, *Veritatis splendor*, n. 81.

84 Bellarmine, *De Controversiis*, 15.2.5.10, vol. 4, 993.

85 Ibid., 15.2.5.10, vol. 4, 994.

86 Ibid., 15.2.5.10, vol. 4, 993.

87 Leo X condemned the following proposition of Martin Luther: "39. The souls in purgatory sin without intermission, as long as they seek rest and abhor punishments."

DS 779. "De fide...etsi non definita" Franc. X. De Abarzuza, O.F.M. Cap. *Manuale Theologiae Dogmaticae* 2nd ed. (Madrid: Ediciones Studium, 1956), 2:401; Louis Billot, *Quaestiones de novissimis* (Rome: Universitatis Gregorianae, 1946), 9. Garrigou-Lagrange noted, "This common doctrine has not been solemnly defined, but is based on Scripture and tradition." Reginald Garrigou-Lagrange, O.P., *Life Everlasting*, trans. Patrick Cummins, O.S.B. (St. Louis: B. Herder, 1952), 62; J. M. Hervé, *Manuale Theologiae Dogmaticae*. Vol. 4. 16th ed. Westminster MD: The Newman Bookshop, 1943), 553; Sylvester Joseph Hunter, S.J. *Outlines of Dogmatic Theology* (London: Longmans, Green and Co., 1896), 3:427; Bernhard Jungmann, *Tractatus de novissimis* (Ratisbonæ: F. Pustet, 1874), 8; Heinrich Lennerz, *De novissimis* (Rome, Universitas Gregoriana, 1950), 100; Ludwig Ott, *Fundamentals of Catholic Dogma* ed. James Canon Bastible, trans. Patrick Lynch (St. Louis: B. Herder Book Company, 1958), 474-75; Christian Pesch, "*De novissimis hominis,*" *Praelectiones Dogmaticae*, 3rd ed. (Freiburg im Breisgau: B. Herder, 1911), 9:278-280; Joseph Pohle, *Eschatology or the Catholic Doctrine of the Last Things: A Dogmatic Treatise* adapt. and ed. Arthur Preuss (St. Louis: B. Herder Book Co., 1929), 13-17; Iosepho F. Sagüés, S.J. "*De novissimis hominis,*" in Aldama, Iosepho A. de, S.J., Richardo Franco, S.J., Severino Gonzalez, S.J., Francisco A. P. Sola, S.J., Iosepho F. Sagüés, S.J. *Sacrae Theologiae Summa* 4th ed. (Matriti: Biblioteca De Autores Cristianos, 1967), 4:839; George D. Smith, Canon, ed. *The Teaching of the Catholic Church: A Summary of Catholic Doctrine* (New York: The Macmillan Company, 1949), 1:1107; Adolphe Tanquerey, *Synopsis Theologiae Dogmaticae* 27th ed. (Paris: Desclée et Socii, 1953), 3:769.

[88] DH 1545/809.

[89] DH 1902/1002.

[90] St. Thomas, *Summa Theologiae*, I-II, q. 114, a. 3.

[91] Bellarmine, *De Controversiis*, 15.5.14, vol. 4, 1002-03.

[92] Second Council of Lyons: "...The souls of those who die in mortal sin or with original sin only, however, immediately descend to hell, to be punished with different punishments..." (DS 464). Council of Florence: "Moreover, the souls of those who depart in actual mortal sin or in original sin only, descend immediately into hell but to undergo punishments of different kinds." DS 693.

[93] DH 1544.

[94] DH 1573/833.

[95] 1 John 5:21. Italics mine.

[96] Iosepho A. de Aldama, , S.J., Richardo Franco, S.J., Severino Gonzalez, S.J., Francisco A. P. Sola, S.J.,
Iosepho F. Sagues, S.J., *Sacrae Theologiae Summa*, 3:251.

[97] DH 1534/802.

[98] 1 Cor. 4:14. 1 Cor. 9:27.

[99] Thomas Kempis admonished the Christian to "pay diligent heed to the motions of Nature and of Grace, because they move in a very contrary and subtle manner, and are hardly distinguished save by a spiritual and inwardly enlightened man. All men indeed seek good, and make pretense of something good in all that they say or do; and thus under the appearance of good many are deceived." He then offered a number of signs to help the Christian. *Imitation of Christ*, III, 54 ff. See also Thomas Aquinas, *Summa Theologiae*, I-II, q 112, a. 5.

Section 4

Justification and the Final Judgment

This final of four dialogues on justification took place at the University of Mary, Bismarck, North Dakota, March 30 – April 1, 2017. Evangelicals and Catholics examined the relationship of justification to the final end and destiny of the human person and of all creation. The dialogue discussed a number of topics covering what happens at death, purgatory, hell, heaven, the final judgment, and eternal life in a new heaven and new earth.

Common Statement

Justification and the Final Judgment

1. Catholics and Evangelicals affirm that the hope of eternal life is rooted in Christ Jesus, our only Savior.
2. Evangelicals and Catholics affirm that justification has as its goal fellowship with the Triune God and final beatitude to the praise of His glory.
3. Catholics and Evangelicals affirm that the grace we enjoy in this life is the beginning of the bliss that shall be ours eternally.
4. Evangelicals and Catholics affirm that justification in Christ is necessarily directed to a life of good works.
5. Catholics and Evangelicals affirm that the faith that justifies must never remain alone but results in faithful obedience that glorifies God and leads to heavenly rewards. However...
    i. Catholics and some evangelicals affirm that faithful obedience of the justified leads to an increased capacity to enjoy the beatific vision.
6. Evangelicals and Catholics affirm that all who are subject to Original Sin are subject to the law of death; it is given to each person to die but once.

7. Catholics and Evangelicals affirm that immediately after death, a divine judgment takes place that immutably decides the eternal destiny of the dead.

8. Evangelicals and Catholics affirm that for every human being there are only two possible final destinies: heaven or hell.

9. Catholics and Evangelicals affirm that at the final judgement, human beings shall be judged according to the works done in this life. However...

    i. Catholics affirm that the justified individual is able to cooperate with the grace of God in such a way that she or he is able to "merit" the attainment of eternal life, eternal life itself, and an increase in glory.

    ii. Some Evangelicals affirm that works validate one's initial justification, but do not secure anyone's final justification.

    iii. Other Evangelicals hold that in the final judgement each individual will be judged on the basis of his or her works; this judgment will always affirm the anticipatory assurance of salvation in the life of the believer based entirely on faith.

10. Evangelicals and Catholics affirm that the punishment of hell lasts for eternity, affecting both soul and body.

11. Catholics and Evangelicals affirm that those who die in the state of original sin and during life committed actual sin are damned. However...

    i. Catholics affirm that all who die unregenerate, i.e. in a state of original sin alone or mortal sin, are deprived of the beatific vision.

    ii. Some Evangelicals hold that all who die without having been regenerated merit eternal damnation on account of original sin even if they have committed no actual sin.

    iii. Other Evangelicals hold that the commission of actual sins is necessary for damnation.

12. Evangelicals and Catholics affirm that inasmuch as the secrets of all people will be revealed on the last day and their works tested as by fire, even the justified should regard the day of judgement with apprehension and godly fear.

13. **Catholics and Evangelicals affirm that before entering eternal glory, the faithful servant must be cleansed of all unrighteousness. However...**
    i. Catholics affirm that the justified dead who at the moment of death have either venial sin or temporal punishment due to sin enter purgatory. The justified souls in purgatory are certain of their salvation and when their period of purgation is completed they will attain beatitude.
    ii. Nearly all Evangelicals deny the existence of purgatory.
    iii. Some Evangelicals affirm that the doctrine of purgatory is contrary to scripture; others affirm that it is not found in scripture.
14. **Evangelicals and Catholics affirm that those who die in a state of grace will see God face to face for eternity.**
15. **Catholics and Evangelicals affirm that in heaven, all the just from every tribe, tongue, nation, and people will join their voices together in worship of the triune God. However...**
    i. Catholics and some Evangelicals would hold that the degree of glory in eternal life is proportioned to each one's good works.
    ii. Some Evangelicals do not emphasize degrees of glory in heaven, nor the reckoning of varying degrees of reward for one's good works.
16. **Evangelicals and Catholics affirm that all the dead will rise bodily on the last day.**
17. **Catholics and Evangelicals affirm that at the end of this age, Christ will come again in glory to judge the whole human race.**
18. **Evangelicals and Catholics affirm that the righteous dead will rise again with the same bodies, newly glorified, that they had on earth.**

Background Paper

The Relationship between Justification and Final Judgment: A Wesleyan View of Judgment, the Goal of Salvation, and Heaven

Rev. Bruce N.G. Cromwell, Ph.D.

John Wesley was a preacher.[1] He famously traveled an estimated 250,000 miles on horseback in his 87 years of life. Preaching two and sometimes three times a day, he preached, it has been claimed, over 40,000 sermons. With a pastoral zeal emphasizing the transformation of the whole person and a compulsion to reach the whole person whether he or she was in a church, field, or factory, the Methodist movement Wesley began reached across the breadth of Britain and continues to be a growing force within Christianity.[2]

John Wesley was driven by the desire to get people into heaven. But equally, he was driven by the desire to get heaven into people and, one might say, to get hell out of them. He stressed what Catholicism might call "deification" and what Eastern Orthodoxy might term "theosis," the ever-increasing participation of the human in the life of God, becoming more and more truly human as we become more and more like the Divine. He was synergistic in detailing how we cooperate with God in working out our salvation and the renewal of the world, completely dependent on God's grace for our redemption and then performing deeds worthy of that redemption. Wesley's position can be simply stated: We cooperate with God in growing in grace and changing into the likeness of Christ.

John Wesley was not a systematic theologian, but this does not mean that he was unfamiliar with theology. Wesley was a pastoral theologian whose primary vehicle for doing theology was the printed sermon. Wesley was a student at Christ Church, Oxford, and became a fellow and tutor at Lincoln College in the University in 1726. While teaching Greek and lecturing on the New Testament, Wesley immersed himself not only in the Eastern Fathers but also in the works of figures from the West such as Thomas á Kempis, Jeremy Taylor, and William Law. He studied writings from the patristic fathers as well, seeking to vindicate many of the doctrines and practices of the Church of England in which Wesley was raised. Upon completion of his master's degree, he returned to Epworth, where his father had been the parish priest. Following in his footsteps, Wesley was ordained on September 22, 1728.

Because he has had many biographers, the details of the life of John Wesley are easily found, and there is no reason to discuss them in greater length in this paper. For our purposes it is enough to highlight that from an early age, Wesley diligently performed his religious duties, studying and working and striving to seek after holiness of heart and life. He endeavored to put his faith into practice, to make it practical and easily imitated by others. Again, he was a preacher and a pastoral theologian. Any systematic approach to his teaching and thought must therefore be discerned through his sermons, his commentary on the Scripture, and his correspondence with particular people. This creates a somewhat challenging task for the Wesley scholar.

It is possible to articulate what Wesley believed and what has been passed down and often continues to be believed by his spiritual descendants with regards to: 1) the final judgment, 2) the goal of salvation, and 3) the new heaven and new earth. As part of the ongoing Catholic-Evangelical Dialogue it is altogether appropriate to discuss a Wesleyan understanding of 4) purgatory, as unfamiliar and uncomfortable as it may be among Protestants. This paper discusses each of these four elements.

The Final Judgment

Looking primarily at three of Wesley's sermons, "The Great Assize," "The Good Steward," and "Of Hell,"[3] one finds a fairly clear explanation of the judgment to come. The only sermon he delivered in a civil court, "The Great Assize" had as its primary text Romans 14:10: "We shall all stand before the judgment seat of Christ." An "assize" was a civil or criminal trial session held by a judge at specific locations at periodic times across England. According to his journals, Wesley began work on this sermon on February 27, 1758, and preached it 11 days later, seeing the assize as the perfect metaphor to describe the judgment to come.

In the sermon, Wesley compares what happens in an earthly courtroom to what will one day occur at the last judgment, where all of humankind, both the just and the unjust, are judged by God. Wesley's belief in the Trinity is clearly articulated here. God the Father is the Judge of justice. God the Son is the divine Advocate for us all. God the Holy Spirit is the reader of hearts.[4]

It is at this place, in the "Great Assize," that all will stand before God and "the books will be opened, the book of Scripture, to them who were entrusted therewith, the book of conscience to all mankind," and "the book of remembrance," which will be laid open before everyone. This is a frightening thing, Wesley says, for "before the devil and his angels, before an innumerable company of holy angels, and before God the Judge of all, thou wilt appear without any shelter or covering, without any possibility of disguise, to give a particular account of the manner wherein thou hast employed all thy Lord's goods."[5]

Everyone will give an account of their works, "a full and true account" of all that was done, whether good or evil.[6] Beyond this, everyone will give an account for "every idle word" spoken during their lifetime[7] as well as "the very thoughts and intents of the heart."[8] Another of Wesley's sermons, "The Good Steward," gives a litany of questions the Judge will inquire of all:

> How didst thou employ thy soul? ...Didst thou employ thy understanding, as far as it was capable, according to those directions, namely, in the knowledge of thyself and me? ...Didst thou employ thy memory according to my will? In treasuring up whatever knowledge thou hadst acquired which might conduce to my glory, to thy own salvation, or the advantage of others? ...Didst thou give me thy heart? ...Was I the object of thy love? ...Was I the joy of thy heart, the delight of thy soul, the chief among ten thousand?[9]

Beyond giving an account of good deeds, the divine inquiry also includes questions about the interior life, questioning how the intentions of the interior life played out through the will and the senses. How one used his or her tongue to give God praise and whether one spoke in a way that honored God was a primary concern: "Didst thou employ it, not in evil-speaking or idle-speaking, not in uncharitable or unprofitable conversation; but in such as was good, as was necessary or useful, either to thyself or others?"[10] The Lord will ask how we used all of the tools entrusted to our care, including our sight, our hearing, our hands and feet and "various members wherewith to perform the works which were prepared for thee,"[11] as well as our stewardship of the resources and gifts we possessed, our finances, our food, even our clothing. We will be asked if we lived

> Not in gratifying the desire of the flesh, the desire of the eye, or the pride of life? Not squandering it away... not hoarding it up to leave behind thee... but first supplying thy own reasonable wants, together with those of thy family; then restoring the remainder to me, through the poor, whom I had appointed to receive it; looking upon thyself as only one of that number of poor whose wants were to be supplied out of that part of my substance which I had placed in thy hands for this purpose?[12]

If the faithful were able to "present thy soul and body, all thy thoughts, thy words, and actions, in one flame of love, as an holy sacrifice, glorifying me with thy body and thy spirit," then they will hear, as Jesus promised in Matthew 25:21 and 23, "well done, good and faithful servant! Enter thou into the joy of thy Lord!"[13] What Wesley is doing is using the final judgment as a way of examining the whole person through the purview of justification as divine transformation through mercy and grace. Throughout his works, Wesley consistently stresses justification by grace, through faith.[14] This justification, this being made righteous, should then be evident in the life of the believer, should be able to be seen, just as a tree is known by its fruit. Those who trust in the grace of God, given through Christ's atoning sacrifice, will receive a sentence of acquittal and will receive "all the pleasures of heaven," which include "the society of angels, and of the spirits of just men made perfect, the conversing face to face with God your Father, your Saviour, your Sanctifier, and the drinking of those rivers of pleasure that are at God's right hand for evermore."[15]

But not all will be pardoned, for not all have accepted Christ or followed Christ. At this point, Wesley states that a great division will take place. Believers will receive a sentence of acquittal, whereas those who have rejected the unmerited grace freely offered by God will be judged appropriately according to their thoughts, words, and deeds. Wesley describes this latter reality in harsh and horrible terms, consistent with how he sees Scripture discussing the judgment of damnation. "The whole beautiful fabric will be overthrown" by fire, Wesley says, referencing 2 Peter, "the connection of all its parts destroyed, and every atom torn asunder from the others."[16] Individuals will experience this fire, too, which is able to "reduce into glass what by a smaller force it had reduced to ashes."[17] The purpose of this fire is to purify and to ready the creation for the new heavens and the new earth, where God will dwell with His people and God will reign with love.[18]

To Wesley, the Holy Spirit used strong language of complete destruction to rouse persons to repent and to believe, motivating them to change their lives and abstain from evil. Given that Wesley's primary vehicle for practicing theology was the written or printed sermon, his writings on heaven and hell were intended to inspire people to freely accept the gift of grace given through Christ, to allow the Spirit of God to change their lives and, therefore, to be assured of the promise of heaven. All needed to bear in mind the coming judgment. Speaking to those gathered at the assize on March 10, Wesley said that "a few will stand at the judgment seat this day, to be judged touching what shall be laid to their charge.... But we shall all, I that speak and you that hear, stand at the judgment seat of Christ."[19] Everyone needs to be prepared, for sin has consequences. And yet until the last breath is drawn, Wesley is insistent that sin is remediable. Whatever we have done, however unjust we may have been, we are covered by the One who is incomparably just. We have but to receive His free offer of grace.

With such a strong emphasis on the need for one to consider the judgment to come, both to life and to damnation, it is somewhat surprising that Wesley spends relatively little time in his works discussing the nature of that damnation. His focus is consistently on God's just and providential purposes, with minimal talk about the specifics awaiting those who have refused God's grace. However, his sermon "Of Hell" does give some insight into how Wesley views the condition that is not blessed but rather "awful and solemn, suitable to [God's] wisdom and justice."[20] He starts with the premise that "the punishment of those who in spite of all the warnings of God resolve to have their portion with the devil and his angels will, according to the ancient and not improper division, be either *poena damni*, what they lose, or *poena sensus*, what they feel."[21]

What the damned lose in all this is God. Hell is separation from God and loss of what is eternally good. With this separation comes the loss of all pleasures, "the enjoyment of which depends on the outward senses."[22] There is the loss of all things that gave value and meaning to this temporal life, the loss of all persons who were loved, and the greatest loss of all, the loss of the hope of heaven—yet another way of describing the entirety of the judgment upon the whole person. Only then will the damned "fully understand the value of what they have vilely cast away."[23]

What the damned feel is unspeakable torment, caused by the "unquenchable fire" and also by the realization of what has been lost. This promised future for all "impenitent sinners" should serve as a guard "against any temptation from pleasure," for the torment is eternal. "What is the pain of body which you do or may endure, to that of lying in a lake of fire burning with brimstone? What is any pain of mind, any fear, anguish, sorrow, compared to 'the worm that never dieth'? That never dieth!"[24] God will once and for all put an end to all sin. "Change your ways!" Wesley essentially pleads, "so that your sin won't be the end of you as well."

The Goal of Salvation

"Changing one's ways" is indeed the goal of Christ's justifying and sanctifying work in a person. Sin is comprehensive, as is judgment, and affects the entirety of the person—mind, body, soul, and spirit. It is total. And yet it is also both a moral and spiritual infection. It is depravity. Salvation given through Christ, therefore, is a comprehensive cure.[25] Justifying and sanctifying grace does more than simply declare one innocent of sin. It makes one innocent, creating a "dynamic reality of sharing in the divine life." In other words, sanctifying grace transforms us into becoming what we were originally created to be.

Wesley ministered to people who often reduced salvation to a moment of decision, rather than a covenant to a changed life.[26] The same happens too often today. Many evangelistic sermons urge a desire to flee the wrath to come, focusing the attention on fearing hell more than on living faithfully in this life with an eye to the next. Whereas we affirm in the creeds *"credo in Deum,"* we nowhere affirm *"credo in diabolum,"* though messages of salvation often urge rejection of the latter more than love of the former.

Christian tradition, particularly in the West, has long discussed the conformity to Christ with the term "deification." This simply means "that we are to become progressively like Christ, transformed into the image of the one who is the very image of God.... It means that we are to grow into mature sons and daughters of God, living a life more and more characterized by the virtues of Christ himself, especially faith, hope, and love."[27] Wesley believed this and saw it as part of his most consistent theme throughout his ministry: holy living and, as he famously proclaimed, Christian perfection.

While a student at Oxford, Wesley was exposed to the *Homilies* of Macarius the Great, and the effect upon him was immense. Through the course of his life, he would read and review these homilies, often using Macarian principles in his own sermons. When Wesley published his 51-volume *Christian Library* around the year 1750, he abridged Macarius' 50 "Spiritual Homilies" in the very first volume.[28] This was followed immediately by Wesley's abridgement of *True Christianity* by Johann Arndt, "the father of German Pietism," who supposedly had many, if not all, of Macarius' *Homilies* committed to memory.[29] The influence of this Eastern Father on John Wesley's theology can hardly be minimized. As Wesley wrote regarding Macarius:

> [H]e continually labours to cultivate in himself and others...the real life of God in the heart and soul, that kingdom of God, which consists in righteousness, and peace, and joy in the Holy Ghost. He is ever quickening and stirring up his audience, endeavouring to kindle in them a steady zeal, an earnest desire, an inflamed ambition, to recover the Divine image we were made in; to be made conformable to Christ our Head; to be daily sensible more and more of our living union with him as such; and discovering it, as occasion requires, in all the genuine fruits of an holy life and conversation, in such a victorious faith as overcomes the world, and working by love, is ever fulfilling the whole law of God.[30]

This recovery of the Divine image, this conformity to Christ our Head, shaped Wesley's teaching on perfection and, in many ways, reflected his greater dependency upon the East over the West.

Another way into this discussion is to consider the parallels between Wesley's sermons and another Eastern Father, Maximus the Confessor.[31] Maximus described the stages of salvation as "the future deification of those who have now been made children of God." Having been changed into children of God in this life, the redeemed could look forward to further and complete transformation in the life to come, into what Jaroslav Pelikan called "participation in the very nature of God."[32] It is a "blessed promise... this grace of deification laid up in hope for those who love the Lord, which already exists figuratively and can be received in advance."[33]

Wesley said that such a change is the ultimate end of the new birth that is worked in a soul through Christ, recapturing and renewing the image of God. This is when "the love of the world is changed into the love of God, pride into humility, passion into meekness; hatred, envy, malice, into a sincere, tender, disinterested love for all mankind. In a word, it is that change whereby the 'earthly, sensual, devilish' mind is turned into 'the mind which was in Christ.' This is the nature of the new birth."[34]

As with both Macarius and Maximus, this recovery of the image of God, this deification, is the result of both an instantaneous gift of grace and a process of growth in that grace. "A child is born of a woman in a moment, or at least in a very short time. Afterward, he gradually and slowly grows till he attains the stature of a man. In like manner a child is born of God in a short time, if not in a moment. But it is by slow degrees that he afterward grows up to the measure of the full stature of Christ. The same relation, therefore, which there is between our natural birth and our growth there is also between our new birth and our sanctification."[35] The faith through which we are saved is not a singular act of belief at a moment in time that cements our standing with God for all eternity. It is a dynamic, ongoing relationship of faith, hope, and love, manifested through our obedience and trust in which we yield to God more and more until He fully fills our hearts and lives.

Wesley's emphasis on this *telos*, this end or goal of one's salvation, is also reflected in some of the hymns written by his younger brother, Charles, whose songs fueled the preaching of the Methodists. Just as

Maximus had written that God "deigned in his kindness that we be one and the same with him... by joining and knitting us closely together with himself in spirit and leading us to the measure of spiritual maturity which springs from his own fullness,"[36] Charles wrote in his 1745 nativity hymn "Let Earth and Heaven Combine":

> He deigns in flesh to appear,
> widest extremes to join,
> to bring our vileness near,
> and make us all Divine;
> and we the life of God shall know,
> for God is manifest below.[37]

The final phrase of the Apostles' Creed declares belief in "the life everlasting." The Nicene Creed ends with profession of belief in "life in the world to come." Both of these indicate, as Wesley is quick to claim, that such life begins not at physical death but at spiritual birth, a rebirth whose transformation prepares and purifies one for the life of the world to come. Becoming one with God is not something that only begins when we leave this life and enter the next. Rather, as the former Bishop of Durham N.T. Wright has claimed, what occurs beyond the grave is life after life after death.[38]

The New Heaven and New Earth

Throughout the Scriptures, we find the salvific work of Christ linked to both creation and redemption. In the Old Testament, God establishes covenants for the preservation of creation,[39] as well as for the redemption of His people.[40] We find observance of the Sabbath grounded in both creation and in redemption from slavery in Egypt. "The Lord made the heavens and the earth, the sea, and everything that is in them in six days, but rested on the seventh day. That is why the Lord blessed the Sabbath day and made it holy."[41] "Remember that you were a slave in Egypt, but the Lord your God brought you out of there with a strong hand and an outstretched arm. That's why the Lord your God commands you to keep the Sabbath day."[42] In the New Testament letter to the Colossians there is further affirmation of this connection, describing Jesus as both "the firstborn of all creation"[43] and "the firstborn from the dead."[44] The Book of Revelation praises

God in hymns celebrating creation and the redemption brought through Christ's sacrifice. "You are worthy... because you created all things."[45] "You are worthy" because "by your blood you purchased for God persons from every tribe, language, people, and nation."[46] In numerous places and in a variety of ways, Scripture reinforces this theme of change, of re-creation, of transformation, and this redemption involves the restoration of all of creation, not just human creation.

Richard Stearns recently wrote that "focusing almost exclusively on the afterlife reduces the importance of what God expects of us in this life. The kingdom of God, which Christ said is 'within you,' was intended to change and challenge everything in our fallen world in the here and now. It was not meant to be a way to leave the world but rather the means to actually redeem it."[47] Such a belief has been foundational in Stearns' work as president of World Vision, a Christian relief organization. The "gospel, the whole gospel, means much more than the personal salvation of individuals. It means a social revolution" based on the work of Christ and the power of the Holy Spirit.[48]

This fits perfectly with Wesley's understanding of the nature and purpose of salvation, the deification or entire sanctification of the believer. It also fits perfectly with Wesley's further understanding of the next life, that of a new creation and a new earth, an understanding that Wesley learned from his study of Christian antiquity.

Augustine emphasized human sin and depravity, tilting the balance toward the original sin of humanity and away from its original goodness, created in the full image of God within the goodness of the created order. This focus was reinforced in 529 at the Council of Orange, which endorsed Augustine's doctrine of sin and grace and further directed the attention of the Western church to human sinfulness and the need for redemption. However, the consequence of an emphasis on sin was an underemphasis on holiness and renewal as normative in the life of a believer.

By the Middle Ages, the Church was established and visible, in buildings, clergy, monastic settlements, and, following Gutenberg, greater access to the printed word. It had always been established and visible, but in the earliest years of Christianity, it was seen in small communities, house churches, and common practices of families and local gatherings. As the Church developed its rich liturgy and its broader visible presence, many people unschooled and unfamiliar in the texts and traditions found liturgy becoming less a thing to do and more a thing to watch. It became less the work of the people and more the work of God done through a priest on behalf of the people. Salvation began to be seen the same way. It was less active salvation to a new way of living, and more passive salvation from the punishment of death. As Howard Snyder has suggested, "The marriage of church and state brought the divorce of heaven and earth." For many in the West, Christianity was seen "as the journey from this world to the next; from the world of fallen matter to the world of perfect spirit."[49]

As we have already indicated above, Wesley was familiar with and strongly influenced by Eastern theology, too. One of the most significant contributions to the church's understanding of salvation and redemption is the recapitulation theory developed initially by Irenaeus of Lyons.[50] He portrayed the plan of salvation as creation-incarnation-recreation. Wesley saw this emphasis on Christ as the "new Adam" as a stark contrast to the creation-sin-redemption model emphasized in the West through the writings of Augustine, Calvin, and other evangelical theologians.

As in Athanasius' *On the Incarnation*, within Irenaeus' *Against Heresies* we find the Christus Victor theme, where God in Christ, through His death and resurrection, has defeated the grave and all the powers of sin and evil. Christ the Victor will return to institute His Kingdom and to reign over all the earth. He will recreate everything, including humanity, into the image of God and the original state of creation. "He commenced afresh the long line of human beings, and furnished us, in a brief, comprehensive manner, with salvation; so that what we had lost in Adam, namely, to be according to the image and likeness of God, that we might we recover in Christ Jesus."[51]

This recovery would happen not in some distant land but rather in the full reconciliation of heaven and earth, with a new heaven and a new earth the result. And so for Wesley, as believers in Christ look forward to the promises of eternal life, there is recognition that the goal of salvation is not escape from the earth but a new creation that heals the divorce between heaven and earth. It is resurrection. It is new life. It is new creation. It is becoming, which, as we have already discussed, is central to Wesley's understanding of heaven as well. He sees Scripture wedding the theme of creation and transformation.

Evidence of this is found throughout Wesley's sermon "The New Creation." After the general resurrection and the final judgment, a new creation is established, a new beginning is made, corresponding perfectly to the new life of the resurrected faithful. That which exists now will be transformed. Air will be purified. Water will be unpolluted. Fire will "destroy no more; it will consume no more; it will forget its power to burn."[52] Everything "will be new indeed; entirely changed as to their qualities, although not as to their nature."[53] That which was lost by "the most deplorable effects of Adam's apostasy"[54] will be regained and restored, for in "the new earth no creature will kill or hurt or give pain to any other."[55]

This ultimate new creation, begun in this life, will be completed in the next. There will be no more death, no more pain, no more sickness or grieving or parting from friends. Rather, the redeemed will enjoy "an unmixed state of holiness and happiness far superior to that which Adam enjoyed in paradise,"[56] for it will be "a deep, an intimate, an uninterrupted union with God; a constant communion with the Father and His Son Jesus Christ, through the Spirit; a continual enjoyment of the Three-One God, and of all the creatures in Him!"[57]

For Wesley, sin triggered a divorce between heaven and earth. The salvation given through Christ was redemption of humanity and all the created order. It was far more comprehensive than saving human souls, or even human beings. It was an ultimate healing of the divide beginning now and finding fulfillment in the future, when the entire created order will be liberated from sin. It is, as Revelation 19:9 suggests, the final marriage of heaven and earth in the new creation.

Purgatory

We have talked about a Wesleyan understanding of the final judgment, the goal of salvation, and the new heaven and new earth. All have as a common theme the synergistic relationship with God and humanity whereby we are saved by grace and yet changed from one form of being into another, bearing fruit worthy of our repentance.

Wesley famously held this change, this transformation, to be what he called the doctrine of perfection, or entire sanctification. And yet Wesley did not believe that this ongoing work of grace in the believer's life made one a saint immediately. He did not believe that full perfection in action was probable in this life, though many of his spiritual descendants seem to claim just that, nor did he believe that he himself had attained this perfection. "I have told all the world I am not perfect; and yet you allow me to be a Methodist. I tell you flat, I have not attained the character I draw."[58] Rather, the change which begins in this life is carried on to completion in the next.

Wesley explicitly described this necessary cleansing, this purging, in multiple places. "Far other qualifications are required, in order to our standing before God in glory, than were required in order to His giving us faith and pardon. In order to this, nothing is indispensably required, but repentance, or conviction of sin. But in order to the other it is indispensably required, that we be fully cleansed from all sin: that the very God of peace sanctify us wholly, even… our entire body, soul, and spirit…. It is necessary in the highest degree, that we should thus wait upon Him after justification. Otherwise, how shall we be 'meet to be partakers of the inheritance of the saints in light'?"[59] And "all holiness must precede our entering into glory."[60] And "none go to heaven without holiness of heart and life."[61] And "all writers whom I have ever seen till now (the Romish themselves not excepted) agree, that we must be fully cleansed from all sin, before we can enter into glory."[62]

The "Romish" understanding is clearly stated in the Catechism of the Catholic Church. "All who die in God's grace and friendship, but still imperfectly purified, are indeed assured of their eternal salvation; but after death they undergo purification, so as to achieve the holiness necessary to enter the joy of heaven."[63] It further states that "the Church gives the name Purgatory to this final purification of the elect, which is entirely different from the punishment of the damned."[64]

As already stated, Wesley readily confessed the truth of Hebrews 12:14, that without holiness no one may see the Lord. He believed that one needed to be fully sanctified and cleansed before being able to enter into the presence of the glory of God. When this happened, however, was less clear in his thinking. The best he could come up with was that the final purification happened at the moment of death. "I believe this perfection is always wrought in the soul by a simple act of faith; consequently, in an instant…. I believe this instant generally is the instant of death, the moment before the soul leaves the body."[65]

Growing up Protestant, I was never really exposed to the doctrine of purgatory. And if I was, it was presented as a Catholic tradition that went beyond the bounds of Scripture, a place where persons needed to pay further penalty for their sins before they could be completely forgiven. Such thinking would not be completely foreign to Wesley, either, who, in his understanding of the Catholic definition of purgatory, saw it as a place where "those who die in a state of grace go into a place of torment, in order to be purged in the other world." This, Wesley stressed, "is utterly contrary to Scripture."[66]

Protestants like to quote Hebrews 9:27, which clearly states that "people are destined to die once and then face judgment." We like to reference Jesus' parable as recorded in Luke 13:23-30. Jesus is asked if only a few will be saved, and in response He says, "Make every effort to enter through the narrow gate. Many, I tell you, will try to enter and won't be able to. Once the owner of the house gets up and shuts the door, then you will stand outside and knock on the door, saying, 'Lord, open the door for us.' He will reply, 'I don't know you or where you are from.'" [67]

Yet the Hebrews passage only says that after we die there is judgment. It does not say when that judgment occurs. Indeed, orthodox theology would stress that the final judgment is yet to come. And the point of Jesus' comments in Luke 13 is less about postmortem repentance and more about genuine transformation and change—again, what Wesley considered the goal of salvation. The owner of the house closes the door, at which point it will be too late for persons to change their lives. They had this opportunity during their lifetime and have squandered it. One should not presume God's grace and forgiveness simply through familiarity.[68] Such an interpretation is borne out when reading the entire chapter, which begins with a parable of a fig tree. "Maybe it will produce fruit next year; if not, then you can cut it down."[69] The demand of Christ is for genuine change. For "not everybody who says to me, 'Lord, Lord,' will get into the kingdom of heaven. Only those who do the will of my Father who is in heaven will enter."[70]

The judgment seat of Christ is after death, at least according to 2 Corinthians 5:10. It seems to involve some sort of purging, something distinct from the final judgment. Moreover, the purification[71] detailed in 1 Corinthians 3 seems to be occurring after death as well. Is it possible that there is a final purging of sin between this life and the next?

Despite what has already been shown, Wesley seems to think so. He says that even in paradise, in what he terms "the intermediate state between death and the resurrection," we will continue to be shaped into the likeness of Christ.[72] This paradise is not heaven, he stresses. It is "the antechamber of heaven, where the souls of the righteous remain, till, after the general Judgment, they are received into glory."[73]

And, though Wesley is careful to distinguish between purgatory as a place of punishment and paradise as a place of refinement, the necessity of such a cleansing is clear. "In paradise the souls of good men rest from their labours, and are with Christ from death to the resurrection. This bears no resemblance at all to the Popish purgatory, wherein wicked men are supposed to be tormented in purging fire, till they are sufficiently purified to have a place in heaven. But we believe, as did the ancient church, that none shall suffer after death, but those who suffer eternally."[74]

Interestingly, Wesley found it permissible to pray for souls in this intermediate state:

> Your fourth argument is, that in a collection of Prayers, I cite the words of an ancient Liturgy, "for the Faithful Departed." Sir, whenever I use those words in the Burial Service, I pray to the same effect: "That we, with all those who are departed in Thy faith and fear, may have our perfect consummation of bliss, both in body and soul." Yea, and whenever I say, "Thy Kingdom come;" for I mean both the kingdom of grace and glory. In this kind of general prayer, therefore, for the Faithful Departed, I conceive myself to be clearly justified, both by the earliest Antiquity, by the Church of England, and by the Lord's Prayer.[75]

Jerry Walls does an excellent job of explaining why the doctrine of purgatory need not be anathema to Protestants.[76] I began to reconcile purgatory with my understanding of paradise and the life to come after reading Jacques Le Goff's work, *The Birth of Purgatory*. I was particularly struck by three simple words he says in a section in which he discusses the *Dialogus miraculorum*, a 13th-century book of hagiography written by the Cistercian Caesarius of Heisterbach: "Purgatory is hope."[77]

Wesley would celebrate this promised hope: "As happy as the souls in paradise are, they are preparing for far greater happiness. For paradise is only the porch of heaven; and it is there the spirit of just men are made perfect."[78] In the last sermon he wrote, "On Faith," Wesley asked, "can we reasonably doubt but that those who are now in paradise, in Abraham's bosom, all those holy souls who have been discharged from the body from the beginning of the world unto this day, will be continually ripening for heaven, will be perpetually holier and happier, till they are received into 'the kingdom prepared for them from the foundation of the world'?"[79]

As disagreeable to the stomach as it may seem for Protestant readers, I find a concept of purgatory to be neither inconsistent with nor contrary to a Wesleyan biblical and theological understanding of the life to come. My sense is that it is mainly just disagreeable to the palate. We are unfamiliar with the taste of the idea.

A Wesleyan, synergistic understanding of grace can profess belief in a sanctification model of purgatory, a model in which one is purified fully before fully seeing God. What is not compatible is a satisfaction model of purgatory, which may imply that additional work beyond the saving power of Christ is necessary for salvation. It is not a second chance, for the choice to accept God's free gift of grace and live out of that grace has already been made. But it can be the necessary completion of the saving work Christ begins in us in this life, remaking us in His image, perfecting us for eternity.

For we Wesleyans believe, with Wesley, in justification by grace, through faith. We believe, with Wesley, in growth in that grace toward the likeness of Christ. We believe, with Wesley, in the redemption of humanity and the redemption of all creation. We can believe, with Wesley, in a period of refinement that prepares one for the new heaven and new earth. And we can also believe, along with Dorothy Sayers, that "purgatory is not a system of Divine book-keeping, so many years for so much sin, but a process of spiritual improvement which is completed precisely when it is complete."[80]

Notes

[1] As, admittedly, am I. My congregation hosts five services every Sunday, two of which are led in English, and with several hundred immigrants and new Americans, as well as many native-born Americans who were not raised "in the Church," clarity and simplicity of communication are paramount. I have similarly tried to focus in this paper on plain understanding, rather than profound exposition.

[2] The World Methodist Council is made up of over 80 Methodist, Wesleyan, and other denominational descendants of John Wesley, including the Free Methodist Church, of

which I am an ordained elder. It represents over 80 million persons in over 130 countries around the world.

3   The writings of Wesley quoted in this paper, and all other subsequent works of John Wesley, are from the Abingdon Press editions of which the late Frank Baker was editor-in-chief. All direct quotations will be taken from these. For the remainder of this paper, I will reference the particular sermon, letter, or writing of Wesley to which I am referring and will cite the section and paragraph numbe4 John Wesley, "The Great Assize," in *Works of John Wesley*, ed. Albert C. Outler (Nashville: TN: Abingdon Press, 1984), 1:359. Wesley is not trying to divide the attributes or roles of the Trinity as Monarchianism or Sabellianism might do. He is simply using pastoral license to depict an economic difference, not an ontological one.

5   John Wesley, "The Good Steward," in *Works of John Wesley*, ed. Albert C. Outler (Nashville: Abingdon Press, 1984), 2:293.

6   Wesley, "The Great Assize," 362.

7   Ibid.

8   Ibid., 363.

9   Wesley, "The Good Steward," 293-94.

10 Ibid., 294.

11 Ibid.

12 Ibid., 295.

13 Ibid., 296.

14 Indeed, earlier papers within this dialogue have stressed the Wesleyan emphasis on justification by grace. His focus on the responsibility of the believer at the final judgment is not a tendency toward Pelagianism but rather a synergistic emphasis on God's grace and our faithful response, a response born out of love and not duty or obligation.

15 John Wesley, "Of Hell," in *Works of John Wesley*, ed. Albert C. Outler (Nashville: Abingdon Press, 1984), 3:43.

16 Wesley, "The Great Assize," 367.

17 Ibid., 368.

18 Ibid., 68-70. Interestingly, when John's nephew Samuel became a Roman Catholic, John wrote to his brother Charles, perhaps in jest, that Samuel "may, indeed, roil a few years in purging fire; but he will surely go to heaven at last." *Letter to Charles Wesley Jr.*, dated May 2, 1784. We will discuss a Wesleyan view of such purgation later in this paper.

19 Ibid., 372.

20 Wesley, "Of Hell," 33.

21 Ibid.

22 Ibid., 34.

23 Ibid., 35.

24 Ibid., 43.

25 This has been discussed at length in the other excellent papers in this series of the dialogue.

26 This is part of the reason for Wesley's lengthy discourse on the necessity of deeds done out of love for God in his sermon "The Good Steward" and other places. Unlike Luther, he most definitely did not see James as an epistle of straw.

27 Daniel A. Keating, *Deification and Grace* (Naples, FL: Sapientia Press, 2007), 87. This truly excellent work ends with a summary of our call, not "to become 'gods' on our own and achieve equal status with God. Rather, we are called to be gods by *participating* in God himself, by being joined to the Incarnate Word through the Spirit. Accurately presented, deification reminds us that in Christ we remain the creatures that we are, and find our joy and delight in being elevated by sheer grace to communion with God and participation in his life and power." Ibid, 124.

28 John Wesley, *A Christian Library: Consisting of Extracts from and Abridgements of the Choicest Pieces of Practical Divinity which Have Been Published in the English Tongue* (London: T. Cordeaux, 1819). The first volume, in which the extracts of Macarius can be found, was first published in 1749. For a more substantial overview of Wesley's use of Western and Eastern Fathers, see Ted A. Campbell, *John Wesley and Christian Antiquity: Religious Vision and Cultural Change* (Nashville: Kingswood, 1991). For greater investigation specifically into the influence of Macarius upon Wesley, see Thomas E. Brigden, "Wesley and the Homilies of Macarius," *Proceedings of the Wesley Historical Society* 8, no. 1 (March, 1911): 6-7; or Howard A. Snyder, "John Wesley and Macarius the Egyptian," *The Asbury Theological Journal* 4, no. 2 (1990): 55-60.

29 See Snyder, "John Wesley and Macarius the Egyptian," 55.

30 Wesley, *Christian Library*, 71.

31 Wesley does not include works of Maximus within his *Christian Library*, but Kenneth Carveley posits that Wesley knew of Maximus via Bernard of Clairvaux, who was influential on the Pietists, to whom Wesley was indebted through his exposure to the Moravians. See Kenneth Carveley, "From Glory to Glory: The Renewal of All Things in Christ: Maximus the Confessor and John Wesley," *Orthodox and Wesleyan Spirituality*, ed. S.T. Kimbrough, Jr. (Crestwood, NY: St. Vladimir's Seminary, 2002), 173.

32 Jaroslav Pelikan, introduction in *Maximus Confessor: Selected Writings*, trans. G.C. Berthold (New York: Paulist, 1985), 10.

33 A. Louth, *Maximus the Confessor* (London: Routledge, 1996), 150.

34 John Wesley, "The New Birth," in *Works of John Wesley*, ed. Albert C. Outler (Nashville: Abingdon Press, 1984), 194.

35 Ibid., 198.

36 Maximus: Ambiguorum Liber, *Patrologia Graeca*, 91. 1097.

37 Charles Wesley, *Methodist Hymn-Book* (London: Methodist Conference Office, 1933), hymn 142, verse 5.

38 I believe I first read this quote from N.T. Wright in his book *The Resurrection of the Son of God* (Minneapolis: Fortress, 2003). In late January of 2017, I was privileged to spend some time with Bishop Wright discussing his latest release, *The Day the Revolution Began*. He used this phrase about life after life after death numerous times.

39 Gen. 9:8-15.

40 Gen. 17:1-8.

41 Exod. 20:11.

42 Deut. 5:15.

43 Col. 1:15.

44 Col. 1:18.

45 Rev. 4:11.

46 Rev. 5:9.

47 Richard Stearns, *The Hole in Our Gospel: What Does God Expect of Us? The Answer that Changed My Life and Might Just Change the World* (Nashville: Thomas Nelson), 2009, 17.
48 Ibid., 20.
49 Howard Snyder, *Salvation Means Creation Healed: The Ecology of Sin and Grace: Overcoming the Divorce between Earth and Heaven* (Eugene, OR: Cascade Books, 2011), 17. Snyder provides one of the best summaries of the new heaven and the new earth that I have read. A Free Methodist pastor himself, Snyder also is a world-class Wesley scholar and represents well the full Wesleyan understanding of salvation and redemption.
50 Wesley was quite familiar with Irenaeus, especially his *Against Heresies*. Wesley discusses the work at length in his letter to Dr. Conyers Middleton, dated January 4, 1749.
51 Irenaeus, *Against Heresies*, 3.18, in *The Writings of Irenaeus*, eds. A. Roberts and J. Donaldson (Edinburgh: T&T Clark, 1848), 1:337-38.
52 John Wesley, "The New Creation," in *Works of John Wesley*, ed. Albert C. Outler (Nashville: Abingdon Press, 1984), 2:504.
53 Ibid.
54 Ibid., 508.
55 Ibid., 509.
56 Ibid., 510.
57 Ibid.
58 John Wesley, letter to the editor of *Lloyd's Evening Post*, dated March 5, 1767, Wesley Center Online, http://wesley.nnu.edu/john-wesley/the-letters-of-john-wesley/wesleys-letters-1767/ (accessed April 14, 2017). For Wesley, it was clearly a matter of *posse non peccatore* rather than *non posse peccatore*.
59 John Wesley, *Answer to the Rev. Mr. Church's "Remarks on the Rev. Mr. Wesley's Last Journal*, dated February 2, 1745, Wesley Center Online, http://wesley.nnu.edu/john-wesley/the-letters-of-john-wesley/wesleys-letters-1745/ (accessed April 14, 2017).
60 John Wesley, *A Letter to the Rev. Dr. Horne*, dated March 10, 1762, Wesley Center Online, http://wesley.nnu.edu/john-wesley/the-letters-of-john-wesley/wesleys-letters-1762/ (accessed April 14, 2017).
61 John Wesley, *Letter to Samuel Sparrow, Esquire*, dated December 28, 1773, Wesley Center Online, http://wesley.nnu.edu/john-wesley/the-letters-of-john-wesley/wesleys-letters-1773/ (accessed April 14, 2017).
62 John Wesley, *The Principles of a Methodist Farther Explained*, dated June 17, 1746, Wesley Center Online, http://www.godrules.net/library/wesley/274wesley_h18.htm (accessed April 14, 2017).
63 *Catechism of the Catholic Church* (Washington, DC: United States Catholic Conference, 1994), 1030.
64 Ibid., 1031.
65 John Wesley, "A Plain Account of Christian Perfection," Wesley Center Online, http://wesley.nnu.edu/john-wesley/a-plain-account-of-christian-perfection/ (accessed April 14, 2017).
66 John Wesley, "Popery Calmly Considered," Google Books, https://books.google.com/books?id=TZBKAAAAYAAJ&pg=PA140&lpg=PA140&dq=Wesley+popery+calmly+considered&source=bl&ots=fUM6D64lpZ&sig=ct6VXMYF3yYn9bhuyWwCxaXwqlg&hl=en&sa=X&ved=0ahUKEwjDhrCNsqfTAhUHyoMKHaRDDFsQ6AEIQTAG#v=onepage&q=Wesley%20popery%20calmly%20considered&f=false (accessed April 14, 2017).

67 Luke 13:24-25.
68 See Luke 13:26-27.
69 Luke 13:9.
70 Matt. 7:21.
71 Particularly verses 12-15.
72 John Wesley, *Letter to Miss B*, dated April 17, 1776, Wesley Center Online, http://wesley.nnu.edu/john-wesley/the-letters-of-john-wesley/wesleys-letters-1776/ (accessed April 14, 2017).
73 John Wesley, "Dives and Lazarus," in *Works of John Wesley*, ed. Albert C. Outler (Nashville: Abingdon Press, 1984), 4:7.
74 John Wesley, *Letter to George Blackall*, dated February 25, 1783, Wesley Center Online, http://wesley.nnu.edu/john-wesley/the-letters-of-john-wesley/wesleys-letters-1783a/ (accessed April 14, 2017).
75 John Wesley, *Second Letter to Bishop George Lavington*, dated November 27, 1750, Wesley Center Online, http://wesley.nnu.edu/john-wesley/the-letters-of-john-wesley/wesleys-letters-1750/ (accessed April 14, 2017). See also his *Letter to the Rev. Dr. Conyers Middleton Occasioned by His Late Free Inquiry*, dated January 4, 1749, Wesley Center Online, http://wesley.nnu.edu/john-wesley/the-letters-of-john-wesley/wesleys-letters-1749/ for a similar justification for prayers for the dead.
76 Jerry L. Walls, *Heaven, Hell, and Purgatory: A Protestant View of the Cosmic Drama* (Grand Rapids: Brazos, 2015).
77 Jacques Le Goff, *The Birth of Purgatory*, trans. Arthur Goldhammer (Chicago: University of Chicago, 1981), 306.
78 Wesley, "On Hell," 35.
79 Wesley, "On Faith," in *Works of John Wesley*, vol. 2, ed. Albert C. Outler (Nashville: Abingdon Press, 1984), 504.
80 Dorothy Sayers, *Introduction to the Divine Comedy 2: Purgatory* (London: Penguin, 1955), 58.

Background Paper

Theological Contours of Monergism in the Final Judgment: A Reformed Understanding

Rev. Chris Castaldo, Ph.D.

The Reformed Position on Monergism

THE WORD "MONERGISM," it seems to this writer, can be unhelpfully ambiguous. So far as we are aware, John Calvin never used the term. It is also absent from the *Catechism of the Catholic Church*. From the outset, then, it is important to clarify precisely what we mean when we speak of the "Reformed position on monergism." Greg Allison's dictionary of theological terms offers a cogent definition:

> In regard to the doctrine of salvation, the Protestant position [of Monergism asserts] that God alone saves human beings. From the Greek (*monos*, "sole"; *ergon*, "work"), *monergism* refers to a *sole source that works* redemption. God is the single agent that operates the salvation of people. By contrast, *synergism* (Gk. *syn*, "together"; *ergon*, "work") refers to two (or more) sources that *work together* in salvation. God and human beings together operate the rescue of the latter group. Justification exemplifies monergism: one agent, God, justifies the ungodly (Rom. 4:5), who do not/cannot contribute anything.[1]

We certainly wish to affirm God's singular role as the *source* of Christian redemption. But do we really want to assert that God is the singular *agent*? Is there not some place for human will and the cultivation of virtue in the outworking of salvation? To be sure, we recognize the fundamental reason for divine acceptance as the imputation of Christ's righteousness alone; but, apart from that ground, does not synergism belong to Reformed soteriology in some fashion?

Our search for clarity is aided by considering the way other Christian traditions reflect upon the issue. Roman Catholic theology speaks in terms of "uncreated" and "created" grace. The former is the grace of God himself gratuitously accepting sinners. The latter is a grace that renovates the human soul.[2] This distinction is not far removed from what Reformed Protestants mean when we speak of "forensic" versus "effective" justification:[3] the work of God on behalf of sinners versus the soul-renewing righteousness, which God imparts by his Spirit.

Our use of the term "monergism" must be qualified. Reformed theology does not wish to say that Christian salvation is entirely monergistic. When monergism is used in regard to salvation, it refers specifically to the ground or basis of justification.[4] It is the ultimate reason why God accepts us: the fundamental cause or basis of our adoption as children of God. The Reformed tradition, like most of Lutheranism, insists that this ground consists in the alien, external, imputed righteousness of Christ applied for us (*pro nobis*).[5] Christiaan Mostert thus summarizes the Reformed position:

> To speak of justification is to speak of the ground of salvation *extra nos*, in a salvific event that expresses the righteousness of God—especially the "right setting" act of God in Jesus Christ—without regard to any claim of our own, not even our faith. Justification is fundamentally about how God deals with humans and the broken, sinful world in which they live. It is above all about grace.[6]

While the above distinction may sound pedantic, it is absolutely crucial. The Reformers consistently distinguished God's work in accepting sinners—the "not guilty" verdict that pronounces sinners to be sons and daughters—from the internal renewal of the Spirit, which involved human volition and was therefore properly synergistic. "Work out your own salvation with fear and trembling," said Paul, "for it is God who works in you, both to will and to work for his good pleasure."[7] These forms of righteousness may be distinguished, but they cannot be separated. They both flow from one's union with Christ. Like the shining sun that emits light and heat, they are distinct, and, yet, they also run together.

It is at this point that the phrase "faith alone" becomes so important to Reformed Protestants. From the earliest days of the 16th-century Reformation, *sola fide* became a catchphrase to describe how one is united to Christ to receive justifying grace. Thus, God justifies apart from any meritorious works on account of the alien righteousness of Christ alone, which is imputed or reckoned to one's account. In the words of Paul the Apostle: "And to the one who does not work but believes in him who justifies the ungodly, his faith is counted as righteousness."[8] If we are forced to use the term "monergism," it should be used of the forensic attribution of divine righteousness, or what is typically called imputation.

While Reformed Protestants assert that we are justified by faith alone, this faith does not remain alone: "For we dream neither of a faith devoid of good works nor of a justification that stands without them," says Calvin.[9] Having entered into union with Christ, one undergoes the sanctifying work of the Spirit, which results in a virtuous life. Such works truly belong to the Christian and are, therefore, a synergism.

Prof. Tony Lane has analyzed John Calvin's doctrine of justification with particular attention to the above details. Lane explains the logic of Calvin's doctrine of so-called "double justification," noting that "God both accepts and rewards the good works of the justified believer, in addition to accepting the believer himself."[10] As such, persons are engrafted into Christ, and their blemished works are covered by Christ's sinlessness, which causes the imperfections of those works to be expunged. In addition to explaining how genuinely good but flawed works may be pleasing to a holy God, the doctrine of double justification enabled Calvin to give an account for the range of biblical data, including the teaching of James, that portrays God as rewarding human works.

It is important to recognize, however, that Calvin did not use justification language to describe internal renewal or the rewarding of human works. Instead, he categorically distinguished the event of justification from the process of sanctification. His terminology for this distinction was *duplex gratia*, or double grace.[11] Even though Calvin affirmed the idea of double justification, meaning that God rewards our virtue in addition to accepting us, he consistently limits the terminology of justification to the forensic activity of divine acceptance.[12]

Calvin's unwillingness to describe God's approval of human works with the language of justification limits the usefulness of his doctrine for ecumenical dialogue insofar as he cannot explain how justification involves the Spirit working in the human soul—an element of justification that is of central concern to the Catholic tradition. In other words, Calvin's doctrine of double grace so bifurcates justification and sanctification that he lacks the linguistic flexibility to articulate a thoroughgoing doctrine of double justification, even though the concept is woven into the fabric of his doctrine.[13]

There were, however, other Reformers in the opening years of the Reformation who were capable of articulating an explicit doctrine of double justification. One such Reformer was Peter Martyr Vermigli (1499-1562), the Italian Augustinian Prior who converted to Reformed Protestantism when he fled north of the Alps to teach with Bucer at Strasbourg. From there he went to Christ Church, Oxford, before eventually returning to the Continent and settling in Zurich, Switzerland. In what follows, we will examine Peter Martyr's doctrine to appreciate how he combines monergism and synergism in justification, particularly with reference to the Final Judgment. The chief source of our inquiry is Vermigli's *Locus on Justification* from his Romans commentary.

Peter Martyr's Doctrine of Double Justification in Eschatological Focus

Vermigli casts an eschatological light upon justification when he explains how God's end-time judgment is currently rendered in the lives of his children.[14] In good Reformed fashion, the basis of this declaration is solely the imputation of Christ's righteousness.[15] However, there is also a need for a present and future experience of justification in which the moral chaos of sin is reformed in sanctification. For Vermigli, it is not sufficient to simply speak of forensic justification without also connecting it to the Holy Spirit's work of internal renewal, which follows. He thus recognizes "two meanings of the phrase 'to justify,' namely, in fact or in judgment or estimation."[16] This is to say that Vermigli includes both forensic righteousness, monergism, and actual righteousness, synergism, in his doctrine of justification.

The presupposition that undergirds Peter Martyr's doctrine—one shared by all Reformed theologians—is the profound sinfulness of humanity.[17] Frank James described this as an "intensive Augustinianism."[18] According to James, "It is [Martyr's] profound conviction that the Adamic fall rendered all of humanity legally guilty before the divine judge and morally corrupt in their souls, thus bringing alienation and condemnation from God."[19] This conviction, perhaps more than any other, is the driving force behind Vermigli's position. The following points of analysis, therefore, will examine the constituent elements of which Martyr's Augustinian doctrine consists, the logic that holds it together, and the implications for how monergism and synergism relate to Final Judgment.

The Forensic Framework of Justification

The problem of human guilt inherited from Adam led Vermigli to affirm the concept of imputation (*imputatio*), a judicial transference of righteousness to the sinner.[20] Simply put, God "confers" the righteousness of Christ so that one is considered or reckoned to be righteous before God (*coram deo*).[21] Vermigli stresses that this only happens by divine initiative. Commenting on Romans 4:1-4, he explains that the concept of imputation is owing entirely to grace and effectively undermines what he regards as the notion of merit. He writes, "[Paul postulates imputation] as an antithesis to merit or debt, so that he to whom something is imputed neither deserves it nor receives it as debt."[22] Furthermore, this imputation is twofold in the sense that the sinner receives the attribution of Christ's righteousness and also the non-imputation of his own sins.[23] Martyr recognizes such imputation as essential to a biblical understanding of justification.

Also in Reformed fashion, Vermigli insists that imputation is *extra nos*, addressing one's legal status, and not a form of righteousness in us (*iustitia in nobis*), which affects the soul. Contrary to medieval Catholic theology, Martyr asserts that this justifying righteousness "does not adhere [*inhaere*] to our souls, but is imputed by God."[24] Martyr also articulates a reverse imputation in which the sinner's guilt is put upon Christ.[25] Such atonement makes full satisfaction for human iniquity, turning guilty rebels into beloved sons.

As to the *result* of justification for the sinner, a couple of particular benefits come to the foreground, namely, absolution and divine favor.[26] The grace of absolution falls into a schema of inaugurated eschatology, in which one is fully and decisively forgiven in the present despite the ongoing presence of sin. This happens by the non-imputation of his guilt and the imputation of Christ's righteousness.[27] Such forgiveness has "already" occurred. The future "not yet" dimension leads one to seek God for forgiveness of current sins while also leading him to pursue a greater apprehension of love.[28]

Along with God's forgiveness, Martyr's forensic justification also results in God's favor, or *Dei favor*.[29] He writes, "Moreover, as to the remission of sins, a blessing promised to us, we should remember that the chief and principal point consists in this: that we are received into favor by God and our sins forgiven us."[30] With such favor, a positive relationship is established between the defendant and the judge, resulting in the former's acceptance. This forgiveness is a decisive event, imparting the status of son or daughter, and, at the same time, it is gradually apprehended in one's moral life. Frank James helpfully explains:

> To [Vermigli's] mind, "forgiveness" is more than a simple, single, judicial act. Forensic justification is like a pebble dropped in a pond; it creates ripples throughout the lifetime of a sinner. Certainly, it does address decisively the legal matter of guilt derived from Adam. However, even after the judicial acquittal, there remains a moral need for the justified sinner continually to seek forgiveness for subsequent sins.... It is this ongoing need for forgiveness, even after justification has been pronounced, that requires a necessary relationship with sanctification....[31]

Internal Renewal by the Spirit

As indicated, Vermigli was concerned to include the cultivation of virtue in his doctrine of justification, even as he clarified and contended for its forensic character. It is noteworthy that at the very beginning of his *locus*, where he unpacks the meaning of the Hebrew verb *tsadac*, he starts by explaining how God endows believers "with his own Spirit and renews them fully by restoring the strength of their minds."[32] Such sensitivity to the Spirit's renewing work is fundamental to Vermigli's doctrine, as evidenced in his description of justification as "the summit of all *piety*,"[33] a synergistic work of the Holy Spirit that leads the regenerated into an experience of godliness.

Reaching back to his first published work, his exposition on the Apostles' Creed (1544),[34] Vermigli similarly emphasized the in-dwelling of the Spirit in producing the outward evidence of righteousness by which one is judged and rewarded on the last day: "From this [divine inheritance]," he writes, "we learn that our salvation does not depend on us, but on that divine election by which grace, the Spirit and faith dwell within us."[35]

An exploration of this synergism is found in Martyr's *1 Corinthians locus, On Justification*. Here we see his concern to include good works in his doctrine of justification:

> A different kind of justification follows this upright life of holiness by which we are clearly praised, approved or declared just. For although good works do not bring that first righteousness which is given freely, yet they point to it and show it is present.... And on this same basis we will be justified by Christ in the last judgment by the remembrance of good works, that is, we will be declared just, on the testimony of mercy shown to our neighbors.[36]

Resembling Calvin's logic, Martyr explains that such good works are buttressed by the imputation of Christ's righteousness, which restores what is lacking in our "weak and mutilated" works,[37] thus comforting the human soul and assuaging our existential pangs of guilt. In this way, one's upright life of holiness functions as a basis of future justification. Such holiness, in effect, is the vindication of one's justification.

Again, Frank James helpfully summarizes:

> In sum, Vermigli embraces both a narrower and stricter forensic understanding of justification, as well as a broader moral understanding, which stresses the necessary relationship between forensic justification and its accompanying benefits of regeneration

and sanctification. Forensic justification, which is based on the imputed righteousness of Christ alone, is necessarily accompanied by the regenerative work of the Holy Spirit, which produces a moral transformation in the sinner, which in turn inevitably produces sanctification and good works.[38]

Vermigli is quite comfortable with the idea of the progressive, synergistic development of holiness, that is, a "habit" (*habitus*) of righteousness in the context of sanctification. Precisely because regenerate ones are having their minds and wills renovated by the renewing work of the Holy Spirit, they "cooperate with the power of God."[39] Such cooperation grows in time and actually becomes a form of inherent righteousness (*iustitia inhaerente*) that leads to further acts of piety.[40] This synergism, in Vermigli's words, is the "inward righteousness which is rooted in us, which we obtain and confirm by leading a continually upright life."[41]

Such moral achievement results in rewards, which come to the faithful as a divine gift. According to Vermigli, "...[W]e will grant that God sets forth prizes and rewards whereby we are moved to live holy lives."[42] He is careful to indicate that this accomplishment leaves no room whatsoever for boasting.[43] Nevertheless, good works are expected to characterize one who has been justified, precisely because of the Spirit's activity of regeneration.[44] Martyr asserts, "Such works are profitable to the regenerate, for by living uprightly and orderly they are renewed and made perfect."[45] Accordingly, for Vermigli a basis of monergism undergirds a larger, ongoing work of synergism.

Relationship of Monergism and Synergism in the Final Judgment

As we have observed in Vermigli, final justification from a Reformed perspective is an eschatological event that recognizes the divine judge as attributing the righteousness of Christ to sinful men and women by a judicial declaration. Justification is fundamentally about how God brings sinners into his long-anticipated kingdom, in which they enjoy the King's favor. Such people "can already be sure of their participation in eschatological salvation" because they stand on the sufficiency of Christ's righteousness.[46]

In addition to maintaining this conventional understanding of forensic imputation, Vermigli, we have seen, includes regeneration and sanctification in the broader confines of justification. He calls this broader vision "a different kind of justification,"[47] insofar as it becomes part of the basis by which we are justified in the final judgment. Vermigli maintains a form of double justification, or *duplex iustificatio*.[48] Too weak and imperfect to withstand the scrutiny of divine holiness on their own, these works are buttressed by the imputation of Christ's righteousness and thereby made acceptable.[49] Such works are pleasing to God,[50] and, while they are never meritorious,[51] they are rewarded on the last day.[52] Furthermore, these works are essential for salvation.

Vermigli's double justification position sheds light on three aspects of the Final Judgment: the ground of our acceptance, purgatory, and assurance of faith. We shall consider each in turn.

The Ground of Our Acceptance

As we analyze the ground of our acceptance before God, it is important to recognize that Catholics and Protestants both make some distinction between justification, which is one's position before God, and sanctification, which is the process by which one grows in holiness. To affirm the remission of sin is to make such a differentiation, at least implicitly. In other words, to have one's sins forgiven creates a legal distinction between what one *was* before God—guilty—and the way one *is* before God because of grace—forgiven. The key difference is that Catholic theology locates the reason for one's ultimate acceptance not simply in one's *righteous status*, as Protestants do on account of one's union with Christ, but in the *renovation of one's soul* by the Holy Spirit, that is, in sanctification, or a state of grace.

Central to Reformed Protestantism is the conviction that justification is not grounded in human works. Instead, faith is the divinely appointed way in which sinners receive forgiveness because it does not rely upon ourselves but looks to the righteousness of another. Faith has been compared to an empty vessel or an open hand with which one comes to receive divine favor. It is not the vessel or the hand itself that possesses the power. The power of justification is found in the finished work of Christ, which is appropriated through the instrumental means of faith.[53]

This should not amount to a legal fiction. Protestants have consistently maintained that saving faith is more than a mere mental assent to the Gospel. Rather, it is an active faith that gives rise to hope and love. The apostle Paul concludes his statement in Ephesians 2:8–9 about the reception of grace through faith by stressing that "we are [God's] workmanship, created in Christ Jesus for good works, which God prepared beforehand, that we should walk in them."[54] Reformed Protestants believe our justification inevitably and necessarily bears the fruit of our salvation in good works. Double justification emphasizes that such works are pleasing to God and rewarded on the Final Day. In this way, synergism has a role in the final judgment, albeit a secondary one.

The Experience of Purgatory

Since the time of the Reformation, the doctrine of purgatory has been a point of contention between Catholics and Protestants. Protestants, given our framework of justification, see belief in purgatory as a failure to grasp the sufficiency of Jesus' atonement. Catholics, on the other hand, regard the rejection of purgatory as indication that Protestants do not sufficiently appreciate divine holiness and the need for justified persons to reflect that holiness. Vermigli's doctrine, however, may help to allay some of the conflict.

According to the *Catechism of the Catholic Church,* purgatory is a "state of final purification after death and before entrance into heaven for those who have died in God's friendship, but were only imperfectly purified; a final cleansing of human imperfection before one is able to enter the joy of heaven."[55] At the center of this doctrine is the following question: How do followers of Christ enter the holy presence of God when they have not yet been made perfect? Protestants recognize that when Catholics talk about purgatory they are *not* speaking about those who are guilty of having committed unconfessed mortal sins. Catholic theology regards such sins as destroying divine love in the soul, making people guilty before God and robbing them of justification, hence the term "*mortal.*" Catholics teach that the only way to absolve mortal sin is through the sacrament of Penance, which restores sinners to grace and life.

A follower of Christ who enters purgatory is typically someone who has committed unconfessed sins. Venial sins are categorically different from mortal sins in that they don't jeopardize one's state of grace. In Protestant terms, they do not cause the loss of salvation. Nonetheless, they are serious offenses and still need *cleansing* and *satisfaction of temporal punishment*. Note that these two expressions are distinct events. *Cleansing* pertains to sanctification. It asks the question, "*How are imperfect people able to enter the presence of the holy God?*" The second reference, *temporal punishment*, pertains to satisfaction. It asks, "*How are venial sins punished when sinful people fail to do penance in this life?*" The answer to both of these questions is purgatory. The logic of purgatory is specifically concerned with these two issues: making believers actually holy and making satisfaction for unconfessed sins. Catholics believe that it is not enough to have simply been forgiven in the past or to have had righteousness imputed. Because entrance into God's holy presence requires the complete sanctification and satisfaction of all sins, cleansing and punishment in purgatory are both essential.

Reformed Protestants differ from Catholics on purgatory because we do not share the same assumptions. Reformed Protestants oppose the formal distinction between venial and mortal sins. Further, we also differ on the practice of interceding for the dead. Lastly, and, most significantly, Reformed Protestants disagree with the concept that God accepts people on the basis of internal renewal. Purgatory is therefore foreign to Reformed Protestant theology. Instead of looking to the cleansing and satisfaction of one's soul through human purgation as the decisive activity that prepares one for God's heavenly presence, Protestants point to the finished work of Christ and his righteousness attributed to believers by grace through faith alone.

How might double justification help to ameliorate the chasm between Catholics and Reformed Protestants on purgatory? In the concluding chapter of his book on purgatory, Catholic theologian Brett Salkeld connects some of these dots in his chapter titled "Jesus Is Our Purgatory." Salkeld explains the proximity between the notion of purgatory and Final Judgment in terms of Jesus our "judging fire." Quoting Eberhard Jüngel, he writes, "In the judgment 'our sin and guilt is revealed with an unsurpassed clarity in the person of Jesus Christ,' but it is also in him that they are overcome."[56]

Because Reformed Protestants understand our identity to be in union with Christ, and our final justification to involve synergistically produced works, we must take seriously the "judging fire" of Christ. Given the deeply personal nature of this encounter, we can expect to experience a combination of dread, consternation, and loss, along with joyful victory. Such dread is a far cry from the Catholic doctrine of purgatory, but it may be understood as a kind of purgation insofar as one is made painfully aware of how short of divine holiness his good works fall in the face of the manifest glory of God.

Assurance of Faith

The question of assurance is concerned with how certain we can be that we truly possess a saving relationship with God. The *Catechism,* which affirms that Catholics "can lose this priceless gift" of faith,[57] explains, "*Mortal sin* destroys charity in the heart of man by a grave violation of God's law; it turns man away from God, who is his ultimate end and his beatitude, by preferring an inferior good to him."[58] The Protestant Reformers affirmed instead that assurance of salvation is available to all genuine believers. This assurance is based on the power of the faithful God who elects, justifies, regenerates, adopts, sanctifies, and preserves his people. It is further grounded on the pledges and prayers of the Son of God and the sealing and transformative operation of the Holy Spirit. We note that this position, common among many of the Reformers at the time of the Reformation, is also contrasted with several other Protestant groups, including the Arminian, Wesleyan, and Anabaptist traditions. These traditions are sometimes closer to the Catholic view in holding that we cannot maintain certainty that those who are saved will persevere in faith until the end of life.

In the "Assurance of Salvation" section of the *Joint Declaration on the Doctrine of Justification,* written and signed by Catholic and Lutheran leaders in 1999, the signers affirm that the faithful can "rely on the mercy and promises of God" in spite of their weaknesses.[59] The Catholic position initially sounds like a firm statement on assurance, sharing the "concern of the Reformers to ground faith in the objective reality of Christ's promise, to look away from one's own experience, and to trust in Christ's forgiving word alone."[60] However, this is counterbalanced with this reminder: "Every person, however, may be concerned about his salvation when he looks upon his own weaknesses and shortcomings."[61] Thus, the Catholic position is conveyed in a way that more clearly appreciates God's saving intention.[62]

The difference between Catholics and Protestants on the subject of assurance is connected to our deeper differences concerning the ground of justification. On the one hand, if one maintains the Protestant conviction that righteousness is forensically imputed—reckoned or attributed apart from works—then it is possible to be sure of one's status as a child of God. The grace that justifies one before God enables him to persevere in faith, since one's ultimate standing before God is not based on meritorious works. On the other hand, if one maintains the Catholic position that the righteousness of justification is defined as grace infused into the soul, there will always be a measure of uncertainty concerning one's acceptance.

Historically speaking, Catholics have often feared that the Reformed Protestant notion of assurance potentially undermines the motivation to live a life of holiness: Why worry about working out your salvation with fear and trembling if the work is done? Catholic salvation maintains that final justification is predicated upon good works that emerge from a state of grace. Assurance, therefore, may easily appear to Catholics as a form of presumption that provides a license to sin (i.e., cheap grace). A nonchalant attitude toward discipleship in some Protestant churches has sadly added to this conception.

It is important to preserve a proper tension between confidence before God on the basis of Jesus' death and resurrection and the warnings of Scripture against presumption and sloth. Paul tells Christians to "work out your own salvation with fear and trembling"[63] as an imperative we must take seriously. Paul then follows his command with a reminder of the reason why Christ's followers could ever hope to obey it in the first place: "for it is God who works in you, both to will and to work for his good pleasure."[64] So while the Bible provides encouragement that God empowers his children to persevere, giving them assurance of salvation, it simultaneously cautions them to avoid the sin of complacency.

Double justification helps one to strike the delicate balance between confidence and caution. As in the relationship between a parent and a child, there is unconditional acceptance because the child enjoys the status of son or daughter. Loving parents do not disown their children, and neither does God disown us. But a relationship involves expectations.

For example, while the crayon drawings by our small children elicit from us enthusiastic acceptance and affirmation, we expect that (healthy) children will progress beyond that initial stage. If no progress is made, parents will grow dissatisfied and concerned. Likewise, God leads his children in the process of sanctification, cheering and guiding them by his Spirit. Such moral achievement has value in God's sight and inevitably bolsters one's confidence before God, even though such relational assurance is not the ultimate basis of one's confidence. On the other hand, the absence of virtuous works in the lives of believers should raise caution flags and lead one toward repentance.

Conclusion

It seems appropriate to conclude this paper with a story from the end of Vermigli's life, as he prepared to stand before God. According to Josiah Simler, in Peter Martyr's final moments, with Heinrich Bullinger and a small group of friends beside him, "[Peter Martyr] was silent in deep personal reflection; then he turned to us and stated with a rather clear voice that he acknowledged life and salvation in Christ alone, who had been given by the Father to the human race as its only savior."[65] This catchphrase, "salvation in Christ alone," is an apt summary of Vermigli's doctrine of double justification that included monergism and synergism on the Final Day. In this way, Peter Martyr's doctrine of justification is "*of* works," because works validate one's initial justification, and, in the broader, secondary sense of the term, also "*by* works," insofar as the future judgment necessitates the tangible fruit of regeneration.

Notes

[1] Gregg R. Allison, *The Baker Compact Dictionary of Theological Terms* (Grand Rapids: Baker, 2016), 139.

[2] Cardinal Avery Dulles, "Justification in Contemporary Theology," in *Justification by Faith: Lutherans and Catholics in Dialogue VII*, ed. H. George Anderson et al. (Minneapolis: Augsburg, 1985), 258-60. John Henry Newman proposed a fascinating doctrine of justification in which one's acceptance is grounded in the uncreated grace of divine indwelling. In 1874, Newman reissued his *Lectures on Justification* as a Catholic, arguing that his basic premise concerning uncreated grace is altogether compatible with Catholic theology. For more on Newman's position and its ecumenical value, see my published dissertation, *Justified in Christ: The Doctrines of Peter Martyr Vermigli and John Henry Newman and Their Ecumenical Implications* (Oregon: Pickwick, 2017).

3   Karl Lehmann and Wolfhart Pannenberg, eds., *The Condemnations of the Reformation Era: Do They Still Divide?*, trans. Margaret Kohl (Minneapolis: Fortress Press, 1990), 48.

4   It is difficult to argue that justification is entirely monergistic when justification involves human volition to exercise the requisite faith that justifies. Peter Martyr Vermigli, for example, describes this faith as that which actively "takes hold and receives" (*"apprehendimus promissiones Dei"*) the promise of forgiveness. Pietro Martire Vermigli, *In epistolam S. Pauli apostoli ad Romanos commentarii*.... (Basel: Petrum Perna, 1560), 1252. For the English translation, see Peter Martyr Vermigli, *Predestination and Justification: Two Theological Loci*, vol. 8 of *The Peter Martyr Library*, trans. and ed. Frank A. James (Kirksville, MO: Truman State University Press, 2003), 1262. Hereafter, Vermigli's Justification *Locus* will be listed as *Romanos*, followed in brackets by pages from Frank James's English translation, [170].

5   On the fundamental nature of Christ's imputed righteousness, see Alister McGrath, "Forerunners of the Reformation? A Critical Examination of the Evidence for Precursors of the Reformation Doctrines of Justification," *Harvard Theological Review* 75, no. 2 (1982): 219-42; (idem, *Iustitia Dei*, 212-13). Berndt Hamm offers a similar portrait, *The Reformation of Faith in the Context of Late Medieval Theology and Piety: Essays by Berndt Hamm*, ed. Robert J. Bast (Leiden: Brill, 2004). For historical antecedents to this position, see A.N.S. Lane, *Justification by Faith in Catholic-Protestant Dialogue: An Evangelical Assessment* (London: T&T Clark, 2002), 138-40.

6   Christiaan Mostert, "Justification and Eschatology" in *What Is Justification About? Reformed Contributions to an Ecumenical Theme*, eds. Michael Weinrich and John P. Burgess (Grand Rapids: W.B. Eerdmans, 2009), 185-206 [187].

7   Phil. 2:12-13, ESV.

8   Rom. 4:5, ESV.

9   John Calvin, *Institutes of the Christian Religion*, ed. John T. McNeill, trans. Ford Lewis Battles (Louisville: Westminster John Knox Press, 1960), 1:798 (3.16.1). Or in the Westminster Confession: "Faith, thus receiving and resting on Christ and His righteousness, is the alone instrument of justification: yet is it not alone in the person justified, but is ever accompanied with all other saving graces, and is no dead faith, but works by love." *Westminster Confession of Faith*, "Of Justification," Chap. 11.2.

10 A.N.S. Lane, *Justification by Faith in Catholic-Protestant Dialogue: An Evangelical Assessment* (London: T&T Clark, 2002), 33.

11 Cornelius P. Venema, "Calvin's Understanding of the 'Twofold Grace of God' and Contemporary Ecumenical Discussion of the Gospel," *MJT* 18 (2007): 67-105 [70]. Or in Venema's words, the "twofold benefit of our reception of the grace of God in Christ as comprising the 'sum of the gospel.'" Cf. Lane, *Justification by Faith*, 24, fn. 15.

12 While Calvin does not speak of believers "justified by work," he conveys a similar idea when he describes acceptance "by reason of works." *Calvin's Commentaries: The Acts of the Apostles 1-13*, trans. John Fraser (Edinburgh: Saint Andrews Press, 1965), 308-09.

13 A technical distinction to keep in mind: "double justification" (*duplex iustificatio*) is concerned with how God rewards our works despite their imperfections, while "twofold grace" (*duplex iustitia*) refers to the two graces of justification and regeneration.

14 Ibid., 1263 [171]. [should this be Romanos?]

15 Ibid., 1194 [100].

16 Ibid., 1182 [88]. The latter of these, justification "in judgment," constitutes the fundamental cause. Immediately after making this statement, Vermigli explains why

the renewal of the Spirit and "way of life acquired from good works" ultimately relies upon forensic imputation to accomplish one's justification, since such works remain "imperfect and incomplete."

[17] Martyr doesn't hesitate using Augustine's phrase *massa perditionis* to describe this plight. Ibid., 1196 [102]: *"Omnes nascentes massa perditionis complectitur, a qua labe homines operibus suis emergere posse, et vendicare sibi iustificationem iuxta sacras literas fieri non potest."*

[18] Frank A. James, "The Complex of Justification: Peter Martyr Vermigli Versus Albert Pighius," in *Peter Martyr Vermigli: Humanism, Republicanism, Reformation*, eds. Emidio Campi, Frank A. James, and Peter Opitz (Geneva: Librairie Droz, 2002), 52-53.

[19] Ibid.

[20] *Romanos*, 1182 [87]: *"Interdum vero iustificat Deus absolvendo a peccatis, adscribendo et imputando iustitiam."*

[21] Ibid., 1201 [107]; 1314 [220].

[22] Ibid., 1194 [100]: "... nos ex operibus non iustificari. Quoque id magis persuaderet, verbum id logizein, quod dicimus imputare, adscribere alicui iustitiam, aut pro iusto aliquem habere urget, et vult habere antithesim ad meritum et debitum, ita ut is cui quippiam imputatur, id non mereatur, neque ut debitum accipiat."

[23] Martyr makes this point by quoting Rom. 4:5 and Gen. 15:6 to assert that God simultaneously forgives sins and credits those who believe with righteousness. Ibid., 1252 [159].

[24] Ibid., 1194 [100]: "Quibus ex verbis non solum ellcimus iustitiam, qua dicimut iustificari, non inhaere animis nostris, sed imputari a Deo..."

[25] Ibid., 1264 [172]: "atque ita, ut ipse in se suscipiat, et portet illorum scelera."

[26] Ibid., 1182 [87]: "Deus absolvendo à peccatis."

[27] Ibid., 1212 [119].

[28] Ibid., 1207 [113].

[29] Ibid., 1217 [123].

[30] Ibid., 1274 [182]: "Quod autem attinet ad remissionem peccatorum, quum nobis promissa sit benedictio, cogitare debemus, caput, & principium eius esse, ut recipiamur à Deo in gratiam, utque nobis peccata condonentur."

[31] James, "Complex of Justification," 51.

[32] *Romanos*, 1182 [87].

[33] Emphasis added, ibid., 1191 [96]. *"Columen totius pietatis."* Calvin uses similar language to describe justification: *"quae pietatis est totius summa"* in Calvin, *Institutes*, 3:15:7. Petrus Barth & Guilelmus Niesel, eds., *Johannis Calvini Opera Selecta*, 2nd ed. (Munich: Chr. Kaiser, 1958), 4:245.

[34] Martyr's work *Una Semplice Dichiaratione sopra gli XII Articola della Fede Christiana* (Basel: John Hervagrius, 1544) surveys Christian doctrine from the viewpoint of the Protestantism that he had recently embraced.

[35] Peter Martyr Vermigli, *Early Writings: Creed, Scripture, Church*, vol. 1 of *The Peter Martyr Library*, trans. and eds. Mariano Di Gangi and Joseph C. McLelland (Kirksville, MO: Thomas Jefferson University Press, 1994), 53.

[36] "Ad hanc rectam vitam sanctorum, consequitur quaedam alia species Iustificationis, qua scilicet laudamur, approbamur, & iusti praedicamur. Nam bona opera licet illam primam iustitiam quae gratis conceditur non afferant, attamen indicant, &

illam adesse demonstrant.... Et hac eadem ratione à Christo in extremo iudicio commemoratione bonorum operum iustificabimur, id est iusti declarabimur, ex testimonio misericordiae proximis exhibitae." Peter Martyr Vermigli, *Corinthios Commentarii*, 19. cf. *Romanos*, 1182 [88].

37 Peter Martyr Vermigli, *The Peter Martyr Reader*, eds. John Patrick Donnelly, Frank A. James, and Joseph C. McLelland (Kirksville, MO: Truman State University Press, 1999), 147.

38 Frank A. James, "Romans Commentary: Justification and Sanctification," in *A Companion to Peter Martyr Vermigli*, eds. W.J. Torrance Kirby, Emidio Campi, and Frank A. James (Leiden: Brill, 2009), 314.

39 Ibid., 1250 [158]: "et gratia, atque spiritu instauratus cum divina virtute una cooperatur."

40 Vermigli quotes Augustine with approval with regard to "the righteousness that adheres in us." ("Augustinum sensisse de iustitia inhaerente.") Ibid., 1320 [226].

41 Ibid., 1299 [205]: "...sed de illa intrinseca nobis inhaerente, quam recte vivendo perpetuo acquirimus, et confirmamus."

42 Vermigli, *Romanos*, 1288 [195].

43 Ibid., 1289 [195]: After arguing thus, he concludes: "Therefore, we must take away all merit, not only in those who are not yet justified, but also in those who have been justified."

44 One way to see this emphasis on renewal and works in Vermigli is in his treatment of James 2:17-16. There are three such places in his Romans *locus*. In these comments he asserts that faith works (1187 [93]), it is accepted by God (1239-1240 [146]), and by works one comes to a fuller knowledge of God (1311 [217]).

45 Ibid., 1290 [196].

46 Wolfhart Pannenberg, *Systematic Theology*, trans. G.W. Bromiley (Edinburgh: T.&T. Clark and Grand Rapids: W.B. Eerdmans, 1998), 3:236.

47 Vermigli, *Corinthios Commentarii*, 19.

48 Ibid.; *Romanos*, 1182 [88].

49 Vermigli, *Corinthios Commentarii*, 19.

50 Vermigli, *Romanos*, 1222-23 [128-29], 1227-28 [133-34], 1290-91 [196-97].

51 Ibid., 1194 [100].

52 Ibid., 1288 [195].

53 John Calvin, *Institutes*, 3.11.7.

54 Eph. 2:10.

55 *CCC* 896.

56 Brett Salkeld, *Can Catholics and Evangelicals Agree about Purgatory and the Last Judgment?* (Mahwah, NJ: Paulist Press, 2011), 93.

57 *CCC* 162.

58 *CCC* 1855.

59 The Lutheran World Federation and the Roman Catholic Church, *Joint Declaration on the Doctrine of Justification (JD)* (Grand Rapids: W.B. Eerdmans, 2000), §34.

60 *JD*, §36.

61 Ibid.

62 The closing sentence of the Catholic position says, "Recognizing [the justified person's] own failures, however, the believer may yet be certain that God intends his salvation." Ibid.

63 Phil. 2:12.

64 Phil. 2:13.

65 Peter Martyr Vermigli, *Life, Letters, and Sermons*, vol. 5 of *The Peter Martyr Library*, trans. and ed. John Patrick Donnelly (Kirksville, MO: Thomas Jefferson University Press, 1999), 60.

Background Paper

"Saved, But Only As Through Fire:" Notes on the Scriptural and Theological Foundations for the Doctrine of Purgatory

DR. WILLIAM B. STEVENSON

COMMENTING ON I CORINTHIANS 3:11-15, the great divine of Old Princeton, Charles Hodge, remarks, "Romanists found their doctrine of purgatory on tradition rather than on Scripture. They are glad, however, to avail themselves of any semblance of scriptural support and therefore appeal to this passage to prove that men are saved through fire."[1] Hodge's summary judgment (which, in fairness, is incidental to the substance of his commentary) is an apt starting point for a Catholic *apologia pro purgatorio* intended for an evangelical audience. This is because it expresses a broadly held Evangelical assumption that purgatory is an accretion of an overweening speculative tradition built on dubious principles and which, under the withering critique of the Reformers, has only lately gone on a desperate search for scriptural warrants.

The assumption is, alas, abetted by the fact that the doctrine of purgatory—along with eschatology generally—has fallen into widespread theological neglect amongst Roman Catholics. This is a fact as curious as it is troubling, since the historically vexed questions of soteriology cannot adequately be resolved without theological clarity about the last things. Put another way, any meaningful talk about the order of means must be done in light of the ends toward which they tend and in which they have their term. Purgatory ought to be of particular interest in this regard since it may be treated under the formal aspect of soteriology (since it is the final sanctification of the just, but imperfect, soul) or of eschatology (since it is the place of departed souls who, upon their particular judgment, have an indefectible assurance of heaven).[2] This essay intends to examine some of the scriptural and theological grounds for the doctrine of purgatory and, further, to indicate how it represents the full flowering of the Church's teaching on salvation by grace alone.[3]

Quid Sit Purgatorium?

Following the Second Council of Lyons (1249), the Council of Florence (1439) declared:

> If those who are truly penitent die in the love of God before having satisfied by worthy fruits of penance for their sins of commission and omission, their souls are cleansed after death by purgatorial punishments. In order that they be relieved from such punishments, the act of intercession of the living faithful benefit them, namely, the sacrifices of the Mass, prayers, alms, and other works of piety that the faithful are wont to do for the other faithful according to the Church's practice."[4]

Father Reginald Garrigou-Lagrange expresses it this way:

> According to the doctrine of the Church purgatory is the place of those souls that have died under obligation to suffer still some temporary pain, due to venial sins not yet forgiven, or to sins already forgiven but not yet expiated. They remain in purgatory until the debt which they owe to divine justice has been fully paid. They pay this debt progressively, not by merit or satisfaction, for the time of merit has gone by, but by satispassion, that is by enduring voluntarily the satisfactory suffering inflicted on them. Their sufferings may be shortened by suffrages made for them and especially by Masses in their favor.[5]

In other words, purgatory is exclusively for those who have been justified by God's grace, but who must be purged of unremitted venial sins and the disordered attachments that naturally prevent the soul from enjoying the perfect beatitude of heaven. The pains of purgatory are not a satisfaction for sin, for no one can merit anything once he is separated from the body; rather, it is the willing[6] and glad suffering of those in love with God who are assured of their final beatitude[7] and who desire nothing other than to complete in themselves "that which is behind of the afflictions of Christ."[8] Moreover, the sufferings of those in purgatory may be mitigated by the prayers and good works done in supernatural charity by those still in this life and able to acquire merit.

This will, of course, appear to principled Evangelicals a confirmation of their worst suspicions about what Catholics understand by grace. Catholics and Evangelicals have on multiple occasions agreed that God's free and unmerited gift in Christ Jesus is the only way to heaven—that we are saved by grace alone. The doctrine of purgatory, however, seems to give the lie to all that by insisting that all but the most holy Christians must endure an indeterminate period of great suffering before entering into their rest. The Good News appears good only by comparison with eternal damnation, and grace, so far from being a free gift, threatens to require perhaps lifetimes of suffering beyond the grave. The ecumenical task, then, is not merely to establish the scriptural grounds of the doctrine, but also to explain it as the outworking of the inner logic of the gospel of grace.

Scriptural Foundations

Amongst the errors of Martin Luther condemned by Pope Leo X in the Bull *Exsurge Domine* (1520) was the proposition that "purgatory cannot be proved from any Sacred Scripture that is in the canon."[9] So clear, it seemed, were the Scriptures on this matter that the pope could put Luther's assertion under the severest censure.[10] Catholic confidence on this point, however, beggars belief amongst Protestants. That our Lord's saying in Matthew 12:32, for instance, should imply the possibility of forgiveness after death is regarded by Protestants as rather "a slender thread on which to hang so great a weight."[11] But as the Arian controversy demonstrates, it is one thing to identify scriptural supports for a doctrine and quite another to establish it as thoroughly scriptural. In the first case, the job involves the simple arithmetic of tallying Bible passages, while the second requires showing the doctrine's necessary place in the *regula fidei*. In one sense, then, almost any text taken on its own will be too slender a thread. Be that as it may, this study will take its initial bearings by particular passages, and so the remainder of this section will examine "the usual suspects," beginning with the controverted book of 2 Maccabees.[12]

It may be objected that recourse to a deuterocanonical text is hardly helpful in an ecumenical discussion. Yet all but the most intransigent biblicist will grant that the texts of the Alexandrian canon, even if they must finally be denied the claim to divine authorship, are nonetheless revelatory of the mind or Zeitgeist of Second Temple Judaism. This is emphatically the case for the books of the Maccabees, which provide an invaluable window into the world of first-century BC Jewish history and piety. The relevant text is 2 Maccabees 12:43-46, in which we read:

> [Judas Maccabeus] would have a contribution made; a sum of twelve thousand silver pieces he levied, and sent it to Jerusalem, to have sacrifice made there for the guilt of their dead companions. Was not this well done and piously? Here was a man kept the resurrection in mind; he had done fondly and foolishly indeed, to pray for the dead, if these might rise no more, that once were fallen! And these had made a godly end; could he doubt, a rich recompense awaited them? A holy and wholesome thought it is to pray for the dead, for their guilt's undoing.[13]

Remarking on this passage in his *Commentary on the Sentences*, Thomas Aquinas says that "we are not taught to pray for the souls of the dead who are in heaven, nor for those who are in hell, hence there must be a purgatory after death, where the souls of the just pay the debts which they did not pay on earth."[14] Now whatever one may think of this episode, e.g., whether it is descriptive or, as Thomas thinks, normative, it cannot be doubted that prayer for the dead was the universal practice of the Jews of the late Second Temple period. We must note, however, that if it were a superstitious abuse of the true religion, it would certainly be of the gravest sort—and the more wondrous that Jesus says not a word against or about it.

The New Testament passages that have been traditionally adduced as scriptural proofs for purgatory are naturally more familiar. The aforementioned passage in Matthew 12, on the unforgivable sin of blaspheming the Holy Spirit, is by itself unlikely to shed much light on the question.

Nevertheless, this "slender thread" of which Hodge spoke seemed strong enough for St. Augustine:

> The prayers of the Church, or of good persons, are heard in favor of those Christians who departed this life not so bad as to be deemed unworthy of mercy, nor so good as to be entitled to immediate happiness. So, also, at the resurrection of the dead there will some be found to whom mercy will be imparted, having gone through those pains to which the spirits of the dead are liable. Otherwise it would not have been said of some with truth, that their sin "shall not be forgiven, neither in this world, nor in the world to come," unless some sins were remitted in the next world.[15]

It is important to recall that this is the voice of the mature Augustine, that is, of the established *doctor gratiae* who has by this time fought and won the battle against the Pelagians. It would be remarkable indeed for a thinker of Augustine's stature to be unaware of such a fundamental contradiction in his own thought if this passage were at odds with anything in his anti-Pelagian writings. It might be true, but to suppose that he is unself-knowing in just this way is, willy-nilly, a claim to know Augustine better than he knew himself.

1 Corinthians 3:13-15 is, of course, the clearest reference we have in the New Testament to a purifying fire associated with the Day of the Lord. It is this passage above all, says John Calvin, with which Catholics "have tainted the golden purity of the divine word with the pollution of purgatory."[16] In the same chapter of the *Institutes* Calvin makes bold to claim that Augustine denied this passage referred to a purgatorial fire. Yet Augustine himself leaves no doubt as to how it is to be interpreted. Commenting on Psalm 38:1,[17] he says that the psalmist prayed this way in order that

> You may cleanse me in this life, and make me such, that I may after that stand in no need of the cleansing fire, for those "who are to be saved, yet so as by fire" (1 Corinthians 3:15). Why? Why, but because they "build upon the foundation, wood, stubble, and hay." Now they should build on it, "gold, silver, and precious stones" (1 Corinthians 3:12), and should have nothing to fear from either fire: *not only that which is to consume the ungodly for ever, but also that*

> which is to purge those who are to escape through the fire. For it is said, "he himself shall be saved, yet so as by fire." And because it is said, "he shall be saved," that fire is thought lightly of. For all that, though we should be "saved by fire," yet will that fire be more grievous than anything that man can suffer in this life whatsoever...[18]

It is evident that Augustine held that there are two fires: one that is eternal and for the unsaved, the other that is temporary and for those who are saved. The latter, he warns, involves a far greater measure of suffering than any cross in this life could.

The common objection to this interpretation is that Paul is referring specifically to Christian teachers who are charged with building up God's Church. The materials that will be tried by fire are the doctrines that have been built upon the sure foundation of Christ himself. This has been the typical way in which Reformed Christians, if not all Evangelicals, have understood this text. Calvin himself interprets it in this way:

> For [Paul] designates them builders of the Church, who, retaining the proper foundation, build different materials upon it; that is, who, not abandoning the principal and necessary articles of faith, err in minor and less perilous matters, mingling their own fictions with the word of God. Such, I say, must suffer the loss of their work by the destruction of their fictions. They themselves, however, are saved, yet so as by fire; that is, not that their ignorance and delusions are approved by the Lord, but they are purified from them by the grace and power of the Holy Spirit.[19]

Certainly many contemporary Catholic exegetes read Paul in a similar way,[20] and really there is no reason to cavil at the notion that the Apostle is referring here primarily to teachers of doctrine—indeed, the context fairly requires it. Still, the specific context does not preclude a more general application of the principle. Calvin even grants that Paul says the "works of all men [i.e., not just teachers] will be tried." In any case, it is not immediately clear why teachers would undergo a fiery trial from which all others charged with building up the Body of Christ are happily dispensed.

To cite every Father of Church who reads 1 Corinthians 3:13-15 in the way Augustine does would be unnecessary to the argument and burdensome to the reader. It will suffice merely to note that he is in very good company. Origen, Basil the Great, Gregory of Nyssa, Cyril of Jerusalem, Jerome, Ambrose, and Cyprian, to say nothing of much later writers such as Thomas Aquinas, all agree in the matter. And while this is not, strictly speaking, a proof of anything, one ought to be very circumspect before going toe-to-toe with such a great cloud of witnesses.

I should say that my purpose in referencing the Fathers at all in a section on scriptural foundations is partly because, unlike modern exegetes, they are permanent authorities in interpreting the Bible. Every competent Scripture scholar has some sense that he will be vindicated or not before the bar of their work. The more important reason, however, is that they had a demonstrable sense of the unity of Scripture that has largely been lost in the modern dogmatic commitment to hermeneutical "methodology"—that is, the insistence on a rule-guided mode of procedure that owes far more to Descartes and Spinoza than to the *analogia fidei*. This is to say that, by and large, the great pre-modern interpreters of the Bible understood that its teaching on purgatory cannot be ascertained by restricting their inquiry to its "clear and distinct" references to purgative fire, prayer for the dead, or the possibility of forgiveness in the hereafter. In fact, all of these point beyond themselves to a more fundamental and pervasive scriptural idea that the Fathers took for granted, namely, that of satisfaction and the corollary notions of debt and credit. A brief examination of these concepts may be useful for grasping, e.g., the continuity between Jesus' emphasis on reward and merit on the one hand, and, on the other, Paul's insistence on the salvific uselessness of works.

In his landmark study of the biblical idea of sin,[21] Gary Anderson explains that in late Second Temple Judaism a dramatic shift takes place in the way the Scripture speaks about sin. In the Old Testament, sin is characterized either in terms of a "burden" that weighs upon the sinner or a "stain" that sullies him. It is, in other words, a "something" that must be lifted or washed away. But by Jesus' time, sin is understood almost exclusively in terms of indebtedness. The sinner is in debt to God and others. Happily, goodness and virtue have the corresponding effect of reversing the debt of sin by funding a "treasury in heaven."[22] This partly accounts for Jesus' extensive use of economic or monetary imagery in his teaching on sin and forgiveness. The language of reward, merit, debt, and satisfaction abounds in the Gospels. It was with a view to preserving the plain sense of this aspect of Jesus' teaching that the Council of Trent's *Decree on Justification* (1547) declared that only an adversary of Christian orthodoxy would "assert that the just sin in all their works if in those works, while overcoming their sloth and encouraging themselves to run the race, they look for an eternal reward in addition to their primary intention of glorifying God."[23] Jesus appeals directly to the ambitious, honor-loving, reward-seeking instinct in his hearers—what Plato called the *thumotic*, or "spirited," element in the soul. In the spiritual life, Jesus praises the calculating, the shrewd, and the acquisitive. Whatever else they may be, the meek who will inherit the earth are certainly not pusillanimous or retiring. Not to put too fine a point on it, but the man of the Beatitudes bears no resemblance to the *Gelassenheit*-style Lutheran. This is particularly important in understanding how the Gospel transforms the ineradicable human wish to satisfy divine justice. The Gospel of Jesus Christ does not expose this instinct as vain or sinful, but only as impotent. Grace does not nullify it, but rather makes it fruitful. This is a biblical truth, but how it may be so takes us beyond the limits of a purely biblical theology.

THEOLOGICAL AND ANTHROPOLOGICAL CONSIDERATIONS

Though the *Ninety-Five Theses* were published in 1517, it would be another 13 years before Luther would definitively deny any necessity of satisfaction for our sins, on the basis that this would bespeak an insufficiency in Christ's own superabundant satisfaction. But this sets up an opposition of nature and grace that is scripturally unwarranted and, not incidentally, formally similar to Marcionism. As Reginald Garrigou-Lagrange so neatly puts it:

> The first and universal cause does not exclude second causes, but grants them the dignity of causality, somewhat like a sculptor who should make statues which live. Thus the satisfactory merits of Christ do not exclude our own, but rather create them. Christ causes us to work with Him and in Him. St. Paul said: "Bear ye one another's burdens, and so you shall fulfill the law of Christ." Again, "I now rejoice in my sufferings for you and fill up those things that are wanting of the sufferings of Christ, in my flesh, for His body,

which is the Church." Certainly nothing was lacking to the sufferings of Christ in themselves, but they lacked fulfillment in our own flesh.[24]

When the order of justice is violated, it must be reestablished by voluntary acceptance of a compensating punishment.[25] David and Moses were each forgiven grave sins; nevertheless, the former was warned that "the sword shall not depart from your house," and the latter was forbidden to enter the land of promise. Contrition and repentence may be enough for forgiveness, but they cannot of themselves restore the order of justice.

At this juncture it may seem to Evangelicals that "a great chasm has been fixed" between Protestants and Roman Catholics at the level of first principles: "Christ has made superabundant satisfaction for our sins and his completed work admits of no augmentation. If Catholics profess to believe this, they can only mean it in some Pickwickian sense, given their understanding of satisfaction." But the Church that univocally condemned Pelagianism as a heresy has not betrayed either its patrimony or its principles. The satisfactory merits of Christ are sufficient to redeem universes of human beings, yet these must be applied to each individual in order to be efficacious.[26] "Just as the first cause does not render useless second causes but gives to them the dignity of causality, so the merits of Christ do not render our merits useless, but arouse our own wills to make us work with him, through him, and in him for the salvation of souls, and in particular for our own soul."[27] One might understandably reply that they would happily forego a "dignity" that is likely to require, as Augustine says, "a fire more grievous than anything that man can suffer in this life whatsoever." Yet it must be remembered that the first and universal cause is not sequentially first, but ontologically so—that is, it is always operative in secondary causes as the condition of their being causes at all. Thus the Christian's meritorious satisfaction is neither an addition to, nor independent of, Christ's own: "I am crucified with Christ: nevertheless I live; yet not I, but Christ liveth in me: and the life which I now live in the flesh I live by the faith of the Son of God, who loved me and gave himself for me."[28] A Christian's satisfaction for sin is necessarily made in intimate union with the Beloved who makes it efficacious and fruitful.

Satisfaction, or reparation, for sins in this life is meritorious; Christ's free gift becomes our merit by participation in his own superabundant satisfaction. Our merits may fluctuate, or be lost altogether, according to the measure in which we become "partakers of the divine nature."[29] Yet while Christ frees us from the debt of eternal punishment, there remain the temporal punishments for sins, mortal or venial, that have already been forgiven. Sanctification is the natural growth of the supernatural organism by which the order of justice is restored according to our share in the cross of Christ. But if temporal punishments are still due at the time of death, purgatory completes that work, though not by way of satisfaction and merit, since mere souls cannot merit. It is, instead, by means of what is called "satispassion," or the voluntary suffering of the saved who are not yet properly attired in the "wedding garments"[30] of the blessed. In other words, purgatory "applies what was lacking on earth in the line of satisfaction."[31] The doctrine of purgatory is God's pledge to those who die in his friendship that they may indeed be "confident of this very thing, that he which hath begun a good work in you will perform it until the day of Jesus Christ."[32]

Beyond this, however, there are two other reasons for purgatory. First, the justified soul is very often parted from the body with unforgiven venial sins. Second, there will frequently remain in the separated soul the injurious effects of sins that have already been forgiven, which the tradition has called the "remains" of sin. In the first case, venial sins, the sins that are not "unto death,"[33] are expunged in the voluntary satispassion of the soul that died without the contrition required for their remission. These small, usually habitual sins done in thought, word, or deed are committed so often by believers that they routinely go unnoticed and unrepented, and while they do not destroy the life of grace in the soul, they hinder its tendency toward union with Christ. Purgatory is God's gracious provision for their elimination.

The second case involves the soul whose sins have been remitted, but in whom are the "remains" or injurious effects of sin. These are habitual dispositions or inclinations toward created goods that are formed by preceding acts. Such dispositions are naturally weaker than the supernatural charity that the Holy Spirit creates in the justified believer, and so they grow more feeble the longer the believer lives in a state of grace. Now, since many of these disordered dispositions are rooted in bodily appetites, it might fairly be objected that the mere separation of the soul at death would itself be purgative. In one sense this is true, but as inclinations of the rational being, they perdure in the will that is disordered by them. Only the soul and its faculties, then, are purged and perfected.

Such are the theological reasons for the necessity and the existence of purgatory. First, sins already forgiven often demand a temporal suffering. Second, venial sins may still remain. Third, defective dispositions, although their corporeal element disappears, remain as inordinate dispositions of the will. Of these three reasons, the chief is the first. It is, we think, demonstrative because of the revealed principles on which it rests.[34]

Conclusion

In examining some of the scriptural and theological grounds for the doctrine of purgatory, I have not sought to explicate the doctrine in all of its details.[35] More or less exhaustive treatments of the doctrine have been written by much better authors and are readily available. I have set myself the more modest, and safer, task of identifying some of its scriptural and theological foundations. I have also attempted to show how purgatory is a natural outworking of the Gospel of grace; that so far from qualifying or blunting the Good News, it represents the fullest expression of its power.

Finally, viewed under the formal aspect of anthropology, all of the scriptural grounds and theological reasons for the necessity of purgatory converge on what Aristotle calls the "character" (ἦθος)[36] of the soul. They are rooted in the varying states of the souls that enter into their particular judgment. Of those who die in a state of grace, some are creatures fit for beatitude—heavenly creatures—while others must be made so. In this way, the Particular Judgment is less a declaration of positive law than a revelation of what sort of creature now stands before his Lord. What had they become by the time they arrived at the end of all becoming? Of course, if righteousness in Christ is forensic, purgatory must seem an intolerable and monstrous cruelty. But if, on the other hand, as C.S. Lewis put it, "It is safe to tell the pure in heart they shall see God, for only the pure in heart want to,"[37] then the purgative fire must be for those saved but imperfect souls a supreme work of grace by which their desire for heaven is brought to perfection by a purification of their divided hearts.

Since this essay began with an eminent Evangelical thinker, it seems fitting to end it with another. No Protestant writer better expresses the longing of the Christian heart for a final purgation than Lewis. To him goes the last word:

> Our souls *demand* Purgatory, don't they? Would it not break the heart if God said to us, "It is true, my son, that your breath smells and your rags drip with mud and slime, but we are charitable here and no one will upbraid you with these things, nor draw away from you. Enter into the joy"? Should we not reply, "With submission, sir, and if there is no objection, I'd rather be cleaned first." "It may hurt, you know"— "Even so, sir."[38]

Notes

[1] Charles Hodge, *An Exposition of the First Epistle to the Corinthians* (New York: R. Carter & Brothers, 1857), 58.

[2] The Council of Trent takes the former route, treating it in the *Decree on Justification*. The *Catechism of the Catholic Church* adopts the latter approach, devoting a small section to the doctrine under the 12th article of the Creed.

[3] This is not, therefore, an essay of original or creative theologizing, but rather an exposition on some aspects of the Church's normative teaching. Hodge was fond of saying that in all his years at Princeton Seminary, the school had never taught anything new. I should be glad if this essay is likewise successful.

[4] "Item, si vere paenitentes in Dei caritate decesserint, antequam dignis paenitentiae fructibus de commissis satisfecerent et omissis, eorum animas poenis purgatoriis post morte purgari: et ut a poenis huiusmodi releventur, prodesse eis fidelium vivorum suffraggia, Missarum scilicet sacrificia, orations et eleemosynas, et alia pietatis official, quae a fidelibus pro aliis fidelibus fieri consueverunt secundum Ecclesia institute." Hünermann, Peter, Helmut Hoping, Robert L. Fastiggi, Anne Englund Nash, and Heinrich Denzinger, *Compendium of Creeds, Definitions, and Declarations on Matters of Faith and Morals*, 43rd edition (San Francisco: Ignatius, 2012) (hereafter D.), 1304.

[5] Reginald Garriou-Lagrange, O.P., and Patrick Cummins, Patrick, O.S.B. trans., *Life Everlasting* (St. Louis: B. Herder Books Co, 1952), 147.

[6] It should be noted that it is not willed unconditionally, else it would not be punishment. Cf. Thomas Aquinas, *De Malo*, q. 7, a. 2.

[7] The *Catechism of the Catholic Church* stresses the fact that those in purgatory enjoy the assurance of final beatitude even as they are purged from venial sins and from all disordered attachments: "All who die in God's grace and friendship, but still imperfectly purified, are indeed assured of their eternal salvation; but after death they undergo purification, so as to achieve the holiness necessary to enter the joy of heaven." *Catechism of the Catholic Church* (New York: Doubleday, 1995), 1030.

[8] Col. 1:24 (Authorized Version).

[9] D., 1487.

[10] "All and each of the above-mentioned articles or errors, as set before you, we condemn, disapprove, and entirely reject as respectively heretical or scandalous or false

or offensive to pious ears or seductive of simple minds and in opposition to Catholic truth." *D.*, 1492.

11 Charles Hodge, *Systematic Theology*, vol. 3 (New York: Scribner, Armstrong, and Co., 1872), 752.

12 Given the scope of this essay, I will be examining only a few of the many Scripture passages that have been understood by both ancient and modern exegetes to refer to a purgatorial fire for the elect.

13 Knox translation.

14 *IV Sent.*, dist. 21, q. 1, a. 1. Cf., the Appendix to the *Supplementum* of the *Summa Theologiae*: "Now there is no need to pray for the dead who are in heaven, for they are in no need; nor again for those who are in hell, because they cannot be loosed from sins. Therefore after this life, there are some not yet loosed from sins, who can be loosed therefrom; and the like have charity, without which sins cannot be loosed, for 'charity covereth all sins'" [Prov. 10:12].

15 "Nam pro defunctis quibusdam, vel ipsius Ecclesiae, vel quorumdam piorum exauditur oratio: sed pro his quorum in Christo regeneratorum nec usque adeo vita in corpore male gesta est ut tali misericordia judicentur digni non esse, nec usque adeo bene, ut talem misericordiam reperiantur necessariam non habere. Sicut etiam facta resurrection mortuorum non deerunt quibus post poenas, quas patiuntur spiritus mortuorum, impertiatur misericordia, ut in ignem non mittantur aeternum. Neque enim de quibusdam veracitur diceretur in isto tamen remittitur in future." Augustine, *De Civitate Dei*, XXI, 24. For his part, Gregory the Great summarily explains that "in this sentence it is given to understand that many sins can be remitted in this world, but also many in the world to come." ("In qua sententia datur intelligi quasdam culpas in hoc saeculo, quasdam vero in futuro posse laxari.") Gregory the Great, *Dialogorum Libri IV*.

16 John Calvin, *Institutes of the Christian Religion*, Book III, chapter 5, trans. Henry Beveridge (London: James Clarke & Co., 1949), 580.

17 "O LORD, rebuke me not in thy wrath, neither chasten me in thy hot displeasure."

18 Augustine, *Enarrationes in Psalmos*, English translation in the public domain, accessed http://www.ccel.org/fathers2/NPNF1-08/TOC.htm. Emphasis added.

19 Calvin, *Institutes*, III.5.

20 See, for instance, the notes on this chapter in *The Ignatius Catholic Study Bible, New Testament* (San Francisco: Ignatius Press, 2010), 288.

21 Gary Anderson, *Sin: A History* (New Haven: Yale University Press, 2009).

22 Ibid, 22. Anderson prevents us from drawing the facile conclusion that "God is nothing more than a meticulous accountant whose sole task is to keep the heavenly books in balance." Far from it, in fact: "Acts of human generosity funded a treasury that did not play by the rules of a zero-sum economy. Giving alms was like being an initial investor in a company that would eventually rise to the top of the market. The returns one could expect from such an investment would be beyond calculation. God has 'gamed' the system to the advantage of the faithful."

23 *D.*, 1539.

24 Garrigou-Lagrange, 149.

25 Cf. *Summa Theologiae* IaIIae, q. 87, a. 6.

26 Cf. Robert Bellarmine, *De Purgatorio*, ch. 14.

27 Garrigou-Lagrange, 164.

28 Gal. 2:20 (Authorized Version).

29 2 Pet. 1:4.

30 Matt. 22:11.

31 Garrigou-Lagrange, 162.

32 Phil. 1:6 (Authorized Version).

33 1 Jn. 5:16.

34 Garrigou-Lagrange, 163-64.

35 I have, for instance, adverted to prayer for the dead only insofar as the practice indicates an established belief in the forgiveness of certain sins after death and an ultimate satisfaction for these and their remains by which the order of justice is definitively restored.

36 ἦθος must be distinguished from χαρακτήρ. The former term denotes "a stable condition of the soul that makes someone apt to choose in a consistent way...the word refers to active conditions determined by deliberate choices to form oneself in particular ways..." The latter term means "the distinctive mark scratched or stamped on anything, and which is never used in the *Nicomachean Ethics*." Taken from the Glossary and Introduction of Joe Sachs' extraordinary translation of the *Nicomachean Ethics* (Newburyport: Focus Philosophical Library, 2002), 202, xx. There is a very real way in which the difference between Catholics and Protestants on this question is the difference between ἦθος and χαρακτήρ.

37 C.S. Lewis, *The Problem of Pain* (New York: Macmillan, 1944), 145.

38 C.S. Lewis, *Letters to Malcolm: Chiefly on Prayer* (New York: Harcourt Brace Jovanovich, 1964), 107-09.

Background Paper

Nothing Unclean Will Enter Heaven: Justification and Eschatology

Dr. Christian D. Washburn

On October 31, 1517, the 33-year-old Martin Luther posted his 95 *Theses* on the door of the Castle Church in Wittenberg to protest a wide variety of matters that he considered abuses in the Church. Central to this protest was his critique of the Church's doctrines concerning indulgences and purgatory; and while he had not yet formulated his doctrine of justification by faith alone, he already saw, albeit inchoately, the connection between justification and eschatology. The Council of Trent too saw this connection and throughout its *Decree on Justification* desired to reconfirm the deposit of faith on these matters against errors past and present. Thus Trent authoritatively teaches that the "final cause" of justifying grace is both the glory of God and of Christ and life everlasting. Moreover, the council goes on to define that the justified can merit eternal life, the attainment of eternal life, and an increase in glory. Ultimately, justification is of its nature eschatologically oriented to man's fuller perfection, which can be found "only in the glory of heaven."[1] This paper will explore the essential link between the Catholic doctrine of justification and its relationship to man's end. Thus this paper will discuss the four last things: death, judgment, hell, and heaven. Death will be examined as the end of the probationary period on earth, and the particular judgment will be considered in its relationship to justification. The paper will then discuss hell as the abode of those who were never justified or who at the time of death had lost their justification through mortal sin. The paper will then discuss the doctrine of purgatory as the final state of purgation and heaven as the fulfillment of one's justification.

Death

Catholic theology generally uses the term "death" in three distinct ways. Death can refer to death of the soul as the result of mortal sin, to eternal death (hell), and lastly to physical or natural death. Natural death is usually defined as the separation of the soul from the body.[2] It is Catholic doctrine that death is a punishment for sin and that all human beings who are subject to original sin are also subject to death. This teaching is based in part on the following scriptural testimony: "And just as it is appointed for men to die once" and "For as in Adam all die, so also in Christ shall all be made alive."[3] This has given rise to two questions. First, given certain exceptional cases such as Enoch and Elias[4], is death universal? Most theologians have held that Enoch and Elias will eventually die.[5] Second, will those who are alive when Christ returns die? Again the answer is yes. Aquinas holds, for example, that

> it is held with greater probability and more commonly that all those that are alive at the coming of our Lord, will die, and rise again shortly. If, however, it be true, as others hold, that they will never die, ... then we must say in reply to the objection, that although they are not to die, the debt of death is none the less in them, and that the punishment of death will be remitted by God, since He can also forgive the punishment due for actual sins.[6]

Catholic doctrine is clear in teaching that death is the end of the probationary period for man since the human soul undergoes judgment immediately after death.[7] For our purposes the significance of this is that at death those who are not justified will no longer be able to be justified and that the justified are no longer able either to merit or demerit.[8]

The Particular Judgment

Immediately after death, the soul is subject to the particular judgment in which God judges the soul and immutably determines the soul's eternal destiny. Historically, there have been a number of opinions on the judgment and its execution. Vigilantius and Luther seem to have taught a form of soul-sleep in which the souls of the just do not know where they are until the Day of Judgment.[9] Calvin seems to have held that the judgment will not be fully executed until the final judgment. For the development of Catholic doctrine, however, the most important controversy was over the teaching of Pope John XXII (1244-1334). Beginning in 1331, the pope delivered a series of sermons in which he argued that the purified souls of the dead only have a vision of the humanity of Christ and do not enjoy the face-to-face vision of God until the Resurrection.[10] The pope was not proposing his thesis magisterially and even circulated his own sermons, requesting from theologians a theological and doctrinal evaluation of his teaching. Despite the tentative nature of his thesis, John XXII was widely and publicly criticized for his teaching. The pope convoked a commission of cardinals and theologians to study whether his thesis was an open theological question, and they concluded that it was not an open question but rather a serious error. On December 3, 1334, the pope, with great humility, retracted his view in the presence of a notary and the College of Cardinals in the bull *Ne super his*. In this bull, John was clear that "the purified souls separated from the body ... clearly see God and the divine essence face to face."[11] He also went on to affirm that with respect to his previous opinion, he should be understood to have been "discoursing and discussing" the topic "in the disposition of the Catholic faith." He added that if he had said anything in conformity with the Catholic faith, then he approved it, but if it was contrary to Catholic doctrine or to sacred Scripture, he rejected it and submitted "to the judgment of the Church and our successors all that we have said or written on any subjects."[12] John XXII died the following day, December 4, at 89 years of age.

Benedict XII (r. 1334-1342) was elected as his successor and had his predecessor's bull published.[13] The new pope commissioned a group of cardinals and theologians to study the problem. On January 29, 1336, Benedict XII issued the constitution *Benedictus Deus*, in which he declared that its teaching was "to remain in force forever."[14] Benedict solemnly defined that

According to the general disposition of God, the souls of all the saints ... provided they were not in need of any purification when they died, or will not be in need of any when they die in the future, or else, if they then needed or will need some purification, after they have been purified after death—and again the souls of children who have been reborn by the same baptism of Christ or will be when baptism is conferred on them, if they die before attaining the use of free will: all these souls, immediately (*mox*) after death and, in the case of those in need of purification, after the purification mentioned above, since the ascension of our Lord and Saviour Jesus Christ into heaven, already before they take up their bodies again and before the general judgment, have been, are and will be with Christ in heaven, in the heavenly kingdom and paradise, joined to the company of the holy angels. Since the passion and death of the Lord Jesus Christ, these souls have seen and see the divine essence with an intuitive vision and even face to face.... Moreover we define that according to the general disposition of God, the souls of those who die in actual mortal sin go down into hell immediately (*mox*) after death and there suffer the pain of hell.[15]

Benedict's teaching was reconfirmed by Pope Clement VI (r. 1342-1352) and the Council of Florence (1431–1449).[16] This teaching entails that all are judged immediately after death.

Hell

In Catholic theology, the term hell, or "*infernus*," refers to those "secret dwellings in which are detained the souls that are not included in the happiness of Heaven."[17] The term can therefore refer to four distinct things. First, it can refer to the "bosom of Abraham" or *limbus patrum* in which the souls of the just who died before the death of Christ awaited their liberation and triumphal procession to heaven. Catholics understand that this is the meaning signified in the Apostles' Creed when it is said that Christ "descended to hell" (*descendit ad inferos*). Catholics reject any view that would cause Christ to descend to the hell of the damned, as was taught by several Protestant theologians in the 16th century.[18] Second, it can refer to the limbo of the infants (*limbus parvulorum*), in which the children who die with original sin alone suffer natural punishments. Third, it can refer to purgatory. Fourth, it can signify the state and place of punishment for the damned.[19] It is this fourth meaning that is considered hell in the strict sense and to which we now turn.

There are two essential characteristics of hell. First, the punishment of hell lasts for all eternity. There was little controversy in the Church concerning the eternity of hell until the sixth century, when the controversy over Origen's (184/185-253/254) purported doctrine of restoration or "apocatastasis" erupted. In apocatastasis the punishment of hell is essentially a form of temporal purification; after it is completed, all persons, including the fallen angels, would obtain beatitude. In response, the Synod of Constantinople first condemned this theory in 443, and then adopted by the bishops of the Second Council of Constantinople in 553 explicitly condemned anyone who taught that "the punishment of the demons and of impious men is temporary, and that it will have an end at some time, or that there will be a restoration (*apokatastasis*) of demons and impious men."[20] This teaching on the eternity of hell and its punishments was then repeatedly affirmed by the magisterium, both explicitly and implicitly. The Fourth Lateran Council (1215) states that they who have done evil works will receive "perpetual punishment with the devil," and the Council of Trent repeatedly refers to *perpetual punishment, eternal punishment*, and *eternal damnation*.[21]

The second characteristic of hell is that the punishments of the damned are proportioned to each one's demerits. This was taught by the Councils of Lyons and of Florence, both of which declared that the souls of the damned are punished with different (*disparibus*) punishments.[22] Christ, for example, clearly distinguished between the punishment on Tyre and Sidon and the punishment inflicted on the unbelieving inhabitants of Corozain and Bethsaida.[23] St. John says of the corrupt city of Babylon: "Render to her as she herself has rendered, and repay her double for her deeds; mix a double draught for her in the cup she mixed. As she glorified herself and played the wanton, so give her a like measure of torment and mourning."[24]

Catholic doctrine asserts that the nature of the punishment of hell for the unjustified is twofold: the pain of loss (*poena damni*) and the pain of sense (*poena sensus*). The pain of loss consists in the exclusion from the beatific vision. The pain of sense (*poena sensus*), on the other hand, is the suffering caused by material things and is amply testified to in sacred Scripture, particularly by the use of the term "fire."[25] Catholic theologians generally follow St. Thomas' explanation for the existence of this pain of sense. Namely, sins are not performed by a disembodied intellect, but rather the body partakes in some sins and therefore in justice needs to be punished.[26] The one difficulty, of course, with the pain of sense, which would include material fire, is how the soul prior to the Resurrection is affected by it. Most theologians are satisfied to accept this as a mystery; they usually offer St. Thomas' explanation that it is *per modum alligationis*, i.e., through a bond between the fire and the soul.[27]

Catholic theologians generally avoid a consideration of some of Dante's more creative pains of sense, with one exception: fire. This pain has some direct scriptural warrant, and two competing opinions arose over its nature. A few theologians, e.g., Gregory of Nyssa and Ambroisus Catharinus, understood this fire in a metaphorical sense for spiritual pains.[28] Almost all Catholic theologians until the modern period, however, maintained that while "this opinion has not been formally condemned by the church," the existence of a physical fire is the common teaching of both the Fathers of the Church and theologians.[29] Theologians generally adhere to the biblical descriptions of hell as "the furnace of fire,"[30] a "lake that burns with fire and sulphur,"[31] "the fury of fire which will consume,"[32] "flaming fire inflicting vengeance upon those who do not know God and upon those who do not obey the gospel of our Lord Jesus"[33]; according to one, "the fire is not quenched. For every one shall be salted with fire."[34] The basic concern of Catholic theologians in maintaining this teaching is not a crass and uninformed biblical literalism but a wish to preserve the reality of the bodily resurrection. Catholic theologians speculatively discuss the nature of this fire, holding that the fire of hell is unlike fire on earth for several reasons. First, hell's fire never dies out as earthly fire does. Second, earthly fire gives light whereas hell's fire does not. Lastly, due to the nature of the bodily resurrection, earthly fire consumes that which it burns while hell's fire does not.[35]

Lastly, there is the controverted question of whether hell is a "place." Many contemporary theologians dismiss such speculation as "mythological"[36]; however, most Catholic theologians have affirmed that hell is a "place" for two basic reasons.[37] First, they wish to preserve the various biblical descriptions of hell as an "abyss"[38] or "under our feet,"[39] both suggesting a locus. Second, they take seriously the reality of the Resurrection. In the general Resurrection souls will be reunited with their bodies and, if they are human bodies, they will have some real and physical relation to space. For those theologians who consider hell as a place, a secondary speculative question naturally arises concerning hell's precise location. These theologians, including St. Thomas Aquinas and St. Robert Bellarmine, generally hold that it is subterranean.[40]

The doctrine of hell is necessarily linked to the doctrine of justification, for hell, as has been repeatedly and dogmatically taught, is reserved for those who die in the state of sin. This includes those who die in the state of original sin alone, i.e., who had neither received justification nor committed a personal sin.[41] Original sin is the direct opposite of what is referred to in the tradition as the "state of original justice," understood as the inherent condition of human nature as originally found in Adam and as intended for all his progeny by the justificatory decree of God. Hell is also reserved as the punishment for those who have received justification but lost it through personal mortal sin. The opposition to justice in the case of mortal sin is redoubled, for personal sin is not only the ratification of those tendencies and liabilities that, though by no means sin as such, are the consequence of original sin, but also a voluntary rejection of Christ's justice on the part of the individual person. Just in case one might be inclined to view man's incapacity to obtain by his own efforts his ultimate end, i.e., the vision of God, as something rooted per se in the sinful state of the unjustified man, or in the tragically debilitated state of the justified man, Aquinas reminds us that human nature even unblemished could never suffice to attain that end: "the rational creature... excels every other creation in this: that he is capable of the highest good in virtue of having as his ultimate end the vision and enjoyment of God, although the principles of his own nature are not sufficient to attain this but he needs the help of divine grace."[42] Therefore, without justifying grace, beatitude is not possible. If hell is the consequence of the loss of justice, heaven is the consequence of the gift of justice, which is sanctifying grace. Justice and injustice, then, are the intrinsically defining features of heaven and hell.

Purgatory

There are only two *doctrines* that have been solemnly defined by the magisterium concerning purgatory.[44] First, the magisterium has defined that purgatory (*purgatorium*) exists as the place or the state in which the souls of the just who die with venial sin or the temporal punishment due to sin are purged of this sin and attachment to sin. Second, the souls therein can be assisted by the faithful on earth. Both of these teachings have been repeatedly and definitively defined at the Second Council of Lyons (1274), the Council of Florence (1431-1449), and the Council of Trent (1563).[45] In the history of theology there has been a great deal of *theological* speculation about the nature, punishment, and location of purgatory by theologians and mystics. Trent cautions bishops that they should ensure that "in homilies to uninstructed people the more difficult and subtle questions, which do nothing to sustain faith and give rise to little or no increase of devotion should be excluded." They should also avoid "uncertain speculation or what borders on falsehood" and "all that panders to curiosity and superstition."[43]

Scripture also testifies to the act of praying for the dead. For Catholics, 2 Maccabees 12:43-46, in which the prayers and good works of those on earth assist the dead, is decisive. This practice of praying for the dead was continued in the early church, with ancient monuments, early liturgies, and the writings of the Fathers of the Church repeatedly testifying to this. Thus Tertullian (c. 160-220), Cyprian (d. 258), Eusebius of Caesarea (c. 263-339), Ephrem the Syrian (c. 306-373), Epiphanius of Salamis (c. 310-403), Cyril of Jerusalem (c. 315-386), Gregory of Nyssa (c. 335-c. 394), Ambrose (c. 337-397), John Chrysostom (347-407), Sulpicius Severus (363-420), Augustine (354-430), Cyril of Alexandria (c. 376-444), Peter Chrysologus (c. 380-c. 450), Possidius (5th c.), Pseudo-Dionysius (6th c.), Eustratius (6th c.), and Gregory the Great (c. 540-604) all testify to praying for the dead.[46] Moreover, a number of the Fathers either list this practice as of apostolic origin or, like Augustine and Epiphanius, consider it heretical to hold that "sacrifice ought not to be offered for the dead."[47] Therefore, it cannot be true that prayers for the dead entered into Christian thought only on account of "public custom" or simply as a means of appeasing human emotions, as some argue.[48] The Fathers are clear that the purpose of the practice of offering prayers and Mass for the dead is a "help" or "benefit" to the faithful departed. Thus, Augustine, Cyril of Jerusalem, Epiphanius, Eusebius of Caesarea, Gregory the Great, and John Chrysostom all describe prayers for the dead as "helping" or "assisting" the dead.[49] The Fathers do not pray for those in heaven or those in hell, since in both cases they cannot be helped.[50]

While there has been no definitive declaration of the nature of the punishments in purgatory, the magisterium has spoken of the "pains" of purgatory.[51] Catholic theologians generally agree that purgatory contains two types of punishment: the pain of loss (*poeno damni*) and the pain of sense (*poeno sensus*). The pain of loss is due to the loss of the beatific vision and all those goods that accompany it. The precise nature of purgatory's pain of sense is the subject of speculation. The pain of sense is a positive anguish inflicted by God through an external agent as the instrument of punishment; many theologians hold that it is the result of a corporeal fire. This leads to the question: In what way could the pain of sense afflict an immaterial soul separated from the body? The solution offered is similar to the solution we saw above for the souls who are being punished in hell between the particular and general judgments. These pains are generally taken to be rather acute since the poor souls realize that the sin and punishment could have simply been expiated by contrition, confession, almsgiving, or prayer.[52] As to the gravity of this punishment, Catholic theologians generally admit that nothing certain is known; St. Thomas, however, thinks that the slightest punishment in purgatory exceeds the greatest penalty of this life, while St. Bonaventure holds that the greatest penalty of purgatory exceeds those of this life but that the lightest does not.[53]

Given this discussion of punishment, it is appropriate to ask: how does the state of the souls in purgatory differ from those in hell? First, the justified souls in purgatory have a certitude that they will attain beatitude while those in hell have despair. The souls in purgatory have finished their period of probation, and so there is no possibility of falling into sin. Moreover, in the particular judgment, God through His immutable will determines that the end of these souls is beatitude. Second, the punishments of purgatory, although the same as those in hell in a certain respect, are not eternal.[54] Moreover, contemporary Catholic theology would like to emphasize

> the healing and reparative character of purgatorial suffering ... These sufferings tend to be described as the pain attendant upon the purification that comes with assimilation into unimpeded

communion with God. Thus, the International Theological Commission states: "Where there is a delay in reaching the possession of the beloved, there is sorrow, a sorrow that purifies."[55]

At this point it is useful to recall the way that the justified Christian is called to deal with sin on earth. In initial justification, as Trent teaches, man becomes a friend of God in such a way that he is made "innocent, unstained, pure, and guiltless," and all punishment is remitted.[56] Trent notes, however, that "during this mortal life, men, however holy and just, fall at times into at least light and daily sins, which are also called venial."[57] It is for this reason that Trent went so far as to affirm that "the whole Christian life ... ought to be one of continual (*perpetua*) penance,"[58] for the appropriate Christian response to sin, whether venial or mortal, is penance. This penance is comprised of contrition, confession, and satisfaction; the last can be either sacramental or extra-sacramental satisfaction. In either case, through a humble and contrite confession the Christian is led to perform works of satisfaction, which is nothing other than "the full payment of a debt" and "compensation for an injury done to another."[59] It is only by participation in Christ that this satisfaction can be accomplished:

> This satisfaction that we make for our sins is not ours in such a way that it be not through Christ Jesus. For, while we can do nothing of ourselves as of ourselves, we can do everything with the cooperation of him who strengthens us. Thus man has nothing wherein to glory, but all our glorying is in Christ, in whom we live, in whom we merit, in whom we make satisfaction, bringing forth worthy fruits of penance.[60]

For the work to be truly satisfactory—as opposed, for example, to meritorious—the work must involve some aspect of pain or difficulty.[61] It is precisely by undergoing these penances that "we are made like unto Jesus Christ our Head, inasmuch as He Himself suffered and was tempted."[62] This satisfactory work, however, when united to Christ, is not just a payment of debt but also a salutary aid to help the Christian to lead a life in conformity with God's will. First, it helps detach the Christian from sin. Second, it acts as a bridle against future sin. Third, it destroys evil habits by acts of virtue opposed to them. Fourth, it destroys the residual effects of sin.

Unfortunately, some of the justified die without having been united more closely to Christ through making acts of satisfaction (contritely asking for forgiveness for those "light and daily sins") or purging themselves of their inordinate attachments to the people and things of this world.[63] Once in purgatory, they are deprived of the ability to engage in works of satisfaction since their probationary period is over. They can no longer lovingly seek out the cross, uniting their wills with that of Christ's. They are only left with voluntarily accepting and enduring the sufferings offered to them, which theologians call satispassion (*satispassio*). What makes this satispassion effective is the same thing that makes satisfaction effective: union with Christ in divine love.[64] In any case, this suffering unites the souls in purgatory more closely to Christ. Just as satisfaction in the present life not only pays a debt in full but also leads Christians to live a life according to God's will, so too it is with satispassion, for not only is the debt paid through satispassion, but also the poor souls who undergo this voluntary suffering become more virtuous and the attachments of the world fall away.

Finally, Catholic theologians treat, at least briefly, the temporal-spatial dimensions of purgatory. The question of the location has a long history that was given some support from the language of Trent, which uses the noun "purgatorium" for purgatory and describes the souls as detained "there" (*ibi*) in relation to it.[65] St. Robert Bellarmine notes that it is almost "unanimously" held by theologians that purgatory is a place located below the earth in the same place called hell.[66] Virtually all Catholic theologians describe it as both a place and a state. Even so, these theologians have been reluctant to discuss purgatory's precise location.[67] Moreover, a number of theologians also maintain that purgatory is subject to time, unlike either heaven or hell.

Heaven

Justification is the root of salvation, so that in the Scriptures the justified on earth are said to have eternal life now[68] and the guarantee of an inheritance.[69] The souls of the justified, which in the moment of death are free from all guilt of either mortal or venial sin and of the punishment due to sin, enter immediately into heaven and have the beatific vision.

Trent speaks of eternal life both as a grace mercifully promised to the sons of God in their initial justification through Christ Jesus and as a reward promised by God for the good works and merits of the justified.[70] Thus one has a kind of twofold claim on heaven that is in fact due to justice, the justice of God who is faithful to His promises. Note that this twofold claim is based entirely on the promises of God, that is, on His faithfulness to the divine promise extended to man in initial justification and to what He has bound Himself (irrevocably agreed to) in relation to man's works — which means that it is a matter not only of justice but ultimately, and principally, the justice of God. The degree of sanctifying grace in the individual prior to death will determine the degree of the light of glory possessed by the soul in heaven. This light of glory is an additional gift of sanctifying grace, and the degree of the light of glory will determine the degree of our beatific vision.[71] Thus the degree of justification in this life determines the quality of one's vision in the next life.

Boethius classically defines beatitude of heaven as "a perfect state with the aggregation of everything good."[72] This beatitude can be divided into essential and accidental happiness. Essential beatitude consists in the vision of God, the love of God, and the joy of God. The beatific vision of man is that clear and intuitive, but not comprehensive knowledge of God as He is in Himself. Man's intellect is naturally incapable of having this vision, and so a new supernatural faculty, *lumen gloriae*, is bestowed on man in order for him to be able to have this vision of God. Man's will now loves God perfectly, which ultimately involves a freedom from evil, either physical or moral.[73]

In addition to this essential beatitude, there is also the accidental happiness or beatitude, which proceeds from the natural knowledge and love of created things. Part of accidental beatitude are the three classes of aureoles bestowed on the blessed. These aureoles are a kind of exceptional reward for an exceptional victory[74]: the martyrs for their victory over the world, the virgins for their victory over the flesh, and the teachers of the faith for their victory over the devil, who is the father of all lies. This ordering of the aureoles is a matter of excellence so that one accidental gift of beatitude is greater than another. Thus the death of the martyr most closely conforms him to Christ, while the subduing of the flesh of the virgin has a certain likeness to martyrdom that is greater than that of the teacher. These special rewards give to those who receive them an internal joy for the works they performed against the enemies of salvation.

There are two essential properties of heaven that are matters of faith: the inamissibility of heaven and the inequality in the heavenly reward. First, Catholic theologians consider the inamissiblity of heaven to be *de fide* from the Creed's description of heaven as eternal life (*vita aeterna*), the Fourth Lateran Council (1215), and Benedict XII's *Benedictus Deus*.[75] Second, doctrinally one must hold that there is a fundamental inequality in the degree to which one participates in the beatific vision that is proportioned to one's merits on earth. This proposition is taken to be *de fide* from the Council of Florence, which defines that those who go to heaven will be received immediately into the divine presence, but some of these will see God "more perfectly than others, according to the diversity of their merits."[76] Moreover, Trent anathematizes those who deny that one can merit an "increase in glory."[77] There are two basic reasons for this inequality. First, the Scriptures suggest this diversity since Christ will render to each according to his works,[78] glorious bodies will vary in brightness,[79] and there are many mansions in the Father's house.[80] Second, this proposition concerning the degrees of beatitude corresponds in adult believers with their fundamental inequality in both grace and merit.[81] One must be careful to note, however, that this inequality in beatitude is not an absolute inequality, as the Parable of the Workers in the Vineyard[82] makes clear. For beatitude is equal for all according to object—i.e., God Himself—according to the nature of beatitude itself, and according to duration.

Lastly, most Catholic theologians describe heaven as not only a "state" but also a "place." Catholic theologians generally note that while this has never been "expressly" defined by the Church, one cannot deny that heaven is a real place "without great temerity."[83] Catholic theologians provide a number of arguments in favor of heaven as a place, or *locus*. Scripture often describes heaven as a place into which one enters and from which one can depart. In Revelation, St. John describes it as a city with walls. Although clearly a metaphor, the vision would be misleading if heaven is not in some way limited. More convincing, perhaps, a few argue with reference to *analogia fidei* that resurrected bodies, whether Christ's or ours, are material bodies that must have some relation to location.[84]

Notes

1 *Lumen Gentium,* 48.

2 Franc. X. De Abarzuza, O.F.M. Cap., *Manuale Theologiae Dogmaticae,* 2nd ed. (Madrid: Ediciones Studium, 1956), 2:399; J.M. Hervé, *Manuale Theologiae Dogmaticae,* 16th ed. (Westminster, MD: The Newman Bookshop, 1943), 4:552; Sylvester Joseph Hunter, S.J., *Outlines of Dogmatic Theology* (London: Longmans, Green and Co., 1896), 3:426; H. Hurter, S.J., *Theologiae Dogmaticae Compendium,* 12th ed. (Oeniponte: Libraria Academica Wagneriana: 1908), 2:606; Bernhard Jungmann, *Tractatus de novissimis* (Ratisbonæ: F. Pustet, 1874), 3; Albert Knoll, *Institutiones Theologiae Theoreticae seu Dogmatico-Polemicae,* 4th ed. (Augustae Taurinorum: P. Marietti, 1868), 6:126; Heinrich Lennerz, *De novissimis* (Roma: Universitas Gregoriana, 1950), 100; Christian Pesch, *Praelectiones Dogmaticae,* 3rd ed. (Freiburg im Breisgau: B. Herder, 1911), 9:273; Joseph Pohle, *Eschatology or the Catholic Doctrine of the Last Things: A Dogmatic Treatise,* adapt. and ed. Arthur Preuss (St. Louis: B. Herder Book Co., 1929), 5; Joseph Sagüés, S.J., *Sacrae Theologiae Summa,* 4th ed. (Matriti: Biblioteca De Autores Cristianos, 1967), 4:835; Thomas B. Scannell, *A Manual of Catholic Theology* (New York: Benzinger Brothers, 1898), 2:535; François Xavier Schouppe, *Elementa theologiae dogmaticae e probatis auctoribus collecta : et divini verbi ministerio accommodata* (Lyon; Paris: Delhomme et Briguet, 1867), 2:469; George D. Smith, ed., *The Teaching of the Catholic Church: A Summary of Catholic Doctrine* (New York: The Macmillan Company, 1949), 2:1104; Adolphe Tanquerey, *Synopsis Theologiae Dogmaticae,* 27th ed. (Paris: Desclée et Socii, 1953), 3:756. It might be added that this also seems to be the assumption both in Benedict XII's *Benedictus Deus* and in the Council of Florence's decree of union with the Greeks. See DH 530-531/1000 and 693/1304-1305.

3 Heb. 9:27; 1 Cor. 15:22.

4 Heb. 11:5; 2 Kings 2:11.

5 According to St. Thomas Aquinas, Enoch and Elias were preserved in the atmospheric heaven, i.e., an earthly paradise, but not in the empyrean heaven, i.e., heaven properly speaking. See St. Thomas Aquinas, *Summa Theologiae,* III, q. 49, a. 5.

6 St. Thomas Aquinas, *Summa Theologiae,* I II, q. 81, a. 3, ad 1.

7 Louis Billot, *Quaestiones de novissimis* (Rome: Universitatis Gregorianae, 1946), 9. Christian Pesch, *Praelectiones Dogmaticae,* 9:278-80.

8 A few contemporary theologians such as Karl Rahner and Ladislaus Boros have attempted to argue in favor of a "final option" at the moment of death in which the dying person has a last chance to choose his eternal destiny. Karl Rahner, S.J., *On the Theology of Death* (New York: Herder and Herder, 1961), 35–39. Ladislaus Boros, S.J., *The Mystery of Death* (New York: Herder and Herder, 1965), 86–99. For a critique of this theory, see Germain Grisez, *Christian Moral Principles* (Chicago: Franciscan Herald Press, 1983), 445; and Bartholomew J. Collopy, S.J., "Theology and the Darkness of Death," *Theological Studies,* 39 (1978): 22–54.

9 *The Hope of Eternal Life -- Common Statement of the Eleventh Round of the U.S. Lutheran-Catholic Dialogue,* eds. Lowell G. Almen and Richard J. Sklba (Minneapolis: Lutheran University Press, 2011), 27.

10 For a detailed presentation of this controversy, see Appendix IV: Jared Wicks, S.J., "The Intermediate State: Patristic and Medieval Doctrinal Development and Recent Receptions," in *The Hope of Eternal Life -- Common Statement of the Eleventh Round of the U.S. Lutheran-Catholic Dialogue,* 159-70.

11 John XXII, *Ne super his.* DH 991.

12 John XXII, *Ne super his*. DH 991.
13 John XXII, *Ne super his*. DH 990-91.
14 Catholic theologians see this as an early example of an infallible declaration. See Klaus Schatz, "Welche bisherigne päpstlichen Lehrentscheidungen sind 'ex cathedra'? Historische und theologische Überlegungen," in *Dogmengeschichte und katholische Theologie* (Würzburg: Echter, 1985), 404-22. Klaus Schatz, *Vaticanum I, 1869-1870* (Paderborn: F. Schöningh, 1992), 3:331-39.
15 DH 1000-02.
16 DH 1066-67. DH 1304-06, 1314-16.
17 "Verum inferorum nomen abdita illa receptacula signifcat, in quibus animae detinentur quae caelestem beatitudinem non sunt consecutae." *Catechismus Romanus seu Catechismus ex decreto Concilii Tridentini ad Paraochos Pii Quinti Pont. Max. iussu editus*, ed. Petrus Rodríguez et al. (Città del Vaticano: Libreria Editrice Vaticana/Ediciones Univ. de Navarra, 1989), 70.
18 Catholic theology generally has limited the descent of Christ's soul to the *limbus patrum*. Robert Bellarmine, *Disputationes Roberti Bellarmini Politiani Societatis Jesu, de controversiis Christianae fidei, adversus hujus temporis haereticos* (Paris: Triadelphorum, 1613), 2.4.10, 1:417. On the *Book of Concord*, Bellarmine notes, "Sextus error est, quod totus Christus, Deus & homo, ad inferos descenderit." *Judicium de Libro Concordiae*, 4:1196. Or as Gregorio de Valencia writes, "Caeterum sententia Ecclesiae Catholicae CERTA & indubitata est, Christum secundum animam vere ac proprie & substantialiter descendisse ad illum saltem locum infernum, qui fuit *limbus* sanctorum Patrum, non minus quam vere etiam ac proprie & substantialiter secundum corpus fuit positus in sepulchro." Gregorio de Valencia, *Commentariorum Theologicorum Tomus Quartus complectens materias Tertiae Partis ac supplementi D. Thomae*, vol. 4, 578. On this issue in the Fathers, see Jared Wicks, S.J., "Christ's Saving Descent to the Dead: Early Witnesses from Ignatius of Antioch to Origen," *Pro Ecclesia* 17 (2008): 281-309.
19 Compare the manuals on this point to *Catechismus Romanus seu Catechismus ex decreto Concilii Tridentini ad Paraochos Pii Quinti Pont. Max. iussu editus*, 70-71.
20 DH 411. There is some debate over when and by whom these canons were issued. Brian E. Daley, *The Hope of the Early Church: A Handbook of Patristic Eschatology* (Peabody, MA: Hendrickson Publishers, 2003), 188-90. Tanner does not include in his edition of the decrees of Constantinople II the anti-origenist anathemas since he believes that "recent studies have shown that these anathemas cannot be attributed to this council." Norman P. Tanner, S.J., *Decrees of the Ecumenical Councils* (London: Sheed & Ward, 1990), 1:105-6. It may be true that these canons do not form a part of the *acta*; nevertheless, the council fathers, while waiting for the official opening of the council, confirmed the canons. Richard Price, *The Acts of the Council of Constantinople of 553: With related texts on the Three Chapters Controversy* (Liverpool: Liverpool University Press, 2009), 2:271. In any case, these canons were accepted almost universally. The Third Council of Constantinople reconfirms the teaching of Nicaea, Constantinople, Ephesus, and Chalcedon: "with the fifth holy synod, latest of them, which was gathered here against Theodore of Mopsuetia, Origen, Didymus and Evagrius." Tanner, *Decrees of the Ecumenical Councils*, 1:124-25. The Council of Florence affirmed that it "embraces, approves and accepts the fifth holy synod, the second of Constantinople," in which the "many errors of Origen and his followers, especially about the penitence and liberation of demons and other condemned beings, were refuted and condemned." Tanner, *Decrees of the Ecumenical Councils*, 1:580.

21 DH 801/429, 1575/835, 1580/840, 1705/915.

22 DH 858/464, 1306/693. See also DH 926/493a.

23 Matt. 11:22.

24 Rev. 18:6-7.

25 Matt. 13:30-50; Matt. 18:8; 25:41; Mark 9:42ff; Heb. 10:27; Rev. 18:8; 19:20; 20:9.

26 Thomas Aquinas, *Summa contra gentiles*, IV, 89; *Summa Theologiae*, Suppl. 1. 98.

27 Thomas Aquinas, *Summa contra gentiles*, IV, 90; *Summa Theologiae*, Suppl. 1. 98.

28 Gregory of Nyssa, *De anima et resurrectione* (PG 46:67); Ambrosius Catharinus, "De bonorum praemio et supplicio malorum aeterno," in *Opuscula* (Ridgewood, NJ: Gregg Press, 1964), 145-47. Pesch, *Compendium*, 265.

29 Abarzuza, *Manuale Theologiae Dogmaticae*, 2:434; Billot, *Quaestiones de novissimis*, 83; Garrigou-Lagrange, *Life Everlasting*, trans. Patrick Cummins (Rockford, IL: Tan Books and Publishers, Inc., 1991), 127; Hervé, *Manuale Theologiae Dogmaticae*, 4:651; Hunter, *Outlines of Dogmatic Theology*, 3:437; Hurter, *Theologiae Dogmaticae Compendium*, 2:619-621; Jungmann, *Tractatus de novissimis*, 30; Knoll, *Institutiones Theologiae Theoreticae seu Dogmatico-Polemicae*, 187; Lennerz, *De novissimis*, 65; Ott, *Fundamentals of Catholic Dogma*, 481; Pesch, *Praelectiones Dogmaticae*, 9:332-339; Sagüés, *Sacrae Theologiae Summa*, 4:949; *Synopsis Theologiae Dogmaticae*, 3:824-825.

30 Matt. 13:42.

31 Rev. 21:8.

32 Heb. 10:27.

33 2 Thess. 1:7-8.

34 Mark 9:48-49. Both St. Thomas and Bonaventure want to understand texts like this according to the literal sense. St. Thomas, *Light of Faith: The Compendium of Theology* (Manchester: Sophia Institute Press, 1993), 205-06. St. Bonaventure, *Breviloqium*, vol. 2 of *The Works of Bonaventure* (Paterson, NJ: St. Anthony Guild Press, 1963), part 7, c. 6, p. 299-302.

35 Thomas Aquinas, *Summa Theologiae*, Suppl. 1. 97, a. 6.

36 Karl Rahner, S.J., "Hell," *Sacramentum mundi: An Encyclopedia of Theology*, ed. Karl Rahner (New York: Herder and Herder, 1968-1970), 3:8. Hans Küng, *Eternal Life?: Life After Death as a Medical, Philosophical, and Theological Problem* (Garden City, NY: Doubleday, 1984), 141. The English edition of *L'Osservatore Romano* contained the following translation of John Paul II's Wednesday catechesis: "Rather than a place, hell indicates the state of those who freely and definitively separate themselves from God, the source of all life and joy." John Paul II, "Hell is the state of those who Reject God," *L'Osservatore Romano* (August 4, 1999), 7. The Italian daily edition records the passage slightly differently, suggesting that hell is "more" than a place: "L'inferno sta ad indicare più che un luogo, la situazione in cui viene a trovarsi chi liberamente e definitivamente si allontana da Dio, sorgente di vita e di gioia." *L'Osservatore Romano* (July 29, 1999), 4. The Jesuit journal *Civilta Cattolica* offers a slightly more assertive stance, boldly stating that "La dottrina della Chiesa riguardante l'Inferno, quindi, consiste in due proposizioni che si devono credere come verità di fede: *1) esiste l'Inferno*, che non è un <<luogo>>, ma uno <<stato>>, un <<modo di essere>> della persona, in cui questa soffre la pena della privazione di Dio." The editorial then suggests that "Perciò è fuorviante – anche se l'immagine popolare cosi si figura l'Inferno – pensare che Dio, per mezzo dei demoni, infligga ai dannati tormenti spaventosi, come quello del fuoco; . . ." "L'Inferno. Riflessioni su un tema dibattuto," *La Civilta' Cattolica* (July 17, 1999), 111.

37 Abarzuza, *Manuale Theologiae Dogmaticae*, 2:438; Garrigou-Lagrange, *Life Everlasting*, 98; Hervé, *Manuale Theologiae Dogmaticae*, 4:633; Hunter, *Outlines of Dogmatic Theology*, 3:451; Hurter, *Theologiae Dogmaticae Compendium*, 2:626; Jungmann, *Tractatus de novissimis*, 21; Knoll, *Institutiones Theologiae Theoreticae seu Dogmatico-Polemicae*, 174; Pesch, *Praelectiones Dogmaticae*, 9:344; Schouppe, *Praelectiones Dogmaticae*, 477; Smith, *The Teaching of the Catholic Church*, 1:1188; Tanquerey, *Synopsis Theologiae Dogmaticae*, 3:806.

38 Luke 8:31.

39 Num. 16:31.

40 Num. 16:31ff; Ps. 55:15; Matt. 12:40, Eph. 4:9; Phil. 2:10; Rev. 5:3; Rev. 12:9. St. Thomas also appears to consider hell as a subterranean location. *Summa Theologiae* Suppl. q. 97, a. 7. The following is Bellarmine's discussion of the location of hell. "The place (locus) [of hell], I say, is the depth, since on account of the immense crimes by which they offend the divine majesty, the reprobate will be imprisoned in the deepest part of the earth, which is furthest distant from the royal palace which is in the heavens. This is fitting to punish appropriately the pride of the devil and of proud men... From this first woe of the reprobate there follow three others: darkness, tight confinement, and need. Since hell is in the center of the earth where the rays of the sun and the moon and the stars cannot penetrate, there can be no light in it, except that of the sulfurous flames, which serve not to lessen, but to increase the punishment. For that light will give them sight of the demons, their most cruel enemies, and of those men, whether friends or relatives, who were the cause of their damnation. They will see their own nakedness, their deceitfulness, their chains, their torments, all of which they might well wish not to see. Certainly they will not see anything good from which they might derive consolation. Oh, darkness not dark! Darkness because it hides everything good, and yet not dark because it makes visible everything evil." He continues, "The confines of hell are so narrow that they can scarcely hold the bodies of the damned. For the earth is almost an indivisible point in comparison with the immensity of the heavens, and hell encompasses not the whole of it, nor a half, but only the center. Moreover, the number of these damned exceeds the number of the saved... And so who can grasp the tightness of the confines of hell?... Mortals strive to extend and broaden all their field, their rules, their kingdoms, so that for a little while they might boast of their many subjects, and there never occurs to them the narrowness of the confines of hell that awaits them where they will be forced to dwell, not for a little while, but forever, whether they like it or not." Robert Bellarmine, *The Art of Dying Well*, in *Spiritual Writings*, trans. and eds. John Patrick Donnelly and Roland J. Teske (New York: Paulist Press, 1989), 331-32. Robert Bellarmine, *L'Arte di Ben Morire*, in *Roberto Bellarmino Scritti*, ed. Pasquale Giustiniani (Brescia: Editrice Morcelliana, 1997), 3:478.

41 "The souls of those who die in mortal sin or with original sin only, however, immediately descend to hell, to be punished with different punishments..." Council of Lyons II (1274). DH 858/464. "Moreover, the souls of those who depart in actual mortal sin or in original sin only, descend immediately into hell but to undergo punishments of different kinds." Council of Florence (1438-1445), Decree for the Greeks from the Bull *Laetentur coeli*. DH 1306/693. "The affirmation that 'the punishment for original sin is the loss of the beatific vision,' formulated by Innocent III, pertains to the faith: original sin is of itself an impediment to the beatific vision. Grace is necessary in order to be purified of original sin and to be raised to communion with God so as to be able to enter into eternal life and enjoy the vision of God." International Theological Commission, *The Hope of Salvation for Infants who Die Without Being Baptized*, 36.

⁴² Thomas Aquinas, *On Evil*, trans. Jean T. Oesterle (Notre Dame, IN: University of Notre Dame Press, 1995), 211.

⁴³ St. Catherine of Genoa, *Purgation and Purgatory; The Spiritual Dialogue* (New York: Paulist Press, 1979).

⁴⁴ DS 464, DH 1304/693, 1820/983.

⁴⁵ DH 1820.

⁴⁶ Christian D. Washburn, "The Value of Offering Sacrifice for the Dead in the Thought of the Fathers of the Church," *Antiphon* 16.3 (2012): 154-78.

⁴⁷ Augustine, *De haeresibus*, 53 (WSA I/18:47; CCSL 46:323-324). Epiphanius, *Panarion*, 3.1.75.8 (PG 42:513).

⁴⁸ Calvin, *Institutes of the Christian Religion*, 3.5.10, vol. 1, 682-83.

⁴⁹ Washburn, "The Value of Offering Sacrifice for the Dead in the Thought of the Fathers of the Church," 168.

⁵⁰ Ibid., 158-65.

⁵¹ "Ecclesia de hac re nihil definivit." Sagüés, 972. Bellarmine writes, however, "Certum est in purgatorio esse aliquam poenam sensus." Bellarmine, *De Controversiis*, 6.2.10, 2:642. Magisterial evidence of this position can be found in two places. In the Council of Florence's decree, *Decretum pro Graecis*, it is specified that "the souls of these are cleansed after death by purgatorial punishments" (*eorum animas poenis purgatoriis post mortem purgari*). DH 1304/693. At first sight this text seems innocuous enough; however, notice that *poena* is in the plural, and therefore there must be punishments other than simply the deprivation of the beatific vision. The Second Council of Lyon speaks of "punishments" as well. DH 854/464.

⁵² Pohle, *Eschatology*, 83.

⁵³ Ibid., 84.

⁵⁴ *CCC* 1031. CDF, "The Reality of Life After Death" in Austin Flannery, ed., *Vatican II: More Postconciliar Documents* (Grand Rapids: W.B. Eerdmans, 1982), 2:500-04.

⁵⁵ *Hope of Eternal Life*, 83.

⁵⁶ DH 1515.

⁵⁷ DH 1537.

⁵⁸ DH 1694.

⁵⁹ *Catechismus Romanus*, 297. St. Thomas defines satisfaction as "the payment of the temporal punishment due on account of the offences committed against God by sin." Thomas Aquinas, *Summa Theologiae*, Suppl. 1. 12. a. 3.

⁶⁰ DH 1691.

⁶¹ *Catechismus Romanus*, 302.

⁶² Ibid., 300.

⁶³ We can, of course, recall the example of St. Teresa of Avila, who was "very frightened and disturbed" after Christ rebuked her for certain friendships she maintained. In this vision Teresa's will was brought into conformity with that of Christ. *The Book of Her Life*, in *The Collected Works of St. Teresa of Avila*, vol. 1, 2ⁿᵈ edition, trans. Kieran Kavanaugh, O.C.D., and Otilio Rodriquez, O.C.D. (Washington, DC: ICS Publications, 1987), 85.

⁶⁴ While satispassion suffices for the remission of temporal punishment (*reatus poenae*), the theologians following St. Thomas hold that those in purgatory must not just endure

65 DH 1820.

66 Bellarmine states: "Sequitur quaestio quarta: 'ubi sit Purgatorium?' De qua quaestione nihil Ecclesia definivit; sunt autem multae opiniones." After surveying eight opinions held by various Catholic theologians, he concludes, "Theologi fere omnes docent eodem in loco esse, et eodem igne torqueri damnatos, et animas Purgatorii." St. Robert Bellarmine, *Disputationes*, 6.2.6, 2:631, 633.

67 Abarzuza, *Manuale Theologiae Dogmaticae*, 2:419; Hervé, *Manuale Theologiae Dogmaticae*, 4:609; Tanquerey, *Manual of Dogmatic Theology*, 2:428. Bellarmine poses the question and answer, "Ubi sit Purgatorium? De qua quaestione nihil Ecclesia definivit; sunt autem multae opiniones." Bellarmine proceeds to give nine possible locations for purgatory. Bellarmine himself found it most plausible that purgatory is in "a subterranean place." Bellarmine, *Disputationes*, 6.2.6, vol. 2:631, 634.

68 Jn. 3:16.

69 2 Cor. 1:22, 5:5.

70 DH 1545.

71 Garrigou-Lagrange, *Life Everlasting*, 226-227.

72 Boethius, *On the Consolation of Philosophy*, 1.3. PL 63:724.

73 St. Thomas Aquinas, *Summa contra gentiles*, IV. c. 92.

74 St. Thomas Aquinas, *Summa Theologiae*, Suppl. q. 96, a. 1.

75 DH 802/430. DH 1000/530.

76 DH 1305/693 (Florence).

77 DH 1582/842 (Trent).

78 Matt. 16:27; 1 Cor. 3:8; 2 Cor. 9:6.

79 1 Cor. 15:42.

80 John 14:2. There is the difficulty presented by the parable of the laborers in Matt. 19:30 and 20:1-16 or 20:10, since those who labored but one hour had the same reward as those who toiled the whole day. Many Catholic theologians maintain that the point of the story is that the reward is the same, i.e., God himself. While each laborer possesses God, each does not possess God equally.

81 This is not necessarily true for baptized infants since they are incapable of merit, and the initial grace of baptism is equal. St. Thomas Aquinas, *Summa Theologiae*, III, q. 69, a. 8. Suarez, *De baptismo*, q. 69, s. 3, n.1-5. God could bestow grace extra-sacramentally upon infants, thereby rendering their beatitude unequal.

82 Matt. 20:1-16.

83 Hervé, *Manuale Theologiae Dogmaticae*, 4:699.

84 "Paradisum esse locum realem et determinatum, distinctum a loco Inferni et Purgatorii, sententia est communis theologorum, documentis Patrum et Ecclesiae innixa; in ipsum Christus ascendit, et in eo est Bta. Virgo Maria cum corpore suo assumpta, . . ." Abarzuza, *Manuale Theologiae Dogmaticae*, 2:447; Hunter, *Outlines of Dogmatic Theology*, 3:450; "Coelum est locus" Jungmann, 129; Knoll, *Institutiones Theologiae Theoreticae seu Dogmatico-Polemicae*, 6:250; Ott, *Fundamentals of Catholic Dogma*, 476; "theologi communiter affirmant," Sagüés, *Sacrae Theologiae Summa*, 4:910; Schouppe, *Elementa theologiae dogmaticae*, 482; Smith, *The Teaching of the Catholic Church*, 1:1269; "Caelum seu paradisus est status et locus . . .," Tanquerey, *Synopsis Theologiae Dogmaticae*, 3:770.

According to Bellarmine, "The place (*locus*) of heavenly paradise is high above all the mountains of the earth, above all the elements, above all the stars. . . The sublime location (*sublimissimo situ*) of the heavenly city shows us that this place has many privileges and prerogatives over all the other places of the world. First, the higher a place (*locus*) is in this universe, the larger and more spacious it is, since the shape of the universe of created things is seen to be round, with the earth occupying the center of the world and the highest heaven containing in its embrace the last or highest sphere of almost infinite width. Thus just as the place (*locus*) of the blessed is the highest, so it is the most spacious. So too, on the contrary, as the place of the damned is the lowest, it is also the smallest of all. . . . The seat of the blessed is most spacious; the blessed can freely move about from one place to another. And there is no danger of their becoming tired since by the gift of agility they can move from place to place in a moment. . . An even greater pleasure lies in store for the blessed when they enjoy the pure air of heaven, which neither darkness nor fogs nor mists nor blasts of wind nor any pestilence can mar. Meanwhile the inhabitants of hell, wretched beyond all means, are forced to lie in that place of horror in the black fog and smoke of the seething furnace with no hope of purer air." Robert Bellarmine, *The Art of Dying Well*, 334-35.

John Paul II noted in his Wednesday (July 21, 1999) audience on the last things: "In the context of Revelation, we know that the 'heaven' or 'happiness' in which we will find ourselves is neither an abstraction nor a physical place in the clouds, but a living, personal relationship with the Holy Trinity." "Heaven is Fullness of Communion with God," *L'Osservatore Romano*, July 28, 1999, 7.

Contributing Authors: Background Papers

Dr. Christopher Castaldo, Ph.D. is the Lead Pastor at New Covenant Church in Naperville, IL: He earned the Ph.D. from the London School of Theology, was formerly the director of the Ministry of Gospel Renewal at Wheaton College, and is the author of several books including *The Reformation: Is It Over?* from Zondervan Press, 2016.

Dr. Bruce Cromwell holds the Ph.D. in Historical Theology from Saint Louis University and has been the Lead Pastor at Central Free Methodist Church in Lansing, MI since 2007. Dr. Cromwell serves on the Free Methodist denomination's Study Commission on Doctrine and is also the Vice-President of the Free Methodist Urban Fellowship.

Dr. David P. Fleischacker, Ph.D. is Professor of Theology at the University of Mary, Bismarck, North Dakota. He serves as the dean of the School of Arts and Sciences. Dr. Fleischacker's publications can be found in the *Newman Studies Journal, The Thomist, Logos: A Journal of Catholic Thought and Culture, Logos: A Journal of Eastern Christian Studies,* and *Divyadaan: Journal of Philosophy and Education*.

Dr. Steven Hoskins, Ph.D. is Associate Professor of Religion at Trevecca Nazarene University, Nashville, TN, where he has served on the faculty the past twenty-two years. He is an ordained minister in the Church of the Nazarene and the founding President of the Wesleyan Historical Society.

Dr. Cheryl Johns, Ph.D. serves as the Robert E. Fisher Chair of Spiritual Renewal at Pentecostal Theological Seminary, Cleveland, TN. Dr. Johns was a member of the International Roman Catholic-Pentecostal Dialogue, served on the Commission on Faith and Order for the National Council of Churches, and has been active in Evangelicals and Catholics Together.

Dr. Jackie Johns, Ph.D. holds the Ph.D. from Southern Baptist Seminary and is an ordained minister in the Church of God, Cleveland. Dr. Johns serves on the faculty of Pentecostal Theological Seminary as Professor of Discipleship and Christian Formation and was the pastor of New Covenant Church of God, Cleveland, TN, for almost three decades.

DR. DENNIS W. JOWERS, PH.D. is Professor of Theology & Apologetics at Faith Evangelical College and Seminary in Tacoma, WA. Dr. Jowers is a member of the Korean American Presbyterian Church and the author of four books and many articles on apologetics and faith.

DR. DANIEL A. KEATING, PH.D. is Professor of Theology at Sacred Heart Major Seminary in Detroit, Michigan, where he teaches on Scripture, the Church Fathers, Ecumenism, and the New Evangelization. He is the author of *The Appropriation of Divine Life in Cyril of Alexandria* (2004), *Deification and Grace* (2007), *First and Second Peter, Jude* (2011), and co-author of *James, First, Second and Third John* (2017).

DR. GLEN W. MENZIES, PH.D. currently serves as Research Projects Coordinator for the Museum of the Bible's Scholars Initiative in Washington, DC. He is an ordained minister in the Assemblies of God church and from 2001-2015 served on the faculty of North Central University as Professor of New Testament and Early Christianity. He was also Dean of the Institute for Biblical and Theological Studies at North Park from 2011-2015.

DR. WILLIAM B. STEVENSON, PH.D. is Assistant Professor of Dogmatic Theology at the St. Paul Seminary School of Divinity at the University of St. Thomas in St. Paul, Minnesota. He has published articles on philosophy and theology in *The Thomist*, *Moreana*, and *Logos: a Journal of Catholic Thought and Culture*.

DR. CHRISTIAN D. WASHBURN, PH.D. is Associate Professor of Dogmatic Theology, at the Saint Paul Seminary School of Divinity at the University of St. Thomas in St. Paul, Minnesota. His articles have appeared in journals such as *Pro Ecclesia, Annuarium Historiae Conciliorum, The Thomist, Nova et Vetera,* and *Gregorianum*. He is also a member of both the National Lutheran-Roman Catholic Dialogue and the International Lutheran-Roman Catholic Commission on Unity.

DR. MALCOLM YARNELL, PH.D. is the Research Professor of Systematic Theology, Director of the Oxford Study Program, and Director of the Center for Theological Research at Southwestern Baptist Theological Seminary, Fort Worth, TX. Dr. Yarnell served as editor of the Southwestern Journal of Theology, has edited four academic books, and authored The Formation of Christian Doctrine: Royal Priesthood in the English Reformation, 2007.

Annual Dialogue Participants and Consultants

2014

Evangelical Participants
Bonn Clayton, Conservative Congregational Conference
Steve Hoskins, Church of the Nazarene
Glen Menzies, Assemblies of God
Dennis Jowers, The Korean Baptist Church
Bruce Cromwell, The Free Methodist Church
Paul Fleeman, The Salvation Army
Duane Fischer, The Wesleyan Church

Catholic Consultants
Christian Washburn
Daniel Keating
William Stevenson
David Fleischacker
Bishop John Gaydos

2015

Evangelical Participants
Bonn Clayton, Conservative Congregational Conference
Harold Bennett, The Church of God in Christ
Bruce Cromwell, The Free Methodist Church
Jackie Johns, The Church of God
Dennis Jowers, The Korean Baptist Church
Glen Menzies, Assemblies of God
Malcom Yarnell, Independent Baptist Churches
Steve Hoskins, Church of the Nazarene

Catholic Consultants
Christian Washburn
Daniel Keating
William Stevenson
David Fleischacker
Bishop John Gaydos

2016

Evangelical Participants
Bonn Clayton, Conservative Congregational Conference
Bruce Cromwell, The Free Methodist Church
Jackie Johns, The Church of God
Cheryl Bridges Johns, The Church of God
Gregg Allison, Southern Baptist Convention
Dennis Jowers, The Korean Baptist Church
Glen Menzies, Assemblies of God
Steve Hoskins, Church of the Nazarene

Catholic Consultants
Christian Washburn
Daniel Keating
David Fleischacker
Bishop John Gaydos

2017

Evangelical Participants
Bonn Clayton, Conservative Congregational Conference
Christopher Castaldo, New Covenant Church
Bruce Cromwell, The Free Methodist Church
Dennis Jowers, The Korean Baptist Church
Glen Menzies, Assemblies of God
Alan Satterlee, The Salvation Army
Steve Hoskins, Church of the Nazarene

Catholic Consultants
Christian Washburn
Daniel Keating
William Stevenson
David Fleischacker
Bishop John Gaydos

Index of Names

Abarzuza, Francis
    145, 147, 233, 306, 308, 309, 311
Abel
    201
Abelard, Peter
    170
Abraham
    115, 162, 165-169, 179, 187, 188, 192, 193, 201, 204, 255,
Adam
    33-35, 37- 39, 41- 47, 49, 51-53, 55-62, 90, 104, 106, 109, 112, 120, 124-126, 127, 129, 135, 169, 212, 251, 252, 266, 294, 299, and Eve 13-16, 35, 52, 58, 65- 69, 71, 142, 200- 204,
Ahab
    37
Aldama, Josepho
    233
Alexander VII
    124
Allen, David
    99
Allison, Gregg
    261, 274
Althaus, Paul
    99
Amaziah
    37
Ambrose
    58-61, 63, 285, 300,
Ambrosius Catharinus
    298
Ames, William
    49
Anderson, Gary
    285, 291
Anselm
    45, 46, 49, 103,
Aquinas, Thomas
    25, 41, 42, 46-47, 49, 67, 69, 73, 74, 127, 130, 132, 142- 146, 208, 213, 214, 223, 227, 229, 282, 285, 290, 294, 298, 299, 301, 308, 309, 310,
Aristotle
    72, 138, 289
Arminius, James
    20, 23- 25, 27, 30, 85, 108
Armstrong, Chris
    7
Arndt, Johann
    247
Athanasius
    56, 63, 251
Auer, Johann
    144
Augustine
    6, 19, 24-25, 46, 53, 55- 57, 59-63, 68, 72, 89- 91, 94-95, 98, 99, 104-105, 107-108, 112, 120, 136, 139, 146, 147, 183, 184, 188-191, 193, 195, 198, 199, 208, 217, 230, 231, 250, 251, 277, 283, 284, 287, 291, 300, 301

Baasha
37
Balak
36
Bandstra, Andrew
228
Bañez, Domingo
144
Barnes, Arthur
230
Barth, Karl
6, 99
Basil
19, 55, 285
Bavinck, Herman
49, 84, 93, 97, 99, 141, 226
Du Bay, Michel (Baius)
41, 48, 124, 125, 223,
Beatrice, Piero
58, 60, 62, 63
Bellarmine, Robert
127, 130, 134, 141-144, 146-148, 215,
217, 228, 229, 230, 231, 291, 299,
303, 307, 309-312
Benedict XII
147, 295-296, 305, 306
Benedict XVI
31
Berkhof, Louis
48, 141
Bernard of Clairvaux
84, 112, 258
Beza, Theodore
106, 107
Billot, Louis
233, 306, 308
Le Blanc de Beaulieu, Louis
171
Bloesch, Donald
85, 97
Böckle, F.
228
Boethius
304, 311

Boettner, Loraine
120
Bonaventure
301, 308
Bonhoeffer, Dietrich
99
Bonner, Gerald
195
Boros, Ladislaus
306
Brigden, Thomas
258
Brunner, Emil
85, 97
Bucer, Martin
264
Bullinger, Heinrich
274
Busch, Joseph
142
Caesarius of Heisterbach
255
Cain
95, 201
Calvin, John
23, 25, 84, 92- 97, 99, 106-107, 115,
121, 131, 144, 146, 226, 227-228, 230,
251, 261, 263, 264, 267, 275, 277,
283-284, 291, 310
Campbell, Frederick, Bishop
7
Campbell, Ted
258
Canaan
36
Cappadocians
58
Carveley, Kenneth
258
Cary, Phillip
90, 98
Castaldo, Chris
7, 261, 313, 316

Catherine of Genoa
310
Chamier, Daniel
170
Chemnitz, Martin
145
Cheung, Vincent
110
Chrysologos, Peter
300
Chrysostom, John
19, 56, 300, 301
Clayton, Bonn
1, 3, 7
Clement VI
296
Clement XI
124, 126, 128
Clement of Alexandria
19, 54, 60, 62
Clement of Rome
19
Cole, R. Alan
98
Collins, Kenneth
179, 182
Contarini, Gasparo
139
Corbett, John
229
Coulter, Dale
175-176, 182
Cromwell, Bruce
7, 241, 313
Cyprian
19, 55, 61, 63, 285, 300
Cyril of Alexandria
56, 57, 63, 183-184, 190-193, 195, 196, 300
Cyril of Jerusalem
285, 300, 301
Dabney, Robert Lewis
140, 146, 227

Daley, Brian
307
Dante
298
David
37, 74, 157-8, 179, 201, 204, 287
Denzinger, Heinrich
30, 48, 120, 141, 226, 290
Descartes, René
285
Didymus
56, 57, 61, 63
Divjak, Johannes
195
Dulles, Avery, Cardinal
146, 226, 231-232, 274
Dunning, H. Ray
25, 30-31
Ehses, Stephan
147
Eichrodt, Walter
47
Eli
37
Elias (Elijah)
294, 306
Enoch
294, 306
Ephraem the Syrian
19, 57-58, 300
Epiphanius of Salamis
300, 301
Erasmus
91
Erickson, Millard
84, 97
Eusebius of Caesarea
300, 301
Eustratius
300
Feckes, C.
231
Fisher, Duane
7

Fitzmyer, Joseph
194, 229
Fleeman, Paul
7
Fleischaker, David
7, 65, 197, 313
Frame, John
110
Franco, Richardo
233
Fung, Ronald
98
Garrett, James Leo
87, 89, 98
Garrigou-Lagrange, Reginald
233, 280, 286-287, 290- 292, 308, 309, 311
Gaydos, John, Bishop
3, 7
George, Timothy
87, 98
Gerhard, Johann
141
Le Goff, Jacques
255, 260
Gomarus, Francisco
171
Gonzalez, Severino
145, 233
Gorman, Michael
195, 196
Gregory XIII
125, 141
Gregory the Great
291, 300, 301
Gregory of Nazianzus
55
Gregory of Nyssa
55, 285, 298, 300, 308
Grisez, Germain
306
Gutenberg
250

Ham
36
Hamilton, Victor P.
99
Hamm, Berndt
275
Heidegger, J. H.
171
Hermann, Jean
145
Hervé, J. M.
145, 147, 233, 306, 308, 309, 311
Hesselink, John
228
Hodge, Charles
48, 140, 226, 228, 229, 279, 283, 290, 291
Hofius, Otfried
170
Horton, Michael
228
Hoskins, Steven
7, 9, 17, 313
Hunter, Sylvester Joseph
233, 306, 309, 311
Hurter, H.
145, 147, 306, 308, 309
Ignatius of Antioch
19, 72
Innocent X
124
Irenaeus
19, 52-54, 60, 62, 259
Isaac
115, 187, 204
Jacob
204
James the Apostle
114, 115, 166, 167, 168, 187, 188, 190, 192, 193, 263
James, Frank
265, 266, 267, 276, 277
Jansen, Cornelius
124

Jedin, Hubert
  147
Jenkin, William
  49
Jeroboam
  37
Jerome
  227, 285
John XXII
  295, 306
John the Apostle
  75, 187, 224, 297, 305
John Paul II
  74, 75, 120, 209, 215, 229, 232, 308, 312
Johns, Cheryl Bridges
  7, 173, 313
Johns, Jackie David
  7, 173, 182 313-314
Joseph, husband of Mary
  204
Joseph, son of Jacob
  201
Joshua
  201
De Journel, Rouët
  147,
Jovian
  227
Jowers, Dennis
  7, 33, 155, 314
Judas
  113
Judas Maccabee
  282
Julian of Eclanum
  56, 104
Jüngel, Eberhard
  271
Jungmann, Bernhard
  233, 306, 308, 309, 311
Justin Martyr
  19, 52, 61-62

Keating, Daniel
  7, 51, 146, 183, 257, 314
Kelly, J. N. D.
  56, 62, 63
à Kempis, Thomas
  233, 242
Kennedy, Arthur, Bishop
  1, 7
King, J. H.
  175, 182
Knoll, Albert
  306, 308, 309
Küng, Hans
  308
Land, Stephen
  176, 182
Lane, Anthony
  141, 263, 275
Lange, Dietz
  228
Law, William
  242
Leeming, Bernard
  228
Leitch, A. H.
  177, 182
Lennerz, Heinrich
  233, 306, 308
Leo X
  136, 146, 232, 281
Lercher, L.
  146
Lewis, C. S.
  289-290, 292
Lombard, Peter
  84
Longenecker, Richard
  87, 98
Louth, A.
  258
Luther, Martin
  6, 23, 25, 81, 91- 94, 99, 105- 107, 125, 136, 140, 142, 144, 215, 218, 219, 227, 228, 230, 232, 281, 286, 293, 295

Macarius (Pseudo-)
19, 57-58, 247, 248
Macchia, Frank
180, 182
Maddox, Randy
18, 19, 22, 23, 27, 30, 31
Malloy, Christopher
147, 227
Mary
52, 65, 71, 104, 113, 136, 225, 227
Maximus the Confessor
73, 248, 258
McCue, J. F.
147
McGrath, Alister
101, 105, 120, 188-191, 194-196, 275
Melanchthon
93, 106
Menzies, Glen
7, 101, 314
Moo, Doug
170
De Moor, Bernhard
171
Moore, Dennis
7
Moses
34, 38, 74, 156, 185, 201, 204, 215-216, 287
Mostert, Christiaan
262, 275
Mueller, John Theodore
84, 97, 140, 145, 146, 227
Murray, John
46
Newman, John Henry, Cardinal
124, 141, 148, 274
Niles, Samuel
48
Noah
187
Oberman, Heiko
145
Olson, Roger
112, 120, 121

Origen
19, 54, 55, 57, 61-62, 285, 297
Ott, Ludwig
146, 308, 311
Pagels, Elaine
112, 121
Pallavicino, Peter Sforza, Cardinal
142
Panenburg, Wolfhart
100, 275, 277
Pas, Paul
147
Paul the Apostle
6, 34, 38- 40, 43-44, 46, 47, 57, 60, 63, 83, 86-88, 91, 96, 113- 115, 128, 132, 136, 155-170, 178, 184-188, 191, 193, 196, 213, 221, 225, 232, 263, 265, 270, 273, 284, 285, 286
Pelagius
94, 104, 124
Pelikan, Jaroslav
62, 63, 258
Pesch, Christian
146, 147, 233, 306, 308, 309
Pesch, Otto Hermann
219, 228, 231, 232
Peter the Apostle
86, 159, 163, 213
Pharaoh
36
Philo
55, 58, 60
Pinckaiers, Servais
230
Piper, John
110
Pius V
41, 48, 124, 125, 126, 141, 223
Plato
72, 286
Pohle, Joseph
146, 227, 231, 232, 233, 306, 310
Polycarp
19

Possidius
300
Pourrat, P.
228
Price, Richard
307
Pseudo-Dionysius
300
Quinn, Jerome
194
Rahab
167-168
Rahner, Karl
306, 308
Reumann, John
184, 194
Riviere, J.
146,
Rondet, Henri
58, 60, 63
Rückert, Hanns
145
Runyan, Ted
30
Russell, Walter
170
Rybarczyk, Edmund
176, 182
Sagüés, Joseph
141, 146, 233, 306, 308, 310, 311
Salkeld, Brett
271, 277
Satan (devil, Lucifer)
14, 61, 66, 72, 128, 129, 203, 218
Saul
37
Sayers, Dorothy
256, 260
Scannell, Thomas
306
Schatz, Klaus
307
Schaull, Richard
175, 176, 182

Scheeben, Matthias
146,
Schluep-Meier, Christoph
170
Schouppe, François
147, 306, 309, 311
Schrenk, Gottlob
95, 99
Schwarz, Hans
89, 98
Seripando, Girolamo
136, 139, 219
Seth
201
Shea, James P., Msgr.
2, 8
Shedd, William
141
Smith, George D.
233, 306, 311
Smith, Walter George
229
Snyder, Howard
173, 182, 251, 258
Söhngen, G.
228
Sola, Francisco
233
De Soto, Domingo
143
Spaulding, Henry
30, 31
Spinoza
285
Sproul, R. C.
120
Stearns, Richard
250, 258
Stevenson, William
7, 279, 314
Strickler, Jeff
7
Suarez, Francisco
143, 311

Sulpicius Severus
  300
Tanner, Norman
  307
Tanquerey, Adolphe
  146, 147, 233, 306, 309, 311
Taylor, Jeremy
  242
Teresa of Avila
  310
Tertullian
  19, 53, 61, 62, 300
Theophilus of Antioch
  52, 54, 60, 62
Thiselton, Anthony C.
  95, 99
Thomas, Christopher John
  182
Turretin, Francis
  47, 48, 140, 146, 148, 226, 227, 228
De Valencia, Gregory
  229, 307
Vandervelde, George
  142
Vanhoozer, Kevin
  85, 97
Venema, Cornelius
  275
Vermigli, Peter Martyr
  264-270, 274-278
Vigilantius
  295
Vollert, Cyril
  142

Vossius, Gerhard Johann
  171
Walls, Jerry
  255, 260
Washburn, Christian
  7, 123, 142, 145, 211, 226, 231, 293, 310, 314
Watts, Isaac
  111, 121
Wesley, Charles
  248-249, 258
Wesley, John
  19-27, 30, 31, 108, 178-182, 241-260
Wicks, Jared
  306, 307
Wiley, Tatha
  62
Wilckens, Ulrich
  170
Wilkinson, Michael D.
  100
Williams, Colin
  18, 26, 30
Witherington, Ben
  170
Wollebius, Johannes
  148
Wright, N. T.
  170, 249, 258
Yarnell, Malcolm
  7, 83, 97, 98, 314
Yarnold, E.
  147-148

Subject Index

Baptism
42-44, 54, 57, 61-62, 65, 71, 74, 126-128, 134, 136, 138, 146, 180, 185, 190, 193, 195, 203, 214, 221, 226, 232, 296, 311
  Of infants
  15, 53, 55, 57, 59-62, 90, 136, 146, 225

Council
  Chalcedon
  208, 307
  Constantinople
  297, 307
  Ephesus
  191, 307
  First Vatican
  129, 133, 307
  Florence
  143, 147, 233, 280, 296, 297, 300, 305- 311
  Lateran IV
  297, 305
  Lyons
  143, 233, 280, 297, 300, 309
  Nicaea
  220, 307
  Orange
  23, 30, 126, 142, 250
  Second Vatican
  310
  Trent
  23, 30, 42- 44, 72-74, 81, 108-109, 113, 116-118, 120, 124-127, 129-130, 132-139, 142, 145-147, 207, 212-213, 215, 217-224, 226, 228, 231, 286, 290, 293, 297, 300, 302-303, 305, 311

Concupiscence
15-16, 41-46, 61, 68-69, 126, 128, 136, 220

Confirmation
203, 214, 232

Death
14-15, 17, 20, 23, 33-35, 37-38, 44-46, 49, 52-61, 66-68, 72-74, 86, 93, 96, 103, 126, 138, 144, 147, 153, 162, 164, 174-176, 193, 201, 204, 216, 223, 224, 237-239, 249, 251-255, 258, 270, 273, 280-282, 288, 290, 293-296, 303-304, 306, 310

Eucharist
8, 74, 203, 214, 216, 221, 228, 232

Fall of Adam and Eve
13-15, 20, 26, 39, 41-42, 52-53, 57, 59-61, 66-69, 72, 90, 92, 95, 106, 123, 125-130, 132, 140, 143, 202, 205, 265

Grace
9, 14-16, 27-29, 34, 39, 42, 45, 48, 59, 61, 70-75, 79, 81, 84-85, 87-93, 96-99, 102-106, 109, 113-120, 123-136, 139-144, 152, 158, 162-163, 166, 168, 176-181, 188, 191-192, 195, 202-205, 208, 211-228, 231, 233, 237-258, 262-275, 280-281, 284, 286, 288-290, 293, 299, 305, 309, 311

Actual
130, 132, 147, 221-223

Prevenient
15, 17-31, 80-81, 108-110, 118-120, 132, 311

Sanctifying
27, 66-69, 71, 73, 81, 125-127, 130, 132, 136-140, 142, 147, 152, 181, 197, 199-200, 212-213, 217-218, 224-225, 227, 246, 299, 304

Heaven
66, 123, 125, 135-136, 146, 173, 211, 213, 221, 223, 230, 231, 237-239, 241-242, 244-246, 249, 251-258, 270-271, 280-282, 285, 289-291, 293-294, 296, 299, 301, 303-309, 312

Hell
16, 143, 233, 238, 241-242, 245-246, 282, 291, 293-294, 296-299, 301, 303, 308-309, 312

Holy Orders
228

Justice
35, 37, 49, 58, 74, 132-133, 136-139, 159, 163, 177, 184, 189-190, 199, 201, 203-207, 212-213, 218-220, 231, 243, 245, 280, 286-288, 292, 298-299, 304

Original justice
41, 49, 67, 73-74, 123-127, 140, 299

Justification
18, 22, 27, 34, 37, 43-44, 59, 79-81, 83-96, 101-120, 123-125, 130, 132-140, 145-146, 148, 149, 151-153, 155-169, 173, 175-181, 183-195, 197-200, 203-207, 211-221, 224-226, 232, 237-238, 244, 253, 256-257, 261-276, 293-294, 299, 302-304

Law
17, 21, 33-34, 38-40, 42-44, 48, 57, 73, 83, 86-87, 89, 91, 94, 103, 126, 130, 155-170, 185, 191-192, 211, 214-218, 221, 225, 228-230, 237, 247, 272, 286, 289

Marriage
54, 204, 216-217, 229, 251, 252

Merit
15, 44-45, 48, 67, 79-80, 91, 100, 102-103, 108, 117-119, 123, 130, 132, 134-135, 140, 152, 158, 166, 190-191, 204-207, 211, 218-225, 228-232, 238, 245, 263, 265, 269, 273, 276-277, 280-281, 285-288, 293-294, 302, 304-305, 311

Monergism
9, 17, 24-25, 28, 33-34, 39-46, 79, 87, 92, 113, 119, 155, 160, 168-169, 171, 262, 275

Nature of Man
14, 20, 22, 33, 35, 39-47, 55, 57, 68, 73, 74, 84, 89-92, 96, 97, 103, 109, 123-132, 141-144, 179, 181, 185, 202-203, 214, 252, 299

Penance
116, 201, 271, 280, 302

Sacrament of
102, 135, 270

Preternatural gifts
13-15, 125, 141

Purgatory
232, 239, 242, 252-256, 269-272, 279-283, 288-290, 293-294, 297, 300-303, 310-311

Redemption
53, 60, 73-74, 96, 158, 185, 241, 249-252, 256, 259, 261-262

Sacraments
(see also individual headings)
59, 71-72, 152, 202-204, 207, 214, 216-217, 220, 224, 225, 227-228, 232, 302, 311

Sanctification
9, 17, 20, 23, 26-27, 65, 67, 74, 81, 102, 107, 116, 119, 123, 136, 147, 151-153, 168, 169, 173, 176-181, 183-187, 191, 193-194, 197-200, 203-207, 211-212, 224-226, 248, 250, 252, 256, 264-274, 280, 288

Sin
  Actual Sin
      14, 20, 21, 34-35, 40, 46, 59, 143, 224, 233, 238, 294, 296, 309
  Original Sin
      9, 13-28, 30, 33, 35, 40-41, 45-46, 51-62, 65-74, 81, 90, 108, 124-130, 136-137, 143, 175, 201-202, 216, 233, 237-238, 250, 294, 296, 299, 309

Supernatural gifts
      14, 123, 125-127, 137, 140-141

Synergism
      9, 17, 20-21, 26-29, 79, 84, 92-93, 101-119, 173-179, 241, 252, 256, 257, 263, 267-268, 271